How Do Mādhyamikas Think?

Studies in Indian and Tibetan Buddhism

This series was conceived to provide a forum for publishing outstanding new contributions to scholarship on Indian and Tibetan Buddhism and also to make accessible seminal research not widely known outside a narrow specialist audience, including translations of appropriate monographs and collections of articles from other languages. The series strives to shed light on the Indic Buddhist traditions by exposing them to historical-critical inquiry, illuminating through contextualization and analysis these traditions' unique heritage and the significance of their contribution to the world's religious and philosophical achievements.

STUDIES IN INDIAN AND TIBETAN BUDDHISM

How Do Mādhyamikas Think?

And Other Essays on the Buddhist Philosophy of the Middle

Tom J. F. Tillemans

Wisdom

Wisdom Publications, Inc.
199 Elm Street
Somerville MA 02144 USA
wisdompubs.org

Library of Congress Cataloging-in-Publication Data
Names: Tillemans, Tom J. F., author.
Title: How do Mādhayamikas think? : and other essays on the Buddhist philosophy of the middle / Tom J.F. Tillemans.
Description: Somerville : Wisdom Publications, 2016. | Series: Studies in Indian and Tibetan Buddhism | Includes bibliographical references and index.
Identifiers: LCCN 2015032359 | ISBN 1614292515 (pbk. : alk. paper)
Subjects: LCSH: Mādhyamika (Buddhism)
Classification: LCC BQ7457 .T55 2016 | DDC 294.3/42042--dc23
LC record available at http://lccn.loc.gov/2015032359

ISBN 978-1-61429-251-7 ebook ISBN 978-1-61429-266-1

20 19 18 17 16
5 4 3 2 1

Cover and interior design by Gopa&Ted2. Set in Diacritical Garamond Pro 10.5/13.

Wisdom Publications' books are printed on acid-free paper and meet the guidelines for permanence and durability of the Production Guidelines for Book Longevity of the Council on Library Resources.

This book was produced with environmental mindfulness.
For more information, please visit wisdompubs.org/wisdom-environment.

Printed in the United States of America.

FSC www.fsc.org MIX Paper from responsible sources FSC® C011935

Please visit fscus.org.

Contents

Publisher's Acknowledgment

THE PUBLISHER gratefully acknowledges the generous contribution of the Hershey Family Foundation toward the publication of this book.

Introduction

THE ESSAYS COLLECTED here are on the Madhyamaka, the "philosophy of the middle" that begins with Nāgārjuna and Āryadeva in the second century CE and evolves throughout Indian, Tibetan, and Chinese Buddhism.[1] Many have appeared previously and are reprinted with a few revisions; some (chapters 5, 7, and 12) are new. As in my previous work on other Buddhist philosophers, notably Dharmakīrti, these essays zigzag between a historico-philological approach and philosophical analysis. It is a delicate balance. Madhyamaka needs to be understood charitably with the best philosophical reading that textual data and intellectual contexts permit.

The book is loosely organized in terms of four topics: Madhyamaka's philosophical promise (chapters 1 and 2), features of its philosophy of logic and language (chapters 3–7), its ethics and spiritual path to Buddhist enlightenment (chapter 8–10), and its potential contributions to contemporary philosophical controversies (chapters 11 and 12).

This philosophy has had a mixed reception, both in the past and nowadays. It has been taken as the pinnacle of subtlety by its promoters but also vilified, and even simply ignored, by many Buddhists and non-Buddhists alike, one of the frequent objections being that it distorted opposing realist positions willfully and thus refuted straw men. The first essay, "Trying to Be Fair," attempts an initial view of the lay of the land, in a charitable light. The second, "How Far Can a Mādhyamika Refute Customary Truth?" takes up issues of relativism, truth, and ontology. Chapters 3 and 4 deal with the question of whether the Mādhyamika respects universally the law of noncontradiction; the argument is that while a weak, nonadjunctive type of inconsistency may well fit some sūtras and possibly Nāgārjuna, inconsistency of any sort is considered as a fault by the time of the sixth century and is thus not endorsed by major Mādhyamikas such as Candrakīrti, Bhāviveka, and their successors. Chapter 5, "Prasaṅga and Proof by Contradiction in Bhāviveka, Candrakīrti, and Dharmakīrti," takes up a crucial application of the law of noncontradiction: *reductio ad absurdum*, or *prasaṅga*, which has long been considered the preferred strategy of the Mādhyamikas who follow Candrakīrti (commonly known as *prāsaṅgikas*) to expose the internal flaws of philosophical positions while not taking a position of their own. The use of proof by contradiction in the Mādhyamika thinkers Candrakīrti and Bhāviveka is contrasted with that of Dharmakīrti, a sixth/seventh century non-Mādhyamika metaphysical realist, who along with the founder of the Epistemological School, Dignāga (fifth century), is sometimes the direct adversary, and often the *éminence grise*, in so many later Indo-Tibetan Madhyamaka debates.[2] Chapter 6, "Apoha Semantics: What Did Bhāviveka Have to Do with It?" is the most historical and philological chapter of the book. It shows how close the relationship between Epistemologists and Mādhyamikas was historically in India, as the dominant semantic theory adopted by the leading Indo-Tibetan Buddhist thinkers seems to have been quite significantly influenced by the sixth-century Mādhyamika Bhāviveka. Chapter 7, "What Happened to the Third and Fourth Lemmas in the Tibetan Madhyamaka?" takes up problems that arise in Tibetan interpretations of the third and fourth lemmas in the famous tetralemma, or *catuṣkoṭi*, whose use Mādhyamikas claimed as essential to their abstention from all theses (*pakṣa*, *pratijñā*) or philosophical positions (*abhyupagama*). The question arises whether Mādhyamikas can and should accept a law of double-negation elimination (*pratiṣedhadvayena prakṛtagamana*; *dgag pa gnyis kyis rnal ma go ba* "understanding the main [proposition] by means of two negations") and whether they respect De Morgan's Laws. The issues are real, even if the formulation of the problem was skewered in thinkers like Gorampa (Go rams pa), Khedrup Jé (Mkhas grub rje), and others due to syntax-provoked ambiguities in the Tibetan language that led them to widely confuse statements of the form "neither φ nor ψ" with those of the form "not both φ and ψ."

From logic and language we turn to ethics and the Buddhist spiritual path. Chapter 8, "Madhyamaka Buddhist Ethics," examines, inter alia, whether a Mādhyamika's reliance on scriptural authority to settle ethical issues can be justified, as Candrakīrti claims, on the basis of what the world itself recognizes (*lokaprasiddha*). The Candrakīrtian argument is, however, an interesting failure. The upshot is that traditional Buddhist ethics founded on the law of karma involves a type of epistemic protectionism that, if left unchallenged, prices Buddhism out of secular ethical reflection. Chapter 9, "Reason, Irrationality, and Akrasia (Weakness of the Will) in Buddhism," looks at recurrent arguments from the eighth-century Mādhyamika Śāntideva that suggest a recognition of incontinence, or weakness of the will, as a significant factor in Buddhist ethics. "Yogic Perception, Meditation, and Enlightenment," chapter 10, is a reexamination of the philosophical themes in the key eighth-century debate between the Chan monk Heshang Mohoyen and the Indian Mādhyamika paṇḍit Kamalaśīla.

The final two chapters are applications of Madhyamaka to contemporary problems in the philosophy of mind and ontology. "On Minds, Dharmakīrti, and Madhyamaka" argues that the usual Buddhist defenses of mind will fare badly against modern eliminative materialism; a Madhyamaka approach would hold more promise. Chapter 12, "Serious, Lightweight, or Neither: Should Madhyamaka Go to Canberra?" looks at how Madhyamaka might find a place in current metaontological debates on the legitimacy and merits of pursuing philosophical questions of what there really is. "Canberra" refers not only to the political capital of Australia but also to a philosophy department that is especially associated with the revival of interest in metaphysics in analytic philosophy. Should a modern Madhyamaka philosophy also tread the Canberran path? Perhaps the Svātantrika could. Prāsaṅgika-Madhyamaka, however, is best seen as a quietist philosophy that is fundamentally out of step with most of the new analytic metaphysics as practiced in Australia and elsewhere.

* * *

The theme that comes back repeatedly in the essays is indeed quietism, or the Mādhyamika's reasoned disengagement from all philosophical theses, and hence debates (*vivāda*) about them. Here is how Nāgārjuna put it in verse 50 of his *Yuktiṣaṣṭikā*:

> Superior individuals have no theses (*pakṣa*, *phyogs*) and no philosophical debates; how could there be any opposing theses for those who have no theses [themselves]?[3]

That quietism is not just prudential advice—like what we find in the Pāli canon—to avoid destructive and fruitless discussions with hostile adversaries. Nor is it, in my opinion, a dishonest refusal to show one's own hand, as the non-Buddhists regularly caricatured Mādhyamikas in calling them *vaitaṇḍika*: "cavilers," "sophists." At its best, it is a defendable truth: that one *cannot reasonably* have philosophical theses and take sides in debates on how things really are in themselves, or how they are in an ultimate fashion. Finally, quietism is not only a stance for philosophers who argue. It figures in meditation and practice too, as Mahāyānists generally agree that there comes a point on the Buddhist spiritual path where views (*dṛṣṭi*, *darśana*), and indeed all conceptual thinking (*vikalpa*, *kalpanā*), are to be left behind. Where that point is—either at the beginning or the end of the path—

constitutes the subject of the well-documented historical confrontation between Chan and Madhyamaka whose philosophical issues are my focus in chapter 10. Suffice it to say here that both Chan and the Madhyamaka recognized that—sooner or later—Buddhist practice is quietistic.

There is, however, an obvious tension here. As the articles in the present book show, there are such ample Madhyamaka contributions to typical philosophical controversies in logic, language, causality, epistemology, and ethics, to name a few, that the question naturally arises as to how such inquiries *could* be pursued if Mādhyamikas supposedly remained unengaged, advocating instead the *āryatūṣṇīṃbhāva*, the "silence of the noble ones." What room, if any, do quietistic Mādhyamikas leave for truth claims? Can they engage in philosophical debate in some limited way? The answers to these questions are complex and will vary considerably from one thinker to the next and from one period to the next. Let us look at some of the varieties of quietism in more detail.

One possible—admittedly speculative—way to understand Madhyamaka quietism would be to see it as resulting from a certain tolerance of contradiction. As developed in chapter 3 and 4, the author(s) of the Prajñāpāramitā and other sūtra literature, and perhaps Nāgārjuna, could be read as regularly asserting and denying the same statements *p*, *q*, *r*, and so on, so that *p*, *q*, and *r* are affirmed for the worldly reasons that the common man would give but are also denied from an ultimate point of view, as there is nothing that has an ultimately existing "intrinsic nature," or *svabhāva*, or in other words, *really is what it is anyway*—that is, independently of all relations it might enter into and whatever one might say or think about it. Affirmations and denials of the same statements cancel each other out, leaving disengagement from both and suspension of belief. Nāgārjuna, read in this way, would be quietistic in not himself making truth claims.

Interesting as it may be, such reliance on paradox, however, cannot easily be read into post-third-century writers like Candrakīrti who respect strictly the law of noncontradiction. Their quietism turns on other considerations. A common traditional Indian and Tibetan interpretation of Candrakīrti (what I term in chapter 2 "typical Prāsaṅgika Madhyamaka") holds that things lack real intrinsic natures and—what is the same—that things are therefore false appearances (*ābhāsa*, *snang ba*) that merely, in an oft-repeated stock phrase, "exist from the point of view of mistaken minds" (*blo 'khrul ba'i ngor yod pa*) or, less literally, "just seem to be thus and so to the mistaken." This generally unpacks as the idea that for Mādhyamikas there are no genuine "sources of knowledge" (*pramāṇa*, *tshad ma*), because what people term "right understanding" is nothing more than a type of "seeming to be right" that meets with widespread acceptance by the world, which in any case invariably labors under illusions. This is a strongly antirealist way of reading Madhyamaka: there is nothing "out there" that really is what it is anyway and can be represented correctly by our thoughts and language; minds and conventions make the world's entities, which work as they do because people believe in them.[4] Mādhyamikas are then quietists because they shun any and all deeper questions about what there actually is and content themselves with what the world acknowledges (*lokaprasiddha*); they thus use *reductio ad absurdum* of others' positions to demolish them but don't affirm anything that they themselves hold to be true. In this book, unless otherwise indicated, I'll generally read Candrakīrti in this way—as a "typical Prāsaṅgika." Such is the book's default setting: Candrakīrti read in a natural Indian fashion. In some chapters nothing much turns on it, but sometimes it is important. Chapter 5 on *prasaṅga*, for example, turns on this "typical Prāsaṅgika" reading.

Other Mādhyamikas, such as Tsongkhapa (Tsong kha pa, 1357–1419) and his followers—"atypical Prāsaṅgikas"—think quite differently. They do accept that there are sources of knowledge (*pramāṇa*) and thus have a much greater place for beliefs and truth claims—there are true/right answers, where "true" is not just "seeming to be true," "generally thought to be true," "believed in," et cetera. In their logic, although they adopt the moniker Prāsaṅgika, they believe and prove truths in a minimalist fashion not involving a metaphysics of intrinsic natures. Crucially, then, they insist upon a split between how things are confusedly grasped in the fashion of a metaphysical realist committed to intrinsic natures and how they are understood innocently and rightly without such commitments. The daunting task for these quietists, then, is to disentangle the innocent from the confused, and stay unengaged on positions that involve the latter.

A thought such as this in which there is a richer place for truth and reality is, in my opinion, considerably more sophisticated and promising than the global error theory or fictionalism of the typical Prāsaṅgika. I fully recognize that it is going to be disturbing to some to read that a fourteenth-century Tibetan philosophy may have been, in certain significant respects, clearer and even much better philosophy than that of the Indian thinkers on which it was based. That evolution toward sophistication should be unsurprising to the historian who recognizes that traditional religious thinkers are regularly obliged to disguise their innovations and creativity. Nonetheless, it means that much of the effort to read Tsongkhapa and other later Mādhyamika thinkers back onto Candrakīrti or Nāgārjuna is strained. Let's be clear: Madhyamaka changes significantly over time, sometimes for the better.

But could this type of Madhyamaka philosophy work? Or would its acceptance of sources of knowledge, right answers, truth, and reality entail that the Mādhyamikas came full circle and had to accept fundamental entities with fully fledged intrinsic natures? In chapter 2, the limited realism and truth that these atypical Prāsaṅgika Mādhyamikas conserved is explained in terms of a form of *deflationism*, where there is nothing more to be said about truth and real facts other than platitudes like the so-called T-sentences of a semantic theory of truth: <*p*> is true if and only if *p*, "'Snow is white' is true in English if and only if snow is white."[5] Of course, a bottom line of deflationary truths and facts is thin fare for those who expect more from an account of truth and reality or from a Buddhist religious philosophy of liberation. Deflationism does nonetheless retain the crucial minimal features of the concepts of truth, objectivity, and reality, namely that truth involves an all-important contrast between being right and just seeming to be right and that any viable concept of reality thus needs a difference between what is the case (or what has been the case all along) and what just seems to be the case or is widely believed to be so. This is quite a lot, and it comes without metaphysical strings attached. It brings no commitments to one who rejects *svabhāva* and is thus already disinclined to ontology. The radical point is thus that such deflationary truths and facts may be all the Mādhyamika Buddhist needs for his idea that true and false statements, existence and nonexistence, realities and unrealities are established customarily (*vyavahāratas*), by genuine sources of knowledge, and never ultimately (*paramārthatas*).[6]

What then is the place for philosophy? Svātantrika-Mādhyamikas like Bhāviveka, Śāntarakṣita, and Kamalaśīla not only make truth claims but have a much greater place for positive, constructive, philosophical theorizing than their Prāsaṅgika counterparts. Indeed, I have argued that one of the most important differences between the two is that Svātantrikas reinstate much of the ontology, philosophy of language, and epistemology of Dignāga and Dharmakīrti as customary (rather than ultimate) truths.[7] The Prāsaṅgikas, by contrast, have no interest in such constructive philosophizing, and thus their quietism also ranges over ontology and epistemology even when transposed to customary truth: they generally have nothing constructive to offer as a theory of universals, particulars, negative facts, perception, memory, reflexive awareness, and the like.

In chapter 12, I try to make sense of this wide-ranging quietism by making a distinction, following Kit Fine, between purely quantificational and ontological questions—roughly those that ask, in an innocent, noncommittal way, whether there is an x such that x is F and those that ask whether the x that is F really exists; the latter questions do, thus, involve ontological commitment. Much of science and common sense's interest in what there is arguably involves the first sort of question. For example, when a mathematician has found a number that has the property *F*, it is trivial and of no metaphysical import to infer "There is an *x* such that *x* has *F*." Philosophical debates on the existence of universals, absences, nonnatural properties, numbers, and the like have, of course, been generally framed in terms of questions of the second sort. If, however, we were also to regard the existence of universals, absences, and so forth in the purely quantificational way, then it might well become harmless and even obvious that we should accept them. And doing so would not be a philosophical thesis at all but just an acceptance of uncontroversially true statements coupled with a dismissal of the philosopher's sense of the strangeness of the entities concerned. I would contend that something along those lines is a plausible rational reconstruction of the Prāsaṅgika quietist's move when he grants that there are universals and so on but stays clear of all philosophical/metaphysical debates about them.

Not surprisingly, many modern writers would not agree with a purely negative, quietistic, characterization of Prāsaṅgika-Madhyamaka and insist that it also has, or perhaps just should have, a minimal positive philosophical explanation of why the things of the world are precisely the ones they are. That positive account is presented as a corollary of the Mādhyamika's idea of emptiness, and it goes something like this: because objects have no (i.e., are empty of) genuinely real intrinsic natures and thus have no real way of being as they are anyway, then it must be minds, human society, and language (and possibly other factors) that somehow bring about the things of our world. The Mādhyamikas, so it is claimed, are after all providing a positive account of the genesis of objects, even if it is not a full-fledged ontology of real entities.

The most plausible of such positive accounts are formulated in terms of pragmatism: we adopt, or even choose, certain objects that are "convenient fictions," useful to us in meeting our needs and furthering happiness, and we reject or ignore those that are not. Jay Garfield, in the introduction to his translation of Nāgārjuna's *Mūlamadhyamakakārikā*, put his version of that positive Madhyamaka account in terms of choices of useful mereological sums. Others, like Mark Siderits, but in a broadly similar vein, speak of us adopting "conceptual fictions"—tables, chairs, personal identity—because of our interests and needs. We can, for our purposes, take the two positions together. Here is the version in Garfield 1995, 89–90:

> To say that it lacks essence [i.e., *svabhāva*], the Mādhyamika philosopher will explain, is to say, as the Tibetans like to put it, that it does not exist "from its own side"—that its existence *as the*

> *object that it is—as a table* [Garfield's italics]—depends not on *it,* nor on any purely nonrelational characteristics, but depends on us as well. That is, if our culture had not evolved this manner of furniture, what appears to us to be an obviously unitary object might instead be correctly described as five objects: four quite useful sticks absurdly surmounted by a pointless slab of stick-wood waiting to be carved. Or we would have no reason to indicate this particular temporary arrangement of this matter as an object at all, as opposed to a brief intersection of the histories of some trees. . . . The table, we might say, is a purely arbitrary slice of space-time chosen by us as the referent of a single name and not an entity demanding, on its own, recognition and a philosophical analysis to reveal its essence.

What is being maintained here, if I have understood correctly, is in part the recognizable antirealist position that entities of the world being what they are depends not only on things but "depends on us as well." We carve out our worlds for our own reasons.[8] Thus, the components of our world—tables, chairs, chariots, people—are what they are because of a set of largely collective decisions; for the world as we know it, and not another, was somehow found useful to our interests (especially interests conditioned by preexisting social institutions) or was even chosen because of its utility.[9] And this is not a blind causal process, like an evolutionary acquisition of thumbs or digestive enzymes. Instead, some brute, unstructured objects, like pieces of wood and chunks of metal, were *interpreted* as belonging together and thus structured as tables and chairs for strategic reasons. We could have taken them otherwise—it was arbitrary—but we did not because we somehow saw that it was not in our advantage as rational agents. The parallel might be with a group of rational agents' economic decisions aiming for prospective profits.

Any philosopher who deliberately stays close to ordinary usage should feel uneasy here. After all, we commonly understand what it is ordinarily to choose rationally some thing or person or to choose an alternative course of action, but what would it mean to stretch that further and say that people also choose the entities of their worlds? Of course, people ordinarily do have interesting and sophisticated ways to answer legitimate questions about the origins of specific things—for instance, "Why are there planets, human beings, wars, and so forth?" These can be answered with complicated reasons from science or simpler ones from common sense. But a story about how we interpret things to make up useful mereological sums or adopt "conceptual fictions" like tables, people, and planets for reasons of convenience is never *that* type of answer. (We know what it means for vanadium to be used in making steel alloys or in flow batteries but not what it means for vanadium *to exist* because of our uses.) For a Mādhyamika who places store on what the world acknowledges, something would seem to be going badly wrong. Instead of the usual talk about how various things come about, why they exist, how they are used, and so on, we are attempting to extend that talk and say, in philosophical terms, how acceptance of anything at all is grounded in virtue of a further type of fact—namely, decisions about utility. And that step beyond is suspect.

It is not only suspect, but such an account of why things exist *could not* be given on the wide scale Garfield's and Siderits's position would demand. Indeed very large scale or exclusive appeals to usefulness and human ends to explain the existence of objects and people would seem to involve a vicious circularity, for in order to determine ends and usefulness to them in human enterprises, we already need to have a world in its broad outlines, with people and many macroscopic objects too. In short, usefulness of carts, tables, and the like to people *presupposes* a context in which there are people, their environments, and their complex interactions with a lot of quite different sorts of objects. If strategies to further human ends were themselves responsible for the genesis of all these entities, their genesis would seem to become unintelligible.[10]

Actually, the Mādhyamikas themselves do not seem to have used their own part-whole argumentation to come up with anything like Garfield's positive account of how thought, language, or societal transactions lead us to choose mereological sums strategically. True, reasons of utility *do* explain why buddhas or bodhisattvas supposedly describe the world in such and such fashion to guide disciples along the path—what is commonly known as "skill in means" (*upāyakauśalya*), where teachers make pedagogically useful statements that should not be taken at face value but need exegesis (*neyārtha*) to get their message across. But that is not what is going on here. The question facing us is whether ordinary beings *themselves* rely on reasons of utility to choose the world they have and whether the world thus "depends on us as well" in this fashion. The Buddha's pedagogy and pragmatic skill in means just concern his methods for teaching others.

We do find numerous statements to the effect that everything is a mere designation (*prajñaptimātra*), dependently arisen, designated in dependence on something else (*upādāya prajñapti*), empty of intrinsic natures, and that intrinsic natures are superimposed (*samāropita*), and so on and so forth. It is well known that Nāgārjuna (in the *Mūlamadhyamakakārikā*) and Nāgasena (in the *Questions of King Milinda*) held that a chariot or the self is *prajñapti*/

paññati. The temptation may indeed be great to gloss these terms, as does Siderits, as meaning "convenient designator"[11] or a "useful fiction."[12] But let's be clear: "convenient" and "useful" are additions. Siderits admits as much in his account of customary/conventional truth in Vasubandhu and the Abhidharma (an account that he seems to apply to Madhyamaka too):

> A sentence is said to be conventionally true if and only if it is assertible by the conventions of common sense, where these are understood as standards based on utility.[13]. . .
>
> These accounts are extrapolations from what is actually said about conventional truth (*saṃvṛtisatya*) and ultimate truth (*paramārthasatya*) in the Abhidharma literature. . . . Vasubandhu says that the conventions for the terms "pot" and "water" having been made, the statement "Pots and water exist" is conventionally true. And since he has made clear that the relevant conventions involve the aggregation of either spatial parts or atomic properties, it seems fair to say that these conventions, and thus conventional truth, reflect the pragmatic standards of common sense.[14]

Is this actually fair to say? It is one thing to give a negative account (as Mādhyamikas or Ābhidharmikas do) of why objects like pots and water are unfindable under analysis and are mere designations (*prajñapti*, Pāli: *paññati*) or are customary truths/realities (*saṃvṛti*, *sammuti*) that are commonly accepted; it is another to move to justificatory talk about the convenience and usefulness of certain designations and thus introduce pragmatism and talk of strategies. Although the second move is easy to make,[15] it does not seem to be there, explicitly or implicitly, in the Abhidharma/Abhidhamma accounts of *paññati* (designation, concepts), *sammuti* (convention, consensus),[16] nor in the well-known Madhyamaka etymological explanations of three uses of the term *saṃvṛti* as "what is real for the obscured," "what arises dependently," and "what is governed by agreement."[17] Indeed, significantly enough, when Buddhists do provide accounts—over and above the world's own explanations—as to why we experience and accept the customary realities we do, the account is often framed in terms of a moral causation: karma accumulated in past lives and ripening in the present in unfathomable ways. Or sometimes it is said that we have "beginningless tendencies" (*anādivāsanā*) to experience things in a certain way.[18] Or it is simply said that such are our customs and practices, our *vyavahāra*. In any case, our making choices for reasons of utility doesn't seem to play any role in the explanation. It is not said that we interpret otherwise unstructured brute data in certain ways because we aim at useful fictions or sum individuals. We could perhaps go further: arguably, the Buddhist account of how all things come to be in terms of humanly unfathomable karma, "beginningless tendencies," and custom is itself a backhanded admission that constructive philosophical accounts of the origin of everything cannot be given and should not even be attempted.[19]

So much for the texts. It will probably be replied that the point is more about what the Mādhyamikas *should say* philosophically than what they did say. In other words, even if they did not fully, or properly, develop their own philosophy of emptiness (*śūnyavāda*) in that constructive pragmatic way, they would nevertheless need the pragmatic complement to avoid an otherwise incomplete picture. They would need some such account to develop their own ideas of how *vyavahāra*—customs, accords, societal transactions and practices—determine our acceptance of things. Many are, for example, the attempts to explain the evolution of cultural phenomena in broad accordance with the same evolutionary game theories initially developed in biology.[20] Why then not also our strategic choices of mereological sums?

Let's expand the debate a bit to see how a modern Mādhyamika could resist that seemingly constructive pragmatic explanation of how our world as a whole comes to be. Indeed, whether self-professed quietistic philosophies *should* nonetheless admit such a constructive counterpart is not just a Madhyamaka matter but in many respects an East-West problem. It is well known that Wittgenstein, in his later philosophy, repeatedly invoked forms of life and linguistic/social practices when confronted with philosophically inspired questions about how understanding and meaning are possible. This has led many commentators to see him as providing the makings of actual philosophical answers to those questions in terms of societal practices, or even "social pragmatism." Such is, in effect, the positive, constructive reading of the *Philosophical Investigations* and other works of Wittgenstein that we find in Crispin Wright and others, and which is contested by philosophers like John McDowell, for whom it is a serious, albeit very seductive, mistake.[21] On a strongly quietist reading like that of McDowell, Wittgenstein's point is that our most basic understandings do follow customs in which we have been trained but without the overintellectualization that comes from seeking interpretation and choice "all the way down."

It is not controversial to say that we have customary practices within which the useful is valued. No doubt, too, our practices generally have little or no place for mereological sums when the components would be so discontinuous as to make the sum impossible to use. And a good number of entities—clearly so in the case of tables, carts, borders, and stock markets—are obviously unintelligible taken independently of customary practices in which they figure. Indeed, if the Mādhyamika is right, all are. The controversial philosophical step is to say that we therefore somehow interpret otherwise neutral data to pick out what sums and kinds are useful to us in those practices and that this explains why we have the world we do and not another.

Much of the *Philosophical Investigations* and *Remarks on the Foundations of Mathematics* is consecrated to the "paradoxes of rule-following" and seeks to show in detail how no one could ever understand basic facts—like someone's linguistic behavior being in keeping with a particular rule—if such an understanding were itself an interpretation of data that could always have been taken otherwise.[22] We thus arrive at Wittgenstein's given: customs, forms of life, are the ground or bedrock beyond which the philosopher's justificatory quest is misguided, as it is a search for one set of reasons and one interpretation too many.[23] Something analogous may well be going on in the Madhyamaka idea of *vyavahāra* admitting of no analysis (*avicāra*), or "being fine as it is unanalyzed" (*avicāraramaṇīya*).[24] To say that designated things depend on *vyavahāra* is thus to arrive as far as one can go: justificatory reasons stop there and can go no further in spite of the philosopher's constant temptation to uncover ever more interpretations and choices. Why *should* the modern Mādhyamika stop there? Well, for one thing, those Wittgensteinian paradoxes apply to rule following across the board: in arithmetic, in meaning such and such by words, and interestingly enough, they would also apply to rules of how to group things together under kinds or combine things to make mereological sums. If rule following was an interpretation, we would never know which rule we, or anyone else, were following, and which kinds or sums people (ourselves included) intend.

How then would the Madhyamaka idea of an unanalyzable *vyavahāra*, "fine as it is," fit into such an updated picture? The Madhyamaka—indeed the Mahāyāna in general—consecrates considerable effort to show that it is impossible that our ideas of entities are copies of, or somehow dictated by, entities as they are intrinsically. They are unintelligible without rule-governed contexts—customs and practices. But that would not mean that they *owe their being to human strategic choices and interpretations*. Following rules and customs could better be seen as no more a strategic choice or interpretation than would be a drowning person's understanding of the word "Help!"[25] It would be a natural fact in need of no further justification and analysis, "as much part of our natural history as walking, eating, drinking, playing" (*Philosophical Investigations* §25). The point in saying that the customary is unanalyzable would then be this: there is no deeper account to explain entities, and indeed our lives, being what they are, whether in terms of intrinsic natures or in terms of strategic choices. The felt necessity to ground forms of life on something else (how reality is intrinsically, our reasoned choices, interpretations, what have you) is the mistake. Quietism, be it Madhyamaka or Wittgensteinian, is a type of vigilance.

* * *

It remains for me to acknowledge people who have helped me along the *madhyamā pratipad* over the years, especially Jacques May, a consummate scholar of Buddhist Studies and uncompromising Madhyamaka quietist, and the late Geshé Tamdin Rabten (Dge bshes Rta mgrin rab brtan), with whom I and a number of other Westerners of my generation studied Dbu ma/Madhyamaka and Tshad ma/Pramāṇa in the 1970s and early 1980s. The ideas in this book would not have taken the form they did without the backdrop of exchange with Mark Siderits, Jay Garfield, and Georges Dreyfus, who all hold quite different positions from mine. The debt to them is obvious throughout, and I thank all three of them for years of debate on Madhyamaka. Shōryū Katsura, David Seyfort Ruegg, Graham Priest, Yasuo Deguchi, Arindam Chakrabarti, Eli Franco, Dan Arnold, Sara McClintock, John Dunne, Malcolm Eckel, Johannes Bronkhorst, José Cabezón, Jiří Holba, Jan Westerhoff, Koji Tanaka, Bronwyn Finnigan, Helmut Krasser, Birgit Kellner, David Higgins, Pascale Hugon, Vincent Eltschinger, Ken Liberman, and Stephen Batchelor all deserve my heartfelt thanks for hearing me out, sometimes correcting unclarities, and often helping me formulate ideas in one way or another. Sincere thanks to David Kittelstrom and the team at Wisdom Publications for their editorial rigor. There are many others who have helped.

Some of the papers here came out of my lectures, seminars, and conversations at the University of Lausanne in the former Department of Oriental Languages and Cultures. I was blessed with excellent doctoral students over the years. I also have a great debt to the Center of Buddhist Studies at the University of Kathmandu, where I presented ideas in annual conferences and in intensive courses, and to my students at the University of Vienna for a delightful class on Indo-Tibetan Buddhism as philosophy that stimulated me every week throughout the summer semester of 2012.

Finally, a book such as this one, a collection of articles written over more than a decade, will inevitably have some repetitions, changes of perspectives, and other inelegances. With the exception of chapter 1, the original articles have been left mostly as they were, as it was practically not feasible to do otherwise. Some translations and terms might also merit rethinking, and on occasion the philosophical analyses were too cautious, perhaps because Buddhist studies was, for a long time, so cautious about the methods of analytic philosophy in general. The more serious problems, however, are the philosophical implications that I did not see or only dimly understood. I can only hope that others will see them more clearly than I did.

Notes to the Introduction

1. The translation of *Madhyamaka* as "philosophy of the middle" is in keeping with Seyfort Ruegg 2010. Should the term be *Madhyamaka* or *Mādhyamika*? The attempt to see the former as the word for the school of thought and the latter as the word for the adherents to this thought is, as Jacques May pointed out quite some time ago, not grounded in rigorous data from Sanskrit texts. Even if *Madhyamaka* might be more of a designation of the system, *Mādhyamika* is attested for both, viz., the system and its adherents. The situation in Sanskrit is *not* parallel to that in Tibetan where *dbu ma* and *dbu ma pa* do respectively designate the philosophical system and its adherents. See May 1979, 472. In what follows, we have adopted this new convention of distinguishing between *Madhyamaka* (the school, the philosophy) and *Mādhyamika* (the adherents, the philosophers). Avoiding orthographic chaos is probably enough of a justification.
2. For a summary presentation of my views on Dharmakīrti's philosophy, see Tillemans 2011a—that is, the *Stanford Encyclopedia of Philosophy* entry, plato.stanford.edu/entries/dharmakiirti.
3. *Che ba'i bdag nyid can de dag // rnams la phyogs med rtsod pa med // gang rnams la ni phyogs med pa // de la gzhan phyogs ga la yod //*. Tibetan text in Lindtner 1990, 114.
4. For antirealist interpretations of Madhyamaka, see Siderits 1988 and 1989 and Westerhoff 2011.
5. On the problems and advantages of a deflationary theory of truth and its T-sentences for Madhyamaka, see Priest, Siderits, and Tillemans 2011.
6. Deflationism might capture philosophically important features of Madhyamaka, but it would be wildly bizarre to imagine that simply thinking about deflationism or concentrating on it is somehow what Buddhists promote as a *path* to enlightenment. Our claim is just that it might describe in philosophical terms what the quietistic Prāsaṅgika perspective on truth would have to be like. Buddhist paths—sūtra or tantra—involve many quite sophisticated psychological techniques and ethical practices that induce personal transformations in ways that philosophizing about truth theories cannot. Also, without additional understanding of how intrinsic natures are somehow incoherent, a deflationism would be little different from the commonsense realism that Madhyamaka diagnoses as confusedly grasping at reifications. Cf. MacKenzie 2009. Many of these same considerations would apply, *mutatis mutandis*, to quietism and the abstention from philosophical positions.
7. See Tillemans 2003. The terms Svātantrika and Prāsaṅgika are, as is relatively well known by now, Sanskritizations of the Tibetan terms *rang rgyud pa* and *thal 'gyur ba*. This should be borne in mind. Jay Garfield has finally convinced me that it is pedan-

tic to put an asterisk in front of these Sanskritizations. For more on these and related Tibetan terms for subschools of the Madhyamaka, see chapter 2, note 7.

8. Cf., for example, Hilary Putnam's "internal realism," according to which the world is not independently as it is because the various "carvings" into kinds and individuals are brought about by our cognizing minds.
9. Cf. Siderits 2003, 8: "[O]ur ontological intuitions are being guided by our institutionally arranged interests," by which he decribes how we assemble various parts to make a cart because we have an institutionalized use for such an entity—transportation—but not for cart parts scattered all over a battlefied.
10. Amber Carpenter (2015, 14–15) makes the same point about people being clearly presupposed in explanations that turn on human ends.
11. See Siderits 2007, 49. "'I' is what they call a 'convenient designator,' a word that refers to something that is just a useful fiction. The person is that useful fiction. The person is a whole made of parts. And wholes are not themselves real things, only the parts are. I think that 'I' must refer to one and the same thing every time I use it because I have forgotten that the person is a useful fiction. I have forgotten that 'I' is just a useful way to talk about all the parts taken together."
12. See, e.g., Siderits and Katsura 2013, 23.
13. Siderits 2003, 7.
14. Siderits 2003, 14.
15. Indeed Guy Newland and I made that conceptual slide in an earlier publication entitled "An Introduction to Conventional Truth." See the Cowherds 2011, 12: "Which wholes are created and focused upon and which are not is largely a matter of tacit common agreements about what is useful to the human form of life."
16. Y. Karunadasa has done admirable studies on the Theravāda Abhidhamma notions in which he shows in detail that common agreement or consensus is essential to *sammuti* and *paññati* but never suggests that the Buddhist claims that people use reasons of interest or usefulness to settle upon one particular agreement rather than another. See, e.g., Karunadasa 1996.
17. See Newland and Tillemans 2011.
18. The Vaibhāṣika schools have a bewildering variety of causal accounts of how karma works to create the world. See, e.g., Bareau 1955. In the Mahāyāna, Yogācāra's causal account of the world's genesis typically turns on the *ālayavijñāna* (storehouse consciousness), in which karmic seeds and tendencies are "planted" and come to maturity—this is part and parcel of their idealism. In *Madhyamakāvatāra* 6.89 and *Bhāṣya*, Candrakīrti interprets the sūtra passages that state that all is mind alone (*cittamātra*) to be expressing the Abhidharma principle that everything in the world, be it animate or inanimate, is caused by karma, which is itself dependent upon mental factors. What is important for our purposes is that in such accounts, considerations of utility *do not figure at all* to explain why we have the world and the sentient beings we do. They are purely causal. Note, finally, that the Buddhist Epistemologists' theory of *apoha*, especially in its Dharmakīrtian version, is more complicated in its emphasis on human interests in the construction of common properties and kinds (see Dunne 2011a). Dharmakīrti's Yogācāra maintains that various inherited imprints/tendencies (*vāsanā*) and other causal processes lead us to understand kinds as we do. Does his apohavāda then also maintain that we somehow *choose* how to understand them or interpret them in the ways we do for various reasons, and that in principle those choices

could always have been radically different, perhaps yielding weird sum individuals and funny composite kinds like GRUE (i.e., things observed to be green before time *t* or not so observed before *t* and blue. See N. Goodman 1983)? Functions are no doubt important in defining kinds for Dharmakīrti and avoiding realism about universals; it is not clear to me how much liberty he leaves us to choose for our reasons.

19. To get an idea of the philosophical work typically done by the term *anādivāsanā* from Dharmakīrti to Klong chen pa, see p. 123–24n12, and p. 198n27.

20. There are a considerable number of attempts to apply evolutionary games theory to cultural phenomena, from altruism, senses of fairness, to social contracts. See Alexander 2009.

21. See, e.g., McDowell 1998, 277: "Readers of Wittgenstein often suppose that when he mentions customs, forms of life, and the like, he is making programmatic gestures towards a certain style of positive philosophy: one that purports to make room for talk of meaning and understanding, in the face of supposedly genuine obstacles, by locating such talk in a context of human interactions conceived as describable otherwise than in terms of meaning or understanding. But there is no reason to credit Wittgenstein with any sympathy for this style of philosophy."

22. Cf. *Philosophical Investigations* §201: "It can be seen that there is a misunderstanding here from the mere fact that in the course of our argument we give one interpretation after another; as if each one contented us at least for a moment, until we thought of yet another standing behind it. What this shews is that there is a way of grasping a rule which is *not* an *interpretation*, but which is exhibited in what we call 'obeying the rule' and 'going against it' in actual cases." See also chapter 1 on Wittgenstein's "paradoxes" that arise when we *interpret* behavior as in conformity with such and such a rule.

23. Cf. *Philosophical Investigations* §226: "What has to be accepted, the given, is—so one could say—forms of life." Ibid. §217. "I have exhausted the justifications . . . my spade is turned." Finally, cf. *Remarks on the Foundations of Mathematics* VI–31 (cited and discussed in McDowell 1998, 242): "The difficult thing here is not to dig down to the ground; no, it is to recognize the ground that lies before us as the ground."

24. See chapter 1, page 23. A quietistic interpretation of the Madhyamaka stance about the world's things existing customarily (*vyavahārasat*) is not that thought, language, and human transactions actually create them but that one cannot intelligibly come up with any undergirding for them that would be radically outside, or beyond, thought, language, and transactions. Those two interpretations are not the same. To take a provocative Tibetan formulation: there is no other way of establishing things (*'jog byed gzhan med pa*) besides, or beyond, our *vyavahāra*. See chapter 11, page 209–10 on the differences between an antirealist and a quietistic interpretation of the Madhyamaka idea that things are what they are because of, or in a context of, thought, language, and human transactions.

25. Cf. *Remarks on the Foundations of Mathematics* VI–35 (cited in McDowell 1998, 240): "How do I know that the colour that I am now seeing is called 'green'? . . . If I am drowning and I shout 'Help!,' how do I know what the word Help means? Well, that's how I react in this situation.—Now *that* is how I know what 'green' means as well and also know how I have to follow the rule in the particular case."

Madhyamaka's Promise as Philosophy

1. Trying to Be Fair

MADHYAMAKA, the philosophy of the middle, is one of the principal interpretations of Mahāyāna Buddhist scriptures and has a lineage of several prolific and revered thinkers in India, Tibet, and China, beginning with Nāgārjuna and Āryadeva in about the second century CE and going on to Candrakīrti and Bhāviveka in the sixth century, Kamalaśīla and Śāntarakṣita in the eighth, and a host of illustrious Tibetan exponents, not the least of which was Tsongkhapa (Tsong kha pa) in the fourteenth century. It has fascinated Western writers from the end of the nineteenth century on, including the major figures in Buddhist philology, like Theodore Stcherbatsky, Louis de La Vallée Poussin, and Étienne Lamotte, and even some well-known philosophers, like Karl Jaspers. Practitioners of Buddhism in the West inspired by, or belonging to, one or another Tibetan school often faithfully endorse the hierarchy of Indian thought as found in the genre of Tibetan works known as *grub mtha'* or *siddhānta*, the doxographical literature that maintains that Buddhist philosophy culminates in the Madhyamaka. The point is incontestable: Madhyamaka, whether in the East or in the West, has often been revered for its depth and has stimulated many of the best minds in Buddhism and in Buddhist studies. I'll attempt a working philosophical introduction and will seek to bring out what I think is promising philosophically. I will not do a survey of the history and literature of the school, as others have done that already and much better than I can here. I will, however, approach that philosophy in a slightly more backhanded way than is usual. To see what is promising we first need to look seriously at a potentially darker side to Madhyamaka, for there are interesting and well-informed contemporary critics of Madhyamaka who have seen deviousness and fraudulence where most everyone else saw depth.

The first article in this direction was that of Richard Robinson (1972) entitled "Did Nāgārjuna Really Refute all Philosophical Views?" For Robinson, the principal complaint was that Nāgārjuna and the Madhyamaka school were attributing to their opponents notions and positions to which these opponents themselves would never agree. The second major article was a follow-up to Robinson by Richard P. Hayes (1994), "Nāgārjuna's Appeal," in which the author argued that not only did this Mādhyamika regularly misrepresent his opponent's positions and thus refute a man of straw, but that his key arguments only appear to work because of a systematic equivocation upon the polysemic term "intrinsic nature" (*svabhāva*). While Robinson saw a strategy of deliberate misrepresentation, Hayes added equivocation to the would-be sins of Nāgārjuna.[1]

That there would be this strong negative turn some time or another is to quite a degree understandable. After all, what could be more irritating to a good, serious scholar than a general idolatry of a philosophy that seemed to him to be a series of bad arguments, misrepresentations, and sloppy or deliberate plays on words? The temptation is great to buck the tide of exaggerated claims. Nonetheless, the Robinson-Hayes type of reaction is short on charity, leading to more heat than light. Worse, it is sometimes short on some potentially relevant information on the complicated points it treats. Indeed, as we shall see, the later Indian and Tibetan Mādhyamika scholastic had taken up accusations similar to those Robinson and Hayes are leveling and had some solutions that involved considerable ingenuity and in some cases, I would argue, significant insights. I think it is clear that at least the impatient tone of Robinson's and Hayes's articles is unfair: the Mādhyamika philosopher is much, much less of an amateur; or to put it more strongly, he is less of a trickster or fraud than Robinson and Hayes make him out to be.

It would be too involved and technical in the present context to undertake a blow-by-blow analysis of the passages that modern critics of the Madhyamaka cite. Nor fortunately do I think we need to do this, as we can get our points across with a reconstruction of some general strategies in this school's argumentation. But before we delve into that, it is worthwhile to point out that the argumentation is not *just* what should make or break this philosophy, or other philosophies, for us. Even if certain of the different sorts of arguments that we find in these Madhyamaka texts might seem unconvincing to us, as they probably often do, it would nonetheless be a mistake to thereby dismiss Madhyamaka thought in general. To take a parallel, I think that many people, other than perhaps certain die-hard analytic philosophers, would think it strangely narrow to dismiss the philosophies of St. Thomas Aquinas or René Descartes purely because of the unconvincingness of the Five Ways or the ontological argument—it would be seen as narrow because somehow these philosophies are more than just those arguments; they involve a certain systematic vision, approach, and method of thinking that is of interest and can be developed further, even if many of the actual arguments that Aquinas and Descartes themselves gave might often leave us less than converted. It may be that someone formulates other arguments to arrive at essentially Thomistic or Cartesian conclusions. So I think it may be with Nāgārjuna and the Madhyamaka: even if some of the reasoning that he gave in the second century leaves us puzzled in the twenty-first, the philosophic vision is of interest and could well find support in arguments possibly quite different from those of Nāgārjuna himself. In the last chapter of this book, I suggest some ways in which this update could be pursued. In short, I think the Madhyamaka should be of interest to contemporary scholars, because the system and philosophic vision should be of interest. On the most general level the Madhyamaka is trenchantly asking the question "What is a thing?" This question, as well as the Mādhyamika thinker's attempted answers, should be of interest to philosophers, be they analytic philosophers concerned with issues of realism, antirealism, and quietism, or so-called continental philosophers, such as the Heideggerians meditating on *Die Frage nach dem Ding*.

I

For our purposes, that is, to try to reopen the debate on Madhyamaka in a fairer way and bring out some of what seems promising in the Madhyamaka vision, we need to do two things: have a working description of what Madhyamaka is and dispel, to some degree at least, the accusations of sleight of hand and amateurism.

The Madhyamaka is in the first place a philosophy that denies, across the board, that things (whatever they might be) have any intrinsic nature (*svabhāva*). This lack of intrinsic nature, or what it terms "emptiness of intrinsic nature" (*svabhāvena śūnyatā*), is considered the ultimate truth (*paramārthasatya*) or ultimate reality. Now there have been certain interpretations of Madhyamaka that have tended to go in the direction of taking this ultimate truth as a kind of permanent absolute, much more real than the phenomena of our ordinary world, which are supposedly just widespread illusions that the world shares in common due to its general ignorance of this absolute. On the other hand, we also find in Indian and Tibetan literature a carefully developed position that the ultimate, or emptiness of intrinsic nature, is itself nothing more real than the ordinary things that make up our world. To say, therefore, that ordinary things lack intrinsic nature is not to describe a genuine reality lying behind or separate from them but is rather to give the final and best account of how ordinary things are; indeed this "no-intrinsic-nature-ness" (*niḥsvabhāvatā, naiḥsvābhāvya*) is just itself without any intrinsic nature, no more no less.

No-intrinsic-nature-ness is supposedly, however, something that is difficult to realize, something extremely subtle that has a deep effect upon us when we do realize it. Following the usual canonical descriptions, a superficial understanding of "no-intrinsic-nature-ness" even inspires terror, but a genuine understanding is a liberating experience.[2] Why would this realization be liberating at all, and what would this liberation be like? Of course, there are elaborate scholastic accounts as to how this liberation comes about, who has it, and when. However, I think the fundamental Madhyamaka stance is that people's thought and language is through and through pervaded with an almost instinctive and confused reification: we grasp at things, and hold that, if they are to exist at all, things must possess consistent intrinsic natures that are what they are completely independently, in themselves. The emotional and ethical life of people is then supposedly directly conditioned by this systematic reification. One of the many surprising Madhyamaka positions is that the ordinary person is also fundamentally in the dark about how he or she reifies ordinary things. Instead of the Madhyamaka advocating a simple acquiescence in the banal, there thus are significant discoveries to be undertaken. Understanding emptiness and being liberated is understanding the ordinary, or the so-called "customary truth" or "customary reality" (*saṃvṛtisatya*),[3] as is, stripped of our all-pervasive reifications of intrinsic natures and related confusions; it is an understanding of *saṃvṛtimātra*—what is just customary, as is, and no more.[4]

So much for the basic picture of Madhyamaka as I see it. Clearly the key term here is *svabhāva*, intrinsic nature. Broadly speaking, a recurrent semantic feature of the term, whether in Madhyamaka or in other philosophies, is that *svabhāva* is something or some property that exists objectively and genuinely occurs in, or qualifies, certain things; it is thus to be contrasted with an appearance that is absent from, or fails to correspond to, the thing themselves. Thus, to take the stock Indian analogy: when a striped rope is seen as a snake, the pseudo-snake that appears is not present in, or corresponding to, the striped rope. In the Madhyamaka texts we find this fundamental sense expressed in terms of designations and their bases: to say that something has an intrinsic nature and is not just a mere appearance or a mere designation (*prajñaptimātra*) due to language and thought means that it withstands logical analysis and that it is findable or obtainable by reason in the "basis of designation." The pseudo-snake is obviously not findable anywhere in the striped rope—a fact that any worldling can verify—but if we switch to a more sophisticated level, that of ultimate analysis of the mode of being of things, then according to the Madhyamaka, nothing is fully findable in its bases, and in that sense, nothing has intrinsic nature.

Note that the formulation I have adopted in terms of *x* having a *svabhāva* implying that *x* and its properties are findable when one searches logically, or equivalently, that *x* and its properties have the ability to withstand logical analysis (*rigs pas dpyad bzod pa*), is not literally what occurs in the texts of Nāgārjuna himself. However, the locution "ability to withstand logical analysis" and variants upon this terminology *are* prominently used by most major Indian Mādhyamika writers, who say that customary things exist for us only insofar as they are not analyzed (*avicāratas*), or to take the striking formulation of Śrīgupta and Atiśa, they are "fine [only] when not analyzed" (*avicāraramaṇīya*).[5] "Findable/obtainable/perceptible as existent under analysis" figures in such texts as, for example, *Madhyamakāvatāra* 6.160, where Candrakīrti discusses the so-called sevenfold reasoning (*rnam bdun gyi rigs pa*) and says that when yogins analyze things, the latter are not found (*rnyed pa*) to have any of the seven possible relationships to parts.[6] Under analysis, wholes are neither identical with nor different from their parts, meaning that when we look for, or analyze, what we take to be the intrinsic nature of something like a cart in terms of possible part-whole relations, we come up empty-handed: we don't find (apprehend/perceive) any coherent, unassailable version of what this cart or its cartness could be. And in that sense, we don't find any real thing: the customary cart only exists unanalyzed. These ways of interpreting Nāgārjuna are probably present in one way or another in all the important currents of Indian Madhyamaka philosophy and especially so in the later Indian Madhyamaka works, such as those of Candrakīrti, Jñānagarbha, Śrīgupta, Śāntarakṣita, and Kamalaśīla. There is a quasi consensus among commentators on this unfindability under analysis, and I see no reason to deny that, on this very broad characterization at least, they may well have gotten Nāgārjuna pretty much right.

As we shall discuss shortly, Richard Hayes also focused on something like this sense of *svabhāva*, but instead of speaking of it being a type of analytically findable identity or intrinsic nature, he spoke of it as being identity *simpliciter*. Thus for him this usage of *svabhāva* meant just what something is, its identity, as opposed to what it is not, its difference from other things.[7] This is not far from accurate as a general account but nonetheless lacks a very important feature in Madhyamaka contexts. The term *svabhāva* can indeed mean identity, what something is—as for example in Abhidharma texts or when Mādhyamikas themselves endorse the generally recognized verity that fire has the *svabhāva* of heat—but it is always more than that in the polemical contexts where it is being refuted by the Madhyamaka. In those contexts, it is an identity that withstands analysis—that is hence real and not just customary; it is consistent and does not dissolve into contradictions when subjected to logical analysis. This is why I prefer to speak of this sense of *svabhāva* as an "analytically findable intrinsic nature" or "analytically findable identity," thus bringing out the fact that the Mādhyamika is arguing against *real* identity, what something really is. In their polemical attributions of *svabhāva* to "realists," or advocates of "real entities" (*bhāva*), the Mādhyamikas always take this *svabhāva* as involving a reification, a misguided attempt to confer some sort of an ultimate status to things, a *bhāvasvabhāva.* As I will try to show below, this idea that realists, and indeed we ourselves, are constantly engaged in reification—that is, a type of distorting projection—is the thread that ties the would-be double use of the term *svabhāva* together. Before we get to that, however, let us very briefly look at Nāgārjuna's own use of *svabhāva.*

In chapter 15 of his most important work, the *Mūlamadhyamakakārikā*, Nāgārjuna develops what seems to be a different use of "intrinsic nature" from that which we have termed "analytically findable identity." In the first two verses he speaks instead of an intrinsic nature as something that "cannot arise due to causes and conditions" (*na saṃbhavaḥ svabhāvasya yuktaḥ pratyayahetubhiḥ*) and as that which is "not fabricated and is not dependent on anything else" (*akṛtrimaḥ svabhāvo hi nirapekṣaḥ paratra ca*).[8] It is this sense that Robinson would take as the point of departure for his critique, arguing that Nāgārjuna foists upon his innocent opponent an acceptance of an absurd and self-contradictory *svabhāva* (after all, would anyone actually acknowledge that things are independent of causes and conditions?) and proceeds to an all-too-easy refutation of his opponent by saying that *this* cannot exist.[9] Equally it is this second sense of *svabhāva* that Hayes would seize upon to show that the Madhyamaka arguments' seeming persuasiveness will evaporate when we diagnose the equivocations between the first and second senses of *svabhāva*. Let us term these two aspects intrinsic-nature-as-findable-identity and intrinsic-nature-as-independent-existence.[10] As I had mentioned earlier, Hayes spoke of the first sense as identity *simpliciter*, but it's worth our while to stress that it is actually a type of *analytically findable* identity, or analytically findable intrinsic nature. So I'll deliberately take the liberty of modifying Hayes' formulation a bit and add the qualification of "findability" to identity.

Now, I think that it is quite clear that Nāgārjuna himself made a conscious attempt to fuse these two would-be separate aspects of *svabhāva* in some sort of mutually implicative relationship. In his *Mūlamadhyamakakārikā* 18.10, we find:

> *pratītya yad yad bhavati na hi tāvat tad eva tat /*
> *na cānyad api tat tasmān nocchinnaṃ nāpi śāśvatam //*

> Whatever *x* exists in dependence [upon *y*], that *x* is not identical to *y*, nor is it other than *y*. Therefore it is neither eliminated nor eternal.

The passage is in effect stating that whatever exists dependently—in other words, whatever lacks independent existence—also lacks findable identity, for being a findable identity means, according to Nāgārjuna, that one should be able to say rationally, in a way that stands up to analysis, that a thing is either identifiable with, or is something different from, the things it depends upon. In short: if *x* and *y* are dependent, they do not have independent existence; if they do not have independent existence, they do not have a findable identity. And providing that this "if then" paraphrase of Nāgārjuna's verse is right, it follows by applications of *modus tollens* that whatever *x* and *y* have findable identity must also have independent existence and will not be dependent on anything. The route from findability to independence is thus short: for Nāgārjuna, a findable identity entails independence. If we add the term "intrinsic nature," it looks like the following entailment holds for Nāgārjuna: intrinsic-nature-as-findable-entity entails intrinsic-nature-as-independent-existence.

There is another famous passage in the *Mūlamadhyamakakārikā* that rather clearly supports our contention that Nāgārjuna himself saw a link between findability and independence and thus between the two aspects of the semantic range of the supposedly equivocal term *svabhāva*. This is the extremely well-known verse 24.18, which makes a series of equivalences or mutual implications, including one between being dependent and being something just simply designated by the mind on the basis of other things, especially its parts:

> *yaḥ pratītyasamutpādaḥ śūnyatāṃ tāṃ pracakṣmahe /*
> *sā prajñaptir upādāya pratipat saiva madhyamā //*

> Dependent arising, that we declare to be emptiness. This [emptiness] is [equivalent to] being a designation in dependence. And it [i.e., emptiness] is precisely the middle way.

Without going into a detailed exegesis of this rich and complex verse, we can fairly readily see that an attempt is once again being made to connect the concepts of dependence and unfindability or, equally, findability and independence. Being a designation in dependence upon something else has to be understood as being just a designation and no more (*prajñaptimātra*): the thing in question cannot be found if we subject it to analysis. What is dependent, then, is unfindable under analysis.

We'll come back to the type of argumentation strategies used by Nāgārjuna, but in any case, I think we already should have an inkling that a relatively natural reading of Nāgārjuna is to take him as accepting a very close link between the two aspects of *svabhāva*. In fact, I strongly suspect that the link is not just a conditional in one direction but is rather a biconditional; in other words, *x* has independent existence *if and only if x* is analytically findable. Besides findability under analysis implying independence, it looks to me that Nāgārjuna would also accept the converse, that if something were to be of a genuinely independent intrinsic nature (namely, independent of causes, parts, and all activities to understand it), it would have to be somehow findable under analysis—for example, as something completely distinct from parts or from any kind of causal history, and present in an object independently of any conventions, customs, or cognitive and linguistic processes. It would be a genuine absolute completely other than the relative. The candidates for this sort of absolute would be things like nirvāṇa or the "unconditioned" (*asaṃskṛta*), and it is not surprising that Nāgārjuna subjects them to a trenchant critique of unfindability under analysis. In short, it looks like, for Nāgārjuna at least, findability under analysis and independence are two equivalent, mutually implicative, notions. If we say that sometimes the use of the term *svabhāva* seems to highlight one aspect and sometimes the other, that does not mean that term *svabhāva* is thereby equivocal: we may well have two ways to unpack one and the same concept. If that is right, then the minimum result of our discussion up to this point is that it should begin to look rather doubtful that Nāgārjuna is guilty of the gross equivocation of which he is accused by Hayes. He may perhaps have been wrong, he may have even done something that we cannot easily follow, but he did not just simply play on two different senses.

II

A few words about Robinson's paper and the charge that the Mādhyamika pursued a sophistical strategy of misrepresenting his opponents as accepting an absurd and contradictory notion of *svabhāva*. Robinson had argued: "The validity of Nāgārjuna's refutations hinges upon whether his opponents really upheld the existence of a *svabhāva* or *svabhāva* as he defines the term."[11] He then proceeded to survey the various opponents' positions to see whether "Nāgārjuna succeed[s] in refuting all views without making any assumptions that are not conceded by the adherents of the particular view under attack."[12] I won't evaluate the actual list of "axioms" that Robinson attributes to the Mādhyamika himself and their nonacceptance by the Mādhyamika's opponents, as fortunately we need not enter into the details of this rather complicated picture. I maintain that the accuracy of those details is in any case a secondary debate. Instead, what is significant for us here is Robinson's general line of argument that the Mādhyamika philosopher is just practicing sleight of hand *because* he attributes to his opponents things they do not accept.

It is in fact quite unfair to accuse Nāgārjuna of deliberate misrepresentation *simply* because he attributed to his opponent things that the same opponent would reject, even vociferously. Certainly if an opponent did not recognize something attributed to him, that in itself would not necessarily mean that he was misrepresented, for it is a natural and even inevitable part of many genuinely philosophical debates between truth seekers that at some point one group says what the other actually thinks, or what they *must* think if they are to remain consistent with their own basic principles. Of course, there are good and bad, fair and unfair, ways to do this, but the simple fact of one party adopting such a move in a debate does not in itself mean that it is misrepresenting the other or playing, what Robinson calls, a type of sophistical "shell game."

The issue can be reformulated: Are Mādhyamikas then being sincere and fair to their opponents, and (often or mostly) doing truth-seeking philosophy, or are they just playing at disingenuous word games, purporting to convey significant truth but actually being quite disinterested in whether anything they say is true at all (what an analytic philosopher like Harry Frankfurt would designate with the technical term "bullshit")?[13] I think the texts would tend to back mostly the former view, even if the dichotomy is a little simplistic and the line that we want to draw between truth seeking and sophistry is often shaded. In any case, Mādhyamikas, or at least many Mādhyamikas, were quite aware that misrepresentation was a charge *they* had to answer, and they tried to answer it (as far I can see) with sincerity. Of course, it might be that they were in the long run unsatisfying in their answers, but it's very hard to agree that they were just performing a *trompe l'oeil* or deliberately setting up their opponent with facile self-contradictions.

For example, the eighth-century Indian writer Kamalaśīla, in his *Madhyamakāloka,* was confronted with the objection that his opponents would not themselves acknowledge the logical reasons that the Mādhyamika was using, and that therefore the reasons would be "unestablished" (*asiddhahetu*). He replied with rather detailed arguments showing that his adversaries *would have to accept* the reason, in spite of their vociferous denials, because it was entailed by other propositions that they did explicitly accept. The tactic of argumentation is clear and figures repeatedly in the discussion of the "neither one nor many" argument (*ekānekaviyogahetu*) in the *Madhyamakāloka,* from folio 215b to 218a in the Sde dge edition (henceforth "D.").[14] Indeed Kamalaśīla systematically takes up the objections of numerous sorts of Buddhist and non-Buddhists who argue that they have been misrepresented by the Mādhyamika who alleges that things *they* accept (God, atoms, space, consciousness, and so on) are neither single entities nor several different entities (and are hence unreal). Kamalaśīla's reply is always the same: the adversary accepts by implication, or has in fact accepted (*shugs kyis na khas blangs pa nyid, khas blangs pa kho na*), that the pseudo-entity to which he subscribes is neither one thing nor many different things, because he accepts such and such a property of this entity, and that property in fact implies being neither one nor many. The key Tibetan term *shugs kyis na* that is used here probably translated a Sanskrit original term along the lines of *sāmārthyāt,* "indirectly," "by implication." One example passage from *Madhyamakāloka* should suffice to show how such "acceptance by implication" works:

> *gang dag gis lus la sogs pa rdul phran bsags pa tsam yin pa'i phyir rdul phra rab rnams so so re re gcig pa nyid du kun brtags pa de dag gis kyang sbyor ba dang bsags pa sogs pa'i chos su khas blangs pa'i phyir shugs kyis na gcig pa nyid dang bral pa nyid kyang khas blangs pa kho na yin te /*
>
> Those who imagine that each atom individually is one thing since the body and other such [gross objects] are just simply collections of atoms do in fact also accept by implication that [the atoms] lack oneness, for they accept that [the atoms] have properties (*chos*), such as being junctions or collections [of parts].[15]

Nor should it be thought that this use of "acceptance by implication," or perhaps more simply "implicit acceptance," was an occasional flash in the pan of one Indian thinker; it looks to me to be a more or less basic Indo-Tibetan Madhyamaka argument strategy. In Tibet, the same basic general method of attributing positions by implication was often known as presenting what the "opponent's position ends up being" (*khas len pa'i mthar thug pa*) or, less literally, "the upshot" of his views. One also finds in certain texts the related notion *rigs pas 'phul ba*, "forcing [a position upon the opponent] through logical reasoning" or *'phul mtshams kyi rigs pa*, literally and suggestively translated as a "logical reasoning that pushes one's limits."

Interestingly enough, although the term *'phul mtshams* is not, to my knowledge, found in any dictionary, including the three-volume *Tibetan-Tibetan-Chinese Dictionary*, or *Bod rgya tshig mdzod chen mo*, a quick search of the Asian Classics Input Project database of Tibetan collected works (*gsung 'bum*) reveals that *'phul mtshams* occurs eighty-two times—if we were to add the variants like *rigs pas 'phul*, *'phul nus pa'i rigs pa*, and so on, we would be into hundreds of occurrences, largely in later commentaries, but also occasionally in Tsongkhapa's works, like his *Dbu ma dgongs pa rab gsal* on Candrakīrti's *Madhyamakāvatāra*. It seems to have escaped lexicographers, and so it escaped Western researchers on Madhyamaka too.[16] That said, I have the strong impression that it was, and still is, pretty much common knowledge among many Tibetan monks. Indeed, this technique of logically imposing principles upon recalcitrant opponents was, according to the late Geshé Tamdin Rabten, essential in actual Geluk monastic debates on Madhyamaka and was typically used when someone wanted to show that having an intrinsic nature, or equivalently "being truly established" (*bden par grub pa*), or being truly established as such and such a thing, would imply its being such and such in "complete independence from everything whatsoever" (*gang la'ang bltos med*).[17]

In fact, this implication of complete independence from causes, parts, and also from the cognizing mind is amply attested in the texts and is not just an oral tradition. It figures, for example, in an extract from Se ra Rje bstun Chos kyi rgyal mtshan's *Skabs dang po'i spyi don* that I translated a number of years ago.[18] I think the implication in question is a compactly formulated version of the principle that we were stressing earlier in looking at the two verses from Nāgārjuna: namely, that findability under analysis, or findable identity, implies complete independence. What is noteworthy in the present context is that this implication, according to experienced debaters like Geshé Rabten, is known as a case of *rigs pas 'phul ba*. Of course, it would allegedly hold whether the opponent liked it or not—his protests would just be grounds for more debate, a debate that could, nevertheless, be quite sincere and truth-seeking.

III

Let us now take up anew the problem of the link between findability and independence. While it should be clear that the Madhyamaka, with its strategy of implications, upshots, and imposed principles, is probably a much more sophisticated and interesting philosophy than Robinson and Hayes made it out to be, its use of these implications between findable identity and independence is a particularly important step and is, admittedly, not an easy one to fathom. Perhaps at some point much further down the road we might come to the conclusion that we should give up on it all and go back to detecting misrepresentations, equivocation, and other forms of sloppy thinking. But I think that Robinson and Hayes were far too quick in taking that step. So how does the link work? If we grant, as I think we should, that Mādhyamikas were not cunningly equivocating on *svabhāva* and misrepresenting their opponents, then how did *they* think that the seeming gap between findability and independence should be bridged?

There is unfortunately no quick answer. To arrive at a charitable interpretation of Madhyamaka thought that would start to answer that question, we need to be clearer on how the mass of seemingly diverse arguments in Madhyamaka might work together. I can see at least three argument strategies that are relevant in this context, all three present in varying degrees in Madhyamaka texts, although for the purposes of this paper I'll have to be brief and concentrate on broad outlines rather than on the detailed exegesis of specific textual passages. Here are the three:

1. Selective use of pan-Indian philosophical debates
2. Etymological and purely semantic arguments
3. Nonobvious facts about our mental makeup and way of seeing the world.

We first turn to what I am calling "the selective use of pan-Indian debates." A good example of this is found in Dharmapāla's commentary on Āryadeva's *Catuḥśataka*, where this sixth-century Vijñānavāda commentator on Madhyamaka examines the possibility of vision and other sensory experiences, and embarks on a detailed analysis on whether the subtle matter of the eye has contact with its object.[19] The problem thus is whether the senses act at a distance. This is a bona fide pan-Indian debate, known as the problem of *prāpyakāritvavāda* ("action by contact") and *aprāpyakāritvavāda* ("action without contact"), and interestingly enough, Dharmapāla accepts the critique of each side against the other.[20] This acceptance of the absurdities raised by both sides means that the Madhyamaka can then move to the desired conclusion that all possibilities of *genuine* vision are riddled with faults, and that it is hence impossible that people do *really* see anything. For Dharmapāla, Āryadeva's end was best served by showing that both sides of the debate were untenable—the two adversaries' refutations were both accepted, with the result that the eyes, objects, and perceptions were shown to be without intrinsic nature, unable to resist a thorough examination, and hence unfindable under analysis.

We see a similar strategy at work in the Madhyamaka arguments on causality—for example, whether effects and causes are essentially identical or different. Causality was regularly examined in terms of two alternatives, *satkāryavāda* and *asatkāryavāda*, or the "theory of the effect existing or not existing" at the time of the cause; predictably Nāgārjuna's conclusion is that neither alternative is possible.[21] We also see this use of pan-Indian themes in Nāgārjuna's use of the recurring controversy on parts (*avayava*) and wholes (*avayavin*)—whether parts are identical to or different from wholes, or whether wholes are somehow more or less real than parts. Here too the conclusion is that none of the alternatives are satisfactory and yet, if something genuinely had intrinsic nature, it would have to fit in with one of the two possible positions. The conclusion is immediate: no intrinsic nature.

What is noteworthy for us is that this peculiar type of acceptance of both sides' refutations in pan-Indian controversies *does* make for a bridge between intrinsic-nature-as-independent-existence and intrinsic-nature-as-findable-identity. In *Mūlamadhyamakakārikā* 18.10, cited above, we saw that when *x* was dependent on *y*, the two were neither genuinely identical nor different; at least following Candrakīrti's interpretation in *Prasannapadā*, the argument turns on the *satkāryavāda-asatkāryavāda* debate: the cause would be neither the same nor different from the effect. *Mūlamadhyamakakārikā* 24.18, it will be recalled, made a linkage between being dependent and being a mere designation (*prajñaptimātra*), that is to say, between dependence and being unanalyzable, unfindable. Here Candrakīrti explicitly glosses the verse in terms of the problem of parts and wholes—everything has parts and is dependent upon parts but cannot be found as the same or different from the parts.

Whether it is causality or part-whole problems that are at stake, the Madhyamaka very often relies upon the same type of argumentation strategy: use one side of a pan-Indian debate off against the other to show that dependence will imply not being findable, and thus show that findability entails independence. If things were dependent *and* findable under analysis, then the cause-and-effect relationship would be either along the lines of *satkāryavāda* or *asatkāryavāda*, but it is neither of the two; therefore things cannot be both dependent and findable. Similarly for parts and wholes: if things were dependent and findable, then they would be identical or different from their parts, but they are neither; therefore they are not both dependent and findable. The linkage between dependence and being unfindable is thus made by means of an implicit three-step argument:

1. For things to be both dependent and findable under analysis would imply a solution to major pan-Indian debates, such as those concerning part and wholes and causality.
2. These debates have no such solution.
3. Ergo dependence and findability are incompatible and cannot both be asserted.

If things are dependent, they cannot be findable under analysis; their findability entails their independence from causes, parts, and all other factors.

The second approach—etymologies and semantics—is what one finds in *Mūlamadhyamakakārikā* chapter 15 on *svabhāva*, and especially in Candrakīrti's exegesis upon this chapter in his *Prasannapadā*. It is the type of argumentation where the Mādhyamika says that if something has *svabhāva*, the word *svabhāva* is to be analyzed as meaning that the thing has its own being—that is, *svo bhāvaḥ*. Equally, in the world, to say that a property is the *svabhāva* of something is to say that it is "natural," "innate," "intrinsic," and is not "fabricated" by extraneous causal facts, just as heat is said by the world to be an intrinsic nature of fire but not of water (because when we boil water, the heat has to be brought in "from the outside").

As an adequate treatment of the use of semantic arguments in Madhyamaka texts would take us too far afield here, for our present purposes we will again skirt overly detailed textual exegesis. The semantic approach in arguments like the one about fire, water, and heat is probably best viewed as providing no more than approximate illustrations and analogies and not rigorous probative demonstrations about *svabhāva*'s complete independence. Indeed Candrakīrti himself, in the *Prasannapadā*, goes on to stress that actually the heat, because it *is* causally dependent, does *not* have intrinsic nature for the Mādhyamika at all, and he thereby acknowledges rather clearly the approximate and merely illustrative aspect to his discussion about fire, water, and heat.[22] Not only that, but in stressing the limits of the fire-heat case, he suggests that what constitutes the intrinsic nature that he and other Mādhyamikas are refuting is not just the worldly conception of a natural, innate, or intrinsic property like fire's heat, but something more subtle and radical in that it involves *complete* independence. It may be approximately illustrated by reference to the ordinary worldly notion of nature with its partial independence from certain types of (extraneous) causes, but it is not the same as that notion, because it goes much further in its independence. Similarly for the etymological argument about *svo bhāvaḥ*, which immediately precedes the fire-water-heat analogy: this too is explicitly recognized by Candrakīrti to be showing how "it is established, for the world, that intrinsic nature is not a fabricated entity."[23] It is at most indirectly illustrating the type of *svabhāva* that the Madhyamaka is attacking. But once again, that latter *svabhāva* is something rather special and is not simply identifiable with the ordinary notion of intrinsic nature with which the world is familiar.[24]

Finally, the third strategy—invoking nonobvious facts about our mental makeup and way of conceiving the world—is arguably what pins down better the interpretation of the first two as involving a subtle sense of intrinsic nature. An extremely important feature of Madhyamaka philosophy is that it depends heavily on the idea of the Mādhyamika refuting our "superimpositions" (*samāropa*): our inveterate tendencies to distort the world by systematically imposing upon it "intrinsic natures." *Svabhāva* is thus a false projection upon otherwise innocuous objects of our customary world that do not have such *svabhāva*, and the task of the Mādhyamika is to refute these projections but not the customary world itself. This key emphasis on distinguishing subtle superimpositions of intrinsic nature from the otherwise innocuous customary world of ordinary objects is to be found in texts of Candrakīrti, Jñānagarbha, Kamalaśīla, and many others, and perhaps even in those of Nāgārjuna himself, at least if we believe the commentators. To take a passage from Jñānagarbha's *Satyadvayavibhaṅgavṛtti* (D. 12a–b):

> *gzugs la sogs pa'i lus rtog pa'i nyes pas ma sbags pa gzhan gyi dbang gi bdag nyid rnam par shes pa tsam snang ba dgag par mi nus pa 'ba' zhig tu ma zad kyi / byed na byed pa po la mngon sum la sogs pas phyir gnod pa kho na byed do //*

> We cannot negate physical things, visible matter and the like, which are untainted by conceptualization's corruptions, are of a dependent nature, and are appearances to simple [nonconceptual] cognition. Not only is this impossible, but if we did [negate such things] then the person who performed [this negation] would in fact be subsequently refuted by direct perception (*pratyakṣa*) and other [sources of knowledge].

Compare Kamalaśīla in the *Madhyamakāloka* (D. 180a):

> *des na dngos po rnams kyi ngo bo nyid kun rdzob pa la yang gnod pa ni mi byed kyi / 'on kyang de la bden pa'i rnam pa nyid du sgro btags pa sel ba'i phyir rab tu sgrub par byed pa kho na yin no //*
>
> We do not invalidate the customary natures of entities but instead just prove [the absence of real intrinsic nature] in order to exclude what is superimposed (*sgro btags pa = samāropita, adhyāropita*) upon the [customary entities] as their aspect of being true/real (*bden pa'i rnam pa*).

Finally, Candrakīrti also stressed that there had to be an all-important distinction between things and the intrinsic nature (*svarūpa = svabhāva*) of things. *Prasannapadā* 58.10–11:

> *tasmād anutpannā bhāvā ity evaṃ tāvad viparītasvarūpādhyāropapratipakṣeṇa prathamaprakaraṇārambhaḥ / idānīṃ kvacid yaḥ kaścid viśeṣo 'dhyāropitas tadviśeṣāpākaraṇārthaṃ śeṣaprakaraṇārambhaḥ / gantṛgantavyagamanādiko 'pi niravaśeṣo viśeṣo nāsti pratītyasamutpādasyeti pratipādanārtham //*
>
> Thus, when [Nāgārjuna] says "entities do not arise" in this way, first of all [it is pointed out that] the initial chapter [of the *Mūlamadhyamakakārikā*] was written as a counter to superimpositions (*adhyāropa*) of false intrinsic natures and then that the remaining chapters were written in order to eliminate whatever distinctions are superimposed anywhere, the [passage] is designed to show that dependent arising has absolutely no distinctions at all like goers, places to be gone over, and going, and so on.

Some remarks. First, all three authors regularly speak in one way or another of superimpositions (*adhyāropa, samāropa*), be they superimposed intrinsic natures (*svabhāva, svarūpa*), distinctions (*viśeṣa*), or aspects (*ākāra*)—the differences are essentially those of wording. Kamalaśīla's words, "what is superimposed upon the [customary entities] as their aspect of being true/real (*bden pa'i rnam pa*)," take on special significance because they show that this is a *reification*, a way of making things appear to us as much more real than they are. Second, in his article "On *samāropa*," Teruyoshi Tanji says quite rightly about the passage cited from *Prasannapadā*:

> Candrakīrti asserts that, strictly speaking, the effect of *samāropa* is not a thing but the own-being [i.e., intrinsic nature] of a thing, as he observes that . . . [*tasmād anutpannā bhāvā ity . . . pratipādanārtham*]. This observation [i.e., the passage in *Prasannapadā* 58.10–11], being the summary of the subjects of the chapters in the MMK [i.e., *Mūlamadhyamakakārikā*], expresses aptly the core of Candrakīrti's philosophy of emptiness. It is so important and cardinal that the meaning of all the other statements in his commentary ought to be estimated by way of meeting the view of this observation."[25]

I agree. In brief: at least for Jñānagarbha, Kamalaśīla, and Candrakīrti, refuting superimpositions (that is, reifications of things rather than customary things themselves) is what Madhyamaka thought is essentially about.[26] Mādhyamikas would thus refute superimposed versions of causes, parts, wholes, people, things, what have you, but not the causes, parts, wholes, and so on themselves upon which the superimpositions are made. It is here, in the reliance upon the contrast between superimpositions and the ordinary, that we see clearly that the *svabhāva* which the Mādhyamika is refuting is not just an ordinary and familiar property or nature like heat, impermanence, being blue, and so on—it can and should be distinguished (albeit with difficulty) from ordinary things. The result, however, of it not being identifiable with ordinary things is that it is nonobvious, and that it therefore needs some kind of in-depth investigation to recognize it for what it is.

Note in passing that while it seems clear that we must see Candrakīrti, Kamalaśīla, and other commentators as recommending an interpretation of Nāgārjuna as refuting superimpositions, the status of the "innocuous" customary things that remain is disputed. Many Indian and Tibetan thinkers (whom I term in chapter 2 "typical Prāsaṅgikas") hold that without intrinsic natures, the ordinary things themselves are just falsities (*mṛṣā*), deceptive appearances: they are not existent objects of reliable cognitions, "sources of knowledge" (*pramāṇa*), but fictions that are commonly but wrongly thought to be real. They may be innocuously accepted, indeed must be accepted, in appropriate practical contexts, but they are no more than *that*: false, fictional, but necessary. It is an interpretation that finds a natural confirmation in the recurrent Buddhist image of the customary world being just like the hairs and other such hallucinations that appear to people suffering from myodesopsia, or "floaters" (*timira*).[27] Others, however, hold that while the superimposed intrinsic natures are indeed thoroughly nonexistent and false, the remaining customary entities are not. Instead the customary entities, stripped of the superimpositions (though that is difficult), are the objects of sources of knowledge and thus exist and are real in a stronger sense than do mere fictions that are just commonly thought to exist. I won't delve into these issues further here. They are the subject of the next chapter. Suffice it to say that while the first account, "typical Prāsaṅgika," is a very natural Indian reading, the second account may well be philosophically more promising.[28]

In any case, if we adopt the commentarial approach and methodology of Candrakīrti, Kamalaśīla, Jñānagarbha, *et alii* on which we have been insisting, the use of semantical arguments, etymologies, and pan-Indian debates will have to be interpreted accordingly as refuting superimpositions. The Mādhyamikas were not seeking to eliminate customary entities—be they taken as commonly accepted fictions or objects of *pramāṇas*—nor even our customary and thus innocuous notion of natures, intrinsic properties, and so on (notions that the worldling does undoubtedly have and use);[29] rather they were seeking to refute a peculiar reified version of intrinsic nature, one that at most exhibits analogies to the customary notion. The pan-Indian arguments are being used to undermine superimpositions, or perhaps more exactly, the notions of parts, wholes, and so on as corrupted by a subtle, erroneous, superimposition that is responsible for them being reified. Both sides in such debates can have no consistent solution when what are at stake are notions corrupted by reifications.

What light would this threefold account of Madhyamaka argumentation bring to the link between findability and independence? The first problem would be exegetical: to look at some of the passages that Hayes discussed and try to see whether Nāgārjuna's arguments could work better and make better sense once we saw them as directed against a rather special target of things corrupted by superimpositions. I think they might well make better sense, in that the equivocations and nonsequiturs that Hayes diagnosed with regard to verses like *Mūlamadhyamakakārikā* 1.5 seem to disappear when we see *svabhāva* as always involving *both* analytically findable identity and independence. Similarly for the other verses that troubled Hayes. True, the verses highlight, at one time or another, one of the aspects of *svabhāva*, but the other aspect is always implicitly present. And if that is so, then the complicated analysis that Hayes gives us would be largely unnecessary and moot. Indeed, instead of hastening toward a reading discerning equivocations, we could adopt what Paul Grice once termed the "Modified Occam's Razor":

senses are not to be multiplied beyond necessity.[30] If we need not do what Richard Hayes did with Nāgārjuna, I think we had simply better not do it.

IV

I could imagine that defenders of Robinson's and Hayes's debunking of Madhyamaka might well say the following: if we avoid the charges of refuting straw men and equivocation by making *svabhāva* nonobvious in this way, we may have temporarily sheltered Nāgārjuna and company from the charge of sleight of hand but at the price of fuzz and obscurantism. Why should we believe that people see the world through these mysterious types of superimpositions of *svabhāva*? Indeed, strictly speaking, I have not taken up *that* question. After all, my rather longish argument so far has not actually been that the Mādhyamika philosopher is *right* but rather that he is not tricky, sloppy, equivocal, or amateurish. Now if one *also* wanted to argue that people who have not understood emptiness are inveterate realists and *do* make something like the superimpositions that the Mādhyamikas say they do, then the argumentation would have to go in a rather different direction.

First of all, quotations from Indian Buddhist scriptures would offer relatively little help. There is no shortage of passages from Buddhist sūtras that can be cited to show that people are ignorant and hence get the world systematically wrong, but such quotations would not be persuasive to anyone other than an already convinced Mahāyāna Buddhist. More controversially, I do not think that the mass of argumentation that one finds in Nāgārjuna's *Mūlamadhyamakakārikā* would *by itself* convince people that realists must make the superimpositions of *svabhāva* that Candrakīrti and others say they do. True, the *Mūlamadhyamakakārikā* does show a number of recurring dialectical strategies[31] in its attempts to find contradictions in all the major realist views in Indian philosophy. But there is no single overarching diagnosis to show that realisms all go wrong due to invariably involving a pernicious superimposition of *svabhāva*. Instead of a clearly articulated "master argument" to this effect, we have *ad hoc* counterarguments against each candidate view, with the conclusion being that nothing is fully real or has *svabhāva*. I suspect, then, that a big part of what perturbed Robinson, when he asked "Did Nāgārjuna Really Refute All Philosophical Views?" was the inconclusiveness of this procedure. There is no assurance that better views will not be found later by more sophisticated realist thinkers and that they will not, at some point, carry the day to show that some things *do* have *svabhāva* after all.[32]

Contrast the *ad hoc* approach with the sweeping range of the commentarial approach, where it is one and the same superimposition that always recurs and is responsible for the contradictions. On this type of reading, the structure of the argumentation becomes:

1. Any realist view always involves superimposition of *svabhāva.*
2. Superimpositions of *svabhāva* always lead to a finite number of recurring inconsistencies.
3. No realist views are or will be acceptable.

The quantity of argumentation needed can be drastically reduced and the emphasis shifts to understanding the mechanism of superimposition. But again, in the spirit of Robinson, it would be replied that we need arguments to establish the first two steps. Are these available? Not as much as some would like. One way to look at the matter would be to say that the zigzags of the twenty-seven chapters of the *Madhyamakakārikā* and their commentators might make one aware, or uncover, the superimpositions that we have. The parallel might be with the back-and-forth exchanges between Wittgenstein and his imagined opponents to *tease* out the hold that the picture theory or a certain conception of meaning and necessity has on thinking. Similarly, perhaps with *svabhāva*: running through the conceptual tangles in formulating a viable part-whole relation, account of causality, agency, perception, and so on brings the implicit turns of superimposition to the fore. There is probably no hard demonstration that we always make such superimpositions, however, if we mean by that an argument that would be convincing to the unsympathetic or unbelieving.

Another sort of approach could be marshaled, namely the specific psychological—or better, phenomenological—investigations that later Tibetans develop to uncover how people perceive and think of objects. When imagining unjust accusations, desirable outcomes, great praise, anger, and so on, the I stands out as if separate and real; the passions, in effect, bring out the latent grasping at *svabhāva* and thus uncover the place of the superimpositions in one's *Lebenswelt.* Investigations of this sort are especially found in Geluk Madhyamaka writing, in, for example, the *Dbu ma'i lta khrid* "Guidance on the Madhyamaka View" texts. And the recurring general theme of the need to "recognize what is to be refuted" (*dgag bya ngos 'dzin*)[33] figures in major texts such as the "Insight" (*lhag mthong*) chapter of Tsongkhapa's *Lam rim chen mo*; such recognition is often said to be the hardest and most essential step in Madhyamaka and needed so that the numerous Nāgārjunian reasonings neither refute too much (*khyab che ba*)—the customary things themselves—or too little (*khyab chung ba*)—purely speculative or theoretical notions not relevant to our actual experience.[34] Proper recognition enables the Gelukpa to use the "reasoning that forces [the opponents'] limits [of what they accept]" (*'phul mtshams kyi rigs pa*) of which we spoke earlier. Without that recognition it supposedly falls flat.

What kind of investigation is this and what might its results show? Certainly, if this can be said to be a type of phenomenology, it is very different from the usual Husserlian sort in that it does not use "bracketing" to arrive at the given latent structures of consciousness. Instead of suspension of judgment (*epoché*) to discern the given without biases and projections, the Tibetan Mādhyamika has various meditative techniques and, especially, thought experiments to exaggerate projections and bring them out more starkly. Those techniques presuppose key principles in the Buddhists' moral philosophy, in particular, the idea that underlying the passions is always *satkāyadṛṣṭi* (the false view of the personality). Grasping the I or phenomena as completely independent entities is thus not considered to be a state of mind that is *just created* when our thinking is clouded with pride or anger and absent otherwise. The opposite is so: it is allegedly there constantly. Part and parcel of every thought that beings who do not experientially understand emptiness might have is such a hypostatized intentional object. The task is again to tease it out.

V

Why *tease* it out? Why *not* just say clearly and starkly that people grasp at inherent natures, independence, findable identity, and so forth and that it is all wrong? Is that not what philosophers should do: say clearly what they think? If these superimpositions can only be teased out but not argued for more clearly, are they to be taken seriously? A Prāsaṅgika Mādhyamika has a potential response to this question, even if it might, at first sight, seem evasive. It would go something like this: bringing superimpositions of *svabhāva* out into stark clarity by simply describing them and saying they are wrong is actually counterproductive, for how could one readily distinguish between superimposed intrinsic natures and the innocent customary things? The danger is that one takes the superimposed as the innocent and then vociferously denies that there is anything wrong at all.

Indeed, the subtlety of the superimposition, and hence the difficulty in distinguishing it from the customary reality that should be conserved, is a key position of Gelukpa Prāsaṅgika commentators, who speak of the average man's life-world as a kind of "mixture" (*'dres pa*) between customary truth (which is innocent) and reification (which is not), as if there were two parts (*cha*) that normally appeared to the average man as one. It is also implicit in Candrakīrti's discussion of *saṃvṛtimātra*, the "merely customary"—merely customary things are not to be identified with what the average man sees and conceives but are, according to Candrakīrti, the ordinary as understood only by those who can see the world free of reifications, those noble ones (*ārya*) who have understood emptiness and are free of grasping things as being true (*satyābhimāna*). For these Mādhyamika writers, there is thus a sense in which grasping at *svabhāva* can only thrive in the shadows and is misunderstood when formulated in stark clarity for all to see. We may perhaps be able to tease it out in an indirect fashion, but direct formulations have no force. The risk is, in effect, a Robinson-like response that one was being attributed something absurd that one never accepted at all.

An illustration from another context may be of use in showing the possible dangers involved. The extreme difficulty of distinguishing the "purely ordinary" from the ignorant person's hybrid combination of ordinary-plus-superimpositions is not unlike that which, in another context, Wittgenstein faced in trying to separate what is right and wrong in our views about following rules. We easily think that when we follow a rule, like adding 2 to numbers from 0 on, the results are all already strongly determined and implicitly present from the start—Wittgenstein's well-known phrase is that we think rule-following is grounded in a "superlative fact."[35] The problem is that if grounding is what we require, we never could actually determine which such fact of the matter was at stake: the rule we (or anyone else) think we are following when we come up with a finite series of calculations like 0, 2, 4, 6 . . . 100 may be "add 2 to *n*," but it may just as well be "add 2 to *n* until 100 and then add 7." The behavioral sample is in accord with both. The same type of argument can always be repeated, *mutatis mutandis*, when new behavioral data is added to the sample. The conclusion in *Philosophical Investigations* §201: "This was our paradox: no course of action could be determined by a rule, because any course of action can be made out to accord with the rule." Nonetheless, someone then asks, "But *are* the steps then *not* determined by the algebraic formulae . . . in a *queer* way, the use itself is in some sense present." To this Wittgenstein replies, "But of course it is 'in some sense!' Really the only thing wrong with what you say is the expression 'in a queer way.' The rest is all right."[36]

One of the more interesting and persuasive analyses of the complexities inherent in philosophical reform of seemingly acceptable common-sense beliefs is that of Saul Kripke in his *Wittgenstein on Rules and Private Language*. The dangerous phase invariably comes in when we feel the need to formulate clearly what we deny and thus filter it out from what is acceptable in the common-sense belief; in other words, a problem arises when we try to explicitly separate the deep-seated queer way of taking things from what is all right, ordinary, and innocuous.

> For in denying that there is any such fact, might we not be expressing a philosophical thesis that doubts or denies something everyone admits? . . . We merely wish to deny the existence of the "superlative fact" that philosophers misleadingly attach to such ordinary forms of words, not the propriety of the forms of words themselves. Whenever our opponent insists on the perfect propriety of an ordinary form of expression (e.g., that "the steps are determined by the formula," "the future application is already present"), we can insist that if these expressions are properly understood, we agree. The danger comes when we try to formulate what we *are* denying—*what* "erroneous interpretation" our opponent is placing on ordinary means of expression.[37]

The trap that one can fall into is a type of misplaced demand for clarity. It is also a risk when one demands that a Buddhist clearly distinguish superimposed intrinsic natures from the customary things, for the superimpositions at stake are close to a type of "superlative fact": a hard-to-isolate queer way of taking things that is held as necessary for the ordinary to be what it is. Indeed, the Mādhyamika thinker incurs the danger of being simply dismissed as absurd when he lays out a general thesis as to *what* he is denying. From the Mādhyamika philosopher's own point of view, it is arguably defensible, and perhaps even profound, that this *svabhāva must* be nonobvious if it is not itself to be misconstrued and trivialized.

If we follow Mādhyamikas this far, then the starting point of the problem that Hayes and Robinson had in taking Nāgārjuna seriously is that they demanded such generalized theses about what was to be denied. In setting out what *svabhāva* was in the form of axioms and theorems, they had already guaranteed that the Madhyamaka thought would be seen to be absurd: the queer way of taking the ordinary had lost all its potent grip and all its interest. No doubt there will be something disturbing here to the analytic reader intent on giving summaries of such and such a philosopher's theses, for if a Madhyamaka philosophy is to receive a just and serious treatment, then the otherwise laudable intellectual work of formulating clear theses and general principles may not be without risk of superficiality.

VI

Where does this longish discussion of the merits of Madhyamaka leave us? The French philosopher Jacques Bouveresse has often argued vigorously for the need to denounce hollow rhetoric (*la rhétorique creuse*) in philosophy, with its deliberate use of equivocations, sophisms, and clichés. The problem he so rightly sees is the pursuit of "rhetorical difficulty" (*la difficulté rhétorique*), deliberate obfuscation, and *imposture* to give the appearance of profundity.[38] His prime target was, of course, the French philosophical establishment of the day, especially the followers of Althusser and Lacan; nonetheless, his is a generalizable stance. Richard Robinson and Richard Hayes, in effect, would argue that the difficulties of Madhyamaka philosophy too are essentially of that rhetorical sort, with its equivocations and deliberate avoidance of clarity. My argument, however, has been that the Madhyamaka is not guilty. Fundamentally, I would see the value of this philosophy as lying in its generalizable rejection of an unattainable, but very seductive, ontological perspective rather than in its blow-by-blow attacks on individual metaphysical positions, a theme I attempt to develop in the final chapter of this book. What is important is thus the recognition of what is to be negated: a certain strong conception of intrinsic nature and reality being as it is anyway, and the distinctness of that strong conception from innocent realism and truth.[39] Indeed, a Buddhist diagnosis of the deep-seated penchant toward ontology should be especially relevant to us now that reflections on realism, the legitimacy of metaphysics, and other such metaontological issues are coming to the fore in a modern philosophy confronted with a revitalized analytic metaphysics. One may of course have reasons to revise, nuance, or even significantly add to the Buddhist diagnosis, but it is not to be set aside as mere facile equivocations and hollow rhetoric.

Notes to Chapter 1

1. Cf. Hayes 1994, 325: "To the various fallacies and tricks brought to light by Robinson in his articles, we can now add the informal fallacy of equivocation as outlined above. That is, not only did Nāgārjuna use the term 'svabhāva' in ways that none of his opponents did, but he himself used it in several different senses at key points in his argument."
2. See Tillemans 1990, 1:99ff. and 122ff.
3. The term *satya* means both "truth" and "reality." Although this ambiguity does not in itself present inextricable problems, it does make for some inelegance in translation.

It's one of those semantic problems where one has to be forewarned and reluctantly learn to bite the bullet. On this and other matters concerning customary/conventional truth, see Newland and Tillemans 2011. In the present book, I have adopted the terms "customary truth / customary reality," rather than "conventional truth / conventional reality," because I think "convention" tends to convey the idea of a more or less conscious and arbitrary agreement (or choice) for pragmatic reasons, along the lines of rules of the road, whereas "custom" better includes the behavior patterns and forms of life that are essential to *saṃvṛtisatya* and *vyavahāra* (customary transactions); we follow those customs more or less blindly and not as a choice or interpretation. "Custom" is, then, a deliberate allusion to passages from Wittgenstein, such as *Philosophical Investigations* §198: "A person goes by a sign-post only in so far as there exists a regular use of sign-posts, a custom." Regularly following sign-posts, like other cases of rule-following—counting, meaning something with language, adding, and so on—is above all how we live. On these themes, see introduction above, pages 11–12.

4. See Candrakīrti's *Madhyamakāvatārabhāṣya* ad *Madhyamakāvatāra* 6.28. Translated in La Vallée Poussin 1910, 304–5.
5. See, e.g., Candrakīrti, *Prasannapadā* 67.7 (ed. Louis de La Vallée Poussin): *naitad evam / laukike vyavahāra ithaṃvicārāpravṛtter avicārataś ca laukikapadārthānām astitvāt.* "No, it's not so, for in the world this type of analysis does not operate with regard to customary transactions, and entities for the world exist [only] from a nonanalytic point of view." See also ibid. 71, n. 1a. On the term *avicāraramaṇīya* and Jñānagarbha's emphasis on no-analysis (*avicāra*), see p. 42 and 138 in Eckel 1992.
6. *Madhyamakāvatāra* 6.160ab: *rnam bdun gyis med gang de ji lta bur / yod ces rnal 'byor pas 'di'i yod mi rnyed.* It is not clear what the Sanskrit corresponding to *rnyed pa* is here, but it is likely to be *labdha*, as it is in 6.23, or possibly *prāpta/upalabdha.* The basic idea of things being fundamentally unfindable (*na labdhaḥ / labdhāḥ*) is already present in the *Samādhirājasūtra* 32.96: *dharmo na labdho buddhena yasya saṃjñā utpadyate* "The Buddha has not found any dharma of which a notion arises."
7. Hayes 1994, 305 and 311.
8. A similar statement concerning *svabhāva* being independent is also to be found in Candrakīrti's *ṭīkā* to verse 288 of the twelfth chapter of Āryadeva's *Catuḥśataka*: *tatrātmā nāma bhāvānāṃ yo 'parāyattasvarūpasvabhāvaḥ.* "There, what is called ātman ('self,' 'identity') is entities' intrinsic nature (*svabhāva*), the essence (*svarūpa*) that does not depend on anything else." See Tillemans 1990, 1: 126.
9. See Robinson 1972, 326.
10. Hayes's terms are respectively *svabhāva*1 "identity" and *svabhāva*2 "causal independence." See Hayes 1994, 312.
11. Robinson 1972, 326.
12. Robinson 1972, 327.
13. Frankfurt 2005. Critics wanting a considerably harder edge might well prefer McGinn 2008.
14. = Peking edition (P.) folio 238b–241a.
15. Sde dge edition (D.) folio 216a–b.
16. David Rawson has kindly pointed out to me that *rigs pas 'phul mtshams* does have an entry in a new dictionary, i.e., Sgom sde Lha ram pa 2013: *gzhan gyi khas blangs la gzhigs nas nan gyis rigs pas gnod byed brjod pa / skyon de gzhan gyis dngos su khas ma blangs kyang / khyod ltar na skyon 'di dang 'di lta bur 'gyur ro zhes rigs pas gnod*

byed brjod pa / 'di la 'phul mtshams zhes kyang zer /. "After one has examined the other's position, one pressingly states a logical refutation. Although the other does not explicitly acknowledge that fault, nonetheless one states the logical refutation saying 'Following you, such and such type of fault would ensue.' One also speaks of 'pushing limits' (*'phul mtshams*)."

17. In my own time as his student in the 1970s and early 80s I often had heated arguments with him where I presented my own Robinson-like objections.
18. Tillemans 1984. See especially page 364 (text fol. 26a6): *khyab ste / bden grub kyi gcig yin na gang la'ang bltos med kyi gcig yin dgos / de yin na cha bcas ma yin dgos pa'i phyir /.* "The entailment holds because if anything were to be truly one, it would have to be one [thing] which does not depend on anything [else] whatsoever, and in such a case it could not have parts."
19. See pages 156–59 and notes 290 and 299 in volume 1 of Tillemans 1990.
20. On the general outlines of this debate in Indian philosophy, see chapter 18 in Mookherjee 1980.
21. There are several arguments involved here involving fairly clearly discernible pan-Indian controversies invoking widely accepted principles, often from grammatical analysis. For example, my colleague Johannes Bronkhorst has traced how Nāgārjuna used a certain pan-Indian preoccupation concerning the correspondence between words and things to argue that statements like "X causes Y" or "X makes Y" cannot resist analysis, because the effect Y does not yet exist at the time of X. See Bronkhorst 1999.
22. See *Prasannapadā* 260.9–10: *tad evam akṛtakaḥ svabhāva iti lokavyavahāre vyavasthite vayam idānīṃ brūmo yad etad auṣṇyaṃ tad apy agneḥ svabhāvo na bhavatīti gṛhyatāṃ kṛtakatvāt /.* "So thus, when in the world's customary transactions it is established that intrinsic nature is what is not fabricated, we now assert that it should be understood that heat is not the intrinsic nature of fire either, for it is produced [from causes and conditions]." Cf. also chapter 15 in de Jong 1950 and 1972 on this and other uses of *svabhāva*.
23. *Prasannapadā* 260.5: *kṛtakaḥ padārthaḥ sa loke naiva svabhāva iti vyapadiśyate.*
24. Compare Stephen Yablo's intuitive characterization: "You know what an intrinsic property is: it's a property that a thing has (or lacks) regardless of what may be going on outside of itself"' (Yablo 1999, 479). Cf. also Dunn 1990, 178: "Metaphysically, an intrinsic property of an object is a property that the object has by virtue of itself, depending on no other thing." One common version of intrinsicness coming from Jaegwon Kim is that *F* is an intrinsic property if and only if it is possible for a "lonely object" (i.e., an object that doesn't coexist with any other objects distinct from it) to be *F.* See J. Kim 1983. It should be clear that when *these* authors are speaking of no dependence on outside forces, other things, loneliness, and so on, they are *not* saying that an intrinsic property (e.g., an object's mass or atomic composition) is completely independent of any and all factors whatsoever, past or present. A lonely object that has a certain electrical charge, for example, may have depended for that charge on past objects or past moments of the object that are now all nonexistent but did cause the present charge to come into being. Madhyamaka-style independence, however, would rule out that property of having a charge as intrinsic, because it depends upon causes.
25. In Tanji 2000, 353. See also my remarks on Tanji's article in Tillemans 2001a.
26. One way to arrive at a more-or-less similar interpretation of Nāgārjuna as refuting

superimposed reifications is to say that the Madhyamaka tetralemma (*catuṣkoṭi*) is refuting propositions implicitly or explicitly qualified by an operator "ultimately" but is not attacking unqualified propositions. Thus, for example, Nāgārjuna would be refuting "Ultimately, such and such is the case" but not the simple statement "Such and such is the case." See Tillemans 1999, 197, 135–38. Cf. Claus Oetke 1991, 318, where we are advised to interpret Nāgārjuna's refutations as of the form "On the highest level of truth, it is not so that there are *x* such that *x* is such and such."

27. I thank David Higgins, and especially his wife Dr. Naseem Janmohamed, for the information about floaters. Cf. Higgins 2013, p. 125n318: "Rab rib (Skt. *timira*) is often, though incorrectly, translated as *cataracts* or *glaucoma*. It seems rather to describe an optic condition known as *myodesopsia*, more commonly known as 'floaters.' In those afflicted, deposits of varying size, shape and consistency within the vitreous humour cause them to perceive hair-like floaters (often what look like falling hairs) in the visual field." See the National Eye Institute website for information on floaters: http://www.nei.nih.gov/health/floaters/floaters.asp. *Timira* has sometimes been translated as *opthalmia*, an inflammation of the eye, especially the exterior, sometimes following penetrating injury and sometimes involving seriously reduced vision, pain, floating spots, and increased sensitivity to light. That seems to concord less well with descriptions of *timira*.

28. See introduction and chapter 2. What Nāgārjuna himself thought, however, will probably remain elusive. At the end of the day, we may well come to Paul Griffiths' conclusion that Nāgārjuna's texts, by themselves, straight with no commentarial chaser, may be simply too indeterminate to answer philosophers' questions about their precise meaning. See Griffiths 2000, 24: "The first difficulty is one endemic to all scholarship on Nāgārjuna. It is that Nāgārjuna's works are, in this reviewer's judgment, insufficiently precise and systematic to make debates about what he really meant, philosophically speaking, very useful."

29. See note 23 above.

30. See Grice 1991, 47.

31. See the introduction in Siderits and Katsura 2013.

32. On this scenario, the structure of Nāgārjuna's dialectic would be something like this: (1) Positions *A* . . . *F* are the major realist views of the time and can each be shown to be inconsistent by various *ad hoc* arguments. (2) The Mādhyamika thus can continue to hold, with weak justification, that nothing is fully real, has *svabhāva*, and so on. Mādhyamikas would thus have no "master arguments" but only great skill and staying power in offering counterarguments to their specific opponents. The parallel is with skeptics who have no theoretical stance of their own but are talented and always willing to provide counterarguments of equal force (*isothenia*) in cases that come up. Cf. M. Williams 1988. My only argument here is that while this *could* account for Nāgārjuna—indeed we have insufficiently precise information from Nāgārjuna's own texts to decide what he *himself* meant on difficult issues (see note 28)—it is in any case not the superimpositions approach of the commentators. *If* we wanted to defend such a skeptical reading of Nāgārjuna, it would imply that the commentators made a significant break with Nāgārjuna's own approach.

33. The Dalai Lama gives a number of such methods to recognize the object to be refuted, both with regard to persons and to phenomena. See his "Key to the Middle Way" in Dalai Lama and Hopkins 1975. An interesting Buddhist thought-experiment is

to imagine a trade-off of one's own old and decrepit psychophysical components for those of the youthful, omniscient, bodhisattva Mañjuśrī. At that point, the "exchanger" (*brje pa po*), the self whom we feel would benefit, appears as if it were fully real, separate and independent from all its components, indeed everything other than it. For Buddhists, such a separate "self" is of course an illusion, but it stands out vividly when "just like a merchant seeking [potential] profit, [the old person] would sincerely grasp at making an exchange." See Tillemans 1993, 36.

34. For a good translation of this chapter, see Tsong-kha-pa 2002. The usual Geluk strategy to give an Indian source for *dgag bya ngos 'dzin* is to cite Śāntideva's *Bodhicaryāvatāra* 9.140 (Tib. 139), but this is unconvincing and does not fit well with Indian commentators, like Prajñākaramati. See P. Williams 1995. Better to say that Tibetans made an important and creative addition to Madhyamaka philosophy and then had to hide their innovativeness.
35. See Wittgenstein 1953, §192.
36. See §195 in Wittgenstein 1953. This Wittgensteinian theme of queerness versus the ordinary is a major preoccupation of Stanley Cavell in his exegesis of the opening passages of the *Investigations* discussing the seductiveness of St. Augustine's theory of language. Cf. also his idea of the "uncanniness of the ordinary," e.g., p. 153–178 in Cavell 1988.
37. See Kripke 1982, 69–70.
38. Bouveresse 2006. See also Bouveresse 1998, 101: "[O]n ne fait pas assez de différence entre la difficulté technique, qui est normale sur certains sujets et que l'on peut surmonter, et la difficulté rhétorique, qui n'est pas normale et souvent insurmontable."
39. Note that this formulation deliberately places the accent on the thinking human's ideas of realism and truth. It would not apply easily to animals or lower forms of life. Now the later Indian Mādhyamikas, and especially the Tibetans, make a distinction between "speculative" (*kun brtags = parikalpita*), or philosophically motivated, superimpositions of reality, real selves, and so on and those that are innate (*lhen skye = sahaja*) to all living beings. The latter sort might look more to us like unconscious basic biological drives, even a kind of lowest common denominator to life, such as a survival instinct. It could thus well be objected that my account might bear on the first sort but would not concern the latter.

    So be it. On a general level, Buddhists, like most other traditional Indian philosophers, wish to take a big-tent approach where all forms of sentient beings are somehow suffering from the same thing, are all reborn in saṃsāra, all have the same fundamental mental make-up, can all be liberated from the myriad varieties of alternating high and low rebirths, etc., etc. Of course, the Buddhist would say that in *not* adopting that big-tent approach, I've just focused on *parikalpita* and have not gone far enough to eliminate innate grasping. If, however, one takes rebirth out of the Buddhist picture—or at least rejects as unintelligible the idea of rebirth as a lower animal—much of that turn to lowest common denominators will no longer be needed. Getting clear about the varieties of human thinking is probably the best we can intelligibly do.

2. How Far Can a Mādhyamika Reform Customary Truth? Dismal Relativism, Fictionalism, Easy-Easy Truth, and the Alternatives

I

A FAMOUS SCRIPTURAL PASSAGE cited in Candrakīrti's *Prasannapadā Madhyamakavṛtti* and *Madhyamakāvatārabhāṣya* goes like this:

> *loko mayā sārdhaṃ vivadati nāhaṃ lokena sārdhaṃ vivadāmi / yal loke 'sti saṃmataṃ tan mamāpy asti saṃmatam / yal loke nāsti saṃmataṃ mamāpi tan nāsti saṃmatam /*

> The world (*loka*) argues with me. I don't argue with the world. What is agreed upon (*saṃmata*) in the world to exist, I too agree that it exists. What is agreed upon in the world to be nonexistent, I too agree that it does not exist.[1]

Clearly the passage is taken as an account of customary truth (*saṃvṛtisatya*) by the Madhyamaka; that is, it is cited by at least certain Mādhyamika philosophers to show the sūtra source for their view that one should accept "customary truth," or truths for the world, as being only as the world accepts them. But what does *that* mean and what does it imply? It might well seem to imply an extreme conservatism that nothing the world ever endorsed could be criticized or rejected and that, on the customary level at least, a Mādhyamika's principal epistemic task is just to passively acquiesce and duplicate.

Let me characterize this version of customary truth as a "dismal position," as I think we would agree that the potential flattening of truth and knowledge's normative roles that such duplication brings is indeed quite unattractive: it is a trivialization of the idea of truth to think that we could somehow settle what *is* true by periodically taking inventories of what people believe to be true at given times and places. Indeed brute reliance on polls and inventories for determining truth has to remain unacceptable whether we are democratic and count each person as one, or assign some greater weight to the opinions of the currently respectable group of clerics and famous cognoscenti.

Who, if anyone, held such a dismal position on customary truth? Something close to this was repeatedly *criticized* by the Mādhyamika Kamalaśīla as being the view of some anonymous opponents who held that things were established as such and so because people simply accepted them to be established in that way (*dam bcas pa tsam gyis grub pa* = *pratijñāmātreṇa siddha*).[2] Kamalaśīla appears to have been duly horrified by the consequences that ensue when instead of justifying one's views with "sources of knowledge" / "epistemic instruments" (*tshad ma* = *pramāṇa*), we are satisfied with simple *belief*. As he puts it, "it would follow absurdly that everything whatsoever would established by everything" (*thams cad kyis thams cad 'grub par thal bar 'gyur ba*).[3]

This worry, for Buddhists, about the negative outcomes when people collapse the distinction between things being so and merely being believed to be so goes back at least to Dharmakīrti, and possibly further. As we see in *Pramāṇavārttika* 4.9, Dharmakīrti was concerned that any discrimination between good and bad reasoning would be just "wiped out" (*lupta*) if we established things as so or not so (*tattvātattvavyavasthiti*) "by the force of people's thoughts" (*puṃsām abhiprāyavaśāt*).[4] (Also, Dharmakīrti seems to have been quite familiar with going accounts of different cultures' weird ideas and sexual mores; he often alluded to them sardonically in his *Pramāṇavārttika* and other works in order to argue that social acceptance didn't give any claim to truth or goodness.) In fact, the flaws in basing justification purely on what people think is a theme that is often repeated in Buddhist epistemology. I think that this worry about the dismal view, if pushed a little bit further, is also one about relativism. While the failure to distinguish between *p* being so and *p* being believed to be so does not by itself constitute or entail relativism, the additional move comes quite easily. In effect we get relativism when we accord equal truth-status to opposing statements because we hold that truth is not a one-place predicate but a two-place predicate like "*p* is true for . . . ," "*p* is true in such and such a mindset/culture," and so on. Although it's difficult to be categorical, it seems to me plausible that Dharmakīrti and Kamalaśīla did also reject such a move to a two-place truth predicate that relativizes truth and gives different people with their different mindsets *equal* claims.

While Kamalaśīla does not explicitly give the name of a particular individual or school in India as the holders of the method of *pratijñāmātreṇa siddha*, some important aspects of his depictions do suggest that he might have been thinking of the sixth-century Prāsaṅgika-Madhyamaka philosopher Candrakīrti, or at least (to be even less committal) someone like him. What Kamalaśīla rails against, in the *Sarvadharmaniḥsvabhāvasiddhi*, is someone who relies exclusively on what is acknowledged (*grags pa* = *prasiddha, pratīta*) by the world. Here is what Kamalaśīla says in that text:

> One should analyze the production of entities with logic (*rigs pa* = *yukti*) and scripture (*lung* = *āgama*). Suppose it were thought, "Why should we analyze it when [a fact such as] the production of sprouts and the like being conditioned by seeds and so forth is just simply acknowledged (*grags pa* = *prasiddha, pratīta*) by everyone from cowherds on up? Judicious people (*rtog pa dang ldan pa* = *prekṣāvat*) should not analyze in order to ascertain the natures of entities (*dngos po* = *vastu, bhāva*), because [if they did,] it would follow that there would be no end [to such analysis] and it would follow that it would not be judicious." This is not right, for they would not ascertain [things] through sources of knowledge (*tshad ma* = *pramāṇa*), and moreover it is possible that what is [generally] acknowledged is wrong. Otherwise [if analysis using *pramāṇa* were unnecessary], no one who applied himself to what he had himself acknowledged would ever end up being unreliable about anything at all.
>
> To take some examples: it is [generally] acknowledged that perishing is something that has a cause [although this is actually wrong],[5] and though people [generally] acknowledge that matter and the like are external objects, this can be undermined (*gnod pa* = *bādhā*) by sources of knowledge if it is subjected to analysis. In the same way here, too [with regard to the production of entities], what people acknowledge could also turn out to be false, and hence one really should analyze it. As for scripture without any logic, it would leave judicious people discontent. It is scripture grounded by logic that cannot lead astray, and so first of all we should analyze [things] logically.[6]

Indeed, Candrakīrti does seem to have been someone who held the stance that the customary is what is "just simply acknowledged" (*grags pa* = *prasiddha, pratīta*); he is, I think quite rightly, depicted by Tibetan scholastics as a "Mādhyamika who practices in accordance with what is acknowledged by the world" (*'jig rten grags pa ltar spyod pa'i dbu ma pa*).[7]

There are a number of other telltale indications that strike one immediately in the *Sarvadharmaniḥsvabhāvasiddhi* passage, notably the admonition by Kamalaśīla's adversary to avoid analysis of causality, and in particular to leave the relationship between seeds and sprouts philosophically untouched and simply as it is, "acknowledged by everyone from cowherds on up." This naturally brings to mind the famous argument in the first forty verses of chapter 6 of Candrakīrti's *Madhyamakāvatāra*, where we find dismissed in detail the claims of Svātantrika-Mādhyamika Buddhists that cause and effect were essentially different things, even if this variant on the pan-Indian debate about causes being nonexistent at the time of the effect (*asatkāryavāda*) was said by them to be only customarily and not ultimately so. Candrakīrti, as is well known, saw as utterly misguided any such philosophically inspired attempt to analyze causal processes in terms that would go beyond ordinary notions like "This did that," "I planted such and such a tree," "I fathered this boy," "When wood, strings, and manual effort are present, sounds arise from musical instruments," "Rice comes from rice," and the other such deliberately simple and philosophically noncommittal characterizations.[8]

So if the ghostly presence of Candrakīrti, or of some such Prāsaṅgika very much like him, is discernible in the *Sarvadharmaniḥsvabhāvasiddhi* passage that I translated above, as I think it is, we see that for Kamalaśīla the case against the Prāsaṅgika is clear: the Prāsaṅgika fails the basic standards of a rational, intellectual approach—he is not *judicious* (*prekṣāvat*), as he simply *copies* the world and eschews sources of knowledge (*pramāṇa*) that confirm or correct the world's beliefs. This yields the unacceptable consequence that sufficiently widespread beliefs would be right ipso facto about the customary.

II

We now jump about twelve hundred years forward in time. Mark Siderits gives a somewhat more forgiving depiction of Candrakīrti's acceptance of *lokaprasiddha*, "what is acknowledged by the world." What Siderits attributes to Candrakīrti's Prāsaṅgika-Madhyamaka philosophy—as opposed to the Svātantrika-Madhyamaka of Bhāviveka, Śāntarakṣita, Kamalaśīla, et alii—is not the hopelessly dismal view that *everything whatsoever* that people say/believe to be so is indeed so (at least customarily); rather it is the view that the customarily accepted practices and community standards in terms of which people assess truth and falsity admit of no rational criticism or reform and have to be taken as given. In an article entitled "Thinking on Empty: Madhyamaka Anti-Realism and Canons of Rationality," he sees Candrakīrti as rejecting any and all theorizing about the customary and thus advocating only mere description of the practices people do accept:

> On the Prāsaṅgika view, customary truth is a set of brutely given practices which must be taken at face value.[9]

For our purposes, however, we can take both Kamalaśīla's and Siderits's depictions of Prāsaṅgika together, as they both have as an essential feature that Prāsaṅgika thinkers supposedly had no use for any theorizing about philosophy or about our practices at all; they just "read off the surface" (Siderits 1989, 244) and reminded us of what we do and say, with (if we push matters) the relativism that could bring. As will become clearer below, I don't think that every serious interpretation of Prāsaṅgika-Madhyamaka *needs* to result in such an anti-intellectual and antitheoretical view, and I think that fortunately there were some later interpreters who probably did not take customary truth and even Candrakīrti's description of it in that way. However, it does need to be granted in Kamalaśīla's and Siderits's favor that their depiction—namely, that a Prāsaṅgika is voluntarily hamstrung to mere descriptive reminders of what people do, think, and say—does *grosso modo* come quite close to a prevalent Indo-Tibetan view of what it means to accept only what is acknowledged by the world, and is a very natural reading of Candrakīrti's texts. Let me call this "typical Prāsaṅgika." I think that *that* Prāsaṅgika is indeed what left Siderits unenthralled and is what Kamalaśīla detested.

Let's look at the broad lines of how that typical Prāsaṅgika proceeds. As Candrakīrti himself was only a curiously minor figure in Indian Buddhism, it's difficult to say much about how he was actually received in mainstream Indian Madhyamaka, other than as the misguided duplicator and endorser of the world's errors that Kamalaśīla depicts him to be—we are thus obliged to flesh out our picture of Prāsaṅgika by turning largely to Tibet, where from the twelfth century on, Candrakīrti assumed an extraordinarily exalted status. In any case, the crucial point is that most Tibetan interpreters of Candrakīrti, as well as his Indian commentator Jayānanda, will hold that the world's customary truth is *wholly* erroneous (*bhrānta*, *'khrul ba*) from the perspective of "noble beings" (*ārya*), who see things properly; it is grasped as "truly so" in the eyes of the ignorant world but not in the eyes of a wiser being, like an ārya.[10] There is no division, à la Tsongkhapa (Tsong kha pa), into a *part* (*cha*) of the world's truth that is also right—that is, established by sources of knowledge (*tshad ma* = *pramāṇa*)—for āryas themselves and a *part* that is wrong for them. The *wholesale* erroneousness of customary truth is sometimes formulated as that the customary is only "existent from the point of view of mistaken thought" (*blo 'khrul ba'i ngor yod pa*).[11] It is often (but not always) closely linked to the issue about whether Mādhyamikas can accept any sources of knowledge for states of affairs / things in the world: for many (cf., e.g., Jayānanda, Stag tshang lo tsā ba, Pa tshab nyi ma grags), the Candrakīrtian position is interpreted as being that there are no such sources of knowledge (*pramāṇa*) and that customary truth is itself just a series of erroneous inventions. Finally, what is also relevant to us here is the typical Prāsaṅgika take on the consequences of customary existence being thoroughly erroneous and unreal in these ways. For espousing thoroughgoing antirealism and being constrained to accept as customary only what is accepted by the world (*lokaprasiddha*) are clearly linked for many Indo-Tibetan exegetes. A writer like Üpa Losal (Dbus pa blo gsal), for example, explicitly makes that very move. Worldly things are taken by the Prāsaṅgika as completely unable to withstand analysis (= erroneous), and *therefore* the Prāsaṅgika just "reads off the surface" and adopts worldly descriptions. Üpa Losal cites *Madhyamakāvatāra* 6.35 (and *Satyadvayavibhaṅga* 21 of Jñānagarbha!), verses that for him show that it is *because* a Prāsaṅgika does not accept that anything can be real, or (what comes to the same) because nothing can withstand analysis, that he will be a "Mādhyamika who practices in conformity with what is acknowledged by the world" (*'jig rten grags sde spyod pa'i dbu ma pa*).[12]

III

Now why might such a Mādhyamika think that a blanket endorsement of the world's beliefs or its practices followed from her thoroughgoing antirealism? Why would she see herself as in some sense constrained to a kind of "reading off the surface" because of holding that things are all empty (*śūnya*) of intrinsic nature and in some way made up by us? It's not obvious that one follows from the other. Indeed it looks like the whys and wherefores of this typical Prāsaṅgika move are only implicit in the actual Indo-Tibetan texts, at least as far as I can see. Nor are its consequences explicitly drawn. We have to step gingerly outside the Indic and Tibetan literature to get a view on what may have happened and why.

Probably the key move and its consequences are due to Prāsaṅgika thinkers' stands on issues connected with what we now know as *fictionalism*. This is an approach that enables a person to reject commitment to some, or even all, kinds of entities by adopting a type of *pretense* or *make-believe*:

she might see talk of such entities as metaphorical, or might even add to truth claims like "*P* is true" a disclaimer operator that *P* is true "in such and such a story" or "for such and such (mistaken) people," "in such and such a (false) version of history," and so forth.[13] To put things in a Buddhist context, while the world buys into its own wholesale errors, the typical Prāsaṅgika will have none of it and knows that they are false (*mṛṣā*); but nonetheless, as a fictionalist, she can, unduped by the world, still accept a kind of truth of the world's statements; if need be, she will make that clear by prefixing the appropriate disclaimer "customarily . . . ," or "in the world's account," "according to the world," and so on. More exactly, to use the terminology of current writing on fictionalism, the typical Prāsaṅgika can be seen as a *revolutionary* fictionalist who holds that adopting a pretense stance constitutes a type of progress. Instead of saying that the world itself already tacitly plays make-believe (what is known as "hermeneutical fictionalism"), she says that the world is completely mistaken about what it does and that it *ought to learn to say and think the things it does only in terms of pretend-assertions*.[14] The world thus proceeds according to what the Prāsaṅgika sees as an *error theory*;[15] the Mādhyamika, who knows better, nonetheless salvages the world's ideas as customary truth by transposing the totality—or at least a considerable number—of the world's false statements into fictional (that is, customary) truths. Note that in contemporary fictionalism some such move from an error theory to fictionalism is not infrequent, especially in ethical irrealist theories that maintain that while people widely believe that there *are* properties like good and bad, in fact there are only ethical attitudes and standards for ethical reasoning. (Richard Joyce, for example, makes that move in his *Myth of Morality*: it is argued that a philosopher should see the idea of there being actual moral properties as false but nonetheless conserve them as useful regulative fictions.)[16] The advantage of fictionalism, both for an ethical irrealist and for a Mādhyamika Buddhist, thus, is that a philosophical understanding that certain propositions are literally false will not lead one to simply eliminate all talk of the entities and properties in question.

For ethical fictionalists, reasoning can take place within the context of the fiction, internal to the ethical "story," by invoking coherence and consistency, not significantly unlike the way one might speculate about what fictitious characters in a novel would have done or should have done had they remained consistent with their fictitious personalities. Thus while a considerable portion of a story needs to be taken as brutely given, there is room for extrapolation, correction, and reform. All this being said, the Prāsaṅgika seems to have perceived the *desirability* for reform to have been very limited indeed, and seems to have felt that *because* no account could ever be true, the world's story should be accepted intact *by default*. He deftly used a "by default" argument against metaphysical theories, like those of the Yogācāras, that sought to replace false ideas about there being external objects with a true idealist account. The argument here and in cases like it (e.g., against the logicians' ontology) is that the whole effort toward *reform motivated by ontology* is simply not worth the candle, given that nothing more real/true is to be gained.[17]

That much is sweetness and light. What is more troubling, however, is the nagging feeling that Candrakīrti and the typical Prāsaṅgika don't stop there. Instead of making a clear distinction between, on the one hand, a metaphysical/ontological issue, something that might indeed best be left alone, and on the other hand sophisticated scientific theories of the world (that may even proceed without much worries about ontology or anything more than minimalist accounts of truth), it looks like all sophisticated explanation is lumped together and that *sophistication is itself to be ruled out*. Saying, as does Candrakīrti repeatedly in debates with Sāṃkhya and his fellow Buddhists, that rice just leads to rice rather than barley, may well be a very good answer to the various metaphysicians who either think that the effect must really be present in the cause to ensure that causality is not haphazard or who think that cause and effect must be completely separate real entities, but it is of course a bad answer to a plant scientist inquiring about genetic features in rice that explain its growth, yield, color, form, resistance to disease, and so on. The problem is that Candrakīrti seems to have taken the type of answer appropriate to the metaphysical debate as also being the best answer to the second sort of inquiry. And you just cannot please the scientist by saying simply that rice leads to rice.

So although Candrakīrti *does* promote some substantial changes in people's ethical and political ideas and even their ways of reasoning about ethics by pitting some of their attitudes against others,[18] and although he does allow for correction of obviously wrong beliefs and attitudes that depend upon gross misapplications of well-known epistemic standards,[19] nevertheless, in spite of these rudimentary mechanisms for reform, there is the inescapable impression that customary truth is still very much a *dumbed-down truth* for him. Consistency with attitudes and mere diagnoses of obviously faulty sense organs do not take a typical Prāsaṅgika very far in allowing for sophisticated theoretical ideas. Indeed, looking at the bald simplicity of the *Madhyamakāvatāra*'s and *Catuḥśatakaṭīkā's* accounts of human actions and processes (as well as the seeds-sprouts causality), it seems that Prāsaṅgika requires our explanation of those activities be in tune with way the ordinary man describes them in the sense that the explanations must at least be more-

or-less readily accessible and understandable to the ordinary man. In human sciences, we would in effect be left with a version of what the philosopher and argumentation theorist John Woods has termed the Easy-Easy Principle, the idea that not infrequently crops up in antitheoretical circles that "if a kind of human practice is competently performable without technical tutelage, then the theory of that practice must likewise be free of technical or theoretically abstruse content" (Woods 2006, 303–4).

IV

Easy-easy truth, or dumbed-down customary truth, whatever be its possible attraction for a sixth-century Mādhyamika, is not attractive to most of us; nor should it be—technical subjects like logic, linguistics, and economics, not to mention physical science, would just plainly be impossible and would be eliminated in favor of oh-so-readily-understandable common sense. Nor was this easy-easy truth even very attractive to certain later self-styled Prāsaṅgikas in Tibet, namely the followers of Tsongkhapa, who were avid theorists of logic, epistemology, philosophy of language, and other subjects that no doubt were abstruse to the ordinary man. What went wrong and what alternatives are there to keep customary truth from being dumbed down?

First of all, did the world-picture *have* to be that pedestrian for a typical Prāsaṅgika fictionalist? Perhaps not. There may indeed be a non sequitur here (although historically speaking many Prāsaṅgikas, including very likely Candrakīrti, did *think* a pedestrian world-picture followed from their pan-fictionalist stance). A modified parable from Stephen Yablo is interesting. Yablo (2000, 200) argues for the fictional nature of mathematics by a thought experiment that is known as the "oracle argument."[20] Let us suppose that we somehow learned from an oracle that there were no abstract objects; we would nonetheless be able to go on doing mathematics as we always have. Some philosophers suggest that we could just as well take Yablo one step further. We might also be able to go on as before doing creative work in science too if the oracle taught us that there were no macroscopic objects but only real extensionless particulars or some other substitute. Let's even suppose that the oracle taught us that there was nothing at all that existed externally and that Berkeleian idealism was the true account of things. And finally, the oracle takes a whiff of the Delphic vapours and tells us the last word: even Berkeley doesn't cut it; it's all pure fiction, even though so many of us had thought otherwise for so long. Couldn't we still just go on as before doing what we used to do, and even coming up with sophisticated theories by following our epistemic procedures?[21] After all, *in any case* we have been all along following epistemic practices of the world, and those are actually very sophisticated and can even evolve if the need arises.

So it may be that if a Yablo-style parable about fictionalism is right, the dumbing down in typical Prāsaṅgika is not actually a *consequence* of the all-encompassing error-theory and fictionalism but more due to Candrakīrti's and his followers' spectacular underestimation of the level of sophistication of the world's epistemic procedures. One Buddhist way out, then, would be to beef up significantly the Madhyamaka's account of how the world establishes the differences between what it accepts and what it rejects.

Still, if in order to get some such fictionalist account off the ground we needed to explain the ordinary man's cognition and discourse exclusively in terms of an unnuanced error-theory, this is going to end up being a very hard sell. If the sales tactic is (as it often is) to put everything on the back of the supposed *usefulness* of the world's errors, this seems an unpromising approach, especially when those errors are all encompassing. Indeed the problem is to imagine how human thinking and discourse, which according to the typical Prāsaṅgika scenario is pervaded through and through by falsity alone, could ever be of *use* to the degree needed to explain why an enormous number of false beliefs/statements about the ordinary world are and should be considered true in some nondismal way.[22] While we might (like an ethical irrealist) take as "true" *certain* shared errors, like beliefs in such and such actions being good or bad, because such mistaken beliefs make people more respectful, gentle, and the like, it would be hard to see how people's flat-out errors about *every* aspect of everything in the world could lead to significantly useful results.

Does one need to bite *that* bullet in order to be (some sort of) Mādhyamika? Now, philosophically speaking at least, such an error theory and fictionalism would be an extremely high price to pay for rejecting what Mādhyamikas say they reject: metaphysical realism (*dngos po smra ba*), the view that things are what they are because of the properties they have intrinsically, independently of our conceptions (*kalpanā*) of them, our linguistic designations (*prajñapti*), and our actions upon (*pravṛtti*) them. There would seem to be an avoidable overkill in saying that *everything* must be thoroughly erroneous/fictional in order for one to simply reject that things are without intrinsic natures (*svabhāva*). Let us for the moment then put on a philosopher's hat, rather than that of a philologist, historian, or close reader of texts: *atypical* approaches might be, philosophically at least, more promising. We leave Candrakīrtian exegesis and philology temporarily on hold.

If we do that, I think that there are indeed a number of ways to avoid metaphysical realism, ways that somehow jettison the typical Prāsaṅgika idea that customary truth is *wholly* erroneous (*'khrul ba = bhrānta*) for the profane and purely fictional for "noble beings" (*ārya*). I would tend to say that the best way to go, instead of all-encompassing error-theory and fictionalism about customary truth, is to see Madhyamaka's two truths as a rung on a ladder that we climb to finally know better a unitary world, one that was there all along but veiled by conceptually created dichotomies and ignorance. Tibetan Nyingmapa (Rnying ma pa) writers speak of this primordial unity in terms of the "two truths being inseparable" (*bden gnyis dbyer med*).[23] Arguably this may not be far from the radical approach spoken about in Priest, Siderits, and Tillemans 2011, where mastery of the Madhyamaka critique of the world's inveterate realism leads one to a return to truths, unqualified as customary or ultimate. Indeed, why not say that truths had *always* been shared by āryas and the world alike (alas, confusedly)?

There is a point then where the two truths and the Madhyamaka dialectic have done their job, so that truth just straightforwardly fulfills its normative role but without any metaphysical baggage. There is a kind of enlightened deflationism (see Cowherds 2011, chapter 8, on deflationism and other truth theories).[24] One considerable advantage of deflationism over typical Prāsaṅgika error-theory/fictionalism is that it has no problems whatsoever accommodating far-reaching criticism and amendments to going worldviews. People can simply be dead wrong about some would-be deflationary "truths," or they can fail to understand and believe genuine truths because they are too technical or theoretical. Truths can remain as sophisticated and elusive as they often are. Fortunately they don't all have to be dumbed down to the level of easy-easy accessibility.

But now let's suppose we keep the two truths. What then? We could have an *atypical* Prāsaṅgika approach like that of Tsongkhapa: customary truths *simpliciter are* established as full-fledged truths for *both* the ordinary person and the ārya alike by full-fledged *pramāṇas* and are not just mere falsehoods that we widely believe in. Error only comes in where the ordinary person—and fortunately not the ārya, who knows better—grasps otherwise innocent things like *F*s and *G*s as having intrinsic properties (*svabhāva*). Here too, just as on the radical scenario, deflationism would seem to fit the bill better than fictionalism and error theory in that it would enable truth to be fully fledged (not just make-believe) and its normativity to be conserved.[25] What exists would be a series of deflationary facts, and the truth of the beliefs, propositions, and so on about them that are accepted by the world and the āryas alike would be explainable simply as deflationary truths. A "REALLY" operator could be introduced to account for Tsongkhapa's repeated admonitions that nothing is ultimately or REALLY (*don dam par*) the case. Thus the Mādhyamika could cheerfully accept the truth of "*p*," and also "not REALLY *p*" (see Cowherds 2011, chapter 8). Note too, however, that both "*p*" and "not REALLY *p*" would be no more than deflationary truths—this might capture Tsongkhapa's idea that everything, even emptiness and the denials of intrinsic nature, is only customarily established (*tha snyad du grub pa*).

Let me, however, close on an untraditional—indeed slightly heretical—note. These *atypical* thinkers are no doubt some of the most subtle thinkers in Buddhism, and not surprisingly their stances are often in a significant and recurring tension with what the Indian texts actually say (on a natural reading of the Sanskrit). Now, I had said earlier that *typical* Prāsaṅgika is a very natural close reading of Candrakīrti. Indeed I would be prepared to argue that, philologically and historically speaking, it is the way these Indian texts are most naturally read. I think, for example, that it's incontestable that on a usual understanding of the Buddhist Sanskrit terms *loka* ("worldling") and *ārya*, they will be taken as standing in sharp contrast, along the lines of a typical Prāsaṅgika interpretation like that of Gorampa (Go rams pa). Tsongkhapa's contrary exegesis here is not convincing even if the philosophical gain may be considerable.[26] One can multiply these sorts of examples. Does it detract from an atypical thinker that he had to read Candrakīrti in the strained way he did? No, but it certainly does often put him in a very different light from the way the tradition depicted him. The positive point is that someone like Tsongkhapa emerges as a highly creative Mādhyamika with a steel-trap philosophical mind. The irony is that he may well have the merit of making Candrakīrti a better philosopher than he actually was.

Notes to Chapter 2

1. The Tibetan equivalent of *loko mayā sārdhaṃ vivadati nāhaṃ lokena sārdhaṃ vivadāmi* is found in *Trisaṃvaranirdeśaparivarta* (chapter 1) of the Ratnakūṭa D. The Sanskrit of the whole quotation is found in Candrakīrti's *Prasannapadā* ad *Mūlamadhyamakakārikā* 18.8 (ed. La Vallée Poussin, 370.6–8), where the source is only identified as a "scripture" (*āgama*); see also *Madhyamakāvatārabhāṣya* ad 6.81 (ed. La Vallée Poussin, p. 179) for the Tibetan. Note that Candrakīrti's source seems to be a Sanskrit version of what we find in Saṃyutta Nikāya III, p. 138 (ed. Léon Feer): *nāham bhikkhave lokena vivadāmi loko ca mayā vivadati // na bhikkhave dhammavādī kenaci lokasmiṃ vivadati // yam bhikkhave natthi sammataṃ loke paṇḍitānam aham pi tam natthīti vadāmi // yam bhikkhave atthi sammataṃ loke paṇḍitānam aham pi tam atthīti vadāmi //*. "Bhikkhus, I do not dispute with the world; rather, it is the world that disputes with me. A proponent of the Dhamma does not dispute with anyone in the world. Of that which the wise in the world agree

upon as not existing, I too say that it does not exist. And of that which the wise in the world agree upon as existing, I too say that it exists" (trans. Bodhi 2000, 949). The Pāli, however, in contrast to the *āgama's* Sanskrit quoted in *Prasannapadā* (as well as the Tibetan translation), has the term *paṇḍitānam* in this passage and the discussion that follows. Thus the Saṃyutta speaks about that which the wise (*paṇḍitānam*) in the world (*loke*) agree upon as existing/not existing, rather than just that which is agreed upon as existing/not existing in the world. The difference is significant, because it means—as the subsequent discussion explicitly shows in the *Khandavagga* of the Saṃyutta (see Bodhi 2000, 949–50)—that the Buddha accepts "impermanent, suffering, changing [*skandhas*] matter," and so on as existent and holds that "permanent, stable, eternal, unchanging matter," and so on is nonexistent. He thus would accept an ontology proposed by the wise—by qualified experts in the world. The Sanskrit, however, simply says that the Buddha accepts what is accepted in the world; experts are not mentioned. Such is the interpretation that Candrakīrti would adopt and that arguably has the potential for populist "dismal positions" on existence and truth in a way in which the Pāli reading does not. I thank Stephen Batchelor for pointing out the difference between the Sanskrit and Pāli here.

2. "Acceptance" and "belief" are sometimes differentiated in fictionalist philosophies (e.g., that of Bas van Fraassen's *The Scientific Image*); I'm not using these terms technically here and am treating them as interchangeable.
3. See for example, *Sarvadharmaniḥsvabhāvasiddhi* P. 327b7–8: *dam bcas pa tsam gyis ni 'dod pa'i don 'grub pa ma yin te / thams cad kyi(s) thams cad 'grub par thal bar 'gyur ba'i phyir ro //.* "The intended point is not established simply because of being accepted (*dam bcas pa tsam gyis = pratijñāmātreṇa siddha*), for [if it were] then it would follow absurdly that everything [whatsoever] would be established by everything."
4. See Tillemans 2000, 18.
5. The allusion here is to the common Buddhist position that perishing is actually without a cause (*ahetukavināśa*)—the point is that perishing (*nāśa*) and nonexistence (*abhāva*) are not real entities and thus cannot be effects. Although people obviously think that a pot is destroyed by hitting it with a hammer, the Buddhist maintains that what actually results is a mass of potsherds (*karparasaṃhati*) and not, strictly speaking, the perishing of the pot. The history and details of the arguments concerning this *vināśitvānumāna* (inference of things perishing) are discussed extensively in Mimaki 1976; for an appraisal of this line of argument, see also Tillemans 2011b, section 1.3.
6. Kamalaśīla, *Sarvadharmaniḥsvabhāvasiddhi*, P. 312a8–312b6: *rigs pa dang lung dag gis dngos po rnams kyi skye ba dpyad par bya'o // gal te 'di snyam du myu gu la sogs pa'i skye ba sa bon la sogs pa'i rkyen can gnag rdzi yan chad la grags pa kho na yin na de la dpyad par bya ci dgos / dngos po'i bdag nyid gtan la phab pa la ni rtog pa dang ldan pa rnams dpyad par rung ba ma yin te / thug pa med par thal bar 'gyur ba'i phyir dang / rtog pa dang mi ltan pa nyid du thal bar 'gyur ba'i phyir ro snyam du sems na / de ni rigs pa ma yin te / tshad mas gtan la ma phab pa'i phyir dang / grags pa yang log par srid pa'i phyir ro // de lta ma yin na rang la grags pa'i ngor byas te 'jug pa rnams su yang gang la yang bslu bar mi 'gyur ro // de la dper na 'jig pa yang rgyu dang ldan pa nyid du grags la / gzugs la sogs pa yang phyi rol gyi don nyid du grags zin kyang / dpyad pa byas na tshad mas gnod pa srid pa de bzhin du 'di la yang grags pa brdzun pa'i ngo bo yang srid pas dpyad par bya bar rung ba nyid do // de la lung rigs pa dang bral ba ni rtog pa dang*

ldan pa rnams rangs par mi 'gyur la / rigs pas brtan por byas pa'i lung yang don gzhan du drang bar mi nus pas de'i phyir re zhig rigs pas dpyad par bya'o //.

7. = *'jig rten grags sde pa, 'jig rten grags sde dang mthun par spyod pa, 'jig rten grags sde spyod pa'i dbu ma pa.* See Mimaki 1982, 27ff. The 'Jig rten grags sde pa, etc., are regularly considered to be the Prāsaṅgika—that is, Candrakīrti and his school—but sometimes certain other thinkers, like Jñānagarbha, are also included. On the terms for Madhyamaka subschools, including the Sanskritizations of Tibetan terms (e.g., *thal gyur ba* = *Prāsaṅgika, and *rang rgyud pa* = *Svātantrika) see Mimaki 1982, 53: "Tous les termes utiles pour classer les sous-écoles des Mādhyamika, tels que Sautrāntika-mādhyamika, Yogācāra-mādhyamika, 'Jig rten grags sde spyod pa'i dbu ma pa, Svātantrika et Prāsaṅgika sont une invention des auteurs tibétains."
8. See *Madhyamakāvatāra* 6.32–33. On Prāsaṅgika-style music-making, see *Madhyamakāvatārabhāṣya* ad 6.35 (ed. La Vallée Poussin, p. 121): *dper na shing dang rgyud la brten byas la / lag pa rtsol ba byas pa gsum tshogs na / sgrog byed pi wang gling bu la sogs pas / de dag las skyes sgra yang 'byung bar 'gyur /.* The passage is quoted from the *Lalitavistara* 13, verse 114 (ed. Vaidya): *yathā tantri pratītya dāru ca hastavyāyāma trayebhi saṃgati / tuṇavīṇasughoṣakādibhiḥ śabdo niścarate tadudbhavaḥ //.* "For example, in reliance upon the strings, wood, and manual effort, three [factors] are conjoined; musical instruments like the *tuṇa* and *vīṇā* ('lutes') then issue a sound that arises due to these [factors]."
9. Siderits 1989, 242.
10. This is how they generally take *Madhyamakāvatāra* 6.23 and other passages that show that ultimate truth is the domain of the āryas, who see rightly (*samyagdṛś*), and *saṃvṛti* (lit. "covered truth") the domain of the ignorant, who see wrongly/falsely (*mṛṣādṛś*). See 6.23: *samyagmṛṣādarśanalabdhabhāvaṃ rūpadvayaṃ bibhrati sarvabhāvāḥ / samyagdṛśāṃ yo viṣayaḥ sa tattvaṃ mṛṣādṛśāṃ saṃvṛtisatyam uktam //.* "All things bear a double nature constituted by correct and false views [of them]. The object of those who see rightly is said to be the truth, whereas the object of those who see falsely is said to be *saṃvṛtisatya*." Cf. Go rams pa, *Dbu ma spyi don nges don rab gsal*, 384c: *bden pa gnyis yul can gyi blo rmongs ma rmongs sam brdzun pa mthong ba dang / yang dag mthong ba'am / 'khrul ma 'khrul gyi sgo nas 'jog dgos pas yul can gyi blo'i sgo nas 'jog pa ni rgya gar gyi thal rang thams cad mthun par snang la //.* "The two truths must be brought about by the thoughts of subjects, thoughts that are [respectively] deluded or not deluded, see falsely or see rightly, are mistaken or not. Thus they are brought about by [different] thoughts of subjects; all Indian Prāsaṅgika and Svātantrika would seem to agree on this." See chapter 1 in Thakchoe 2007.
11. See, e.g., a modern Jo nang pa textbook, the *Rgyu 'bras theg pa mchog gi gnas lugs zab mo'i don rnam par nges pa rje jo nang pa chen po'i ring lugs 'jigs med gdong lnga'i nga ro* of Yon tan bzang po. In the section on the two truths (p. 116) we find statements like: *de ltar gyi kun rdzob bden pa / chos can / khyod don dam bden pa ma yin te / khyod gshis kyi gnas lugs su ye shes dam pa'i spyod yul du mi bden pa'i phyir / der thal / khyod kyi rang bzhin na rnam shes 'khrul ngo tsam du zad pa gang zhig / 'phags pa mchog gi ye shes kyi gzigs ngor rnam yang ma grub pa'i phyir / kun brdzob bden pa yin na rnam shes 'khrul ngo tsam du zad pas khyab ste.* "Take such customary truth as the topic: it is not ultimate truth because it is not true as an object of the highest wisdom about the absolute. This follows because in its nature it is nothing more than a mere perspective of mistaken consciousness and is never established from the perspective of

the noble, supreme wisdom. If something is a customary truth, this implies that it is nothing more than a mere perspective of mistaken consciousness."

12. Mimaki 1982, 170–73.
13. Cf. Stanley 2001, 37: "On a fictionalist view, engaging in discourse that involves apparent reference to a realm of problematic entities is best viewed as engaging in a *pretense.* Although in reality, the problematic entities do not exist, according to the pretense we engage in when using the discourse, they do exist." See Yablo 2001 for four philosophical varieties of fictionalism; adding the operator yields meta-fictionalism. Note that Garfield 2006 promotes a fictionalism as an interpretation of Madhyamaka.
14. On revolutionary and hermeneutical fictionalisms, see Burgess and Rosen 1997; see also Matti Eklund's entry "Fictionalism" in the *Stanford Encyclopedia of Philosophy.*
15. The typical error-theorist is J. L. Mackie, who holds an irrealist position about moral properties: they don't exist, but people have sophisticated and structured beliefs that they do and act, think, and talk as if they do. Sensible people (= certain philosophers), however, know better. See Mackie 1986. See M. E. Kalderon's "standard formulation" of error theory: "The sentences in the target class express propositions that represent the putative subject matter but are systematically false" (Kalderon 2005a, 105). For a celebrated attempt at a global irrealism, see N. Goodman 1978.
16. See also Joyce 2005, 298ff.
17. *Madhyamakāvatāra* 6.48cd: *svapne 'pi me naiva hi cittam asti yadā tadā nāsti nidarśanaṃ te //.* "Indeed, given that in a dream the mind does not [really] exist for me either, then you have no [valid] example [to show how mind is real while external objects aren't]." Tsongkhapa, in his *Rtsa ba'i she rab kyi bka' gnad brgyad,* p. 17, lucidly concludes: *des na tha snyad pa'i ngor don sems gnyis ka yod par mtshungs la / de kho na nyid sems pa'i ngor don sems gnyis ka med par mtshungs pas / don med la sems yod par mi rigs so /.* "So, from the point of view of customary transactions (*tha snyad* = *vyavahāra*), [physical] objects and the mind are the same in existing. From the point of view of one contemplating the [ultimate] truth (*de kho na nyid* = *tattva*), both are the same in not existing. Therefore, [for the Mādhyamika] it is incoherent that the object be nonexistent and the mind existent."
18. In the initial four chapters of the *Catuḥśataka* and Candrakīrti's *Catuḥśatakaṭīkā* thereupon, Āryadeva and Candrakīrti deal with a famous series of four "illusions" (*viparyāsa*) that are supposedly present in the confused minds of worldlings: taking transitory life as permanent, what is painful as pleasurable, what is dirty as clean, and what is selfless as having a self. Translation in Lang 2003 and 1986; Sanskrit fragments in Suzuki 1994. For the canonical schema of four *viparyāsa*, see *Abhidharmakośabhāṣya* of Vasubandhu ad 5.8, translation La Vallée Poussin 1923–31, 4: 21. To résumé the critique in the *Catuḥśataka* and *Ṭīkā* concerning the *viparyāsa*: the ordinary person's confidence about the future is based on self-deception about his mortality (1.6–7); worldlings' attitudes to mourning are inconsistent (*'gal ba* = *viruddha*) so that they mourn what on reflection does not deserve it (1.13); pleasure and happiness are rare, contrary to widespread opinion; it is pain is that is prevalent (2.4); people might think that work is a source of happiness, but it is a largely meaningless and slavish exertion to survive (2.18); attitudes about beauty and cleanliness are confused and would be seen to be wrong if we reflected upon them (3.3–5); possessiveness makes no sense (3.11); kings (and other so-called "superior individuals") are more like social

parasites, dependent upon others' work—they have no reason to feel justified of their status (4.2); a king who is violent, corrupt, or cruel deserves to be denounced, even though he claims to provide protection or to be the "father of the people" (4.11–13), and so on and so on.

19. See *Madhyamakāvatāra* 4.25: *vinopaghātena yad indriyāṇāṃ ṣaṇṇām api grāhyam avaiti lokaḥ / satyaṃ hi tal lokata eva śeṣaṃ vikalpitaṃ lokata eva mithyā //*. "Indeed, what the world considers to be apprehended by the six faculties without impairment, that is true just according to the world; the rest is thought to be false simply according to the world." Skt. in *Bodhicaryāvatārapañjikā* in Vaidya 1960, 171. The examples in the *Catuḥśatakaṭīkā* of attitudinal changes are often somewhat weird and comical. Thus, for example, Candrakīrti's commentary to CŚ 3.25: discovering that one's wife is actually a flesh-eating demoness (*piśācī*, *sha za mo*) is said to produce profound changes in one's attitudes and desires toward her (sic!). Cf. also his commentary to CŚ 3.23: when butter has been smeared on a cat's nose, the cat thinks his food is buttery and hence more attractive (*ghṛtaliptabīḍālanāsikasvādanavat*). The point is of course that the cat, or more generally anyone whose senses are altered or impaired, can be said to have wrong beliefs and inappropriate attitudes about things because his epistemic process is understood (even by ignorant worldlings) to be faulty.
20. The idea initially figures in Burgess and Rosen 1997, 3.
21. See Eklund 2005, 559–61, for the extension of Yablo's oracle argument.
22. Cf. Stanley 2001, 46: "The problem facing a brute error theory of a discourse that is epistemically central . . . lies in explaining how a discourse laced through with falsity can nevertheless be useful. On the view we are considering, this problem amounts to explaining how a discourse that expresses mostly falsities may communicate true propositions."
23. A radical Tibetan Buddhist way, which alas I only rather dimly understand, is what we seem to find in the writings of the eleventh-century Nyingmapa thinker Rongzom (*rong zom chos kyi bzang po*). The idea seems to be that Madhyamaka talk of customary truth as erroneous shows the inherent limitations of a dialectical system (*mtshan nyid kyi theg pa*) as it dissects and discriminates between right and wrong, rejection and acceptance, enlightenment and delusion, while the two truths are to be seen as inseparable (*bden gnyis dbyer med*). See chapter 3 and note 235 et passim in Köppl 2008. Rongzom's key stance seems to be a kind of suddenism: a state of absence of error (i.e., purity and enlightenment) is not to be reached gradually by a process of dispelling error, but error is by its nature already pure and thus is itself enlightened (*de yang 'khrul ba bsal nas ma 'khrul ba zhig bsgrub tu med de / 'khrul ba ngo bo nyid kyis rnam par dag pas sangs rgyas pa yin te / de bas na chos thams cad ye nas mngon par rdzogs par sangs rgyas pa'o /*).
24. That is, Priest, Siderits, and Tillemans 2011. To my knowledge, the first attempt to interpret Buddhist ideas in terms of deflationism/minimalism was Perrett 2002.
25. Note that if we still wished to go the fictionalist route, it would be a hermeneutical fictionalism, perhaps à la Yablo: we could say that ordinary people and āryas alike do *themselves* talk about *Fs* and *Gs* in a fictionalist way, but the ordinary man somehow also adds a corrupting superimposition. The usually cited difficulty in saying that ordinary people somehow talk in a make-believe fashion is that it is not at all clear what that means, for phenomenologically speaking they don't think they do or feel they do.

26. On Tsongkhapa's exegesis of "the world" (*loka*) as *including* āryas (and not in contrast to them, as typical Prāsaṅgikas would have it), see the article by Sonam Thakchoe, "Prāsaṅgika Epistemology in Context," in chapter 3 of Cowherds 2011.

Logic and Semantics

3. How Do Mādhyamikas Think? Notes on Jay Garfield, Graham Priest, and Paraconsistency

SEVERAL PHILOSOPHERS and Buddhist studies specialists have taken up the question of whether the philosophers of the Madhyamaka school use some form of deviant logic, or a logic that would not recognize fundamental theorems such as the law of double-negation elimination, the law of excluded middle, and even the law of noncontradiction. Often this investigation has focused on the tetralemma (*catuṣkoṭi*), with very varied results. In some writings problems about excluded middle or the interpretation of negation in the tetralemma have tended to take precedence over earlier interests about Madhyamaka respect or lack of respect for the law of noncontradiction. Indeed it's probably fair to say that, in Buddhist studies at least, attributing contradictions to Nāgārjuna has increasingly fallen out of vogue, such an attribution often being considered, by those of a philosophical bent, as tantamount to a trivialization of Madhyamaka's approach as exclusively mystical or even irrational. Some argue, more or less intuitively, that contradictions are rationally unthinkable. Others invoke a more sophisticated formal problem that anything and everything would follow from a contradiction, so that all reasoning would become indiscriminate; contradictions thus could supposedly never be tolerated by rational individuals on pain of "logical anarchy." In any case, the underlying idea is that, if the Madhyamaka is not to be trivialized as irrational—and indeed I agree it should not be so trivialized—it would have to rigorously respect the law of noncontradiction.

In what follows, we need to be clear on two terms: (1) a logic will be said to be *paraconsistent* if it does not allow every statement to be derived indiscriminately from premises that are contradictory. In short, paraconsistent logics are those in which, contrary to classical logic, a contradiction does not lead to "logical anarchy" or "explosion"; (2) a philosophy is *dialetheist* (accepts a double truth, *aletheia*) if it accepts that there are at least some statements of contradictions that are true. Paraconsistency and dialetheism clearly are separable for logicians who are interested primarily in the formal handling of inconsistency, all the while maintaining skepticism about there actually being any true contradictions. The two do, however, tend to be taken as a package by logicians and philosophers whose thought is inclined toward acceptance/tolerance of contradiction. For our purposes, as we are dealing with the latter type of thinkers, we will not treat paraconsistency independently from dialetheism.

Recently the Australian logician Graham Priest has teamed up with the American philosopher Jay Garfield to significantly elaborate upon certain ideas that they attribute to the second-century author Nāgārjuna. Priest and Garfield reconstruct this philosophy in terms of a radical type of paraconsistent logic and dialetheism, maintaining that there are some Nāgārjunian arguments that can best be interpreted as evidence of a *rational* acceptance of some true contradictions. In other words, Nāgārjuna was (at least implicitly or in a reconstruction of his philosophy) an advocate of a robust and full-fledged form of dialetheism and thus accepted that, for some statement ϕ, ϕ and not-ϕ were both true, but he did not accept that this implied a logical anarchy where any and all statements were derivable. Priest and Garfield's joint paper, "Nāgārjuna and the Limits of Thought," certainly does not endorse a laissez-faire acquiescence in any and all contradictions; it does, however, seek to argue that *some* statements of contradictions can be best taken as true given the basic principles of Madhyamaka thought, notably those along the lines of "the ultimate truth is that there is no ultimate truth" or "all things have one nature: no nature." These Buddhist positions, and others of a logically similar structure and supposedly to be found in Western thinkers like Kant, Wittgenstein, and Hegel, have the characteristic that Graham Priest has diagnosed as being at the "limits of thought," in that they involve totality paradoxes. The dialetheism comes in when we say that specific sorts of totalities, or "inclosures," exist and that there are at least some things that both are and are not in them.[1]

I. My Own Take: I Can Readily Accept a Limited Type of Paraconsistency/Dialetheism in the Prajñāpāramitā and Nāgārjuna, but Priest and Garfield's Robust Form of Dialetheism Seems to Me Unlikely

Graham Priest and Jay Garfield seem to have read my introduction to *Scripture, Logic, Language* as showing that I, like them, accepted Nāgārjuna's "sincere endorsement of contradictions" (Priest 2002, 250n2). Well, no doubt, finding out what that book's *svamata* (Tib. *rang lugs*, own take) on paraconsistency and dialetheism might actually be is a difficult task, especially as my views had evolved considerably since an earlier article (reprinted as chapter 9 in Tillemans 1999). It is probably by now high time to set out as clearly as I can what I do accept.

In my introduction to *Scripture, Logic, Language* I had wanted to indicate that my previous views about Buddhist works not exhibiting any logical deviance still applied to later (i.e., post-fifth-century) writers but that originally things were not so neatly classical. I said:

> I don't now know how to exclude that the *Prajñāpāramitāsūtra*s are most simply and naturally read as having more or less the contradictions they appear to have. Indeed, that [Edward] Conze-[Jacques] May scenario fascinates me more and more.[2]

I was essentially imagining an attempt at a more-or-less literal and unhedged interpretation of certain passages in the Prajñāpāramitā sūtras and in early Mādhyamika writers like Nāgārjuna, an interpretation that would be independent of and even opposed to that of the later commentators. I found myself in a position where I could no longer rule out an interpretation of this sort on formal grounds or because all contradiction supposedly would be irrational or lead to unlimited anarchical implication. Indeed, the prospect of trying to tread this paraconsistent path seemed to me worthwhile, even heady, in that it seemed to be an attempt to take the provocative and disturbing aspects of the Mādhyamikas' writings seriously, straight no chaser, and not explain them away with sophisticated *ad hoc* solutions or additions to the texts designed to accommodate a type of prescriptive common sense about what was needed so that an author like Nāgārjuna would supposedly be minimally rational.

In *Scripture, Logic, Language*, I had spoken about a natural and simple, literal reading of passages in the Prajñāpāramitā sūtras that suggested acceptance of contradiction. I was thinking primarily of the "signature formulae" of the *Vajracchedikāprajñāpāramitāsūtra*.[3] These are the oft-repeated statements throughout the sūtra that say that X does not exist or is not the case and that we therefore say that X does exist or is the case. For example, the Buddha doesn't have any distinctive marks and that is why one says he does. Here is a passage from *Vajracchedikā* 8 (ed. Conze):

> *buddhadharmā buddhadharmā iti subhūte 'buddhadharmāś caiva te tathāgatena bhāṣitāḥ / tenocyate buddhadharmā iti //*

> The dharmas special to a buddha, the dharmas special to a buddha, these the Tathāgata has taught to not in fact be/have dharmas special to a buddha. Thus they are said to be dharmas special to a buddha.

Let us leave aside the somewhat tricky question as to how we take the Sanskrit compound *abuddhadharmāś ca* (as a *bahuvrīhi* or as a *tatpuruṣa*; I tend to opt for the latter, as do most translations in Buddhist canons). In any case, the simple and natural reading of the passage, for the moment at least deliberately neglecting commentaries, is that this signature formula is denying something and then later affirming it. We shall delve more into the mysteries of such statements, as well as the commentaries, below.

As for Nāgārjuna, I was only secondarily thinking of his use of the tetralemma: what impressed me was the possibility of a more-or-less literal interpretation of his system in the sixfold logical corpus (*rigs tshogs drug*). At some points (e.g., in his *Ratnāvalī*) he endorses various Buddhist doctrinal positions (e.g., karmic retribution), and at other points (i.e., in the *Mūlamadhyamakakārikā*) he clearly denies that there are any such things at all. The fabric of his system, again neglecting commentaries, seems to suggest contradictoriness not unlike that to be found in the signature formulae of the *Vajracchedikā*: such and such that is said to be so in certain texts, chapters, and elsewhere, or even in the same paragraph, is said not to be so. My own mentor, Jacques May, many years ago interpreted Nāgārjuna using Hegelian ideas of the contradictoriness of all things; Edward Conze also held a view on the Prajñāpāramitā as accepting contradictions; Gadjin Nagao too, I think, was not far from this. I often thought that the debate about Buddhist acceptance (in some sense) of contradictions, a debate that had gone largely out of fashion in professional Buddhist studies, could be profitably revived once the full resources and rigor of the interpretative tools of nonclassical logics were skillfully brought to bear upon informed textual readings. That is now happening thanks to the considerable impetus of Graham Priest and Jay Garfield, and it is, I think, something of a liberating experience to be able to talk seriously about Madhyamaka and Prajñāpāramitā thought in these terms without getting bogged down in mind-numbing vagueness or excessive philological data too short on theoretical insight.

My own objections to Priest and Garfield's interpretations concern essentially two points: the role they attribute to totality paradoxes in Nāgārjuna's thought and, especially, the type of dialetheism they attribute to him. While we may well be able to find weak contradictions/dialetheism in early texts, it seems unlikely that early authors endorse, or in any way tolerate, the robust, or full-fledged, form of dialetheism of which Priest and Garfield speak. Here is what being weak and being strong/robust means in this chapter: we will speak of an endorsement of a weak contradiction as an acceptance of the truth of a statement ϕ at some point and an acceptance of the truth of not-ϕ at another; an endorsement of a strong contradiction, by contrast, means accepting the truth of a conjoined statement, ϕ and not-ϕ, in other words, $\phi \& \neg\phi$. The move from the weak to the strong variety is not inevitable, and thus a wedge can be driven between a weaker dialetheism (in which weak contradictions are accepted) and the robust dialetheism accepting strong contradictions.

Now, I think there are reasons for taking Nāgārjuna and the Prajñāpāramitā as accepting weak dialetheism. These reasons will be spelled out below. But in any case, these early authors, if they were dialetheist, could not be dismissed *a priori* because of looming anarchical implications or some other specter of irrationality. Formally speaking, their logic would involve a recognizable type of paraconsistency and dialetheism; indeed it would be significantly similar to what Nicholas Rescher and Robert Brandom developed in their joint book, the *Logic of Inconsistency*.[4] In 1992, in a *note liminaire* to a felicitation volume for Jacques May, I had mentioned that Rescher and Brandom's (weak) inconsistency might allow us to rationally reconstruct aspects of a Madhyamaka philosophy in the style of Conze and May. I later discovered that the approach was not unique to Rescher and Brandom; it was, as Koji Tanaka pointed out in his taxonomy of contemporary theories of paraconsistency, initially developed by the Polish logician Jaśkowski and certain other writers, including some of my Canadian compatriots. Tanaka classified these theories as "nonadjunctive" approaches to paraconsistency: they prohibit the move from individual premises, ϕ, $\neg\phi$, to their adjunction $\phi \& \neg\phi$.[5] In other words, nonadjunctive paraconsistency enables one to affirm that ϕ is true and to affirm that $\neg\phi$ is true—a weak inconsistency—without, however, ever admitting the truth of the statement $\phi \& \neg\phi$. This latter statement would be a strong contradiction that cannot be accepted as true in the Rescher-Brandom system if dastardly consequences like explosion are to be avoided. The paraconsistency may certainly be disturbing, but it is not irrational.

II. Priest and Garfield on Nāgārjuna

Although a natural account of the signature formulae of the *Vajracchedikā* and the fabric of Nāgārjuna's six works seems to have their authors granting/

endorsing the truth of ϕ at some point and endorsing the truth of not-ϕ at another, we never, to my knowledge, find them giving a clear endorsement of the truth of the conjunction, ϕ and not-ϕ.[6] My skepticism about finding full-fledged, or robust, dialetheism in Nāgārjuna is obviously going to be out of step here with Priest and Garfield's interpretation. We thus need look in more detail at why Priest and Garfield thought that there were indeed true adjunctions of ϕ and not-ϕ in the Madhyamaka literature and what exactly would be problematic in such a reading of Nāgārjuna.

I have no problems with Priest and Garfield's characterization that what they are doing with Nāgārjuna "is . . . not textual history but rational reconstruction,"[7] providing of course that history and textual evidence do not seriously clash with, or rule out, that reconstruction. Let it be granted that their first candidate for paradox—"The ultimate truth is that there is no ultimate truth'—is arguably a consequence or paraphrase of several passages in the *Mūlamadhyamakakārikā* and in that way can perhaps be claimed to be the thrust of Nāgārjuna's philosophy, if not actually his words.[8] The second—"All things have one nature: no nature"—is in fact close to an historically attested interpretation of some passages in *Mūlamadhyamakakārikā* 15 about the three characteristics of any intrinsic nature (*svabhāva*): nonfabricated, independent of other things (*nirapekṣaparatra*), and always fixed. It is especially Candrakīrti's interpretation of these passages—notably his *Prasannapadā* on 15.2—that brings in the idea that Nāgārjuna does not just refute intrinsic natures, he accepts that there is at least one such nonfabricated, independent, and unchanging fixed nature of things: their emptiness (*śūnyatā*).[9]

I should not go into very many technical details here about how Priest and Garfield formally present the paradoxes that they see in Nāgārjuna; I will confine the presentation of inclosure schemata to a long note.[10] In any case, Priest and Garfield claim that the Nāgārjunian paradox is one like paradoxes in set theory, where in the case of some totality, or "limit of thought," defined in a certain way, there will be objects that both are included within it and are outside it. They argue that if we suppose with Nāgārjuna that all things are empty, then the totality of empty—that is, natureless—things will itself have a nature—being empty—and that this nature will be both in and not in the totality of empty things. Formulated as an inclosure paradox, it looks potentially interestingly similar to other totality paradoxes, like those of Cantor and Russell.

The connection with other logical paradoxes, if it could be established, would itself be quite important, as it would serve in part to answer a charge that these Nāgārjunian paradoxes are simply "rhetorical paradoxes" along the lines of "The Golden Rule is that there is no Golden Rule," "I can resist everything except temptation," and other such cute duplicitous sayings, which are no more than attention grabbers.[11] Undeniably, there is a penchant for such enigmatic, provocative styles of expression in Indian philosophy so that it would be rather silly to say that *every* use of words in an apparently contradictory fashion in a Sanskrit text is a case of an author embracing dialetheism or saying something exotic of logical interest. The saving grace of Priest and Garfield's Nāgārjunian paradoxes, if they are right, would be that these paradoxes would be cases of a wider East-West phenomenon, inclosure paradoxes, and would thus not be simply a matter of provocative style. They would be logical paradoxes in the same way that Russell's and Cantor's paradoxes are.

Although the Nāgārjunian paradoxes would be interesting for comparative philosophers in that they would be East-West discoveries of consistency problems with totalities, there are, it seems to me, some serious problems if we wish to abide by the spirit and letter of Indian texts and say that Nāgārjuna would also advocate true strong contradictions that he would see as stemming from totality paradoxes. Consider what we do know about the spirit of Indian discussions of totalities. Indeed, inconsistencies in the notion of a totality *do* explicitly and repeatedly figure in Indian philosophy's arguments about the coherence of the notion of *sarva* ("all," "the totality," "the universe"), but these derivations of inconsistencies are certainly not *endorsed* by Buddhists as cases of dialetheism or genuine true contradictions, strong or weak. They are instead used by Naiyāyikas, like Uddyotakara in his *Nyāyavārttika* to *Nyāyasūtra* 2.2.66,[12] to *refute* Buddhist doctrines, like the semantic theory of *apoha*, by *reductio ad absurdum*. The non-Buddhist Naiyāyika argues, for example, that the Buddhist theory of *apoha*, where the term X signifies non-non-X, is impossible in the case of a word like "the totality," "all" (*sarva*). The reason is that the Buddhist would (absurdly) have to admit that there was something, be it a set or a property or an individual, that was outside the totality of things. For, given the principle that any word X signifies non-non-X, "the totality" would express the negation of nontotality (*asarvanivṛtti*); the hidden premise is that there always must be something to negate, a real, existing negandum. Of course the problem then is that this "something outside the totality" would have to be both outside and not outside the totality of things.

Whatever the value of Uddyotakara's attack, the Buddhists, including Mādhyamikas like Kamalaśīla in his *Madhyamakāloka* and Śāntarakṣita in the *apoha* chapter of his *Tattvasaṃgraha*, repeatedly take great pains to show that these supposed contradictions in the notion of a totality are *not* contradictions at all and that there is a way to preserve consistency in the *apoha* theory by saying that "something outside the totality" (*asarva*) is just a conceptual invention: it is not necessary that an *asarva* actually be real to be the negandum in non-nontotality. In short, the most explicit and frequent discussions about contradictions stemming from totalities are those between non-Buddhists and Buddhists; the Buddhists defend themselves by arguing that acceptance of totalities does *not* lead to any inconsistencies at all. The Buddhists never, as far as I know, *accept* any explicitly formulated argument to the effect that *sarva*, the universe, the totality, would indeed be contradictory in the strong or weak senses of contradiction. It would thus be odd that, for them, totality arguments should nonetheless be the major vehicle they use to show true strong contradictions concerning emptiness and other cardinal principles of their philosophy. Earlier, I spoke about the Nāgārjunian paradoxes being supposedly distinguishable from insignificant rhetorical paradoxes because they would turn on major East-West problems about totalities. If I am right in arguing that Buddhists generally do not seem to view totalities as involving contradictions, then the paradoxical passages that Priest and Garfield cite could well also diminish in significance: they would become more like anomalies or enigmatic expressions than evidence of common East-West fellowship in discerning contradictions at the limits of thought.

Turning to the letter of the texts, I would argue that not just are totality arguments used differently in Indian philosophy from the way Priest and Garfield would have them used, but that it seems rather implausible to say that Nāgārjuna himself accepted any true strong contradictions at all: indeed he seems to give pretty good textual evidence that he does not. For example, in *Mūlamadhyamakakārikā* 25.14 he gives what looks like a clear prohibition against strong contradiction:

> *bhaved abhāvo bhāvaś ca nirvāṇa ubhayaṃ katham / na tayor ekatrāstitvam ālokatamasor yathā //*
>
> How could both nonbeing and being pertain to nirvāṇa? Just like light and darkness, both are not present in one place.

Even more explicit in banning true strong contradiction is Candrakīrti's commentary on this verse:

> *bhāvābhāvayor api parasparaviruddhayor ekatra nirvāṇe nāsti saṃbhava iti // bhaved abhāvo bhāvaś ca nirvāṇa ubhayaṃ katham / naiva bhaved ity abhiprāyaḥ /*

> For being and nonbeing too, there is no possibility for the two mutually contradictory things (*parasparaviruddha*) to be present in one place—that is, in *nirvāṇa*. Thus "how could both nonbeing and being pertain to nirvāṇa?" The point is they could not at all.

The argument is situated in the context of the fourfold negation of the tetralemma (*catuṣkoṭi*), where an opponent suggests that nirvāṇa both is and is not; in short, the opponent is advocating that a true strong contradiction would apply. Nāgārjuna and Candrakīrti reply that such a true contradiction is not possible. Now, there is no indication whatsoever that their reasoning is restricted to the isolated specific case of nirvāṇa. It looks rather clearly generalizable: no true strong contradiction in this case because no true strong contradictions at all. To suggest otherwise and say that there are some true strong contradictions in certain specific cases makes for a circumscribed rejection of the third lemma of the tetralemma that is hard to reconcile with fundamental texts of the Mādhyamikas. Indeed, there is solid evidence (e.g., in the work of Nāgārjuna's disciple Āryadeva, in Candrakīrti, and in others) that the essence of the Madhyamaka method is that the rejection of the four lemmas in the tetralemma is and must be generalizable, and that it is the way a Mādhyamika should *always* proceed in criticizing philosophical positions. This is the point of the famous verse 22 in Āryadeva's *Catuḥśataka* 14, which advocates negating all four positions:

> *sad asat sadasac ceti sadasan neti ca kramaḥ / eṣa prayojyo vidvadbhir ekatvādiṣu nityaśaḥ //*

> Being, nonbeing, [both] being and nonbeing, neither being nor nonbeing: such is the method that the wise should always use with regard to identity and the like [i.e., all other theses].

Again, it would be quite odd if a Buddhist were to allow that, in spite of verses like this, Nāgārjunian totality paradoxes nonetheless yielded true strong contradictions that were exceptions to the rejection of the third lemma.

III. Nāgārjuna and the Prajñāpāramitā Unhedged

Let me try to make the best case I can for a paraconsistent, dialetheic interpretation of Nāgārjuna and the Prajñāpāramitā sūtras. Instead of totality arguments suggesting some form of paraconsistency and dialetheism, as

Priest and Garfield have things, it is the whole system that suggests a type of paraconsistency/dialetheism on a natural reading; in particular it is the use of the two truths, customary (*saṃvṛtisatya*) and ultimate (*paramārthasatya*).

Here is what I take to be a key problem in early Madhyamaka and Prajñāpāramitā texts. Suppose the Buddhist author says (more or less explicitly) that ϕ is true and also says that not-ϕ is also true, as the Mādhyamikas and the author(s) of the Prajñāpāramitā sūtras are wont to do when they say that dharmas, aggregates, Buddha marks, karma, suffering, and so on exist and also say that they do not exist, that they are empty. Are hedges and parameters, like the qualifiers "customarily" and "ultimately," implicit or somehow built into ϕ and not-ϕ, respectively, so that there is only a pseudo-appearance of contradiction?[13] Or is it the same statement, without any implicit parameters, whose truth is being endorsed (for one set of reasons, say, customary) at some point in the text and rejected (for another set of reasons, say, ultimate) at other points in the text?

By way of illustration of the two approaches, let us go back to the signature formulae of the *Vajracchedikā*: X does not exist / is not the case, and thus we say that X does exist / is the case. For example, the Buddha doesn't have any distinctive marks, and that is why one says he does. Now, these types of statements can be and have been approached in both above-mentioned ways. We could do what the eighth-century Indian Mādhyamika Kamalaśīla did in his *Vajracchedikāṭīkā*, which was a kind of common later Buddhist interpretative stratagem—namely, clearly differentiate the perspectives involved: the buddha-dharmas and so on are not buddha-dharmas and so on, looked at ultimately, and they are buddha-dharmas and so forth looked at from the point of view of customary truth.[14] We could either add explicit qualifiers right into the wording of the respective affirmative and negative statements (as did, for example, the Tibetan writer Tsongkhapa), or we could leave the actual wording in the sūtra unchanged but say, as did Kamalaśīla, that qualifications of perspective have to be understood as implicitly present. In any case, for our purposes, the result is more or less the same: appearance of any contradiction (strong or weak) vanishes. There would be nothing more logically provocative here in endorsing both statements than there would be in endorsing the statements "It is ten o'clock" and "It is not ten o'clock" when we also know that the first statement concerns Eastern standard time and the second concerns Pacific time.

The alternative approach, à la Conze et al., is one that leaves the provocation of the signature formulae intact: we would say that the same completely unparameterized statement is being affirmed and negated. In short, no explicit parameters nor implicit timezone-like switches of perspective along the lines of Tsongkhapa or Kamalaśīla but only, at most, different kinds of supportive reasoning as to why the one statement is true and why its denial is true. Thus the sūtra author(s) would have good reasons to say that dharmas or Buddha marks do exist (e.g., to account for truths that must be accepted in the world, or at least among Buddhist worldlings) and other good reasons to say they do not (e.g., to give an account of their ultimate status, emptiness). Indeed, this move might well bring out just how close and inseparable customary and ultimate truths are for early Mahāyāna Buddhist authors: as Nāgārjuna had himself often repeated, the customary truth/reality, saṃsāra, is nothing but (*eva*) the ultimate, nirvāṇa, and vice versa. Put in our terms, the two truths are so close that the very same unparameterized statements about dharmas, aggregates, suffering, and so on, are both asserted and denied.

There is, I think, a good reason to prefer the second style of interpretation and be suspicious about the imposition of hedges and parameters and other attempts at nonliteral nuancing of early Madhyamaka writings. Simply put, if we can read Nāgārjuna and the Prajñāpāramitā without qualifiers and pretty much literally in their acceptance and rejection of the world and Buddhist schemata, let's go ahead and do it: they are interesting, rational, and intelligent as is, and charity may not require anything more; there is no need for our prescriptive common sense. This is about the most straightforward and persuasive exegetical argument I can think of for interpreting these writers as embracing paraconsistency and dialetheism.

A not infrequent, but in my view less persuasive, argument is that a nuanced and finessed approach would invariably be wrong, or even be a travesty of the Madhyamaka approach, because it would bring in philosophical theses by the back door and thus fatally weaken the whole quietist project that Nāgārjuna sought to promote. Indeed there is a traditional Sakyapa interpretation of Madhyamaka thinking that goes a considerable distance in fleshing out this argument: I am thinking of the *Lta ba'i shan 'byed* of the fifteenth-century Tibetan writer Gorampa (Go rams pa Bsod nams seng ge, 1429–89), probably the most explicit traditional source I know for a potentially coherent, unparameterized interpretation of Nāgārjuna and the Prajñāpāramitā. Gorampa's target was of course Tsongkhapa, who advocated adding qualifiers like "ultimately" (*don dam par*), or "truly" (*bden par*) to the typical negative statements made by Mādhyamikas: things are not ultimately/truly produced, are not ultimately/truly existent, and so on and so forth for all properties a person might wish to attribute.

Gorampa's main point in his refutation of Tsongkhapa was that if a Mādhyamika commentator adds that kind of ultimate parameter and thus gives a nonliteral interpretation of Nāgārjuna's negative statements, he has in effect denatured the whole Nāgārjunian dialectic to the degree that it will no longer be able to accomplish its (religious) purpose of quietening philosophical speculation and attachment—and irenic quietism, or complete "freedom from proliferations" (*spros bral*, Skt. *niṣprapañca*), is, for Gorampa, the main point of the Madhyamaka's negative dialectic. His alternative is thus to take literally the idea of *yod min med min*, "not existent, not nonexistent," and not add any qualifiers like "ultimately" or "truly," the danger being that, by negating "ultimately ϕ" instead of ϕ itself for any statement, the Mādhyamika thinker will arrive at smugness about being free of positions but will in fact remain as attached to the truth of ϕ as any other realist philosopher. Qualifiers and hedges, so the argument can be paraphrased, make everything a little too neat and refute only straw men.

This argument, however, does not look to me to be as telling against *all* Mādhyamika uses of parameterization as Gorampa would want it to be. Gorampa (and critics like him) would surely be right in opposing the tendency of many followers of Tsongkhapa to rather glibly trot out the provisos "truly" or "ultimately" whenever the philosophical going got tough. However, differentiating between "truly X" and "X" can be more than that and can reflect a repeated self-examination—that is, a type of phenomenological analysis of our *Lebenswelt*—to discern nonobvious recurring features of how we superimpose true/ultimate status upon otherwise innocent customary things. In fact, Tibetans have argued that recognizing what is to be refuted (*dgag bya*) and what is to be conserved (true existence and customary existence, respectively) is one of the most difficult, and most necessary, points in a sophisticated Madhyamaka philosophy. As I have argued elsewhere, this approach is more in step with later Indian Madhyamaka thought than is generally conceded.[15] The upshot would be that Gorampa's traps of parameterization would tell against an overly facile or dogmatic resort to the tactic. No doubt, much use of qualifiers was often little more than rote repetition of doxa, but I think that it was not always and need not be.

In any case, let us suppose we adopted an unqualified reading either because simplicity and naturalness are (all other things being equal) better than complex additions and hedges, or perhaps because of Gorampa-style quasi-religious arguments. Where does this unhedged interpretation of Nāgārjuna and the Prajñāpāramitā take us in terms of logic? I would say the following: it leads to a type of paraconsistent logic according to which Nāgārjuna will in certain discussions admit that ϕ is true (for worldly, doctrinal, or even Abhidharmic reasons) and in other contexts that $\neg\phi$ is true (for reasons involving the emptiness of intrinsic nature); however, Nāgārjuna will recognize no good reasons at all to ever admit the truth of the conjunction $\phi\&\neg\phi$. There will be no such reasons, because Nāgārjuna, as I had argued earlier, is deeply respectful of the third negation in the tetralemma, a negation that he generalizes to apply to every statement. In short, we end up with Nāgārjuna accepting nonadjunctive paraconsistency and weak dialetheism. He could not however hold strong dialetheism if the Mādhyamika is not to run afoul of his own prohibitions. For Nāgārjuna, there is no ϕ such that $\phi\&\neg\phi$ is true.

Up until now my argument has been essentially that whatever the philosophical merits or demerits of blocking the move from weak to strong, Nāgārjuna and the Prajñāpāramitā, interpreted quite literally, *do* seem to have blocked precisely that move. But given that adjunction generally seems an obvious and inevitable logical operation to most people, why might a Mādhyamika nonetheless embrace a nonadjunctive approach, apparently tolerating weak contradiction but eschewing the strong? If we stay in the spirit of Gorampa, the beginnings of an answer could be found in the Mādhyamika thinker's quietism, her refusal to engage herself on how things really are. Asserting a strong contradiction of the form $\phi\&\neg\phi$ could quite easily be taken (and was supposedly so taken by certain non-Buddhists) as a definite position with perhaps a commitment to there actually being a contradictory state of affairs, while stating ϕ at some point (for worldly reasons) and then its negation at another (because of emptiness) would have the effect of annulling commitment to what was previously stated, and thus would be considerably less likely to engage one in a position or thesis. Indeed the same process of annulment would apply to stating $\neg\phi$ and then denying it too, resulting in a return to a perspective where ϕ can be once again endorsed but without hypostasis, grasping at how things really are. A nonadjunctive use of the two truths may thus be a systematic use of inconsistency in the service of quietism: no position would escape annulment.

The logic of Nāgārjuna would be paraconsistent/dialetheic but with nonetheless well-defined areas in which classical logic would function. Nonadjunctive paraconsistency and weak dialetheism would, as I have been arguing, apply in a general manner to the so-called six logical works (*rigs tshogs drug*) of Nāgārjuna, which sometimes treat of things worldly and then deny those same things elsewhere in discussions of emptiness, *śūnyavāda*. They would also apply when Nāgārjuna discusses the ultimate status of things in systematically negative terms: they would thus apply to discussions of emptiness, like in the tetralemma, where Buddhists endorse $\neg\phi$, $\neg\neg\phi$, but do not endorse the adjunction $\neg\phi\&\neg\neg\phi$, nor *a fortiori* $\phi\&\neg\phi$.[16] Also, if we wish, the passages that Priest and Garfield took as evidence for Nāgārjunian dialetheism could still be taken as showing paradoxes: the relevant inclosure schemata would just have to be reinterpreted in terms of weak contradictions rather than the strong variety. Paraconsistency and dialetheism (of any sort) would not, however, figure in ordinary discussions about purely customary matters, like the usual and banal reasoning about fires on smoky hills, sound being impermanent, fire being hot, and other such discussions about nonultimate states of affairs acknowledged in common by Mādhyamikas and realists. Nor would they be applicable in the numerous *reductio ad absurdum* (*prasaṅga*) arguments where Nāgārjuna seeks to show inconsistencies in his opponents' positions. These *reductio* usually proceed by deriving ϕ at some point and $\neg\phi$ at another; adjunction of the two gives the needed contradiction. Clearly a Mādhyamika debater could not allow even weak contradictions if he were to hope to vanquish his realist opponent by playing according to the rules of the latter's own game.

IV. Caveats and Conclusions

I think that this is about as far as I can go in making the case for paraconsistency and dialetheism in early Madhyamaka and the Prajñāpāramitā texts. In any event, later Madhyamaka philosophy in India or Tibet—or in other words Nāgārjuna's philosophy as viewed by commentators from about the sixth century on—is another story and *is* much more inclined to parameterization. It is also much more conservative about consistency. There are more explicit prohibitions against *virodha/viruddha* (contradiction), a fact that makes it more difficult to read the later Mādhyamika scholastics as tolerating or advocating any weak or strong contradictions. Significant too is that the later Mādhyamika writers were, with one or two exceptions, under the spell of Dignāga's and Dharmakīrti's logic, so that there was an attempt to harmonize Madhyamaka thought with a logic for realists. Numerous examples of disambiguation, parameterization, and other relatively predictable moves of paradox resolution can be given. Suffice it to stress for our purposes that true (strong or weak) contradictions are anathema for the logicians of the Dignāga-Dharmakīrti school and that there is every reason to think they are too for later Mādhyamikas, like Kamalaśīla, Śāntarakṣita, and many others, who saw themselves as under the same constraints as their logician coreligionists. There was a significant change in orientation between Nāgārjuna and later commentators (especially those of the majority Svātantrika persuasion), and that change was largely due to the overwhelming influence of the Dignāga-Dharmakīrti school on Indian Buddhist thought.[17]

Would this evolution mean that later Indian or Tibetan Madhyamaka thought, with its parameterization and classical logic, is inauthentic or without philosophical value as a development of Nāgārjuna's stance? Of course not, unless authenticity and value demanded no evolution, a kind of pure doctrinal deep-freeze. Indeed, many of the more significant philosophical analyses in Nāgārjuna as viewed via later Mādhyamikas—for example, the identification of what is to be refuted (*dgag bya*) and its distinction from what is customarily so, the part-whole arguments, causality, dependence and intrinsic natures, the critique of epistemology—do not seem to depend necessarily upon an acceptance of paradox. These subtle analyses and others can be and were pursued by later Indo-Tibetan thinkers using a classical logic; there is no reason at all to think that these people badly missed the boat. While I have been arguing that the early Madhyamaka and Prajñāpāramitā literature may well be best read as dialetheist, it would be a somewhat stultifying mistake to see the whole, or even the essentials, of this philosophy, or of Buddhism for that matter, as turning irrevocably on a use of nonclassical logic and acceptance of contradiction.

In conclusion, I would maintain my historical hypothesis first advanced in *Scripture, Logic, Language*: not only did the philosophical debates and doctrines evolve over time with Buddhist scholastic thinkers, but the logic seems to have evolved away from a rather complex architecture to one of increasing homogeneity, simplicity, and classicalness.[18] Logical simplification also happened elsewhere in Indian thought. A number of researchers[19] have looked at Indian and Tibetan logicians' problems in explaining their theories of good reasons: with time the formal aspects became ever simpler even though the philosophical analyses often became increasingly subtle. Something similar seems to have happened in the case of the Madhyamaka.

Notes to Chapter 3

1. For the technical details on what an inclosure is, see note 10 below. The joint article by Priest and Garfield, "Nāgārjuna and the Limits of Thought," appears in Priest 2002 as well as in Garfield 2002. My page references are to Priest 2002.
2. See Tillemans 1999, 18.
3. I owe the phrase "signature formula" to Paul Harrison, who has long worked on the *Vajracchedikā*.
4. Rescher and Brandom 1980. See Tillemans 1992b, 11–12.
5. See Tanaka 2003, 29–30.
6. The only potential counterevidence here might be the "positively formulated" tetralemma found in *Mūlamadhyamakakārikā* 17.8, which states that everything is real (*tathya*), everything is not real, everything is both real and not real, and everything is

neither, and that this is what the Buddha taught. However, as Candrakīrti and other commentators make clear—and the overwhelming use of the negative tetralemma in Nāgārjuna seems to bear out—this series of positive statements is an exceptional case and is best seen as a graded hierarchy of provisional stages aiding specific disciples (with diminishing degrees of obscuration) on their way to understanding emptiness. It seems that the verse essentially provides a hermeneutics to resolve the seeming conflicts among the extremely diverse views preached in the scriptures: the lowest view is realism's affirmation of things, then its denial, an acceptance of both and then the rarefied "neither-nor" position for the "scarcely obscured" student. The contradiction in the third lemma is thus best seen as at most a pedagogically useful transitional stage for certain individuals, as is the affirmation in the first; it does not represent the dominant Nāgārjunian standpoint, in which a fourfold denial of all such positions clearly is key. See Seyfort Ruegg 1977, 5–7, 63–64n71.

7. Priest 2002, 251.
8. It is worth mentioning, however, that later Tibetan commentators would hedge this statement to make a distinction between ultimate truth and what is ultimately established (*don dam par grub pa*) so that we end up with the tamer principle that the ultimate truth is the ultimate truth but, like any other dharma, is not ultimately established. The ultimate truth would not be that there is no ultimate truth but rather that nothing is ultimately established. I take this up in chapter 4. It is a very plausible exegesis if one is resolved to eliminate paradox and hold that Madhyamaka follows classical logic.
9. See Candrakīrti, *Prasannapadā* (ed. La Vallée Poussin), 264.12–265.2: *atha keyaṃ dharmāṇāṃ dharmatā? dharmāṇāṃ svabhāvaḥ. ko 'yaṃ svabhāvaḥ? prakṛtiḥ. kā ceyaṃ prakṛtiḥ? yeyaṃ śūnyatā. keyaṃ śūnyatā? naiḥsvābhāvyam. kim idaṃ naiḥsvābhāvyam? tathatā. keyaṃ tathatā? tathābhāvo 'vikāritvaṃ sadāiva sthāpitā. sarvadānutpāda eva hy agnyādīnāṃ paranirapekṣatvād akṛtrimatvāt svabhāva ity ucyate.* Note that in this vein there is also an important passage from the *Aṣṭasāhasrikāprajñāpāramitāsūtra* quoted by Bhattacharya (1986, 113n2) in connection with Nāgārjuna's *Vigrahavyāvartanī* 29: *prakṛtyaiva na te dharmāḥ kiṃcit. yā ca prakṛtiḥ sāprakṛtiḥ, yā cāprakṛtiḥ sā prakṛtiḥ sarvadharmāṇām ekalakṣaṇatvād yad utālakṣaṇatvād.* "By their nature, these phenomena are not anything at all. Their nature is a nonnature; it is their nonnature that is their nature, for all phenomena have the same nature: they have no characteristics." Skt. of *Aṣṭasāhasrikā* (ed. Vaidya), 96. See also the use of the passage in Priest 2002, 266. In fact, this would-be paradox comes up elsewhere, notably in a sūtra closely connected with the tathāgatagarbha literature, the *Jñānālokālaṃkāra*, in which the paradox of nature being nonnature is used to explain why the uncompounded (*asaṃskṛta*) and compounded (*saṃskṛta*) are not two different things. See Study Group 2005, 106: *yatra notpādo na sthitir na vyayaḥ / tad ucyate trimaṇḍalapariśuddham asaṃskṛtaṃ yathaivāsaṃskṛtas tathaivan* [sic] *saṃskṛtaṃ boddhavyam / tat kasya hetoḥ / sarvadharmāṇāṃ yaḥ svabhāvaḥ sa asvabhāvaḥ tatra nāsti dvayam iti /.* "What has no production, no abiding and no destruction, that is said to be the 'uncompounded that is pure in the three spheres.' One should understand the compounded in precisely the same way as [one understands] the uncompounded. Why is that? The nature of all dharmas is their nonnature; there is no duality there."

Finally, on the senses of *svabhāva*, there is an extensive and burgeoning literature;

for starters, see de Jong 1972. For Tsongkhapa's nonparadoxical reading of these and related passages, see Magee 1999.

10. Here, briefly, is how it goes. The key formal notion that they introduce is that of an "inclosure": a totality set Ω is an inclosure if (1) its members have a property ϕ and have a certain property ψ and (2) there is a "diagonalizing" function δ that assigns to each subset x of Ω whose members have ψ a new object that is not in the subset x but is still in Ω. Applying that function δ to Ω itself, we get an object that both is and is not a member of Ω. Symbolically, here are Priest's conditions for an inclosure:

    $\Omega = \{y{:}\phi(y)\}$ exists, and $\psi(\Omega)$.

    For all x such that x is a subset of Ω and $\psi(x)$, $\delta(x)$ is not a member of x and $\delta(x)$ is a member of Ω.

    See Priest 2002, 134, for the inclosure schema. In the Nāgārjunian inclosure paradox, Ω is the set of all empty things—things without intrinsic nature; these things have the property ψ, having a common intrinsic nature. The diagonalising function δ assigns to the subset x the nature of the things in x. Since $\delta(x)$ is a member of Ω, it does not have an intrinsic nature. Subset x, however, has the property ψ and thus consists of things that do have a common intrinsic nature. Therefore $\delta(x)$ is not a member of x. Applying δ to Ω itself, we have the result that $\delta(\Omega)$ is a member of Ω and $\delta(\Omega)$ is not a member of Ω. The nature that δ assigns to Ω is emptiness. Thus emptiness is empty of intrinsic nature and is not empty of intrinsic nature.

11. On the distinction between logical and rhetorical paradoxes, see Rescher 2001, 4. See Tillemans 1999, 195–96 on some examples of the stylistic tendency in Indian philosophy to use seemingly paradoxical modes of expression. Often it is quite clear (e.g., by looking at autocommentaries) that these are only rhetorical paradoxes.

12. See Uddyotakara, *Nyāyavārttika*, 687: *na punaḥ sarvapada etad asti, na hy asarvaṃ nāma kiṃcid asti yat sarvapadena nivartyeta.* "For the word *sarva*, though, this [exclusion] is not to be. Indeed, there is nothing at all called *asarva* (what is outside the totality) that would be negated by the word *sarva*." For further references to the debates concerning *sarva*, see also Keira 2004, 92n139. The same objection of potential contradiction figures in discussions of totalities in other contexts, e.g., Buddhist accounts of "knowledge of all"—omniscience (*sarvajñātā*)—and the Buddhist doctrine of everything being momentary. The Buddhist reply is again the same attempt to dissipate the apparent contradiction.

13. Cf. Priest 2002, 151, on parameterization: "The stratagem is to the effect that when one meets an (at least prima facie) contradiction of the form P(a)!, one tries to find some ambiguity in P, or some different respects, r1 and r2, in which something may be P, and then to argue that a is P in one respect, P(r1,a), but not in the other, ¬P(r2,a). For example, when faced with the apparent contradiction that it is both 2 p.m. and 10 p.m., I disambiguate with respect to place and resolve the contradiction by noting that it is 2 p.m. in Cambridge and 10 p.m. in Brisbane."

14. See for example Kamalaśīla's discussion on the sūtra's formula concerning "heaps of merit," *bsod nams kyi phung po*, in Kamalaśīla, *Āryaprajñāpāramitāvajracchedikāṭīkā*, 296–97.

15. See chapter 1, sections III–V, and Tillemans 2004.

16. An interesting question, which can only be very briefly taken up here, is how the Mādhyamika blocks the move from $\neg\phi$, $\neg\neg\phi$ to $\phi\&\neg\phi$. Is it because he does not accept adjunction or because he (also) does not accept a law of double-negation

elimination? The status of the latter law is unclear among Indian and Tibetan Mādhyamikas. Many contemporary scholars have thought that *paryudāsa* (implicative) negation is subject to the law of double-negation elimination, but that the *prasajya* (nonimplicative) negation in the tetralemma must not be subject to such a law. Unfortunately, all this is nonobvious and cannot be taken for granted, varying rather with the philosophical stances of the schools. Some Tibetan Mādhyamikas do go in that direction but using other terms. Gorampa uses the term *dgag pa gnyis kyis rnal ma go ba* (understanding the positive via two negations), which clearly corresponds to a law of double-negation elimination. He argues that the Mādhyamika does *not* accept such a law; see, e.g., the argument against Tsongkhapa in Gorampa's *Lta ba'i shan 'byed,* 51–52. Tsongkhapa, by contrast, takes it as virtually self-evident that Mādhyamikas, indeed everyone, must accept double-negation elimination. See his use of *dgag pa gnyis kyis rnal ma ston pa* in his *Rtsa shes ṭīk chen*, 43–44. In fact, as Pascale Hugon has pointed out to me, the term is Indian in origin and is found in the third chapter of Dharmakīrti's *Pramāṇaviniścaya.* We find there the phrase *pratiṣedhadvayena prakṛtagamanāt* (*Tib: dgag pa gnyis kyi rnal ma go ba'i phyir ro,* D. 224b). It seems clear that Dharmakīrti at least, and possibly the Mādhyamikas that felt strong affinities with his thought, recognized double-negation elimination. My thanks to Pascale Hugon for references to Dharmakīrti and to José Cabezón for reminding me of the importance of the term in Gorampa. These issues concerning double negation are taken up more fully in chapter 7.

17. I have taken up the subject of the Svātantrika-Madhyamaka debt to the logicians in Tillemans 2003.
18. Tillemans 1999, 17: "[O]n this scenario Buddhist thought would have a history of going from the very provocative logic of certain Mahāyāna sūtras, and perhaps even Nāgārjuna, to the tamer logic of the scholastic. The later Indo-Tibetan scholastic, not surprisingly perhaps, would turn out to have an increasingly conservative reaction to the original writings of their tradition, arguing that the paradoxical or provocative aspects just cannot be taken at face value, but must be explained away with qualifiers and hedges."
19. See, e.g., Oetke 1996 as well as the articles by Claus Oetke, Pascale Hugon, and Tom Tillemans in Paul 2004.

4. "How Do Mādhyamikas Think?" Revisited

In the article "How Do Mādhyamikas Think?" reprinted as chapter 3 in this book, I tried to go a certain distance with Yasuo Deguchi, Jay Garfield, and Graham Priest (henceforth DGP) in reading some Buddhist texts as dialetheist.[1] The dialetheism that I saw as plausible for the Prajñāpāramitā sūtras and Nāgārjuna was not the full-blown robust variety of DGP (that is, acceptance of the truth of some statement of the form $p \,\&\, \neg p$) but a nonadjunctive variety, acceptance of p and acceptance of $\neg p$. In short, the adjunctive move to $p \,\&\, \neg p$ is blocked.

I had focused on texts like the *Vajracchedikāsūtra* ("Diamond Cutter Sūtra") with its famous "signature formulae" along the lines of "x does not exist / x is not the case, and therefore we say that x does exist / x is the case."[2] And I had focused on the two truths in Nāgārjuna, trying to make sense of how and why this Mādhyamika thinker says p but also later says $\neg p$. These types of contexts seemed to me a fertile place to look for a form of dialetheism, especially if we took the statements literally. Thus, to take one out of the many signature formulae in the *Vajracchedikā*:

> The dharmas special to a buddha, the dharmas special to a buddha, these, Subhūti, the Tathāgata has taught to not in fact be/have dharmas special to a buddha. Thus they are said to be dharmas special to a buddha.[3]

Looking at Nāgārjuna's corpus of writings in his "six collections of reasoning" (*rigs tshogs drug*), we find in one context an acknowledgment of the existence of karma, reincarnation, causality, and so on and then in another context the denial of their existence. What we don't seem to find in the Prajñāpāramitā sūtras or in Nāgārjuna is an assertion of $p \,\&\, \neg p$ (strong dialetheism), just a seemingly weak inconsistency where, to take the case of Nāgārjuna, p is asserted somewhere for one set of reasons (call them "customary") and $\neg p$ is asserted somewhere else for another set (call them "ultimate").

The other important difference in my position vis-à-vis that of DGP was that my hypothesized Buddhist dialetheism didn't get much beyond the third century. It did not apply to the commentarial literature. For me, the texts that lend themselves to this kind of interpretation did *not* include any Indo-Tibetan commentarial literature, be it Candrakīrti, the Svātantrikas, Tsongkhapa (Tsong kha pa), Gorampa (Go rams pa), or what have you. One reason for my choice was that although it is probably textually underdetermined whether the Prajñāpāramitā sūtras and the Nāgārjunian corpus actually *do* endorse contradictions, at least they don't have explicit prohibitions against them. If one has some significant philosophical reasons for doing so, one *can* thus plausibly read them in a limited dialetheist way without running up against a lot of problematic textual counterevidence. In short, there may well be no passage that is a clincher *for* dialetheism, but at least there is room to go in that direction if the philosophical spirit moves you. On the other hand, the commentarial literature has numerous seemingly quite explicit prohibitions against contradiction (*virodha*, *viruddha*) that are just very hard to talk away. In my earlier article (see chapter 3) I had cited Candrakīrti's general rejection of *parasparavirodha* (mutual contradiction). One could add to that other admonitions of Candrakīrti to the effect that a rational individual must give up positions when he sees that they are contradictory: in a famous passage in *Prasannapadā* 1, Candrakīrti forcefully tells us that not doing so is tantamount to stubborn shamelessness (*nirlajjatā*) or just plainly being out of one's mind (*unmattaka*):

> *atha svābhyupagamavirodhacodanayāpi paro na nivartate, tadāpi nirlajjatayā hetudṛṣṭāntābhyām api naiva nivarteta / na conmattakena sahāsmākaṃ vivāda iti.*
>
> But if the opponent did not desist even when confronted with a contradiction (*virodha*) in his own position, then too, as he would have no shame, he would not desist at all even because of a logical reason and example. Now, as it is said, for us there is no debate with someone who is out of his mind (15.9–10).

Of course one can wiggle and squirm a bit and say that Candrakīrti's pronouncements about espousers of contradictions being demented have to be nuanced and presuppose a realist opponent and so forth, and that in some sense Candrakīrti didn't actually mean it to apply to himself.[4] But why bend over backward in this way? Candrakīrti's own Madhyamaka espousal of contradictions would certainly have to be extraordinarily discrete if he is not to be accused of the very same shamelessness and irrationality with which he charges his opponents. More plausible is that Candrakīrti, and pretty much every other major Buddhist thinker in the sixth century, had come to respect the law of noncontradiction as applying to themselves and their opponents alike. This was probably largely due to the influence of logicians—Buddhist or Naiyāyikas—and the fact that the Buddhists were participants in debates with Buddhists and non-Buddhists alike in which *any* contradiction meant simply incurring ignominious defeat (*nigrahasthāna*). They adopted what I have called elsewhere a "standard conception of rationality," according to which knowing acquiescence in contradiction is excluded.[5]

If one says, as I do, that earlier philosophers seem to have been more tolerant of or somehow looser about inconsistency, then one also has to accept that a rigorous sixth-century observance of noncontradiction would represent a significant difference from the sūtras and Nāgārjuna. There would be an evolution in the tolerance/intolerance of inconsistency and indeed in the way to do philosophy. I think that an evolution over history is indeed what happened, not just on questions of consistency, but on several major issues and in orientation, so that an interpretation that might be quite natural for Nāgārjuna is not natural at all for many subsequent commentators. For example, whereas arguably the early Madhyamaka of Nāgārjuna has much in common with a skeptic's quietistic suspension of belief about any and all positions, later Madhyamaka—especially when under the influence of Buddhist epistemology—redefines quietism and goes much more in the direction of promoting some positions and rejecting others, and thus often enters the fray of philosophical debate to advance what *should* be believed.[6]

Why then might one think that Candrakīrti (and others?) do somehow espouse contradictions? DGP focus on a passage in Candrakīrti's *Prasannapadā* chapter 15 where it is claimed that the intrinsic nature (*svabhāva*, *prakṛti*) of things is to have no intrinsic nature (*naiḥsvābhāvya*). They also focus on the supposed paradox that there are no ultimate truths and yet it is ultimately true that everything is empty, sometimes condensed as the paradox that the ultimate truth is that there is nothing ultimate or that there is no ultimate truth. This is not, in fact, explicit in texts but is essentially a reconstruction of some ideas from Nāgārjuna and his commentators. Another paradox for DGP (one that would figure more explicitly in sūtra and tantra texts) is that the ultimate is supposedly ineffable and yet the Buddhists regularly give longish explanations as to why this is so. DGP give other enigmatic, seemingly paradoxical, passages in their 2008 article—some from Chan texts, some from Indian sources—but the three Indian Madhyamaka paradoxes are clearly the ones they take the most seriously. We'll do likewise.

Now none of DGP's three paradoxes is widely accepted as genuine by the later Indo-Tibetan tradition. I say that because all are countered intelligently and explicitly by important commentators. Here is how some of the commentators and later scholastic thinkers do it. As always, they will say in one way or another that the problematic textual passages should not or cannot be read literally but need to be parameterized. For example, one should add the qualifiers "ultimately" (*paramārthatas*) and "customarily" (*vyavahāratas*) to take out the sting of contradiction. But there are more explicit disambiguating strategies to defuse DGP's three paradoxes. To take the first, Tsongkhapa and Geluk (Dge lugs) writers were certainly aware of a potential problem here and took pains to show there are two senses of nature (*rang bzhin* = *svabhāva*) at play in the relevant passages in the *Prasannapadā*—this is laid out in William Magee's study "The Nature of Things: Emptiness and Essence in the Geluk World" (Magee 1999).

To take the second, again the Geluk have an interesting way to defuse this: they make a split between ultimate truths (*don dam bden pa* = *paramārthasatya*) and ultimate existence (*don dam par yod pa*, *don dam par grub pa* = *paramārthasat*, **paramārthasiddha*). Thus there are ultimate truths, and an ultimate truth is indeed an ultimate truth, but nothing (not even an ultimate truth) ultimately exists![7] Finally, the ineffability problem was taken up by many people in India and Tibet. I published an article, "How to Talk about Ineffable Things," that discusses Dignāga's and Dharmakīrti's ways.[8] (Note that *apohavāda*, "the theory of exclusion," is not *just* to be found in Yogācāra or the Buddhist Epistemological school; a large number of Mādhyamikas were also Dharmakīrtian *apoha* theorists.) The idea in Dharmakīrti's *apoha* theory turns on making a distinction between language describing things' features by a kind of mirroring process versus language simply being causally connected with things. For the *apoha* theorist the former is impossible—hence the ineffability—and the latter is how language works. In any case, commentators fairly commonly explain how one can talk about ineffable things (*avyapadeśya*, *śabdāviṣaya*, *anabhilāpya*) in one way or another without incurring paradox.

Besides the move of the *apoha* theory just outlined, another way to do it is to claim that the direct experience of what *x* is like, be it emptiness or brown sugar, is indeed ineffable to one who is inexperienced, but that apart from *that* one can cheerfully talk a lot about *x*. There is no shortage of such commentarial moves to preserve consistency.

Could we just wave away those strategies and adopt the radical methodological principle to read *all* seemingly paradoxical passages literally? I think that would be overkill and leave us with too many pseudo-paradoxes. So do DGP in their 2008 article. There are some virtues in staying literal and taking the original at face value, but unless we have filtering criteria, we will have far too many spurious "paradoxes" being put forth by authors who cannot plausibly be taken as dialetheists. Paradoxical rhetoric is widespread in India—non-Buddhists engage in it and Buddhists authors themselves adopt it; some even adopt it in their verse texts, only to explain it away later in their autocommentaries to those same verses.[9]

For DGP, however, the three bedrock cases supposedly stand out from the mass of pseudo-paradoxes:

> [S]ome contradictions in some Buddhist texts *cannot* be defused. To suppose that one ought to defuse them would be to misunderstand.[10]

Well, I'm afraid that begs the fundamental question at issue. Indeed it is not obvious that DGP's last statement is true. After all, the fact is that the three "paradoxes" DGP mention were defused regularly and often in very intelligent fashions by Indo-Tibetan thinkers. Here is a potentially better tactic to find Buddhist paradoxes: instead of claiming that some would-be contradiction in a text simply *cannot be defused*, show that there is a substantial benefit for a particular Buddhist philosophical system if the text is read as tolerating inconsistency. In effect, we need to argue for significant *systemic* advantages for Mādhyamika Buddhists (and not only for a modern dialetheist philosophy building on the recurrence of inclosure schemas in both the East and the West). Now if we go that way, my problem is that I'm not convinced that there is that kind of *significant Buddhist pay-off* in DGP's paradoxes. Why would a Madhyamaka philosophy, including that of Candrakīrti and perhaps other later commentators (like Tsongkhapa? Gorampa?), be significantly furthered by accepting a contradictory notion of nature or an inconsistent version of ineffability? That's not clear to me. On the other hand, suppose that instead of DGP's examples, we focused on the two truths' discussions in early Madhyamaka and Prajñāpāramitā. (What I am calling "two truths discussions" would include the *Vajracchedikā*'s signature formulae as well as Nāgārjuna's affirmations and negations of the existence of karma, dharmas, people, buddhas, and so on.) And suppose that instead of putting Nāgārjuna, Candrakīrti, and later commentators together, we just took early Madhyamaka and Prajñāpāramitā, seeing the main lines of their project as a form of quasi-skeptical suspension of belief in all positions. Taking these kinds of statements literally, without parameters, seems to me to be a way one could arrive at that skeptical form of quietism important to Nāgārjuna and the Buddhist author(s) of the Prajñāpāramitā sūtras.

What is the gain for that Nāgārjunian quietism if we read the texts literally and did *not* parameterize statements of two truths? Let me put it this way: if one *does* parameterize the statements, one is not negating the same statement p that one asserts, and thus it becomes thoroughly possible to hold p, suitably parameterized, all the while accepting a suitably parameterized $\neg p$. There is then a real danger of ending up with a Madhyamaka philosophy that will leave customary truths perfectly intact and unimpacted by talk of emptiness and ultimate truths. Some traditional scholars, like Tsongkhapa, have seen that as desirable, especially because it allows a Buddhist to conserve ethics and hold positions easily by relegating it all to the domain of the customary. But there are others for whom it would leave the Madhyamaka missing the mark of quietism and becoming part of the problem, in that this "overly philosophical" Madhyamaka would make for more and more "conceptual proliferation" (*spros pa* = *prapañca*). I brought in Gorampa as a representative of the second camp, that is, no parameterization, because he had precisely that objection: for him, the parameterized Madhyamaka failed to lead to the religious goal of quietude.

The question then arises as to why weak dialetheism would better lead to a Buddhist suspension of all beliefs than the strong variety. Why would one *ever* block adjunction, as intuitively it seems very hard to resist the move from asserting p and asserting $\neg p$ to asserting the conjunction $p \& \neg p$? Leave aside the textual arguments to the effect that the Prajñāpāramitā sūtras don't seem to make that adjunctive move and that Nāgārjuna doesn't make it either and, indeed, would seem to rule it out in negating the third lemma of the tetralemma, namely, $p \& \neg p$. The systemic reason I would see is that if we accept a strong dialetheist's conjunction $p \& \neg p$ as an ultimate truth, this is tantamount to having a very definite (quasi-Hegelian) position on how things are.[11] Nonadjunctive dialetheism could, I think, do better to preserve the irenic positionless Nāgārjunian standpoint. In short, a possible connection between nonadjunctive dialetheism and Nāgārjunian quietism would be like this: because one negates (for various reasons) precisely what one has asserted (for other reasons), each statement undermines the other—one will not fully believe either; or better, one will not believe either—to capture how things really are.[12]

It will be replied that this nonadjunctive program would have to involve a "cancellation view of negation" if it is to work to its quietistic end of suspension of belief. I would tend to agree, although formal issues do remain.[13] Part of the nonadjunctive program I have sketched out *is* a "cancellation view of negation": asserting $\neg p$ just cancels out an assertion of p instead of adding more information; asserting p and asserting $\neg p$ ends up asserting no content at all and not committing oneself to anything. The cancellation view seems to have had quite a number of proponents in the history of Western thought, from Boethius and Abelard to J. N. Findlay and P. F. Strawson. So did Indians themselves ever subscribe to that particular view of negation? One could make a pretty strong case that they did. One indication is that the dominant metaphor in the Sanskrit terms for negation—*pratiṣedha*, *niṣedha*, *bādhā*, *kṣati*, et cetera—is that of "blocking"/"stopping" (*pratiṣedha*, *niṣedha*), "annulling" (*bādhā*), or "destroying/nullification" (*kṣati*, *bādhā*)." Negation of *p* is conceived in quasi-psychological terms as stopping, destroying, nullifying, and so on a belief in *p*. And turning to Indo-Tibetan Madhyamaka, the *prasajyapratiṣedha* (nonimplicative/simple negation) that they claim to use is a kind of pure annulment with no positive information. (To take an odd but suggestive description, the usual way the Indian idea of *prasajyapratiṣedha* is formulated in elementary Tibetan logic texts—for example, the chapter on negation in Yongs 'dzin Phur bu lcog, *Yongs 'dzin bsdus grwa che ba*—is that there is no positive dharma that is "projected" [*'phen pa* = *kṣipta*] in the "space left behind by the elimination of what is to be negated" [*dgag bya bcad pa'i shul du*].) I won't dwell on dominant metaphors any further, but yes, I think the texts—Buddhist and non-Buddhist alike—often do suggest that Indo-Tibetan thinkers looked at negation in terms of a type of cancellation view. It seems that, historically, it was a fairly natural view to hold, East and West.

Finally, a brief word on Gorampa and an article by Constance Kassor.[14] What I did *not* do—but what Kassor seems to think I did—was to take Gorampa *himself* to be an advocate of nonadjunctive, or weak, dialetheism. In fact, I would agree with most of Kassor's fine characterization of Gorampa's philosophy and her distinction between Gorampa's philosophical approach—accepting parameterization, positions, and Madhyamaka's need to adhere to the law of contradiction—and his religious quietistic approach, in which he rejects parameterization and all positions, including dialetheism. I would not, however, easily agree with her tentative attribution to Gorampa of a (strong) dialetheism on the ultimate level—she seems to think he would, or would have to, endorse an ineffability paradox like the one that DGP find in Indian texts. My disagreement is, in part, because (as I mentioned earlier) I'm not convinced that talk of ineffability is always, or even usually, a sign of one endorsing dialetheism. But to go further, I don't see a very plausible case for there being *any* dialetheism in India or Tibet much past the third century or so. Most people, including Gorampa, are just too respectful of the law of noncontradiction, especially because of the enormous influence of the Dignāga-Dharmakīrti school. So in short, I doubt we can find any Indian or Tibetan *commentator* on Madhyamaka or Prajñāpāramitā who advocated dialetheism, and certainly not Gorampa Sönam Sengé. I took Gorampa as being an interesting case of someone who advocated no-parameterization and quietism—and *that's all.* There was no suggestion here, nor I hope in anything else that follows in the article,[15] that Gorampa himself was a dialetheist of any variety, weak or strong.

Notes to Chapter 4

1. See Deguchi et al. 2008; my earlier article was focused on Garfield and Priest's joint article, "Nāgārjuna and the Limits of Thought," published in Garfield 2002 and in Priest 2002. I will treat these articles as complementary and just speak of "the position of DGP." I will also take up certain objections that they raise.
2. In fact, there are quite a number of potentially paradoxical passages in sūtras that do not belong to the Prajñāpāramitā corpus. The *Śraddhābalādhānāvatāramudrāsūtra*, for example, has a repeating series of formulae applied verbatim to various basic Buddhist concepts. For example, D. 7b: *bdag ni bdag dang dbyer med pa bdag med pa'i ye shes la gnas kyis / gzhan dag kyang bdag dang dbyer med pa bdag med pa'i ye shes la dgod do zhes dbugs 'byin pa rnyed par 'gyur te / de la bdag dang dbyer med pa bdag med pa ni bdag gi rang bzhin gang yin pa pa'o / de ci'i phyir zhe na / bdag med pa ni bdag gi rang bzhin las gzhan ma yin pa'i phyir te / bdag gi rang bzhin las bdag med pa gzhan med pas bdag gi rang bzhin nyid bdag med pa ste.* "One will be revitalized by thinking 'I will live in the gnosis of no-self that is indistinguishable from the self and will thus inspire others too toward the gnosis of no-self that is indistinguishable from the self.' In this case, 'no-self that is indistinguishable from the self' is the nature of the self. How so? It is because no-self is nothing other than the nature of the self. Since no-self is nothing other than the nature of the self, the very nature of the self is no-self."
3. For Sanskrit text, see chapter 3, page 69.
4. A way out would be to say that Candrakīrti is only banning predication of contradictory properties to objects that would have intrinsic natures (*svabhāva*) but that he accepts contradictions otherwise. Such is the approach of Deguchi, Garfield, and Priest (2013, 427), who argue that all four lemmas of the tetralemma involve only objects with *svabhāva* and hence that the door remains open to acceptance of contradiction so long as one does subscribe to such realist views about objects. The *Prasannapadā* passage does not bear that out—it simply says that acceptance of contradiction is a sign of irremediable craziness or shamelessness. There is certainly no indication in the passage, nor even from the context of the argumentation here, that there are exceptions and that contradiction is, after all, somehow okay for Mādhyamikas, as they are not realists. The disgrace in contradicting oneself looks like something that Candrakīrti would expect everyone to acknowledge as uncontroversial.

   As for the tetralemma, too, it does not look very likely that *svabhāva* figures implicitly in the formulation of the third lemma. The passage from the *Prasannapadā* (see chapter 3, p. 75) banning contradiction doesn't make any caveats about acceptable and unacceptable cases; it just says that contradictory properties are not found in one and the same thing, here too more or less appealing to a principle that everyone recognizes. It is of course often pointed out that the tetralemma is used to reject the possibility of objects with *svabhāva*, or *bhāva* for short. That much is uncontroversial, however one takes the tetralemma's statements, Tsongkhapa-style (with parameters about *svabhāva*) or Gorampa-style (without parameters). A further, controversial step that some people (i.e., Indo-Tibetan writers and modern Geluk-inspired exegetes) make is to take the formulations of the statements of the first and second lemmas as *themselves* parameterized to concern *bhāva*, the reasoning being that otherwise the negations might reject all existence and nonexistence statements as false. DGP subscribe to this: it is a stronger position than just saying the tetralemma refutes *bhāva*. In any case, whatever one thinks about parameterization being implicit or not in the first two lemmas, such parameters about *bhāva* are not clearly required in the Indian formulation of the third lemma. Rather it seems that the logic is that $p \,\&\, \neg p$ is *in any case* false and thus *a fortiori* not true of any object with *svabhāva*, because it is not true of any object at all. Quite possibly DGP were inspired by Tibetan sources, as many Tibetans *did* think that *svabhāva* also had to figure in a duly parameterized formulation of the third and fourth lemmas, without which various absurdities would supposedly arise. As I try to show in chapter 7, this debate and its pseudo-problems stemmed from a muddle due to linguistic ambiguities in the Tibetan formulation of those lemmas. It cannot be taken seriously as exegesis of the tetralemma.

5. See chapter 9, page 159.
6. Later versions of quietism, as in for example, the Svātantrikas or Tsongkhapa, are also often quite different from a Nāgārjunian skeptical suspension of belief. See the introduction to this book on the varieties of Madhyamaka quietism.
7. See Newland 1992, 94: "The distinction between being an ultimate (*don dam yin*) and ultimately existing (*don dam du yod*) is critical in Tsong-kha-pa's system. Emptiness is found, known, and realized by a mind of ultimate analysis, and therefore it is an ultimate truth. However, emptiness is not ultimately existent because it is not found by the ultimate mind analyzing *it*."
8. Tillemans 2011a. See also §2.2 in my *Stanford Encyclopedia of Philosophy* article on Dharmakīrti, found at http://plato.stanford.edu/entries/dharmakiirti/, i.e., Tillemans 2011b.
9. Tillemans 1999, 196.
10. Deguchi, Garfield, and Priest 2008, 399.
11. Cf. Tillemans 2009, 95; chapter 3 above, page 79. Cf. however Deguchi, Garfield, and Priest 2013, 433: "This is not an objection to our view; it *is* our view. We are not quietists." Here then is the parting of the ways: Madhyamaka for me is about quietism and *not* having philosophical positions, and that includes a Hegel-like advocacy of true contradictions.
12. If we want a (partial) parallel with skepticism and their quest for suspension of belief and quietude (*ataraxia*), it is that the skeptic seeks to find for every argument in favor of a proposition a contrary argument for its opposite that has the same force (*isothenia*)—both arguments are equally strong and hence equally undermine belief. A cautionary note is in order here: whereas a writer like Nāgārjuna can well be seen as in many respects following a program not so different from that of a skeptic who seeks to provide counter-arguments against any particular thesis that might be put forward,

this is *not* what most later writers were doing. They had very different orientations, all the while of course having to appear in line with the founder of the tradition.

13. Deguchi, Garfield, and Priest 2013, 433: "The contradiction could function in the way Tillemans envisages only if negation really can be a cancellation operator in Indian logic." On the cancellation view, its historical exponents, and its philosophical prospects, see Priest 1999. One problem in an account like mine is that if cancellation is doing the quietistic work, it would have to be spelled out more clearly how it would somehow combine best with a nonadjunctive approach (rather than a usual approach to conjunction). While it may happen to be so that Indians historically had a cancellation view and that some Buddhists may have had a nonadjunctive approach, the philosophical and formal logical issues about how the two are actually connected remain. Cf. DGP 2013, 433: "What Tillemans really needs is a story about conjunction: one according to which there is a difference between asserting p and $\neg p$ severally and conjointly. An account of negation as cancellation does not provide this. Negation as cancellation is quite compatible with conjunction functioning in the familiar way (Priest 1999)." Point taken. I agree that *this* story needs to be more than just hand-waving about negation as cancellation.
14. Kassor 2013. Cf. Tillemans 2009, 93–94; chapter 3, 77–79.
15. Cf. Tillemans 2009, 95; chapter 3, page 79: "Why might a Mādhyamika nonetheless embrace a nonadjunctive approach, apparently tolerating weak contradiction but eschewing the strong? If we stay in the spirit of Gorampa, the beginnings of an answer might be found in the Mādhyamika thinker's quietism, her refusal to engage herself on how things really are." What I meant by "the spirit of Gorampa" was not nonadjunctive dialetheism but his radical quietism of "freedom from [conceptual] proliferations." This was perhaps not clear enough, unfortunately, and may have mislead Kassor into thinking I attributed nonadjunctive dialetheism to Gorampa.

5. Prasaṅga and Proof by Contradiction in Bhāviveka, Candrakīrti, and Dharmakīrti

I. Two Types of Reductio ad absurdum

Jon Barwise and John Etchemendy, in their introductory logic textbook, give a handy mnemonic description of what it is to prove *not-S* by contradiction or, what is the same, by *reductio ad absurdum*: "To prove *not-S* using this method, assume *S* and prove some sort of contradiction."[1] We can see two ways in which we can "prove some sort of contradiction":

A. Typically, in logical reasoning in philosophy and mathematics, one shows that if *S* is added to a number of premises *P,Q,R*, then the conjunction of *P,Q,R,S* would lead to a contradiction, and then one says that if (or because) *P,Q,R* are all true, *S* must be false and hence ¬*S* ("not-*S*") must be true. This is the type of proof by contradiction that, for example, the Greeks used to prove that the square root of two is irrational. Note that if we wish to prove the truth of *S* in this way, we must accept that *P,Q,R* are true. We would in that sense be committed to the truth of *P*, *Q*, and *R*.

B. We can reason that the conjunction of *P,Q,R* and *S* leads to a contradiction, and is in that sense internally inconsistent, but nonetheless remain unwilling or unable to say which of the conjoined statements are true and which must be negated. We are only prepared to say that *P&Q&R&S* implies some contradiction and hence that ¬(*P&Q&R&S*) is the case. We can leave the matter in suspense and go no further toward saying which of *S*, *P*, *Q*, and *R* is actually false. This is typically what happens when we feel that a theory, a story, or a testimony is contradictory but abstain from saying where exactly it goes wrong and what is really so. Or, if we know our interlocutor's mindset and are intent on leading her to determine which of the conjuncts is to be abandoned, we simply present her with the internal inconsistency of her statements, knowing that the truth of *P*, *Q*, and *R* will be so deeply held by this person that she will naturally and inevitably end up doing what we want her to do—that is, to negate *S*. We, however, need not be committed to the truth of *P*, *Q*, and *R*. Let us speak of this method as being that of "internal inconsistency without commitments." It is a method that a cross-examining attorney can use to make hostile witnesses reveal what they believe to be true. It suffices to point out that their stories are inconsistent, and then let them do the rest, with at most a few nudges here and there to keep them on track.

There is another variant on method B. Suppose that for a certain single statement S, it could be determined (a priori) that if S were true, $\neg S$ would also follow from it. It then follows that S is not true and hence that $\neg S$ is true. Such is the type of reasoning that we use when we want to show that square circles or barren women's children do not exist; it is also used to show the falsity of certain self-refuting statements like "Everything I say is false." In short: if so-and-so were a barren woman's child, then she also would not be a barren woman's child, and hence she isn't. Note that here we prove $\neg S$ simply from the internal inconsistency of S; other statements need not be accepted as true.

It is my contention that Bhāviveka, and Svātantrikas in general, promoted method A and that, in its essentials, method A is what is involved in moving from a *prasaṅga* (absurd consequence) to a *prasaṅgaviparyaya*—the contraposition of the consequence, in which it must be true that the reason qualifies the subject (*pakṣa*) and implies the property being proved (*sādhyadharma*). Candrakīrti in his famous debate with Bhāviveka is, however, advocating B, and this is what he himself seems to favor as a Prāsaṅgika. Finally we will turn to Dharmakīrti's *Pramāṇavārttika* 4.12 and the related passages at the beginning of his *Pramāṇaviniścaya* 3, where Dharmakīrti describes how *prasaṅga* and *prasaṅgaviparyaya* operate. There he elaborates method A; interestingly enough, he used B but denied that it could yield any real knowledge.

II. Bhāviveka

We begin with the sixth-century thinker Bhāviveka.[2] He accuses an earlier coreligionist, Buddhapālita, of wrongly commenting on *Mūlamadhyamakakārikā* 1.1, the programmatic verse that, inter alia, denies that anything can be produced from, or by, itself. Buddhapālita's misstep was supposedly that he formulated the refutation of production from self as a faulty *prasaṅga* (*reductio ad absurdum*), one that when *contraposed* will imply a statement that no Mādhyamika can accept. The argument in Bhāviveka's own commentary on the *Madhyamakakārikā*, his *Prajñāpradīpa*, and hence in the first chapter of Candrakīrti's *Prasannapadā*, is often talked about but still baffles many. To see that *prasaṅga* and its contraposition in the needed detail, we need to backtrack a bit and go step by step.

For starters, what Buddhapālita said is this:

> *na svata utpadyante bhāvāḥ / tadutpādavaiyarthyāt / atiprasaṅgadoṣāc ca /*
>
> Things/entities are not produced from themselves because their production would be pointless [i.e., futile] and because there would be the absurdity [of an infinite regress of productions].

If this is taken as a *prasaṅga*, then, at least according to Bhāviveka's understanding, we get:

> It would follow absurdly that things are produced pointlessly and without end, because they are produced from themselves.

Now, this *prasaṅga*, according to Bhāviveka, must yield the following *viparyaya*, or contraposed reasoning:

> Things are not produced from themselves because their production has a point and has an end.

From here it is a short step to a statement that Mādhyamikas cannot accept, for given that things are produced but not from themselves, they must be produced from something else. And that would result in *siddhāntavirodha* (contradiction with one's philosophical tenets) in that it would contradict the fundamental Madhyamaka philosophical stance that the negation must be nonimplicative (*prasajyapratiṣedha*) and that things are neither produced from themselves nor from something else.[3]

Bhāviveka's logic is in essence as follows. We all know as true that (1) things' production has a point and has an end (it does not go on and on over and over again). We also all know that (2) if something existent were produced from itself, it would be produced pointlessly and over and over again. If we add the opponent's principle (3) that things *are* produced from themselves, we get the absurdity stated in the *prasaṅga*: things' production would be pointless and endless.

Clearly for Bhāviveka the first two statements must be conserved and are true, so that it is the third that is negated. And that is what we find in the *prasaṅgaviparyaya*: the truth of the first and second are established by *pramāṇas* (sources of knowledge), and *that is why* the third must be negated.

To look at Bhāviveka's argument in Indian terms, the first statement is cited as the *hetu* (reason) in the *prasaṅgaviparyaya*, and the second is the *vyāpti*, the entailment or, more literally, "pervasion." Although the second statement (i.e., the *vyāpti*) is not explicitly given by Bhāviveka himself in either the *prasaṅga* or the *viparyaya*, it is certainly accepted by him as true. Indeed, not stating *vyāpti* explicitly is nothing surprising: it is quite routine in Indo-Tibetan argumentation.[4] In any case, the *vyāpti* unpacks as the following universal generalization: "if something existent were produced from itself, it would be produced pointlessly over and over"; its logically equivalent contrapositive formulation is "if anything existent is not produced pointlessly over and over—if its production has a point and an end—then it is not produced from itself." These statements are essential to the *prasaṅga* and *prasaṅgaviparyaya* respectively.

Now let the first statement (the *hetu*) be *P*, the second statement (the *vyāpti*) be *Q*, and let the statement "Things are produced from themselves" be *S*. (We don't need an *R* here.) In Bhāviveka's hands, the *prasaṅga* is a *reductio ad absurdum* along the lines of our method A, where the conjunction of *P*, *Q*, and *S* yields a contradiction and where the proponent of the reasoning proves $\neg S$ precisely because he is committed to *P* and *Q* being true. I might remark that when I speak of an absurdity or contradiction being derived, there is a slight unclarity here, because the *prasaṅga* itself only explicitly derives one statement, the assertion that things' production would be pointless and without an end. To get a genuine contradiction we obviously need to conjoin the absurd statement with what I termed statement 1, that production has a point and so on. Then we would get a clear contradiction that things' production would both have and not have a point.

III. Candrakīrti

Turning to the second kind of use of *reductio ad absurdum*, namely, what I have been terming the method of "internal inconsistency without commitments," this is, I believe, what we find advocated by Candrakīrti in his reply to Bhāviveka. Candrakīrti, as is well known, replies that showing an internal contradiction in an opponent's position is enough to convince someone who is not "out of his/her mind" (*unmattaka*) to give it up; he also replies that the Mādhyamika proponent is not obliged to put forth a contrapositive form, nor accept its component statements as being true. Such a stance is part and parcel of what it means for a Mādhyamika not to have any theses and thus not himself make truth claims. Let us take two representative passages:

> *Prasannapadā* 1.15.7–10: *tasmān nirupapattika eva tvadvādaḥ svābhyupagamaviruddhaś ceti / kiṃ tanmātreṇa codite paro nābhyupaiti yato hetudṛṣṭāntopādānasāphalyaṃ syāt / atha svābhyupagamavirodhacodanayāpi paro na nivartate / tadāpi nirlajjatayā hetudṛṣṭāntābhyām api naiva nivarteta / na conmattakena sahāsmākaṃ vivāda iti /*
>
> So your own position is simply illogical and contradicted by what you yourself accept. When criticized by [us saying] just this much, then why would the opponent not accept [that things are not produced from themselves], so that [the additional step] of using a reason and an example would then accomplish something? But suppose the opponent does not even desist when criticized as having a contradiction with what he himself accepts. Then too, due to his lack of any shame [at contradicting himself], he would not desist at all, not even because of a reason and example. Now, our argument is not with someone who is out of his mind.
>
> *Prasannapadā* 1.23.3ff.: *prasaṅgaviparītena cārthena parasyaiva sambandho, nāsmākaṃ svapratijñāyā abhāvāt / tataś ca siddhāntavirodhāsambhavaḥ /*
>
> It is only the opponent who is linked to the contraposition of the absurd consequence and not we, for we have no thesis of our own. And therefore we do not have a contradiction with [our] philosophical tenets.

In effect, Candrakīrti seems to be arguing that Bhāviveka has imposed upon him a type-A use of *reductio ad absurdum* (with the ensuing commitment to the truth of certain statements and hence the implied *siddhāntavirodha*), whereas he himself was only using a type-B method of internal inconsistency without commitments. The opponent—but not Candrakīrti himself—accepts that things are produced from themselves; from this and other statements acceptable to the opponent, a contradiction follows. Candrakīrti himself goes no further than to show that the conjunction of the statements accepted by the opponent yields a contradiction, but he does not himself say (or more likely, refuses to say) which statements are actually true and which must be negated. He does, of course, know what the opponent's probable reaction will be, and therefore he himself can stand back and assert no more than that $P\&Q\&R\&S$ will imply $\neg(P\&Q\&R\&S)$ or, equally, that $P\&Q\&R\&S$

implies internal consistency, namely, *P&Q&R&S* and ¬(*P&Q&R&S*). No more than that. In short, we have a method designed to show internal inconsistency that is coupled with a (fallible) prediction that rational individuals in a particular dialectical situation will behave in such and such ways.

IV. Implicative Reversal and Contraposition

An exegetical excursus is badly needed at this point. For, before going on, we have to take up, in broad outlines at least, David Seyfort Ruegg's carefully developed opinion that the talk of *prasaṅgaviparītārtha* or *prasaṅgaviparyaya* in *Prajñāpradīpa* and *Prasannapadā* 1 is *not* to be taken in the straightforward technical way of the contraposition of the consequence—that is, in the way I outlined above. Seyfort Ruegg takes up the *prasaṅga* and two contrapositions (formulated by Jeffrey Hopkins on the basis of a major Gelukpa author) and argues that in fact, in Bhāviveka's objection, it is *not* contraposition that is at stake at all:

> [Bhāviveka's objection] apparently involves the idea not of contraposition but of implicative reversal, namely that a negation of production from self would imply the affirmation of production from an other.[5]

Seyfort Ruegg is thus perfectly aware that later Gelukpa writers *did* say there were *prasaṅga* and *viparyaya* at stake like those I have sketched out but sees this as an interpretative error of imposing a later understanding of *viparyaya/viparītārtha* on an earlier one. I would respectfully disagree: the Gelukpas and Jeffrey Hopkins had things essentially right.

Now, part of Seyfort Ruegg's argument is that Buddhapālita's own words *tadutpādavaiyarthyāt / atiprasaṅgadoṣāc ca* use the ablative and hence state reasons rather than absurd consequences. That is, they are being used to say "because . . . ," rather than "it follows that . . . ."[6] I don't think that this is a particularly strong argument, because the actual form of Buddhapālita's reasoning is far from obvious and is controversial among scholastic writers in spite of Buddhapālita using two ablatives. Indeed the passage can be taken (as we even see in some Tibetan monastic manuals) as meaning "Things are not produced from themselves, because if they were, then their production would be pointless." In effect "because if they were, then their production would be pointless" would express the consequence, "It follows that things' production would be pointless, because they are [supposedly] produced from themselves."

Although Seyfort Ruegg does not himself stress this, some of the strongest evidence for his position, as far as I can see, is that it concords with Avalokitavrata's interpretation of Bhāviveka's *Prajñāpradīpa*. Here is briefly how that interpretation goes. In his *Prajñāpradīpa* commentary, Avalokitavrata argues that Buddhapālita's reasoning is a statement vulnerable to criticism (*sāvakāśavacana, sāvakāśavākya* = *glags yod pa'i tshig*) because it is not a valid reason, and that for it to be a valid reason, the property being proved (*sādhya*, i.e., "not being produced from self") must be changed to a negative (*viparītārtha*) like "being produced from other things." Similarly Buddhapālita's bad reason "because its production is pointless" must be amended to "because its production has a point." So Avalokitavrata is *not* talking about *prasaṅgas* and their contrapositions but about amending Buddhapālita's argument so that it would have a valid reason and not be criticizable as badly formulated.

In an earlier article (Tillemans 1992a) I had sketched out this interpretation by Avalokitavrata and translated representative passages from his *Prajñāpradīpaṭīkā*—the interpretation was, incidentally, *also* known and even incorporated in a very complex fashion by the Gelukpas and others into some of their explanations of the Bhāviveka-Candrakīrti debate. A part of the problem was that Bhāviveka and Avalokitavrata did not actually speak of the argument against production from self as being a *prasaṅgavākya* at all but rather characterized it as a *glags yod pa'i tshig*—that is, a *sāvakāśavacana* or *sāvakāśavākya*, "a statement that offers an occasion [for a critique]," "a vulnerable statement." Candrakīrti on the other hand *did* represent Bhāviveka as using the term *prasaṅgavākya*. It is significant that Candrakīrti does clearly speak of *prasaṅgavākya* and *prasaṅgaviparītena arthena* and not just the *viparītārtha* and *prakṛtārthaviparyaya* spoken about by Bhāviveka and Avalokitavrata.[7] A natural reading is that, irrespective of what Avalokitavrata might have thought, Candrakīrti took the debate as being about *prasaṅgas* and contrapositions in the usual technical sense, especially so because a nontechnical, looser sense in terms of "implicative reversal" is not readily found elsewhere for these terms.

However, we can go considerably further than what I wrote in 1992. Toshikazu Watanabe (2013), independently of my earlier unpublished investigations, has looked at the passages in *Prasannapadā* 36.11–37.2 dealing with Bhāviveka's criticism of Buddhapālita's arguments. He examined in particular the *prasaṅga* refuting any production from "other" (*paratra*)—causes that would be radically other than their effects. Here too, as Watanabe shows, Bhāviveka's criticism of the *prasaṅgaviparyaya* as leading (again) to contradiction with Mādhyamika philosophical tenets (*siddhāntavirodha*) presupposes a normal contraposition of the *prasaṅga*, one that a later logician (Dharmakīrtian or Gelukpa) would find fully familiar. The logical structure of this argument and its contraposition is thus the same as that of the earlier refutation of production from self. What one says about the one will hold for the other.

On the other hand, an interpretation of the whole controversy—be it Bhāviveka's or Candrakīrti's understandings—by relying on Avalokitavrata's commentary is impossible to comprehend in that normal fashion. The problem is that an "implicative reversal" and Avalokitavrata's proposed amendments are not generalizable logical moves at all, whereas contraposition is; it is one that is actually quite ordinary in both Western and Indian logic. To attribute "implicative reversal" or amendments here means in effect that we do not know why this move is being made, for either it seems to be an *ad hoc* tactic, or worse (but less likely), it is one that simply relies on errors in logic.

The best course of action, as far I can see, is thus to discard Avalokitavrata's interpretation as creating more trouble than it is worth.[8] As I hope the central arguments of this paper show, the Bhāviveka-Candrakīrti controversy can have a simpler, and logically understandable, explanation when seen as turning on the technical senses of *prasaṅga* and contraposition, an interpretation in which Candrakīrti's statement that he is not bound to accept the *prasaṅgaviparyaya* becomes a justifiable stance in keeping with some recognizable and defensible features about the use of *reductio ad absurdum*. On a methodological level, I think that such a gain in theoretical elegance would be considerably more important than ambiguous philological evidence and counter-evidence from competing commentators. What is at stake is, in effect, an application of the principle of charity, privileging elegance of interpretation and rational reconstruction. When faced with complicated arguments in dense Sanskrit or Tibetan, philological analysis is easily blind: logic counts.[9]

Finally, I think that it is particularly relevant that on the technical interpretation of *prasaṅga* and *prasaṅgaviparyaya*, Candrakīrti can conserve his "thesislessness" and actually establish that the opponent's position (i.e., the conjunction) is false by using what seem to be recognizable theorems in a classical logic. In other words, he is showing that *P&Q&R&S*, which is a conjunction of various individual statements, is false.[10] The only thing he is not doing is committing himself to which individual conjunct is true and which is false. In that sense he himself stays thesisless and leaves the hard (but predictable) choice of what to reject to his adversary.

V. The Use of Recognizable Logical Theorems

I mentioned that on this interpretation of the Bhāviveka-Candrakīrti debate, we would see that Candrakīrti uses "recognizable theorems." But which ones? The basic point is this: If $P\&Q\&R\&S$ also imply $\neg(P\&Q\&R\&S)$, then we *can* validly infer $\neg(P\&Q\&R\&S)$. If we look at the history of logic, as depicted by William and Martha Kneale, it is clear that variants upon this type of argument pattern were formulated in Stoic logic ("If the first, then the first; if the first then not the first; therefore not the first"). The theorem that a statement that implies its negation must be false is what figures implicitly in Plato's rejection of Protagoras's relativism ("If it were true, it would also be false; therefore it is false"). In short, the theorem relied upon is the following: $(P\rightarrow\neg P)\rightarrow\neg P$. This is a tautology, but its applications can be vast, as we shall see.

Note that this same theorem is what is at stake when someone argues against a liar-type sentence, like "Everything I say is false," saying that if it were so, then it would not be so, and that therefore it is not so. Arguably too, this strategy seems also to be what we find in St. Thomas Aquinas' *De Veritate*, "From the destruction of truth it follows that truth exists, because if truth does not exist, it is true that truth does not exist and nothing can be true without truth. Therefore truth is eternal."[11]

There are other theorems that underlie arguments that proceed along the lines of "such-and-such a statement implies its opposite and hence the opposite is so." We have seen $(P\rightarrow\neg P)\rightarrow\neg P$. We can also obtain a similar theorem by inserting the contradiction $P\&\neg P$. Thus, for example, $(P\rightarrow(P\&\neg P))\rightarrow\neg P$ is equally a tautology. So in that sense, when I speak of Candrakīrti relying upon "recognizable theorems," the plural does have a point: there may indeed be more than one, and it is admittedly hard to pin him down. Note too that if instead of these theorems, we redistribute the negations and take $\neg P$ as the starting point and show that it implies P, we can thereby infer P, and with this redistribution of negation signs we get the infamous *consequentia mirabilis*. This seems to be what is behind St. Thomas's argument, which states that the nonexistence, or destruction, of truth (if true) would imply that it exists undestroyed, and hence we can infer that truth exists undestroyed (= eternally). It also seems to be the theorem behind Descartes' *cogito ergo sum*, where the reasoning is that if there were nothing, not even a thinking subject, there would at least be something, the thinking subject, and thus there is a thinking subject. Candrakīrti thus seems to be in good company, reasoning in recognizable ways, even if he certainly would have used these theorems only for negative ends and not to establish substantive metaphysical claims a priori. His quietistic reluctance to countenance substantive truth claims of how things are would probably be even stronger if someone argued that he could justify such a claim a priori by an argument that conjures a truth from the "fact" that its falsehood would imply its truth.

What about Bhāviveka? Was he rejecting these theorems outright? The worst-case scenario is that in imposing the demand for a *viparyaya*, he may have missed something fundamental about logic and hence may even have embarked on a sterile debate. But what is much more charitable and likely is that Bhāviveka had other deep-seated reasons, not of a purely logical order, to reject an argument strategy turning on simple internal inconsistency.

The problem is this. Method B, unlike method A, would not end up *obliging* an opponent to acknowledge any specific individual statement in the conjunction as true or false: it would only oblige him to acknowledge that the conjunction is not true and thus give up *something* in previously cherished positions. That may be all that a quietist advocate of no-theses, no-*prapañca* (no conceptual proliferations), like Candrakīrti, needs in order to guide people to the irenic standpoint that he considers genuine Madhyamaka. But the problem is that there is *no* guarantee that it will work to guide people to truth, to what they *should* believe. It was then probably not enough for Bhāviveka, who emphasized that Mādhyamikas advocated knowledge and positions; he advocated *pramāṇas* leading to determinate customary truths.

VI. Dharmakīrti

Finally, we turn briefly to certain thinkers of the *pramāṇavāda* school, notably the Buddhist logician Dharmakīrti and his successors, some of whom were not only logicians but also Mādhyamikas of the broadly Svātantrika orientation of Bhāviveka.

Which methods did they use? With a little analysis we can readily see that it is indeed the type-A use of *prasaṅga* and *prasaṅgaviparyaya* that is described and promoted. Dharmakīrti's *Pramāṇavārttika* 4.12bcd is the classic source:

> *parakalpitaiḥ / prasaṅgo dvayasambandhād ekābhāve 'nyahānaye //*
>
> An absurd consequence is [drawn] by means of the opponent's conceptual constructs (*parakalpitaiḥ*); as the [consequence's] two terms are necessarily connected (*sambandhād*), it serves to negate the second term in the absence of the first.

The *prasaṅga* at stake in the parallel discussion in *Pramāṇaviniścaya* 3 and in Manorathanandin's commentary on the *Pramāṇavārttika* is as follows:

> *sāmānyasya paropagatānekavṛttitvād anekatvam āpādyate*
>
> It follows absurdly that the universal is several things because, as the opponent accepts, it is present in several different things.

The contraposition (*viparyaya*) is:

> The universal is not present in several different things (*nāneka-vṛttitva*) because it is not [itself] several things.

This then looks clearly like the type-A use of *reductio*. After deriving the absurdity from the conjunction *P,Q,S*, the key step is to say that *S* is false because *P* and *Q* are true.[12]

So did Dharmakīrti have any place *at all* for what we are terming the type-B use of *reductio*, the method of merely showing internal inconsistency of a conjoined ensemble of statements? No doubt, Dharmakīrti was extremely sensitive to inconsistency in treatises (*śāstra*) and scriptures (*āgama*) and in the tenets (*siddhānta*) they propound, and not surprisingly he thought that any inconsistent ensemble of statements was discredited. Indeed, he goes on at length about how certain Brahmanical scriptures and treatises are inconsistent in their accounts of liberation, in that they state that passions (*kleśa*) such as desire and the like (*rāgādi*) are the root causes of immorality (*adharmamūla*) and yet they also say that purification of such immorality is to be accomplished by bathing (*snāna*) in the Ganges and other such practices that have nothing to do with the passions. In short, the Brahmanical treatise is inconsistent in that one of its main statements about passions being the root of immorality is contradicted by statements about the would-be remedy—this "remedy" would, in effect, imply that passions are not the root causes at all but that something else is.[13]

Such a refutation of the trustworthiness of a scripture is essentially a use of method B, showing internal inconsistency of a conjunction of propositions. Dharmakīrti, like Bhāviveka, however, also holds that merely showing inconsistency of *P*, *Q*, *R*, and S does not establish any genuine knowledge of specific truths. However, the reason given why that is so is somewhat different from that given by Bhāviveka. For Dharmakīrti, an examination (*parīkṣā*) of inconsistencies is characterized as *na vāstavī*, not bearing upon real facts, or real entities (*vastu*), at all but only on words and concepts; in

Devendrabuddhi's commentary, we are told that merely finding a contradiction in a set of scriptural statements does not give any significant information (literally "genuine knowledge" *don dam rtogs pa*) about real entities or their actual properties.[14] And in *Pramāṇavārttika* 4.98–101 Dharmakīrti argues that we need an *extra* procedure to determine what is actually so. What is needed to determine specific truth and falsity is a *pramāṇa* "grounded in reality"—that is, more literally, one that "operates due to real entities" (*vastubalapravṛtta*).[15]

VII. Some Questions and Speculations

Dharmakīrti's position is complex. It is clear that he adds important metaphysical requirements about "grounding in reality" that a Mādhyamika would not easily endorse. And method B is wanting not *just* because it does not tell us *which individual statements* are true, but because genuine knowing also requires understandings that are grounded upon real entities. Now given that metaphysical requirement about grounding in reality, an interesting problem arises as to whether we can genuinely know the truth of ¬(*P*&*Q*&*R*&*S*) when that statement is only derived because the conjunction *P*,*Q*,*R*,*S* is shown to be inconsistent. Is it still a full-fledged fact about the real world? And could one know that fact a priori without relying on any other *pramāṇas*? Interestingly enough, the thrust of his philosophy of logic would seem to be to say "no" to both. One indicator is Dharmakīrti's treatment of the liar-statement "Everything said is false" and other self-refuting statements (like "My mother is barren") in *Pramāṇavārttika* 4.93–101. He, in effect, says that reasoning simply from words and concepts cannot establish that everything said is false nor can it establish that it is not so that everything said is false. The same holds for "My mother is barren," "There are no sources of knowledge," and so on. If we proceed purely a priori, we can only know that a statement like "Everything said is false" implies itself as well as its opposite, and that the two propositions "clash" or "obstruct each other" (*pratibandhaka*), but there is no specific invalidation (*bādhā*) of either of them; we do not actually know which is true and which is false unless there is an extra *pramāṇa* grounded in reality, such as an independent confirmation that people sometimes do say true things. We seem to have, in effect, a thoroughgoing rejection of a priori reasoning as being able to establish genuine truths. Instead, facts about reality need to be established by reasoning linked to reality (that is, involving a so-called "natural connection" *svabhāvapratibandha*), reasoning that ultimately relies on perceptual input.

This stance would indeed leave logical tautologies, whose truth is determined purely a priori, as having no real purchase on reality.[16] We could even go further and say that presumably other logical laws—like excluded middle, double negation, et cetera—would have to be of a similar status; it would not be a genuine fact that $P \vee \neg P$ or that P if and only if $\neg\neg P$; knowing the truth of a tautology is not like knowing the truth of an individual statement that is grounded in reality.

It is also an important question as to what truth status Candrakīrti himself would assign to $\neg(P\&Q\&R\&S)$. If he would not, like Dharmakīrti, invoke a metaphysical requirement of grounding to say that its truth is not genuinely known, would he then simply accept it as true? Significantly, Seyfort Ruegg 1983 has shown that Candrakīrti does himself seem to accept some negative statements—the conclusions of refutations—and argues that this does not violate his deliberate avoidance of substantive truth claims, or theses (*pratijñā, pakṣa*), about what there is. Philosophically, it would seem that this would have to be the case, as otherwise we have the oddity that Candrakīrti would not even accept the bona fides of his own arguments. I will leave *that* conundrum for another occasion.

VIII. Conclusions

Where does this three-way comparison of uses of *reductio* lead us? In the end, a sixth-century debate turns on quite different, but recognizable, conceptions of what it is to do philosophy. One way to look at this Svātantrika-Prāsaṅgika debate—and there are other significant ways too[17]—is that it turns on the question of whether philosophy is essentially normative in nature.

Bhāviveka, and his successors in this Madhyamaka subschool as well as Dharmakīrti, seem to have recognized that a type-B method showing internal inconsistency of the conjunction of P, Q, R, and S does not constitute a *proof* of the truth of any one of the negated individual statements, in the sense that there is no clear *normative* account why the opponent must admit such and such a proposition to be true. (Method B may tell you that such and such a philosophy will not work, but it does not actually *prove* which specific propositions you *should* actually think to be true or false.) For a Svātantrika or Dharmakīrtian then, the normative dimension is missing in a purely *prasaṅga* method, and that is why the method is inadequate. Prāsaṅgikas who choose method B and the principle that rational individuals will behave in such and such predictable ways would seem to content themselves with psychology and rhetoric. Instead of proving truths that all people should think by a universally valid methodology, they lead people to changes of heart but not truths that they themselves endorse. They rely on techniques that simply do, as a matter of fact, lead to persuasion in specific individuals but cannot be universalized as a proper way to knowledge.

Issues of normativity are significant to how one does philosophy. There is a well-known Kantian opposition between *conviction* (*Überzeugung*), valid for all rational beings or for an (idealized) universal audience, and *persuasion* (*Überredung*), which particular groups of people in particular contexts may feel but which is solely a subjective ground for their personal judgments. One can imagine Bhāviveka's and Dharmakīrti's views transposed into the language of the first Kantian *Critique*. The persuasions to which the Prāsaṅgika leads his opponents via mere *reductio ad absurdum* are not understanding but only "a mere semblance" (*ein blosser Schein*), with "private validity" (*Privatgültigkeit*) and no more; where Candrakīrti goes wrong is that he cannot provide conviction, as he just "talks people into beliefs" and thus fails to meet the rational normative demands that make philosophy the activity that it is. I have no doubt that the Kantians would see Bhāviveka's and Dharmakīrti's points quite clearly.[18] I can also imagine that Candrakīrti would reply in some way to the Kantians and the Svātantrikas that their normative standards are too high and are unattainable. Insistence on conviction would be the last illusion in the Svātantrika's Madhyamaka, a disguised realist metaphysic about truth being thoroughly independent of thought.

Notes to Chapter 5

1. Barwise and Etchemendy 1992, 64.
2. Such is how he now is known ever since the work of Yasunori Ejima, in part because of the Chinese phonetic rendering *Po pi fei jia*; we'll adopt "Bhāviveka" too, instead of "Bhāvaviveka" or "Bhavya."
3. Here is the actual text as found on 14.4–15.2 of La Vallée Poussin's edition of Candrakīrti's *Prasannapadā*: *athaike dūṣaṇam āhuḥ / tad ayuktaṃ hetudṛṣṭāntānabhidhānāt / paroktadośāparihārāc ca / prasaṅgavākyatvāc ca prakṛtārthaviparyayeṇa viparītārthasādhyataddharmavyaktau parasmād utpannā bhāvā janmasāphalyāt / janmanirodhāc ceti kṛtāntavirodhaḥ* [or *siddhāntavirodhaḥ*] *syāt //*. "Here certain people [i.e., Bhāviveka] set forth the following critique: This [reasoning of Buddhapālita] is incoherent because (1) it does not state a [valid] reason and example and (2) it does not eliminate [certain] faults which the [Sāṃkhya] adversary states. (3) Since [Buddhapālita's reasoning] is a statement of an absurd consequence (*prasaṅgavākya*), should one, by contraposing the terms in question [i.e., in the *prasaṅga*], then set out what is to be proved (*sādhya*) and its [pakṣa]dharma as

the contrapositives (*viparītārtha*), one would in that case contradict one's own philosophical tenets (*kṛtānta = siddhānta*), for entities would be produced from other [things] because their production would have a point and because there would be an end to [this] production."

4. It is routine in Indo-Tibetan Buddhist argumentation not to formally state *everything*, even though the strict formal canons in Vāda manuals go on at length about exactly what you should and should not state! Theory versus practice: Vāda rules are regularly streamlined in practice. Indeed, one typically gets the complete formal reasoning (*prayoga*) with *hetu* and *vyāpti* and examples (*dṛṣṭānta*) only in so-called "inferences-for-others" (*parārthānumāna*). The most frequent "working reasoning," however, is "*A* is, or would be, *B* because it is *C*." The implicit *vyāpti* is "All *C*s are *B*s," or equivalently, "All non-*B*s are non-*C*s." This is the type of reasoning used in our debate. See Tillemans 2008b.
5. Seyfort Ruegg 2000, 253.
6. Seyfort Ruegg 2000, 254: "But the first two reasons adduced by Buddhapālita (*utpādavaiyarthyāt* and *atiprasaṅgadoṣāt*) in fact remain reasons in the form in which they appear in Bhavya's text, even if the reason 'because of futility' has indeed been converted there to 'because of usefulness' (i.e., *janmasāphalya* in the PPMV) and the reason 'because of over-extension' (viz. because of being endless) has been converted there to 'because of having an end' (i.e., *janmanirodha* in the PPMV), so that (according to Bhavya) Buddhapālita will be in contradiction with the Madhyamaka *siddhānta*."
7. In Tillemans 1992a, 320, I came to the following conclusion, which I would stick by now as a minimal position: "Personally, I think we must take *Prasannapadā*'s reading of *prasaṅgavākyatvāc ca* as showing that *at least Candrakīrti* took the passages from *Prajñāpradīpa* as arguing that the *prasaṅgaviparyaya* leads to a contradiction with the Mādhyamika's *siddhānta*. Candrakīrti's later discussion (Prasannapadā 23ff.), where he speaks of not having to accept the *viparītārtha* of the *prasaṅga* and thus avoiding contradiction with *siddhānta*, shows beyond reasonable doubt that Candrakīrti *himself* took Bhāviveka's argument as turning on a *prasaṅga* and a *prasaṅgaviparyaya*."
8. Watanabe does the same, presenting a "normal" version of the *prasaṅga* and *viparyaya* and then noting (Watanabe 2013, 177n14) that this interpretation is different from that of Avalokitavrata.
9. For a forceful application of this maxim, see also chapter 7.
10. We can go a bit further: $\neg(P\&Q\&R\&S)$ is true. Arguably, this would not be a substantive truth claim about reality. See the discussion in section VII below on "questions and speculations."
11. Translation in W. and M. Kneale 1962, 202 and 746.
12. The details are as follows: the term *dvayasambandha* (the necessary connection between the two terms) in verse 12 means that there is an appropriate *vyāpti*, or general principle that holds because of a real/natural relation (i.e., *sambandha = svabhāvapratibandha*) between the terms; the *vyāpti* is thus true and hence its contraposition is also true. In the reasoning at hand, "presence in several different things" implies "being itself several things"; the contraposition of this general statement figures in the *viparyaya* and consists in the principle that what is not itself several things is not present in several different things. "In the absence of the first" is a true statement that must be accepted: it is the *hetu* of the *prasaṅgaviparyaya*,

i.e., "not being [itself] several things." The opponent's conceptual construct (viz., the universal's being present in several different things) is in effect the statement that leads to the absurdity (viz. the universal's being several things). It is thus "the second term" that is negated in the absence of the first. See Tillemans 2000, 21–24, for translation and explanation of the verse and Manorathanandin's commentary.

13. *Pramāṇavārttika* 4.107 with the commentarial additions of Manorathanandin (see Tillemans 2000, 150–51): *virodhodbhāvanaprāyā parīkṣāpy atra tadyathā / adharmamūlaṃ rāgādi snānaṃ cādharmaśodhanam //.* "In the case of this [treatise], examination, moreover, consists chiefly in pointing out contradictions [between prior and subsequent statements and is not concerned with facts (*na vāstavī*)]: for example, [contradictions such as when it is said that] desire and so on are the root of immorality and that bathing is what purifies immorality."
14. Devendrabuddhi, in his *Pramāṇavārttikapañjikā* P. 346b5–7, is explicit in saying that this examination of an inconsistent treatise points out contradictions (*'gal ba brjod pa*) but does not concern *what is really so* (*don dam pa ma yin ≈ na pāramārthikā; na vāstavī*). Manorathandin clearly follows him on this in saying that the examination detecting inconsistencies does not concern real facts (*na vāstavī*). See Tillemans 2000, 151n522.
15. On *vastubalapravṛtta* and related concepts like *svabhāvapratibandha* (real/natural connections), see Tillemans 2000, 12. Classic sources for the latter term are to be found in Dharmakīrti's *Svavṛtti* ad *Pramāṇavārttika* 1.14. See also Steinkellner 1971 and 1984.
16. In Tillemans 2000, 140, I was puzzled by his views on liars and the like and said: "This inference [establishing that it is not so that everything said is false] would be valid because the statement ((*P*→*not-P*)→*not-P*) is a theorem . . . [His discussion] here strongly suggests that either he did not know this basic logical theorem. . . . or, perhaps more interestingly from a philosophical point of view, that he did not accept it." It is more the latter: he rejected purely a priori reasoning as leading to knowledge about reality.
17. See Tillemans 2003.
18. The Kantian distinction between conviction (Überzeugung) and persuasion (Überredung) is found in the *Critique of Pure Reason* II (Transcendental Doctrine of Method), chapter II (The Canon of Pure Reason), section III (Of Opinion, Knowledge, and Belief). See Kant 1998, 684–90. The Kantian pair of concepts was first put into the context of argumentation theory in Perelman and Olbrechts-Tyteca (1958), who saw it as pertaining to arguments destined to a universal audience and particular audiences respectively. The conviction-persuasion distinction was applied to the Svātantrika-Prāsaṅgika debate in Tillemans 2003 and will be developed further in my forthcoming article on Nāgārjuna's quietism in the *Oxford Handbook of Indian Philosophy*, ed. Jonardon Ganeri.

6. Apoha Semantics: What Did Bhāviveka Have to Do with It?[1]

I AM AN ADMIRER of the late Paul Hoornaert's translation and study of the fifth chapter of the *Madhyamakahṛdayakārikā* (MHK 5), the chapter consecrated to the critique of Yogācāra. Besides giving a very good translation, Hoornaert often provided quite perspicacious notes, some of which merit being taken up in more detail. One that I think particularly important is his observation that most work on *apoha* "surprisingly ignores Bhāvaviveka's criticism of Dignāga," and that "by anchoring general properties in the nature of individual entities, Bhāvaviveka anticipates Dharmakīrti's corrections to Dignāga's *apoha* theory."[2] This paper then is an attempt to flesh out the details and evidence for those remarks of Paul Hoornaert, a person whom I was unfortunately never able to meet, in spite of our mutual efforts, and for whom I have great respect.

I. The Problem

The sixth-century Mādhyamika writer Bhāviveka (a.k.a. Bhavya, a.k.a. Bhāvaviveka) undoubtedly knew Yogācāra Buddhism well, very well, and although he systematically rejected its key positions on idealism and many other things in *Madhyamakahṛdayakārikā* 5, the information that he gives in doing so helps us better understand the Yogācāra positions themselves. In particular, in MHK 5 we seem to get an interesting version of Dignāga's philosophy of language, or *apoha* (*exclusion*), being used by an unnamed Yogācāra to bolster the Yogācāra theory from Mādhyamika attacks. Now, one way to read Bhāviveka is that he countered the Yogācāra's use of Dignāga's philosophy of language by rejecting *apoha* completely across the board, substituting for it an intuitive appeal to customary truths and a semantic theory that seemed to him more faithful to customary truths than what *apohavāda* had to offer. The consequence, of course, would be that Bhāviveka was *not* an *apohavādin*, that he rejected it just as much as he rejected idealism and other key features of Yogācāra, and that he had little or no place in the *apohavāda* movement.

I think that the situation is much more nuanced. First of all, the evidence is mixed on whether Bhāviveka was himself an adherent of a form of *apoha*. He certainly did not explicitly say he was, and it is rather hard to tell definitively from the outside: the term *apohavādin*, like other labels for philosophical movements, is probably a family-resemblance term picking out several features, each of which is at most common to some (but not all) of the movement's thinkers, so that there probably are no definitive necessary and sufficient conditions for its application. Be that as it may, it does seem that what Bhāviveka elaborated in MHK 5 significantly anticipates, and indeed resembles, what will be a particular variant of the *apoha* theory—the variant that will be developed later by Dharmakīrti and that will become the dominant current in the subsequent evolution of this philosophy. And if that is right, Bhāviveka's position would represent a transitional stage, one that, if better understood, might provide much-needed context and historical antecedents for the ever-increasing complexity of the later developments of *apohavāda*. In what follows, I will use Hoornaert's recently published edition of the Sanskrit text of the MHK and the Tibetan text of the autocommentary, the *Tarkajvālā* (TJ).[3] The translations, however, are my own and exhibit some differences from those of Hoornaert.

II. Dignāga and Dharmakīrti on apohavāda *Semantics: "Pure-*vyāvṛtti*" Theories Versus Buddhist Versions of the* tadvatpakṣa

Apohavāda is an approach used, over time, for a multitude of problems: logical (i.e., substitutivity in propositional attitude contexts like "X knows that . . ." and "X believes that . . ."), metaphysical (i.e., universals), epistemological (i.e., knowledge arising from verbal testimony), and even religious (i.e., critique of the philosophy of language justifying the Vedas). In the fifth chapter of the *Pramāṇasamuccaya* of Dignāga, we find an important attempt to come up with a solution to a recurring, even pan-Indian, dilemma in thought on semantics: *do general words somehow signify, or express, universals or particulars*? Dignāga's point is that general words are not *expressive* (*vācaka*)[4] of real universals (*sāmānya*)—that is, they do not make us explicitly aware of real universals—nor do they express the particulars (*svalakṣaṇa*) distinct from the real universals, as particulars in themselves remain inexpressible.[5]

His solution, then, is to deny both seemingly hopeless approaches: words neither express real universals nor the particulars but rather express a type of double negation—the word "pot" directly makes us aware of the absence of all non-pots. It is this latter two-stepped exclusion that is known as an *apoha* (exclusion) or, equivalently, *vyāvṛtti*; it is what a word directly expresses (*vācya, abhidheya*); being an absence it is unreal, a kind of conceptual fiction, and so enables us to avoid acceptance of *real* universals. The upshot: words still directly express a "something" that fulfills much of the role that a universal like potness or cowness fulfills in most Indian semantic theories in that it is "present" in several different things at any one time. After all, the exclusion expressed by the word "pot" can be thought to qualify the multiple individual pots because these individuals can be grouped together as non-non-pots.

Now from a relatively early time on, there seem to be at least two important directions in the evolution of *apohavāda* semantics. The first, which we can attribute to Dignāga (or at the very least to what must have been a widespread pre-Dharmakīrtian interpretation of Dignāga) and which we shall call the "pure-*vyāvṛtti* theory," is that words *just* express the *apoha* or *vyāvṛtti*, and nothing more. This "pure-*vyāvṛtti* theory" seems to be what is brought out in *Pramāṇasamuccaya* 5.4, where Dignāga argued against an opposing realist position that constituted a kind of seductive middle-ground combining elements of both sides of the pan-Indian dilemma. The position that Dignāga took pains to refute was that words directly expressed the particulars that "have the universal" (*jātimat, sāmānyavat*). Against this he argued that such a view would incur *asvātantryādidoṣa*, faults such as inter alia that words would never express their senses directly and autonomously—the particulars having the universal—but only indirectly and in dependence upon other factors. The key verse from Dignāga is *Pramāṇasamuccaya* 5.4, the first *pāda* of which is:

> *tadvato nāsvatantratvāt*
>
> [A term] is not [expressive] of what has the [universal] (*tadvat*) because it would not be [semantically] autonomous (*asvatantratvāt*).

The point that we can glean from Dignāga's own *Pramāṇasamuccayavṛtti*, Jinendrabuddhi's *Ṭīkā*, and the paraphrases of the arguments in non-Buddhist texts is that if a word like *sat* (existent) signified the *things/substances that possess existence* (*sattvavad dravyam*), then the word *sat* would not be semantically autonomous in that it would signify those substances only via the intervention (*vyavadhāna*) of an intermediary—the universal "existence"—that would be the actual ground for applying (*pravṛttinimitta*) the word. In that case it would be other-reliant (*paratantra*), and not autonomous (*svatantra*), in signifying the *substances that possess existence, in that it could not signify them directly* (*sākṣāt*).[6]

The rest of verse 4 and Dignāga's own commentary spelled out the absurd consequences of this dependence in more detail: such a semantics could not account for the adjective and noun in phrases like *sad dravyam* (existent substance) having "co-reference" (*sāmānādhikaraṇya*) to one and the same individual thing, because a term like *sat* would not directly express individual substances at all, and nor would it logically imply them;[7] equally, it would follow that words could never be applied literally, only figuratively (*upacāra*), as they would apply to things only metonymically via the universal. In short, Dignāga used *vyākaraṇa*, or broadly speaking grammatical considerations, against "the thesis [that a word expresses] what has the [universal]"—the *tadvatpakṣa*, or equivalently *sāmānyavatpakṣa* or *jātimatpakṣa*—by arguing that if a term's meaning became a derivative or indirect matter, other (ordinary) linguistic practices would be inexplicable. His position was therefore that if such practices were to be accounted for, then what was directly expressed could only be a fiction, a quasi universal, the *non-non-X* that consisted in an exclusion (*apoha*, *vyāvṛtti*), and not the possessor of a real universal.

Let us move on to the second direction in the evolution of *apohavāda* semantics. At some point there apparently was the objection that Dignāga's *anyāpoha* theory falls into exactly the same types of absurdities that he leveled against the *tadvatpakṣa*, because the *apoha* theory must maintain that a term for X still supposedly somehow expresses the individual things, Xs, that are differentiated from what is other than X.[8] Following Frauwallner in *Beiträge zur Apohalehre*, this objection is clearly documented in Kumārila's *Ślokavārttika* (Apohavāda) 120 as well as in Śāntarakṣita's *Tattvasaṃgraha* v. 972, 1099ff.[9] In any case, the objection figures prominently in Dharmakīrti's own remarks to *Pramāṇavārttika* 1.64 in his *Pramāṇavārttikasvavṛtti* (PVSV 34.19–21):

> *yad āhuḥ / anyāpohe 'pi śabdārthe tadviśiṣṭasyābhidhānāt tadvatpakṣoditaḥ sarvaḥ prasaṅgaḥ samāna iti tad apy anena prativyūḍham /*

> Some say that even when a word's significance (*śabdārtha*) is an exclusion of other things (*anyāpoha*), all the absurd consequences cited against the position [that words express the individual things] that have the [universal] (*tadvatpakṣa*) will remain the same, because [words] would express something [i.e., a signified thing (*artha*)] that is qualified by that [i.e., an exclusion

> of other things (*anyāpoha*)]. This [depiction of the *tadvatpakṣa* (*tadvatpakṣopavarṇana*)] too is refuted by that [i.e., by the fact that exclusions and things that have exclusions are not different (*vyāvṛttivyāvṛttimator ananyatvena*)].[10]

So now enter Dharmakīrti, who basically grants that the *apoha* theory is, or should be, a harmless type of *tadvatpakṣa*, because it is one with an all-important twist that sets it apart from the realist type of *tadvatpakṣa* that Dignāga had criticized. Dharmakīrti differs from Dignāga (who as we saw rejected *tadvatpakṣa*) in that he argues that the universal (*jāti*) and the particulars having that universal (*tadvat*), or more accurately the *vyāvṛtti* (exclusion) and *vyāvṛttimat* (possessors of the exclusion), are not actually distinct real entities but rather conceptual creations. This gets him off the hook of Dignāga's critique of *tadvatpakṣa*, where the problems had arisen in *tadvatpakṣa* because crucially the universal and the thing that had the universal were taken as genuinely distinct real entities by the opponent. The realist had to hold that a word would express one entity (the things/substances) via the intermediary of the other (the universal); the *apohavādin*, according to Dharmakīrti, would have no such constraint. Here is *Pramāṇavārttika* 1.64, where Dharmakīrti salvages a duly innocuous *tadvatpakṣa* from Dignāga's earlier refutation:

> *tenānyāpohaviṣaye tadvatpakṣopavarṇanam / pratyākhyātaṃ pṛthaktve hi syād doṣo jātitadvatoḥ //*
>
> Thus the depiction [of the faults][11] of the position of [a word expressing the particulars] that have the [universal] is rejected in the case of [a word's] object being an exclusion of what is other. Indeed, there would be a fault if the universal and that which had it were to be separate.

Manorathanandin's commentary to 1.64cd rounds out the argument:

> *jātitadvatoḥ pṛthaktve hi syād doṣa eṣaḥ / na tu vyāvṛttivyāvṛttimator bheda iti nātra tatpakṣoktadoṣaḥ //*
>
> Indeed there would be this fault if the universal and that which had it were to be separate, but there is no difference between the exclusion (*vyāvṛtti*) and that which has the exclusion (*vyāvṛttimat*),

and so the fault leveled against this thesis [i.e., *tadvatpakṣa*] does not occur here.

The argument for rehabilitating *tadvatpakṣa* thus turns on Dharmakīrti's recurring principle that properties (*dharma* = *vyāvṛtti*) and property possessors (*dharmin* = *vyāvṛttimat*) are not actually distinct things,[12] and indeed that a word for a property and a word for a property possessor are both expressing the same exclusion (*vyāvṛtti*) and differentiation (*bheda*).[13] Universals and possessors of the universal are thus both signified by words, not because one real entity is cognized via another, but because both are fiction and any separation between them is purely conceptual and due to subjective causes, such as longstanding habits of language use.

III. Bhāviveka and the Yogācāra

So much for a working presentation of Dignāga's and Dharmakīrti's somewhat technical positions. Here is briefly what I think is going on in MHK 5's discussion criticizing Yogācāra in verses 60–68.

First of all, the general Yogācāra position under attack as we see it in *Tarkajvālā* verses 57–58 and elsewhere is that forms and colors (*rūpa*) and other such things expressed by language do not really exist, that they are just imagined natures (*parikalpitasvabhāva*), and that the words for them are "mere expressions" (*abhidhānamātra*). As becomes equally clear from the rest of the discussion in MHK and the *Tarkajvālā*, the Yogācāra holds that there nonetheless are entities (*vastu*), dependent in nature but inexpressible (*anabhilāpya*) and beyond the imagined natures created by language. All this is recognizably classic Yogācāra, in keeping with the broad outlines of what we find in, for example, Asaṅga's *Tattvārthapaṭala* of the *Bodhisattvabhūmi*, where words are said to designate fictions, and where entities (*vastu*), or mere entities (*vastumātra*), remain beyond the realm of language. However, we find a new wrinkle to this basic Yogācāra doctrine starting in Bhāviveka's verse 60, where the Yogācāra invokes the *apoha* theory to say that what words express (*abhilāpya*) are universals construed as *anyāpoha*/*vyāvṛtti* and thus fictions. In effect, he uses the *apohavāda* to explain precisely *how* language imposes imaginary natures and leaves the real entities (*vastu*) inexpressible. Here is MHK 5.60ab with the beginning of the *Tarkajvālā*:

sāmānyam abhilāpyaṃ hi sāmānyaṃ ca na kiṃcana / nābhilāpātmaśūnyatvam evam apy upapadyate //

> Indeed [according to you, Yogācāra,] what is expressed is the universal, and the universal is nothing [real] at all. In that case, the fact of [universals] being void of the natures conveyed by the words would not make any sense either.

> *khyed cag mngon par brjod par bya ba spyi yin la / spyi ni dper na ba lang ma yin pa rta la sogs pa gzhan dag gis ba lang sel ba ni ba lang gi spyi yin no zhes bya ba lta bur 'dod na /*

> Suppose that you [Yogācāra] hold that what is expressed is the universal and that the universal is as follows: the exclusion of "cow" by [all] other [things] (*gzhan dag gis*), like horses and so forth, which are non-cows, is what constitutes the universal "cow."

Both for historical and philosophical reasons, it seems that the *apohavāda* that is being invoked is most likely that of Dignāga, what we have termed the "pure-*vyāvṛtti* theory," which holds that the object of a word must be *just* the *anyāpoha*, the fictional quasi universal. On Dignāga's position, words express these quasi universals (*sāmānyalakṣaṇa*), while the particulars (*svalakṣaṇa*) are said to be inexpressible. In MHK's Yogācāra chapter there is a substitution of the word *vastu* for *svalakṣaṇa*, but for the rest the position is recognizably in keeping with Dignāga's theory.

Bhāviveka will have nothing of the Yogācāra position about words expressing fictions while *vastu* remain inexpressible. He wants to say, invoking ordinary intuitions, that words *do* signify a *vastu*, though this *vastu* has to be understood as just a customary entity (*saṃvṛtisat*) and not something ultimate or fully real. On the other hand, Bhāviveka does not seem to be ready to simply throw out the *apoha* theory completely, even though he sees grave problems in the pure-*vyāvṛtti* variety. He replies in verses 60–61 that it is not the pure universal (*sāmānya*) that is the object of words but rather the *vastu* that is *sāmānyavat*, the entity that has the universal. Now we have seen that *sāmānyavatpakṣa* is another name for *jātimatpakṣa*—that is, *tadvatpakṣa*; *sāmānyavad vastu* is also an equivalent for *jātivān arthaḥ* / *jātimad dravyam*.

In short, Bhāviveka clearly opts for a *tadvatpakṣa* quite similar to what Dharmakīrti will endorse in PV 1.64. Here again are the relevant passages from MHK and the *Tarkajvālā* (TJ), namely MHK 5.61 along with TJ's introduction and explanation:

TJ: *'o na spyi gang zhig mngon par brjod par bya ba nyid yin par rigs she na / de'i phyir /*

Well then, which universal is suitable to be that which is expressed? Thus [we reply:]

vācyaṃ sāmānyavad vastu tadābhamatihetutaḥ / tasya tenātmanā sattvān na yuktānabhilāpyatā //

It is the entity (*vastu*) that has the universal (*sāmānyavat*) that is expressed, for it is what causes the thought to which it appears. Since it exists as that nature, it is not reasonable that it be inexpressible.

TJ: *mngon par brjod par bya ba'i spyi dang ldan pa'i dngos po ste / gang la sngon po la sogs pa'i khyad par la ma ltos par gzugs nyid kyi spyi yod pa de ni spyi dang ldan pa'i dngos po ste / sngon pa la sogs pa dang / ring po la sogs pa'o // ji lta zhe na / der snang ba'i blo'i rgyu yin pa'i phyir ro // de ni spyi dang ldan pa'i gzugs de'i bdag nyid du yod pas mngon par brjod pa'i yul yin pa'i phyir ji ltar brjod du med pa nyid du rigs ste / brjod du med pa nyid du mi rigs so //*

> [The verse says] *vācyaṃ sāmānyavad vastu*. This means that anything in which [e.g.,] the universal *rūpatva* (being *visible matter*) is present without taking into account differences like blue and so forth is an entity that has the universal, such as [colors] like blue and so forth and [shapes] like long and so forth. How so? Because it [i.e., the entity having the universal] is what causes the thought to which it appears. Since the [entities having the universal] exist as that—as *rūpa*s that have the universal—they are objects of expression [of the word *rūpa*]; so how could they be inexpressible? It is not reasonable that they be inexpressible.

This is unmistakably the *tadvatpakṣa*, very much in the direction that Dharmakīrti will take. There is also other relevant evidence for a possible ancestry for Dharmakīrti's theory. First of all, in verses 61 and 62, Bhāviveka seems to give a causal account as to how the *sāmānyavad vastu* causes the cognition. Such causal accounts linking thought with entities are absent in Dignāga but become *the* major component of Dharmakīrti's position on how thought bears upon the world. I think it is fair to say that this directional change is so important that it represents virtually a new *apohavāda*, one that crucially relies on a causal theory of reference instead of a type of correspondence or logical connection between double negations and things.

Striking too is the resemblance in choice of words. In verse 63 Bhāviveka says: *pṛthag na ca*, which may well be the same idea that finds its way into the verse from Dharmakīrti that we quoted earlier—*pṛthaktve hi syād doṣo jātitadvatoḥ*, "Indeed, there would be a fault if the universal and that which had it were to be separate. [But they are not separate, and so there is no fault.]" MHK thus has a phrase (*pṛthag na ca*, "But it is not something separate") that is in the same philosophical context and that may have become the counterfactual hypothesis (*pṛthaktve*, "If they were to be separate") in the verse from PV 1. It is worth looking at the details in Bhāviveka. MHK 5.63cd reads:

> *tadvat kalpyam ato vastu vācyaṃ ceṣṭaṃ pṛthag na ca /*
>
> So like that the entity [i.e., one said to be a universal] is held to be what is thought about and what is expressed, but it is not something separate [from the natures of the individual *vastu*].

TJ glosses the whole passage as:

> *des na* (*ato*) *spyi zhes bya ba'i dngos po* (*vastu*) *de* (*tad*?) *ni blo'i yul yin pa'i phyir brtag par bya ba* (*kalpyam*) *yang yin la / blos nges par bzung ba'i dngos po la tshig 'jug pa'i phyir de nyid brjod par bya ba* (*vācyam*) *yang yin par 'dod* (*ceṣṭam*) *kyi / ba lang nyid ces bya ba de lkog shal la sogs pa dag las gzhan pa* (*pṛthag*) *ni ma yin* (*na*) *te / 'o na ji lta bu zhe na / dngos po'i rang gi ngo bo nyid las tha mi dad pa yin no //*
>
> So that entity (*vastu*) said to be a universal is held to be on the one hand what is thought about because it is a mental object, and on the other hand it itself is held to be what is expressed because words apply to the entities that are determined by the mind. But what is said to be cowness is not something separate from the things having dewlaps and so forth. [Question:] How so? [Reply:] It is not different from the intrinsic natures of the *vastu* [i.e., individual entities].

The translation of MHK here needs to be taken with some caution. First, it might perhaps be thought that the word *tadvat* is to be taken as the *tadvat* of the *tadvatpakṣa*, "having the [universal]." This actually could make some philosophical sense and might conceivably yield a translation along the lines of "So the entity is thought about as having the [universal]" and so on. However, neither the commentary—or perhaps, more accurately, the Tibetan translator of MHK and TJ—nor Paul Hoornaert read the MHK verse in that way. The Tibetan has simply *des na dngos po de*: "So *that* entity." There is no *de bzhin* or *de ldan* in the Tibetan of MHK or TJ and neither of these Tibetan texts are of help in resolving this issue. Nonetheless, the earlier *pādas* of verse 63 do make a comparison with numbers (*saṃkhyāvat / grangs bzhin*), so that it seems more plausible to take the *tadvat* as a mere continuation of the comparison: "like a number . . . so like that . . ."[14] In short, the context seems to suggest something along the lines of "like that"/"similarly." The passage is not without other difficulties of interpretation—for example, if we follow TJ we obviously at some point will need to give a satisfying explanation as to *how* the *vastu* is said or considered to be a universal (*spyi zhes bya ba*). What TJ tells us is simply that we can or will understand/apprehend/cognize (*gzung*) the universal when the individuals having it have been apprehended (*bzung*). Nonetheless, leaving aside a detailed exegesis of MHK and TJ, what is important for our purposes should come through relatively uncontroversially: it seems likely that in MHK 5.63cd we have a similar core idea to what will occur in *Pramāṇavārttika* 1.64: the quasi universal, and the entities that have it, are not separately existing things.

Now it might be asked why, with this type of evidence, would anyone ever think that Bhāviveka was somehow *not* an *apohavādin*? Intuitively speaking, even on a relatively superficial reading of MHK 5, it would look implausible that Bhāviveka was not an *apohavādin of some sort*. Throughout MHK 5 and TJ there is talk of "absence of dissimilar things" (verse 62, *vijātīyena śūnyatvam*) and "natures differentiated from non-blue and non-lotus" (*anīlānutpalabhinnarūpa*), culminating in verse 65's *apoha*-like justification of co-reference (*sāmānādhikaraṇya*) of "blue" and "lotus" (because the absences of non-blue and non-lotus do not obstruct each other). There seems to be far too much endorsement of key *apohavāda* themes for us to think that all variants on the *apoha* theory are somehow being tossed out.

Nonetheless, the objection is on to something and is certainly not unintelligent. Far from it. After all, potentially troubling is a passage in TJ introducing MHK 5.62 as follows: "Then, if the universal is not the *anyāpoha*, what is the so-called universal?" (*gal te spyi zhes bya ba de gzhan sel ba ma yin na / 'o na spyi zhes bya ba gang yin zhe na*). The importance of this passage has to be relativized by comparing it with MHK 5 beginning at verse 66, which makes it clear that what is rejected is "exclusion *by* others," although "absence of dissimilar things" (*vijātīyena śūnyatvam*) is repeatedly endorsed by MHK and TJ. Indeed in verses 66–68, and already in TJ's commentary to verse 60 (translated above), Bhāviveka discusses and rejects abstrusely an analysis of the compound *anyāpoha* as being an instrumental *tatpuruṣa*, "exclusion by others" (*anyair apoha*; *gzhan dag gis sel ba*). This discussion is complicated and it is not clear to me whom Bhāviveka is attacking, for I personally don't know of anyone who held an interpretation of *anyāpoha*, *anyavyāvṛtti*, *anyavyāvṛtta*, and so on as an instrumental compound—it is usually genitive (exclusion of what is other) or ablative as in "something that is excluded (*vyāvṛtta*) from what is other (*anyasmāt*)." The same oddity was noticed by Hoornaert, who seems to have come to the conclusion that although Bhāviveka *was* criticizing Dignāga, he for some reason deformed Dignāga's position by taking the compound in an unfaithful way.[15] I would suggest that this is right and gives the basis for an explanation of the puzzling passages suggesting outright rejection of *anyāpoha*. In short, there is a rejection of Dignāga's pure-*vyāvṛtti* theory and in this context an (unfair) attribution to him of an instrumental interpretation of the compound. Thus Bhāviveka ends up rejecting *anyāpoha* taken in the Dignāgean way to arrive perhaps at another version of the theory. It looks to me, then, that we may not be dealing with a rejection of all *apohavāda* but only the Dignāgean *apohavāda*, and that the tactics adopted by Bhāviveka may well have involved a certain deformation of this theory.

IV. Conclusions

I have to leave the speculation on Bhāviveka's own affiliations open; what is important is that whatever be the school he would personally endorse, his positions seemed to have found their way, directly or indirectly, into later *apoha* theories from Dharmakīrti onward. Let's take stock of what we have seen so far.

- Dignāga rejected the *tadvat* theory and advocated the "pure-*vyāvṛtti*" theory.
- Bhāviveka in his polemic against Yogācāra criticized what must be Dignāga's theory—the pure-*vyāvṛtti* theory—for leaving individual entities inexpressible.
- Bhāviveka advocates instead a type of *tadvat* theory that anticipates features of later *apohavāda*.

- Dharmakīrti adopts this *tadvat* theory by arguing that properties and property possessors are not separate and that the words for them express the same exclusions.

If this reconstruction of history is accurate, then it looks like Hoornaert was on to something important and that very possibly Bhāviveka did play a role in the development and even transmission of the *apoha* theory. An audacious historical conclusion would be to say that not only is Bhāviveka an *apohavādin* but that he had a clear and direct influence on Dharmakīrti's *apohavāda*—it was his objections to Dignāga as well as his proposed solutions that then led to the position of Dharmakīrti. To be honest, without clear quotations of Bhāviveka in Dharmakīrti's works, I'm not fully convinced of this "lineage" and I'm not sure what kind of evidence would be convincing if it were essentially a matter of similarities and some suggestive choices of words. We might try to find other cases where Dharmakīrti's and Bhāviveka's choices of words are strikingly similar, one potential example being their replacement of Dignāga's notion of "refutation by what is commonly recognized" (*prasiddha*) by "refutation by what is commonly acknowledged" (*pratīti*). (At least in the case of Dharmakīrti, this difference in going from *prasiddha* to *pratīti* is taken to have major philosophical import in *Pramāṇavārttika* 4's section on *pratītibādhā*. Bhāviveka in MHK 3 consecrates a whole section to *pratīti* but doesn't, as far as I can see, attach anything like the importance to this terminological shift as does Dharmakīrti.) I think, however, that similarities of ideas and words will not definitively prove *direct* influence, even if they are suggestive. A more moderate and defensible conclusion would be that Dharmakīrti simply wasn't particularly original in coming up with his *apoha* theory—the basic ideas were already "in the air": he tapped into a discussion in which Bhāviveka and perhaps several others had already somehow participated.[16]

Notes to Chapter 6

1. The present paper has its origins in a conversation with John Dunne and Sara McClintock and a correspondence with Malcolm Eckel and has been presented in different forms and forums, benefiting along the way from the remarks and debates of various attentive colleagues, especially those of Akira Saitō and Shōryū Katsura. See also Saitō 2004.
2. See Hoornaert 2001b, 42n15 and 43n21.
3. See Hoornaert 2001b. The other installments of Hoornaert's translation are Hoornaert 1999, 2000, 2001a, 2002, and 2003.

4. See Richard Hayes's remark on *vācaka* and *vṛtti* in Hayes 1988, 257.
5. Dignāga, in *Pramāṇasamuccaya* and *Vṛtti* 5.2, had argued that if, absurdly, words did express only genuine universals, there would be clashes with basic aspects of Sanskrit grammar. To take what is obviously a frequently occurring phenomenon, an adjectival term supposedly could not express the universal, because then, according to Dignāga, the adjective and the substantive it qualified would express completely different things and could have different grammatical features of case, number, and gender. In fact, the terms are said to be "co-referential" (*samānādhikaraṇa*) and thus must have the same gender, number, and case endings. In short, if one said that the term "white" in "white cow" expressed whiteness, and that this universal, whiteness, was a different entity from cowness or the cows, the grammatical features of adjectives agreeing with nouns would become problematic and unaccounted for—if "white" expressed whiteness, then we would have the problem that *śuklatvam* (whiteness) is, for example, neuter while *go* (ox, cow) is not. If, on the other hand, it was just the particulars that were expressed by general words, then other supposedly irremediable problems would follow, such as that because particulars, like individual cows, are so numerous, we could not possibly be made explicitly aware of them all by the word "cow," and in that sense "cow" could not *express* all the numerous individuals that we might find in pastures everywhere.
6. Here I am relying heavily on the philological work of Ole H. Pind on *Pramāṇasamuccaya* 5. His doctorate thesis from the University of Vienna, i.e., Pind 2009, is as yet unpublished in book form but available as an e-thesis at http://othes.univie.ac.at/8283/.
7. See note 5.
8. How then do general terms come to have anything to do with particulars for Dignāga? The point remains a bit obscure, especially if we see Dignāga apart from the Dharmakīrtian interpretation of his philosophy, although it is clear that he thought they did via this direct expression of the *vyāvṛtti*. For Dignāga, the point seems to turn on a difference between *vācaka* and *vṛtti*, being expressive of and pertaining to: while general terms may pertain to (*vṛtti*) particulars, they are not expressive (*vācaka*) of them, in that they do not make the listener think of any specific individual thing when he hears the general term. See Hayes 1988, 257.
9. See Frauwallner 1932, 261.
10. Translating this passage just as is without additions yields the following terse result: "Some say that even when a word's meaning is an exclusion of other things, all the absurd consequences cited against the *tadvatpakṣa* will remain the same, because there would be expression of what is qualified by that. This too is refuted by that." Our additions follow Karṇakagomin's glosses in his commentary on this passage. See Karṇakagomin's PVSVṬ 153.21–29.
11. It is clear from PVSV that the *tadvatpakṣopavarṇanam* of which Dharmakīrti speaks is the critique that we find in Dignāga's *Pramāṇasamuccaya*, i.e., *asvātantryādidoṣa*. See PVSV 34.21–22 on verse 64: *tatra hy arthāntaram upādāyānyatra vartamāno dhvanir asvātantryādidoṣair upadrūyate.*
12. To get an idea of the broad lines of this position, see PVSV 34.22–35.7 on verse 64: *na cārthāntaram anyasmād vyāvṛttir vyāvṛttād dvayor ekābhidhānād ity uktam / katham idānīm ekasya vyāvṛttasyānyānanugamād anyavyāvṛttiḥ sāmānyam / tadbuddhau tathāpratibhāsanāt / na vai kiṃcit sāmānyaṃ nāmāsti / śabdāśrayā*

buddhir anādivāsanāsāmarthyād asaṃsṛṣṭān api dharmān saṃsṛjantī jāyate / tasyāḥ pratibhāsavaśena sāmānyaṃ sāmānādhikaraṇyaṃ ca vyavasthāpyate | asadartho 'pi / arthānāṃ saṃsargabhedābhāvāt / tasya sarvasya tatkāryakāraṇatayā 'nyebhyo bhidyamānā arthāḥ samāśrayo dhvaniś cāniṣṭaparihāreṇa pravartayatīty anyāpohaviṣaya uktaḥ / tatrānapekṣitabāhyatattvo buddhipratibhāsavaśād eko 'nekavyāvṛttaḥ śabdair viṣayīkriyate tadanubhavāhitavāsanāprabodhajanmabhir vikalpair adhyavasitatadbhāvārthaiḥ /. "The exclusion from other things is not something separate from what is excluded, because both [words for properties and words for property possessors] express the same thing. This has already been explained. [Objection:] Now, how is it that the exclusion of what is other could be a universal, since one excluded thing cannot be present in any others? [Reply:] It is [a universal] because it seems to be that way to the cognition [we have] of it. But there is no universal whatsoever in fact. A cognition based on words ends up combining elements, even though they are not actually combined, because of the influence of beginningless tendencies [to do so]. It is on account of how things seem to be to that [word-based cognition] that universals and co-reference (*sāmānādhikaraṇya*) are established, though they are fictions (*asadartha*), for [actual] things are neither combined [to be a universal] nor differentiated [into the various qualities we think they have.] The basis of all this is the things (*artha*) that are being differentiated from other things on account of their effects and causes. And a word makes one apply oneself [to something] by rejecting what is unintended. For these reasons it is said to have as its object an exclusion of other things. In that case, due to what seems to be so to [conceptual] cognition, [a fictional and conceptually created representation] that is without any relied-upon external nature and is one and excluded [from other things] is taken as an object by words as well as by conceptualizations that arise from the awakening of tendencies instilled [in the mind] through experience of the [particulars], [conceptualizations] that have as objects such superimposed natures."

13. See Karṇakagomin ad PVSV's phrase *na cārthāntaram anyasmād vyāvṛttir vyāvṛttād dvayor ekābhidhānād ity uktam* (translated in previous note) in PVSVṬ 154.7–9: *anyasmād vastunor yā vyāvṛttiḥ sā vyāvṛttān nānyā / dvayor dharmadharmivācinoḥ śabdayor ekasya vyāvṛttibhedasyābhidhānād ity uktam anantaram eva.*
14. MHK 5.63ab: *nāśrayasyāgrahe grāhyaṃ saṃkhyāvat tadgrahe grahāt* /. "[The universal] will not be apprehended when the basis has not been apprehended, for we apprehend [the former] when we have apprehended the latter, just as we do with numbers [i.e., we apprehend 'two, etc.' after apprehending pairs of entities like pots, etc.]."
15. Hoornaert 2001b, 42n15: "The definition of 'general property,' as it is rendered here [in MHK 5.60–68], does not exactly agree with Dignāga's definition. Dignāga does not define the general property 'cow' as the exclusion of cowness by non-cows but as the content of the concept 'cow' or the referent of the word 'cow' that are constituted by excluding the idea 'non-cow' or by excluding the use of any other word but 'cow' upon perceiving a cow." See also Saitō 2004, 30nn4 and 6.
16. Krasser 2012 uses the results of an earlier version of this chapter (i.e., "Dignāga, Bhāviveka and Dharmakīrti on Apoha" published in Krasser et al. 2011) and other considerations to argue quite subtly that Dharmakīrti's dates must be in the mid-sixth century rather than circa 600–660 (as had been generally accepted up until now).

7. What Happened to the Third and Fourth Lemmas in the Tibetan Madhyamaka?

The negation of the disjunction of two statements is logically equivalent to the conjunction of the negations of the two statements; the negation of the conjunction of two statements is logically equivalent to the disjunction of the negations of the two statements. (The laws of logic attributed to Augustus De Morgan [1806–71] and known as "De Morgan's Laws") [1]

HERE IS HOW the recurring schema of four alternatives, or the tetralemma (*catuṣkoṭi*), is presented in a Buddhist Sanskrit text. It is found in numerous such texts (see Seyfort Ruegg 2010, 37–112) and with various formulations, but to choose one we'll start with verse 21 of chapter 14 of Āryadeva's *Catuḥśataka*:

> *sad asat sad asac ceti sadasan neti ca kramaḥ / eṣa prayojyo vidvadbhir ekatvādiṣu nityaśaḥ /*
>
> Existent, nonexistent, both existent and nonexistent, neither existent nor nonexistent, that is the method that the learned should always use with regard to oneness and other such [theses].[2]

Now is not the time for a basic presentation of the Madhyamaka philosophy of emptiness or an exposé on the reasonings to arrive at emptiness and no discursive "proliferations" (*niṣprapañca*).[3] Suffice it to say that the Madhyamaka negates all four lemmas, and this with regard to any philosophical position presented. In short, we are told to negate existence, nonexistence, both and neither, as well as oneness, not-oneness, both, neither, and every other such proposition in its four alternatives.

What will concern us here is primarily the fourth lemma. The Sanskrit term that is often used for the fourth is *na+ubhaya* (*nobhaya*), and like the

Tibetan *gnyis ka ma yin pa*, this term is the least readily comprehensible of the four. Indeed it is ambiguous, suggesting at first sight "not both . . . and . . ." as well as the quite different rendering "neither . . . nor . . ." That said, all major modern writers on Madhyamaka (that I know of at least) opt for "neither . . . nor . . ." Thus, for example, David Seyfort Ruegg in speaking about the Madhyamaka's application of the tetralemma to nirvāṇa takes the fourth alternative as "neither *bhāva* nor *abhāva*" (Seyfort Ruegg 1981, 18), "neither existent nor nonexistent"; Jacques May cites the Madhyamaka tetralemma concerning the permanence of the world and formulates it as: "le monde est éternel, non-éternel, éternel et non-éternel, ni éternel ni non-éternel" (May 1959, 16). Finally, here is how Seyfort Ruegg (2010, 40) summarized the Madhyamaka use of the tetralemma:

> [E]ach position or *koṭi*—the positive one (I), the negative one (II), the one consisting in a combination or conjunction of the positive and negative (III), and the one consisting in the bi-negation of the positive and negative (IV)—is negated.

Seyfort Ruegg throughout his famous 1977 article (reprinted in 2010) on the *catuṣkoṭi* takes this "bi-negation" as meaning "neither . . . nor . . . ," which is certainly correct. To be more technical, taking a bi-negation like "not-*A* and not-*B*" ($\neg A \& \neg B$) as equivalent to "neither *A* nor *B*" ($\neg [A \vee B]$) is an uncontroversial application of De Morgan's laws governing the use of the logical connectives "and" and "or."

One could go on in citing these major modern authors, but the point is that they were *perfectly right* in taking the tetralemma as they took it: the fourth lemma is indeed "neither . . . nor . . ." It is, however, important to have no doubts that (rightly) taking lemma 4 as "neither *A* nor *B*"—as the negation of the disjunction of two statements—is not the same thing as (wrongly) taking it as "not both A and B"—as the negation of the conjunction of the two statements. One commits an egregious logical error, a howler, if one confuses the negation of the disjunction $\neg(A \vee B)$ with that of the conjunction $\neg(A \& B)$. "Neither . . . nor . . ." and "not both . . ." are totally different kettles of fish. Equivalently, to use Seyfort Ruegg's terms, a "bi-negation" is a conjunction of two negated statements, and that is very different from the simple negation of a conjunction of the statements—"not-both . . ." It's easy to see that by De Morgan's laws "not both *A* & *B*" ($\neg[A \& B]$), just implies that either *A* or *B* is false ($\neg A \vee \neg B$) but certainly does not imply the bi-negation $\neg A \& \neg B$ or the negation of the disjunction $\neg(A \vee B)$. On an intuitive level, it's true that a patch that is green all over is not both green and red, given the incompatibility of these colors. However it is obviously false to say that this green patch is not green nor is it red—not green and not red.

Now, as we mentioned earlier, the point of the Madhyamaka method is to negate all four lemmas and in that way end up with "peaceful stilling of all discursive proliferations" (*prapañcopaśama*). These four negations end up rendered quite succinctly in Tibetan as follows:

yod pa ma yin
med pa ma yin
yod med gnyis ka yin pa ma yin
yod med gnyis ka ma yin pa ma yin

In other renderings the negated fourth lemma may sometimes formulated as:

gnyis ka'i bdag nyid ma yin pa min[4]

But these kind of variants and others of that sort make no difference in our understanding at all.

Let's go back to the four lemmas implicit in this formulation, (1) *yod pa*, (2) *med pa*, (3) *yod med gnyis ka yin pa*, (4) *yod med gnyis ka ma yin pa*. While there *are* sometimes formulations of the tetralemma where the fourth lemma is clearer—for instance, what we find in *Mūlamadhyamakakārikā* 18.8: *naivātathyaṃ naiva tathyam* "neither not so nor so"—the very frequent formulations as *nobhaya* / (*yod med*) *gnyis ka ma yin pa* or (*yod med*) *gnyis ka'i bdag nyid ma yin pa* are, however, certainly *not* clear in this way and nor are their negations. Those formulations of the fourth lemma can, with some effort, be understood rightly as "neither . . . nor . . . ," but they are actually very often understood wrongly as "not both . . . and . . ." or "not of the nature of both . . . and . . ." Unfortunately the wrong understanding is a natural superficial reading of the Tibetan *gnyis ka ma yin pa* or *gnyis ka'i bdag nyid ma yin pa*. As we will see, the philosophical understanding of the negated fourth lemma went astray in Tibet because the surface-level meaning of those very words was not clear. We'll see in detail how this played out in a Tibetan debate on Madhyamaka between the Gelukpa (Dge lugs pa) and Sakyapa (Sa skya pa) writers, the former tradition being represented here by Tsongkhapa (Tsong kha pa, 1357–1419) and Khedrup Jé (Mkhas grub rje, 1385–1438), the latter primarily by Gorampa (Go rams pa, 1429–89).

Some of the ground for this paper had already been prepared by José Cabezón, who translated the relevant passages from Gorampa and Khedrup Jé that I will take up and kindly alerted me to an important Tibetan controversy concerning the law of double-negation elimination. There is a point, however, in running through the debate between Gorampa, Khedrup, et al. again, as I think that Cabezón in his two publications (1992, 2007) missed the fact that both Tibetans took the fourth *koṭi* as "not both" rather than "neither . . . nor . . . ," with the result that on Cabezón's interpretation, the logic of the arguments appears irredeemably bad.[5] I will maintain that the arguments were in keeping with perfectly good and comprehensible logic—there are no howlers—but that the problems were in the Tibetan exegesis of Indian texts. Both Gorampa and Khedrup Jé reasoned rightly and intelligently from the same wrong reading of an ambiguous Tibetan phrase *gnyis ka ma yin pa* (*ma yin*).

* * *

We turn now to Gorampa's *Lta ba'i shan 'byed*, where he criticizes Tsongkhapa's use of qualifiers like *don dam du* (ultimately) and *kun rdzob tu* (customarily) in the first two lemmas of the tetralemma. He takes as subject "the consciousness that is empty of object-subject duality" (*gzung 'dzin gnyis stong gi rnam par shes pa*), but he could have taken anything else. The point is generalizable. What is to be noted is that he clearly takes the fourth lemma (*gnyis ka ma yin pa*) in the sense of "not both . . . and . . ." rather than "neither . . . nor . . ." This is clear by his use of double-negation elimination to go from the negation of the fourth lemma to the affirmation of the third. Here is my translation of the relevant passage (ed. Cabezón and Dargyay 2007, 126 and 128):

> *gal te de'i don gzung 'dzin gnyis stong gi rnam par shes pa don dam du yod pa min / kun rdzob tu med pa min ces sogs la sbyar ba yin no snyam na / gzung 'dzin gnyis stong gi rnam shes chos can / don dam du yod pa dang kun rdzob tu med pa gnyis ka yin par thal / de gnyis ka min pa ma yin pa'i phyir /*
>
> *rtags gsal 'bru gnon gyi thog tu dgnos 'gal yin la / khyab pa dgag pa gnyis kyi(s) rnal ma go ba la dngos 'gal yin pas gangs ri'i khrod kyi dge sbyong thams cad 'di la lan gang 'debs bkar gros mdzod cig /*
>
> Suppose it is thought [by Tsongkhapa and his followers] that we have to construe [the lemmas] along the lines of "The consciousness that is empty of object-subject duality does not exist ultimately, is not nonexistent customarily, and so on and so forth." [We reply:] Then let the topic (*chos can*) be the consciousness that

> is empty of object-subject duality; it would follow absurdly that it would be both ultimately existent and customarily nonexistent, because it is not not both of them (*de gnyis ka min pa ma yin pa'i phyir*).
>
> Criticizing the details (*'bru gnon kyi thog tu*) of the reason (*rtags*) and the [absurd] consequence (*gsal*) would lead to direct contradictions (*dngos 'gal*) [with what you hold], and criticizing the details of the pervasion (*khyab pa*) would lead to a direct contradiction with the law of double-negation elimination (*dgag pa gnyis kyis rnal ma go ba*), [which you accept]. So do talk it over with all the monks of the Abode of the Snow Mountains as to what reply (*lan*) you could possibly give here!

Gorampa starts with Tsongkhapa's rendering of the tetralemma duly qualified and then deduces an absurdity—it would be both . . . —from the negation of the fourth lemma—it is not not both of them (*de gnyis ka min pa ma yin pa*). The negation of the fourth is invoked as the logical reason (*rtags*), and the absurdity "it would be both" is the consequence (*gsal ba*) of that reason. Negating the fourth lemma construed as "not-both" would entail formally that we must accept the third—"it is both . . . and . . ."—by the law of double-negation elimination. What is absurd in all this is that instead of negating all four, we've just arrived at the unacceptable result of affirming a contradiction.[6]

The last bit ("Criticizing the details . . .") is indeed complicated, as José Cabezón stressed, as it is formulated in the jargon of possible replies (*lan*) to logical reasonings, namely *rtags ma grub*, *gsal ba la 'dod*, *ma khyab / khyab pa ma byung*, "The reason is not established," "I accept the consequence," "The general principle/pervasion (*khyab pa = vyāpti*) is not right."[7] A follower of Tsongkhapa, in effect, cannot challenge the negation of the fourth by saying that the reason is not established (*rtags ma grub*), as that would contradict his position of negating all four lemmas of the tetralemma. Nor can he accept the absurd consequence (*gsal ba*) as actually true—that something is both ultimately existent and customarily nonexistent. In other words, he cannot say *'dod*, "I accept that this is so," for saying something *is* ultimately existent and customarily nonexistent runs counter to what he (and all Mādhyamikas) would maintain. Finally, Tsongkhapa cannot challenge the pervasion, saying *ma khyab*, "the general principle does not hold." If he did, this would run counter to his acceptance of the law of double-negation elimination. The opponent's being stymied in that way, with no reply, and thus having to give up his position is indeed the mark of such a reasoning's success, as we know from basic sources like *Yongs 'dzin bsdus grwa che ba*'s lesson on *prasaṅga* (consequences / *reductio ad absurdum*).

The other key technical term in this argument is *dgag pa gnyis kyis rnal ma go ba*, literally "understanding the main [proposition] by means of two negations" but less literally "the law of double-negation elimination." The term is found in early *Pramāṇaviniścaya* commentaries, such as that of Ngok Lotsāwa (Rngog lo tsā ba Blo ldan shes rab 1059–1109), and also figures regularly in Tsongkhapa's Madhyamaka texts, such as his commentary on the *Mūlamadhyamakakārikā*, his *Rtsa she ṭīk chen*. However, it is not an original Tibetan term. As Pascale Hugon showed me, it can be traced back to Indian Buddhist logic, and indeed its Sanskrit original *pratiṣedhadvayena prakṛtagamana* is found in the third chapter of Dharmakīrti's *Pramāṇaviniścaya*. We find an occurrence in the two *Pramāṇaviniścaya* Sanskrit manuscripts that she and Tōru Tomabechi have edited:[8] *pratiṣedhadvayena prakṛtagamanāt* (msA 64a2, msB 68a5), which is rendered in Tibetan *dgag pa gnyis kyi rnal ma go ba'i phyir ro* (D. 224b). Note that in some Tibetan texts, including the Sde dge Tripiṭaka passage just cited, *dgag pa gnyis* is followed by a genitive (*kyi*)—Cabezón's text is like that too. Nonetheless, there are several instances where it is followed by the instrumental, and given that we have the Sanskrit *pratiṣedhadvayena* = *dgag pa gnyis kyis*, we can be confident that the Tibetan instrumental (*kyis*) has to be the right reading. Most likely the genitive should be seen to be nothing but a banal scribal omission of the *sa* in the instrumental particle. The term *go ba* (= *gamana*) is often replaced with terms like *ston pa* (e.g., in Tsongkhapa's *Rtsa she ṭīk chen*, 43–44), but this too is of little consequence and can be disregarded for our purposes.

It should be noted that there are also Indian uses of the same or equivalent terms in non-Buddhist Indian texts—like Kumārila's *Ślokavārttika Nirālambanavāda* 125, which uses *pratiṣedhadvayāt vidhir eva*—as well as in Indian Madhyamaka texts such as Candrakīrti's *Prasannapadā* to *Mūlamadhyamakakārikā* 4.5ab and especially Bhāviveka's *Prajñāpradīpa* (D. 80a7) and Avalokitavrata's *Prajñāpradīpaṭīkā* (D. 180b3).[9] But although double-negation elimination does seem to be invoked on relatively rare occasions in those Indian Madhyamaka commentaries, it is not at all clear whether the Mādhyamika himself endorses it as a universally applicable logical law or whether he just uses it in certain situations as a rhetorical stratagem that is recognized by the opponent. In any case, in the context of the *Prajñāpradīpa*(*ṭīkā*) passages that use the term *dgag pa gnyis yod na skabs kyi don go ba* (≈ *pratiṣedhadvaye prakṛtārthagamana*), one gets the impression that the philosophical load it has to bear is not great. The talk of double negation by the Mādhyamika seems to be used incidentally to get fairly uncontroversial points across—for instance, to say to such and such a Sautrāntika that he is not not refuted (*mi gnod pa ma yin*) should make him understand that he in fact is refuted (*gnod pa kho na yin*)![10]

Nor do I know of any definitive, explicit, Indian sources where the Mādhyamikas themselves clearly *reject pratiṣedhadvayena prakṛtagamana* (or something like it) in cases of *prasajyapratiṣedha* (*med dgag*) "nonimplicative negation," and thus in the context of the middle way or tetralemma. In brief, if we just read the Indian Madhyamaka texts without Tibetan commentaries, it is textually underdetermined whether Madhyamaka does or does not accept double-negation elimination *across the board*, for while so-called implicative negation (*paryudāsa*) does seem to obey the law of double-negation elimination, it remains quite debatable whether the nonimplicative negations (*prasajyapratiṣedha*) used in the Indian tetralemma or in formulations of the middle way do actually obey that law.[11]

Be that as it may, Gorampa and Tsongkhapa alike *did* explicitly talk about double-negation elimination in Madhyamaka and particularly in connection with *prasajyapratiṣedha* and the tetralemma, and they had different views about it. Gorampa, in the *Lta ba'i shan 'byed*, for example, cites passages from Nāgārjuna as *his* Indian sources (although the passages are all rather inconclusive and can also be interpreted in keeping with a philosophy like that of Tsongkhapa). Certainly Gorampa *himself* strongly maintained that the Mādhyamika could not accept a law of double-negation elimination as applying to both sorts of negation. And I'm sure he would have a lot of sympathy among modern readers who, like Gorampa, see the *prasajya*-style negation of the tetralemma as a special operator that the Mādhyamika uses precisely *because* it is not subject to double-negation elimination and thus does not force one to affirm positive theses as following from iterated negations. That would arguably be a *good* philosophical reason for a Mādhyamika to reject double-negation elimination.[12] In the present context, however, Gorampa's reason seems to be far less good. He in effect says that the implication of lemma 3 can be blocked only *if* that logical law is not applicable. In short, Gorampa says we should block the move from *gnyis ka ma yin pa ma yin* to *gnyis ka yin pa* because Mādhyamikas shouldn't accept double-negation elimination! This is a *bad* reason, because it is based on a misunderstanding of the fourth lemma as "not both . . . and . . . ," so that its negation would be "not not both . . . and . . ." Not surprisingly, with that wrong understanding of the lemma, Gorampa was worried that an application of double elimination would lead to "both . . . and . . ."

On the other hand, Tsongkhapa, in works like his *Rtsa she ṭīk chen*, shows amply that he thinks the Mādhyamika does indeed accept a law of double-negation elimination, and even in connection with *prasajya*-negations. (That too, of course, is also how Gorampa interpreted Tsongkhapa.) He takes it as virtually self-evident that Mādhyamikas, indeed everyone, must accept double-negation elimination as a universal law. Probably not surprisingly, this attitude is what we see in other Geluk texts on logic, especially the *bsdus grwa* texts, which give the working logical theory for Geluk thought on pretty much all subjects, Madhyamaka or not. The *Bsdus grwa chung*'s lesson on "not being such and such" and "not-not being such and such" (*yin log min log gi rnam bzhag*) shows this acceptance of double-negation elimination explicitly: thus *bum pa ma yin pa ma yin pa, bum pa ma yin pa las log pa* ("it is not not a vase") imply *bum pa yin pa* ("it is a vase"), and *bum pa med pa ma yin* ("the vase is not nonexistent") implies *bum pa yod pa* ("the vase exists"). Indeed, the *Bsdus grwa chung* explicitly says that an even number (*cha*) of negations of *A* is equivalent to *A* and an odd number (*ya*) is equivalent to not-*A*.[13]

To go back to the debate at hand, it is clear that Gorampa was not the first person to argue that the negation of the fourth lemma would result in the acceptance of the third if one granted double-negation elimination. In fact, there were several others who embarked upon interesting and, ironically, even lucid philosophical discussions on the basis of a confused understanding of the fourth lemma. The question of what to do about the looming application of double-negation elimination to the fourth lemma was probably a well-known "problem." Let's be clear: it was actually a pseudo-problem stemming from a misreading of the ambiguous Tibetan, but many otherwise clear thinkers fell into the trap and discussed it intelligently with better and worse solutions.

The youngest of the two great disciples of Tsongkhapa, Khedrup Jé, in his *Stong thun chen mo* (Mkhas grub 1972, 103–4) had already felt the need to reply to some sort of real or hypothetical opponent (*kha cig*) who had "seen" the problem. The textual evidence thus suggests that debate existed well before Gorampa himself and that people had attempted solutions already in the fourteenth century or perhaps before. The *kha cig* ("someone") in question in *Stong thun chen mo* offered one such solution: he obviously accepted double-negation elimination but thought he could avoid having to accept the third lemma by putting in the qualifier "ultimately" (*don dam par*) everywhere in the tetralemma. Khedrup, in effect, criticizes the *kha cig* for putting the qualifier in the wrong place and thus not being able to avoid the absurd consequence of acceptance of the third lemma. He then, of course, puts it in what he takes to be the right place. Here is the passage retranslated:

> *kha cig don dam par yod pa'ang min / don dam par med pa'ang min / don dam par yod med gnyis ka'ang min / don dam par yod med gnyis min pa'ang min zhes smra ba la ni dgnos 'gal gyi nyes pa so na gnas te / don dam par gnyi ga min par smras pa'i rjes su don dam par gnyi ga min pa min zhes smras pas don dam par gnyis ga yin par smras pa'i phyir / de bas na yod pa yang bden par grub pa ma yin / med pa yang bden par grub pa ma yin / gnyis ga yin pa'i phung gsum bden par grub pa ma yin / gnyi ga ma yin pa'i phung gsum bden par grub pa min zhes bya ba'i don yin pas kho bo cag la rgud ci'ang med kyi mngon par mtho ba 'ba' zhig 'byung bar 'gyur ro //*

> When someone (*kha cig*) says, "Ultimately [things] don't exist, ultimately they aren't nonexistent, ultimately they are not both existent and nonexistent, and ultimately they are not not both existent and nonexistent either," then the fault of [asserting] a direct contradiction will remain. This is because after saying that ultimately [things] are not both, [the *kha cig*] then says that ultimately they are not not both, and so he says that ultimately they *are* both [existent and nonexistent]. Thus [we maintain that] the point is rather that [things'] existence is not really established, their nonexistence is not really established, a third alternative (*phung gsum*) consisting in them being both [existent and nonexistent] is not really established, and a third alternative[14] consisting in them being not both [existent and nonexistent] is not really established either. So therefore, there would be no quarrel with us whatsoever, and we'll go nowhere but up to higher states (*mngon par tho ba = abhyudaya*).

Here is our appraisal. Khedrup Jé is absolutely right in thinking that his *kha cig* does not manage to avoid embracing the third lemma, because "ultimately not not both *A* and *B*" would indeed imply "ultimately both *A* and *B*," in particular "ultimately both existent and nonexistent." Also, Khedrup Jé would be right in saying that his own rearrangement of the qualifier *does* work to avoid the problem, because "'Not both A and B' is not really established" does *not* imply "'Both A and B' is really established." In fact, the point of Khedrup's version of the tetralemma is that nothing is ever really established, whatever lemma you might take—a plausible interpretation of Madhyamaka. There would be no question of an unwanted absurd implication of lemma 3 by double-negation elimination. Finally, note that my translation of the *kha cig*'s position differs crucially from that of José Cabezón in that I put the negation within the scope of the operator "ultimately." Thus "ultimately it is not . . ." Cabezón, on the hand, had placed the negation outside the scope of "ultimately"—"it is not ultimately . . ." Philologically, I think one can go either way on that, but logically one way is better than the other, and logical coherence of the rest of the argument counts heavily in choosing a charitable interpretation. I think that a little reflection will show that on the above rendering of *don dam pa . . . min* as "ultimately it is not . . . ," Khedrup's argument against the *kha cig* makes good logical sense, but that if one interprets it as "it is not ultimately . . . ," then nothing that Khedrup claims to follow would actually follow at all.[15]

* * *

We can now step back a bit to see what Khedrup and Gorampa have in common and where they differ. There are three different propositions in question in both Khedrup's and Gorampa's argumentation. They are:

1. Madhyamaka philosophy demands that qualifiers should be systematically added to the tetralemma (in the right places).
2. Madhyamaka accepts the law of double-negation elimination.
3. Madhyamaka takes the fourth lemma as "not both . . . and . . ." (instead of "neither . . . nor . . .").

Khedruup in effect accepts all three. Gorampa rejects 1 and 2 and accepts 3.

Gorampa's positions as well as those of Khedrup on 1 and 2 are intelligent and defendable. They were, and still are, material for a genuinely important debate that has wide-ranging consequences for the interpretation of Nāgārjuna and his successors' thought. Note too that the philosophical interest of Tsongkhapa's, Khedrup's, and Gorampa's respective positions on 1 and 2 remains intact irrespective of what he thinks about proposition 3; 1 and 2 can certainly be discussed on the basis of other, more persuasive, sorts of considerations. Nonetheless, in the confused debate about the fourth lemma, both Khedrup and Gorampa, or more generally, both the major Geluk and Sakya interpretations on the tetralemma, *did* accept proposition 3. And 3 is a muddle. *It is a disastrously wrong exegesis of the fourth lemma.*

How did the muddle happen? It essentially came about because ordinary language, be it Sanskrit or Tibetan, is often insufficiently clear in representing complex distributions of logical connectives like "if . . . then," "not," "or," and "and"; confusion between "not both . . . and . . ." and "neither . . . nor . . ." is largely a linguistic problem rather than a problem due to illogicality or because Buddhists obey some sort of deviant theorems. Not surprisingly when you add a negation to *gnyis ka ma yin pa* and get *gnyis ka ma yin pa ma yin*, it looks superficially like a banal case of a sentence ripe for double-negation elimination: we would get *gnyis ka yin* (it is both) from *gnyis ka ma yin pa ma yin* (it is not not both) just like we get *bum pa yin* (it's a vase) from *bum pa ma yin pa ma yin* (it's not not a vase). This is just what the language suggests at first sight. Nonetheless, that language is misleading and betrays the logical issue, which is that the *nobhaya / gnyis ka ma yin pa* in the fourth lemma *should not be interpreted* as simply "not both . . . and . . ." but as "neither . . . nor . . ." Let's be blunt: much of this particular Sakya-Geluk debate about the third and fourth lemmas did not need to happen at all. It was a confusion where otherwise clear-thinking people tripped over language.

There are two morals to this complicated story, one historical and one methodological. The historical point is that, given the muddle involved, it is probably no wonder that many major Tibetan Mādhyamikas seem to have struggled with the third and fourth lemmas and even devoted considerably less attention to them—much, much less than to the first two lemmas. In Indian passages like Nāgārjuna's *Mūlamādhyamakakārikā* 18.8 and Āryadeva's *Catuḥśataka* 8.15 and 20, the tetralemma's propositions are taken in a hierarchical fashion, and the third and fourth lemmas are very important, as they are considered to be more subtly seductive than the first two (see Seyfort Ruegg 2010, 41–44). That hierarchical perspective, although it was developed significantly in the Chinese Sanlun school by Jizang (549–623) in his *Erdi zhang* and *Sanlun xuanyi* (see Chan 1973, 360ff; Liu 1993) is, as far as I can see, relatively little developed in Tibet. Alas, the fact that some of the more prominent Tibetan thinkers fundamentally did not *understand* the fourth lemma must have been a factor here, as it is hard to imagine how one could take lemma 4 as subtly tempting when one misunderstands it in the way that they did. The methodological moral is that this debate shows, if it ever needed to be shown again, how much ordinary language is often incapable of handling complex formal structures, be it ordinary Tibetan, English, or Sanskrit, and that a surface-level reading of "what the text plainly says," even when philologically/grammatically justifiable, can give a potentially misleading surface-level logic.[16] Nowadays, it is often said (not without some philosophical controversy) that one of the major breakthroughs in modern approaches to logic and language was Gottlob Frege's *Begriffschrift*, which enabled people to see that the apparent logical form—what one understands just from a surface reading—is often not the same as real logical form. The debate about the fourth lemma looks like a good example of what goes wrong when one mistakes the former for the latter.[17]

Notes to Chapter 7

1. Here are De Morgan's Laws in a more succinct form: NOT (*A* OR *B*) = (NOT *A*) AND (NOT *B*); NOT (*A* AND *B*) = (NOT *A*) OR (NOT *B*). In symbols: $\neg (A \vee B) = \neg A \,\&\, \neg B$; $\neg(A \,\&\, B) = \neg A \vee \neg B$. See Copi 1982, 315–16.
2. Text in Seyfort Ruegg 2010, 49.
3. For the basics of the Madhyamaka use of the tetralemma in its philosophy of emptiness (*śūnyavāda*), see Seyfort Ruegg 2010, chap. 3; see also Tillemans 1999, chap. 9.
4. See Mkhas grub, *Stong thun chen mo*, p. 86.
5. Cabezón consistently translates Gorampa and Khedrup's *gnyis ka min pa* as "neither . . . nor . . . ," which would certainly be right generally but it loses the point that Gorampa and Khedrup did not understand it that way. The result is that following Cabezón's version the argument is largely incomprehensible and seems to commit a series of howlers.
6. No Mādhyamika (and certainly not a modern dialetheist like Jay Garfield or Graham Priest) can accept that his negation of all four lemmas, and thus all four possible conceptualizations, would just result in the bald affirmation of number 3, a simple contradiction like being both existent and nonexistent. If there are true contradictions in Madhyamaka, that's not one of them nor the way to arrive at them. See Priest 2002 for his and Garfield's joint article on why a Mādhyamika *is* a dialetheist accepting some true contradictions "at the limits of thought"; see chapter 3 above (Tillemans 2009), which goes a certain distance in the same direction, although for quite different reasons.
7. Cf. however Cabezón and Dargyay 2007, 129: "Based on a careful reading (*'bru gnon gyi thog tu*) of this debate (*rtags sal*), [you will see that you are confronted with] a direct contradiction, and given as well that [to challenge] the pervasion [requires you to] directly contradict the principle of double negation (*dgag pa gnyis kyi rnal ma go ba*) [which you accept], please discuss with all of the monks of this Abode of Snow Mountains what response could be offered to this [predicament, even though it will be to no avail]."
8. Hugon and Tomabechi 2012.
9. My sincere thanks to an anonymous referee who very kindly pointed these sources out to me.
10. *Prajñāpradīpaṭīkā* D. 180b3–4: *de'i lan du 'dir 'grel byed pa nyid kyis mi gnod pa ma yin te zhes bya ba la sogs pa smras te / mdo sde pa na re sun 'byin pa de kho bo'i phyogs la mi gnod ces zer ba de mi gnod pa ma yin te / dgag pa gnyis yod na skabs kyi don go bar 'gyur bas 'di ltar de ni khyod kyi phyogs la gnod pa kho na yin no zhes bya ba'i tha tshig go.* "By way of a reply to this, the commentator here said 'It is not not refuted. . . .' The point is as follows: When the Sautrāntika says, 'The refutation does not refute our thesis,' then [the Buddhist] says that it does not not refute it. When there is a double negation, then the [positive] proposition in question is understood. Hence, in this way, that does in fact refute your thesis."
11. To put things in a slightly backhanded fashion, one point that comes out clearly in the Tibetan controversy between Gorampa and Tsongkhapa is that it shows that the Indian material was sufficiently ambiguous that diametrically opposite positions on double-negation elimination could be reasonably held by intelligent connoisseurs of the Indian texts.

12. There could be other reasons too for a modern Mādhyamika to reject double-negation elimination. In particular she might adopt an intuitionistic logic with its rejection of that law and that of the excluded middle. She might see such a logic as a consequence of a global antirealism taken in the manner of Michael Dummett: namely, the position that there are never any evidence-transcendent ascriptions of truth to statements. See chapter 11, p. 218n19.
13. We rely on the *bsdus grwa* of Yongs 'dzin Phur bu lcog (ed. Kelsang and Onoda).
14. *Phung gsum* (*phung* = Skt. *rāśi*) is used in Indo-Tibetan logical language in precisely the same way as *tertium* in Western discussions of theorems like excluded middle. The point of the discussion here is whether the third or fourth lemmas could be a *tertium*, a third alternative to either affirming "existence" or affirming "nonexistence."
15. Cf. the translation in Cabezón and Dargyay 2007, 310n185: "One individual claims that [the *catuṣkoṭi* requires a simple qualifier—'ultimately'—to each of the four elements, yielding this:] (1) things are not ultimately existent, (2) not ultimately nonexistent, (3) not ultimately both existent and nonexistent, and (4) not ultimately neither existent nor nonexistent. But this does not free this individual from the fault of direct contradiction, for having advocated that things are not ultimately both, by claiming that they are not* ultimately neither, one is [in fact] advocating that they *are* ultimately both." The reasoning in the last sentence would defy logic. Khedrup would be arguing that "by claiming that they are not ultimately neither, one is [in fact] advocating that they *are* ultimately both." The point is rather that by claiming that they are ultimately not not both, one would be saying that they are ultimately both. *Note that this "not" is omitted in Cabezón and Dargyay 2007 but figures in the translation in Cabezón 1992, 106. I have added it because it obviously needs to be there—the Tibetan has *don dam par gnyi ga min pa min zhes smras pas.*
16. This is certainly not the only such case in Indo-Tibetan writings on logical matters. See Tillemans 1999, 180–81.
17. One can, of course, say, as does Glashoff 2004, that it is a well-known fact that formal logic takes away many subtle features of ordinary language. Nonetheless, the minimum to say here is that in cases like the present one, ordinary language is *not* subtle; it is obscure.

Ethics and the Spiritual Path

8. Madhyamaka Buddhist Ethics

WHAT IS THIS elusive discipline called "Buddhist ethics?" As is often the case in modern interpretations and analyses, it is not easy to characterize exactly what a Western-inspired term corresponds to in traditional Indian culture, and sometimes it's not even clear how a particular term is being used in a burgeoning modern secondary literature on the subject. If we look at Indian and Tibetan literature, the closest term to the Western notion of "ethics" seems to be *śīla*, "moral discipline," something that is the subject of monastic Vinaya codes, Abhidharma scholastic, bodhisattva literature, Jātaka tales, narrative Avadāna literature, some Madhyamaka[1] treatises, even tantric texts, and so on and so forth—in short, pretty much everywhere. Modern scholars have devoted significant efforts to the question as to whether there is a recognizable Western ethical *theory*—be it utilitarianism or virtue ethics—that is implicit in all, or at least the most, significant works in this literature. This debate will not be my concern here, although, like Jay Garfield (2011), I too think it is difficult to meaningfully attribute such an overriding ethical *theory* to Buddhism. One danger is that we neglect the extreme diversity of the ethical codes advocated in Buddhist canonical literature and the quite different Buddhisms that we find there. The other danger is that the debate becomes largely focused on the philosophical merits of the proposed Western candidates for such an overarching theory. Indeed, I doubt that one could "see" utilitarianism or virtue ethics in Buddhism and "find" the relevant corroborating passages in the canon unless one were a convinced utilitarian or virtue ethicist oneself.[2]

Almost all Buddhist literature is certainly profoundly ethical in orientation, even if it is not clearly and consistently theoretically oriented. The *śīla* discussions do attempt to tell us what we ought to do and why—to take a very rough and ready characterization of what ethics is about (Thomson 2001, 6). The codes and advice and obligations involve a sense of "should/ought," one no doubt weaker than a Kantian duty but an ethical demand nonetheless. And *śīla* literature does often tell us why—that is, it gives justificatory reasons as to why one should think that such and such ethical demands are genuine and well founded and others are not. The Buddhists are not just moralizers; they give rationales for what they say ought to be done.[3]

Is there in any interesting sense a Madhyamaka Buddhist ethics, an ethics that would be particular to the Middle Way school and follow from or somehow be linked to its subtle analyses of metaphysics? In other words, do the Madhyamaka antirealist, or quietist, philosophies that all things are empty (*śūnya*) of intrinsic nature (*svabhāva*) make any difference to discussions about what people ought to do and why they ought to do it? In many respects Madhyamaka ethics is just general Mahāyānist Buddhist ethics, no more no less. A radical and purely text-based answer thus might be to say flatly, "No, there's no evidence in the texts that would suggest it makes any significant difference at all." One could point out that the position Nāgārjuna and other Indian authors seem to espouse is that typical canonical ethical distinctions remain thoroughly intact in Madhyamaka, though transposed from the level of ultimate (*paramārtha*) to customary (*saṃvṛti*) reality/truth (*satya*). The monastic rules, bodhisattva precepts, love, compassion, and the attention to the law of karma and its often-unfathomable consequences remain unchanged. In the autocommentary to Nāgārjuna's *Vigrahavyāvartanī*, verses 7–8, the opponent is depicted as arguing that without real moral intrinsic natures, the typical Abhidharma list of virtuous and nonvirtuous mental factors (*caitta*) could not exist, nor could there be any liberating (*nairyāṇika*) tropes (*dharma*) or any of the other factors needed for the path.[4] Nāgārjuna, in reply, doesn't contest anything *within* the classifications of what is virtuous, nonvirtuous, liberating, and binding. Instead he seeks to show that the whole Abhidharma-style list remains possible for a Mādhyamika providing it is suitably transposed to the proper level of truth. While he thus devoted very significant efforts toward showing that ethics would not be simply precluded *in toto* by a philosophy of emptiness (*śūnyavāda*), he did not seem to even entertain the idea that *some* important aspects of ethics or ethical reasoning would have to be affected or that some new ethical positions would be demanded.[5]

Often it is said that understanding Buddhist *ultimate* reality leads to one being convinced of the connectedness of all life and that it hence reinforces environmental ethics or universal responsibility; these are themes frequent in popular presentations. In fact this is *not* what I will focus upon for the simple reason that talk of connectedness and the transformative effect of realizations of the ultimate is found, in one form or another, in writings of many major Mahāyānist schools and is not linked exclusively, or even principally, to the Madhyamaka. Indeed, the school in which interconnectedness occupies the strongest place is the Avataṃsaka/Huayan, with its philosophy of the interpenetration of all things and the "unobstructedness between phenomena."[6] I would argue that the Indo-Tibetan Madhyamaka is probably less developed than the Avataṃsaka in this regard.

So leave aside talk of ultimate reality and an ethics of connectedness, important as it no doubt is. The potential changes I wish to take up stem from systemic tensions in Madhyamaka positions on *worldly* reality. I insist on "systemic" to emphasize that what is at stake is rational reconstruction of the system of Madhyamaka thought and not the discovery of some hitherto unknown textual data. (Not surprisingly, rational reconstructions are predominant nowadays in discussions of Buddhist ethics, and especially so when it comes to applied ethical issues, like contraception, responsibilities to future generations, environmental ethics, human rights, and so on that don't have clear textual discussions in canonical literature.)[7] The Mādhyamikas' *śūnyavāda* should, if carried through, have significant implications for their conceptions of what *worldly* reality is and on the epistemology that governs knowledge claims and justification on the level of worldly truths. For ethics, this means a break with certain types of *justificatory reasoning* that Buddhists use on the worldly, or customary (*saṃvṛti*), level.

In a chapter on ethics in a book on Indo-Tibetan Buddhist notions of customary truth, Bronwyn Finnigan and Koji Tanaka (2011) also examine justification in a Madhyamaka approach to ethics, arguing that in a thoroughgoing *śūnyavāda*, genuine justification becomes impossible; in its stead we supposedly only find a weaker type of reasoning to tell Buddhists why they should act and think in certain ways rather than others *as Buddhists*. Now, it is true that in the Madhyamaka and other schools there are many discussions that *are* little more than homiletics and that involve reasoning that would not stand up, or even be intelligible, outside the church. Such is often the case in Candrakīrti's first five chapters of *Madhyamakāvatāra* (cited by Finnigan and Tanaka); it is also what we find in the enormously complicated Svātantrika-Mādhyamika scholastic treatments of Prajñāpāramitā ethical schemata discussed in the Indian commentarial literature centered on the *Abhisamayālaṃkāra* or in the corresponding Tibetan literature. Nonetheless, not all Madhyamaka ethical reasoning is purely or even essentially destined for the already committed Buddhist—far from it. In texts like Bhāviveka's *Madhyamakahṛdaya*, we find direct polemical confrontations with non-Buddhists to show that their ethical pronouncements are wrong and unjustified and that the Buddhists' views alone are justified. There is also a recurring insistence, by Svātantrika-Mādhyamika authors aligned with Dharmakīrti's school, such as Śāntarakṣita and Kamalaśīla, that ethical argumentation should be accessible to an open-minded rational being who provisionally suspends religious commitment; this is the so-called "judicious person" (*prekṣāvat*), who represents an ideal figure in that she adopts positions, ethical and otherwise, purely on the basis of sound justificatory reasoning alone. It is thus incontestable that there *were* such rational strategies for justification in non-Madhyamaka and Madhyamaka Buddhist ethics alike. Mādhyamikas not only thought they were important but that they functioned unproblematically on the level of customary truth.[8]

Of course, one could still maintain that Indo-Tibetan Mādhyamikas were somehow badly wrong about this and that justificatory reasoning *is not* compatible with anything other than metaphysical realism of some form. But this, if right, would end up being the very strong claim that there is a fatal flaw in the numerous sorts of antirealism East and West, namely that such philosophies and ethical justification simply can't mix *a priori*. I don't see that *that* general position is established in Finnigan and Tanaka 2011 or elsewhere.

I think that Finnigan and Tanaka were certainly on the right track in focusing on issues of justification. Where I disagree with them, however, is in their position that the Mādhyamikas' antirealism constrains these thinkers to a type of ethics *without* justification. We'll leave aside the Svātantrika-Mādhyamikas, like Kamalaśīla et al., who clearly rely heavily on the robust justificatory reasoning of the Epistemological school (*pramāṇavāda*) transposed onto the domain of customary truth. The more interesting case is that of the Prāsaṅgika-Mādhyamika. Does Finnigan and Tanaka's position apply better here? Briefly: I don't think we end up with *no* justification; on the contrary, justification for a Prāsaṅgika can remain strong and not simply an affair of the church preaching to the faithful. Justification would, however, become significantly different from what it is generally in Buddhist ethics. This is because evaluation of actions largely in terms of their humanly unfathomable karmic consequences—which *is* traditionally an extremely important part of Buddhist ethical reasoning—becomes especially problematic for the Prāsaṅgika.

What problems does a Prāsaṅgika have with this that others don't? The Prāsaṅgika, more than other Buddhists, is caught between accepting that justification proceeds via the usual tallying of karmic consequences, on the one hand, and a fundamental methodological constraint, on the other, stemming from his views on customary truth. This methodological constraint is that customary truth and the reasoning based upon it must, in some sense, be in conformity with the world's ideas and intuitions. Prāsaṅgikas must remain largely in keeping with what the world acknowledges (*lokaprasiddha*) and should not propose wide-ranging corrections.[9] Let's look at the details. (I will rely on some previous publications giving a more detailed treatment of the Indo-Tibetan ideas and the textual data; the point here is to assess the implications for ethics.)

What an emphasis on conformity with the world and its ways of reasoning means for Buddhist ethics is, in effect, that the world's fundamental moral intuitions, epistemic practices, and norms are reinstated and legitimized as the grounds for justification.[10] And indeed Mādhyamikas do often try to justify fairly usual Buddhist ethical positions in this way. A good example of Prāsaṅgika ethical argumentation that proceeds in terms of the world's moral intuitions and that uses justificatory reasoning destined for the unconvinced is found in the first four chapters of the *Catuḥśataka* (CŚ).[11] In this text of the third-century Mādhyamika Āryadeva and in the *Catuḥśatakaṭīkā* (CŚṬ) of Candrakīrti (sixth century), we find an elaborate discussion of the four "illusions" (*viparyāsa*) that, according to canonical literature (i.e., Abhidharma), are supposedly present in the minds of worldlings: taking transitory life as permanent, what is painful as pleasurable, what is dirty as clean, and what is selfless as having a self. The argumentation follows a pattern. The authors try to show that the world's superficial attitudes on these matters are in conflict with its deep-seated intuitions—if the world reflected, it would recognize the four illusions as indeed illusions. Candrakīrti here, in effect, uses the methodology he uses everywhere else, a form of *prasaṅga* method using *reductio ad absurdum* and "opponent-accepted reasons" (*paraprasiddhahetu*), invoking principles that the world implicitly accepts and will recognize upon reflection.[12] Not only did Candrakīrti in the CŚṬ appeal to propositions that the world recognized, but he proposed an account of the *pramāṇas* (sources of knowledge) that stayed as close as possible to worldly epistemic practices; he deliberately rejected the prescriptive epistemology of the Dignāga school. Indeed in chapter 13 of the CŚṬ he ridiculed prescriptive epistemologists as being "completely unversed in mundane objects" and "intoxicated through imbibing the brew of dialectics" (Tillemans 1990, 177 and 179). The commitment to *lokaprasiddha* in all things epistemic and ethical is abundantly clear.

What difference would such a professed conformity with the world's moral intuitions and epistemic practices make to Buddhist ethics? It is obvious that Āryadeva and Candrakīrti *were* seeking to rationalize and conserve intact a canonical ethical schema and that they did not see their *prasaṅga* method nor their epistemology as in any way placing it in jeopardy. However, unlike the CŚ's discussion of the four illusions, which is largely argumentation about intuitions and does not involve controversial facts, much of Buddhist ethical argumentation *does* crucially rely on problematic facts, typically when actions are evaluated because of their total set of karmic consequences across several lives. While some karmic consequences will be accessible to ordinary reflecting individuals—for example, the general rule that he who lives by violence tends to die by it—many will be completely unfathomable by any ordinary human beings in that they are supposedly unobservable and not inferable from anything observable. These so-called radically inaccessible facts (*atyantaparokṣa*)—like the details of why one comes to have the particular destiny and rebirth one has—are thus supposedly only understandable through scriptures authored by individuals with extraordinary understanding (Tillemans 1999 and 2000). In later Indian and Tibetan Buddhism this extraordinary understanding is increasingly taken to be full omniscience: knowing everything about all.

But there would seem to be a serious problem for a Prāsaṅgika in accepting both *lokaprasiddha* and the usual Buddhist positions on karma. Metaphysical realists could claim that radically inaccessible facts about karma are known by omniscient minds, are as they are intrinsically, really, and irrespective of whatever people might think or whatever intuitions they might have; Prāsaṅgikas, who emphasize *lokaprasiddha*, would logically seem to have a harder time doing that, as such inaccessible things could not be understood by the world using their own epistemic procedures, and might well seem to be contrary to what worldly standards could endorse.

It probably comes as no surprise that Prāsaṅgikas thought that they had a way out. Indeed, although they professed *lokaprasiddha* across the board on customary matters, they certainly did not, for all that, abandon recourse to radically inaccessible facts about karma to justify ethical positions. Let's see how they thought they could do this and see whether it works. It is my contention that it does not work and that this failure, more than anything else, means that Mādhyamikas are in an especially vulnerable position if they wish to continue with much of traditional Buddhist karma-based ethics.

Buddhists, Mādhyamika or not, were certainly aware that persuading people by citing scriptures that weren't understood or believed in, or by invoking the idea that the Buddhists' teacher was a superior individual (*atiśayapuruṣa*) with supranormal understanding, were indeed highly problematic in the eyes of the world.[13] However, instead of simply siding with the world on this, Mādhyamikas sought an ingenious argumentation strategy whereby critical thinkers could supposedly come to accept scriptural propositions and accept that they be used as justificatory reasons in ethical debate. This Buddhist strategy goes back at least to Āryadeva, after which it is taken up by Dignāga (fifth century) and Dharmakīrti (seventh century); most modern Tibetan Buddhists continue to promote it as being a critical approach leading to rational proof of otherwise inaccessible facts; it is regularly espoused by the Fourteenth Dalai Lama. In brief, the procedure in the "triple analysis" (*dpyad pa gsum*) and "scripturally based inferences" (*āgamāśritānumāna*)[14] is that one first ascertains the truth of a scripture's pronouncements on all the observable matters (*pratyakṣa*) it treats as well as on those matters that are rationally accessible (even though unobservable); an immaculate record in these two categories allows one to infer the scripture's accuracy on otherwise completely unknowable matters like karma.

This method is indeed present in Āryadeva's *Catuḥśataka* 12.5, which tells us that when, in an ethical deliberation, there is doubt about the veracity of the Buddha's descriptions of completely obscure karmic consequences, we should be confident in his teachings about them because he was right in other areas, notably the teaching on emptiness.

> *buddhokteṣu parokṣeṣu jāyate yasya saṃśayaḥ / ihaiva pratyayas tena kartavyaḥ śūnyatāṃ prati //*

> When someone entertains doubt concerning the imperceptible things (*parokṣa*) taught by the Buddha, he should develop a [rationally founded] belief in these very things on account of emptiness (*śūnyatā*).

The point is that we supposedly can, with our own critical acumen, determine that the teachings on emptiness are an example (*dṛṣṭānta*) where the Buddha got the facts perfectly right. Therefore, because of his reliability on something essential like emptiness, it is also rational to believe his statements even when we cannot ourselves determine their truth. As Candrakīrti puts it in his *Ṭīkā* to *Catuḥśataka* 12.5:

> *na ca śakyam anena svalpam apy aniścayakāraṇaṃ kiṃcid abhidhātum iti siddha evāyaṃ dṛṣṭāntaḥ / tataś cānyad apy asamakṣārthapratipādakavacanaṃ bhagavato yathārtham iti pratīyatāṃ svanayenaiva tathāgatopadiṣṭatvāt svabhāvaśūnyatārthābhidhāyakavacanavad iti kuto buddhokteṣu parokṣeṣu saṃśayāvakāśaḥ /*

> Now the [adversary] cannot state even the slightest reason for any uncertainty, and thus this example [i.e., emptiness] is indeed proven. Therefore you should understand by means of your very own principles alone (*svanayenaiva*) that the other statements of the Illustrious One, which establish unobservable states of affairs,

> are also true, for they were taught by the Tathāgata, just as were the statements setting forth [that] state of affairs, the emptiness of intrinsic nature. How then could there be any place for doubt concerning the imperceptible things taught by the Buddha?[15]

In short, this (and the slightly more elaborate later idea of *āgamāśritānumāna*) is an appeal to the Buddha's track record in teaching. It's a justificatory argument that one finds in Prāsaṅgika-Mādhyamikas like Candrakīrti, who commented upon Āryadeva, as well as in Svātantrika-Mādhyamikas like Kamalaśīla and Śāntarakṣita, who relied on Dharmakīrti's method in *Pramāṇavārttika* (PV) 1 to prove unfathomable facts inferentially. What is striking for our purposes is that Candrakīrti says that the appeal to the Buddha's reliability proceeds "by means of your very own principles alone" (*svanayenaiva*). *It is clear that Candrakīrti wishes to say that this argument strategy is in conformity with the world and its own epistemic norms.* Candrakīrti, and perhaps Āryadeva, and certainly later Tibetan writers, thus thought that a Madhyamaka philosophy that took customary truth as "what is acknowledged by the world" (*lokaprasiddha*) could *also* engage in a method that stretched the world's acceptance to include propositions about humanly unfathomable karma.

Is Candrakīrti's idea somehow defensible? Do we actually conform to the world's own epistemic standards and practices if we invoke such track records to persuade the unconvinced and doubt-ridden on matters where there are not, and indeed supposedly cannot, be any other empirical evidence or rational arguments? I don't think so. First of all, it's implausible to claim that any major scripture will actually pass the test of getting all empirical and other humanly verifiable matters right. It might get some right, but not all, given that empirical knowledge changes and grows. True, Buddhist writers, like Dharmakīrti and probably Āryadeva and Candrakīrti too, recognized that what really counted was not a track record of 100-percent accuracy on every conceivable trivial matter treated in a scripture or treatise but accuracy on important or difficult principal topics, such as the four noble truths, emptiness, and the like.[16] But what kind of rationally founded belief (*pratyaya*) could one develop in this way? How would all doubts be eliminated, as Āryadeva and Candrakīrti say, by reminding oneself of the rightness of the Buddha's teaching on emptiness, for surely the mere fact of getting one very important thing right is not ipso facto a guarantee on anything else?

Dharmakīrti was quite skeptical about these "scripturally based inferences" and said clearly in his *Pramāṇavārttikasvavṛtti* to PV 1.217 that they weren't actually bona fide inferences at all—*na . . . anumānam anapāyam*—as they lacked certainty (*niścaya*). As he recognized, there are just too many counterexamples where a person is correct on one set of things, be they important or not, but falls down hopelessly on other things. (See, e.g., his *Svavṛtti* to 1.318: *na kvacid askhalita iti sarvaṃ tathā / vyabhicāradarśanāt*, "It is not the case that when one is unmistaken on something, all the rest is similarly [unmistaken], for we see that this [implication] is deviant.") Any observer of human foibles can come up with examples where people get significant things right and fall down on less significant and even comparatively easy matters.[17]

Now, the impression one might get in reading about these types of problems with scripturally based inference is that the issue is just the usual one of the fallibility of induction: we cannot arrive at certainty about the truth of generalizations on the basis of a finite number of confirmations. Indeed, the weakness of induction is a constant theme in Dharmakīrti. But if it were only a matter of the well-known failings of induction to generate certainty, one might also well reply, "So much the worse for Buddhist demands of certainty," and thus become a resigned or even cheerful fallibilist. In that case a fallibilist could say that demonstrated accuracy in certain important matters constitutes at least *reasonable grounds* for supposing accuracy in another *duly related* type of matter. After all, it is indeed so that we proceed by such transfers of credibility in many cases where someone's proven expertise in one set of matters serves as grounds (fallible though they may be) for trusting him or her in another closely related set. (One need only think of expert witnesses in court cases to see that this is indeed common practice.) A suitably fallibilist Candrakīrti would then at least be right in saying that *this* is in keeping with the world's epistemic standards.

The problem with scriptural inference, however, is *not* simply the ever-present uncertainty one finds in inductive reasoning. And so merely embracing fallibilism is not the remedy either. The real catch in transferring credibility from one area to another, if we wish to conform to the world's own norms, is that there must be a type of connection or relevant similarity between the different areas so that the expertise is transferable in a reasonable, albeit fallible, fashion. We are all too familiar with people who are highly qualified in one area—say, economics—who then *think* they can expound on virtually everything else, related or not—say, French literature—and usually with disastrous results. We would say that those would-be experts become unreliable, not because they hadn't at some point understood a lot of significant things rightly or because of some general problem about induction, but because they overstep their qualifications. They take on subjects not clearly related to the area in which they have been recognized to be reliable. The flaw in a fallible appeal to the Buddha's track record is similar: it is not at all clear that reliability concerning important general principles like emptiness *does* reasonably transfer to explanations concerning the details of karma in all their specificity and complexity, because the relationship is not clear. While emptiness of intrinsic nature, as a general principle, may be closely linked with the *general* feature that phenomena arise dependently due to causes and conditions—as Buddhists from Nāgārjuna on have stressed[18]—knowing that much would hardly suggest that one somehow knows the *specific* details of what causes what.

While Āryadeva and Candrakīrti seem to have thought that scriptural inferences were an unproblematic way for Buddhists to argue with any opponents, Buddhist or not, in that such inferences were just another case of the world's extending credence to people on the basis of their past performances, Dharmakīrti's position was no doubt much more nuanced. Dharmakīrti, in *Pramāṇavārttika* 1 and 4, maintained that this type of faith-based reasoning about the specifics of karma would *not* be persuasive to nonbelievers; not only is the reasoning extremely uncertain, but many opponents would simply refuse to recognize its subject matter (*dharmin*), Buddhist accounts of the details of karmic causality. Nonetheless, Dharmakīrti's view was that scriptural inferences, even if they weren't fully bona fide, were still somehow to be used, at least in the "private" context of Buddhists who wished to set out (*pravṛttikāma*) on the spiritual path. While scripture may provide direction (albeit very fallible) in a closed context of believers, it is not at all a proof (*sādhana*) in a public context when appeals to authority are contested. On the one hand, Dharmakīrti would steer clear of outright denial of karma—which no sixth–seventh-century scholastic Buddhist writer could just flatly deny—but on the other hand he knows that he cannot and should not use scriptural descriptions of karmic consequences to clinch debates in the public domain, where rebirth and the causality between lives are either contested issues or too obscure to be admitted in "fact-based" (*vastubalapravṛtta*) debates.

I think that some such distinction between private and public is indeed implicit in his position. But would such a public-private distinction be acceptable in ethical debate? What are the consequences of this move? If we take another type of subject matter, the nature of mind, there is a great difference between a discussion in a private domain, among convinced Buddhists, that cites sūtra or tantra passages on the luminous nature of mind, the subtle consciousness, and so forth and such a discussion in the public domain where the other party is a well-meaning, but non-Buddhist, cognitive scientist working in a secular university. To mix up the private and public domains and say that Buddhist scriptural quotations about otherwise inaccessible features of mind should also be probative for the cognitive scientist would be seen as a violation of norms of rationality. And if one then goes from bad to worse and persists in somehow saying that the scripture is in any case right because it is the words of the Buddha and so on, this would be seen as not far from fundamentalism.

Now, instead of cognitive science, let's take an example of an ethical argument on a contested issue in applied ethics: animal welfare and vegetarianism. People on both sides can and will invoke considerations that are publicly debatable: harm to animals, ecological consequences, health benefits of eating meat or not eating meat, suffering, perhaps rights of animals, speciesism, and so forth. This is recognizably normal argumentation on such an issue. Things are much different when someone seeks to prove their case by a scriptural quote concerning the unfathomable karmic consequences of eating meat! For example, a Buddhist vegetarian may invoke passages from the *Laṅkāvatārasūtra* to the effect that a meat eater will be reborn as a carnivore, or alternatively a meat-eating Tibetan Buddhist might reply to a vegetarian opponent by invoking a (tantric?) teaching that the meat eater will establish a "karmic connection" with the animal whose flesh he eats and will in a future life lead the being to enlightenment, and so on and so forth. Perhaps such ways of thinking would still somehow be meaningful in the private context of committed Buddhist exegetes wondering what their scriptures advise. However, they would certainly become deeply suspect if they left the purely private context of intra-Buddhist exegesis.

Clearly there are huge philosophical problems about holding *any* dual perspectives, be they in philosophy of mind or on ethical and religious issues.[19] Dharmakīrti, if I read him rightly, thought that at least in ethics a purely intra-Buddhist position on key matters, like karma, while publicly unarguable and unable to lead an unbeliever to conviction, could be more than simple irrationality and that it could have a pragmatic (rather than "factual"/"objective") type of justification for ordinary beings embarking upon the Buddhist spiritual path.[20] He seems to have thought that belief in karma would be objectively justified by the perception of yogins and omniscient beings but not by ordinary unrealized people with their cognitive limitations who, short of any better options, were thus forced to rely on pragmatic reasoning.

We don't need to enter into the complex arguments Indo-Tibetan writers used to prove omniscience. The important point for us is that a purely intra-Buddhist private perspective, whether it involves acceptance of scriptural descriptions of karma or appeals to what only yogins or omniscient beings know, should not figure in a normal adversarial debate on ethics between ordinary people. Āryadeva and Candrakīrti thought such a perspective could figure in such public debates, and Buddhists often do appeal to it, but their arguments for the legitimacy of this move—or the idea that in any case it is nothing special, and that people make it frequently in various walks of life—are, as I have tried to show, riddled with problems. It is much more likely that, if we followed the world's norms, switching to a private, intra-Buddhist perspective would be seen as an illegitimate shift, an attempt to promote certain Buddhist ethical ideas in the public domain all the while insulating them from criticism by stressing people's epistemic incompetence.

Recently the philosopher Owen Flanagan (2006), in a lecture on Buddhism and science, confronted much the same problem where Buddhists priced problematic subjects outside critical debate: he coined the term "epistemological protectionism." (This may capture the problem better than the accusations of dogmatism that are sometimes bandied about). Such a protectionist approach would claim that one could cite reasons—scriptural passages, for example—to provide proof in a public debate but at the same time preserve them from criticism by making them unassailable. I think it is clear that in a critical approach to ethics, appeals to humanly unfathomable facts are also protectionist in this way. They too fail to conform to what the world, on reflection, values and demands in debate on contested issues—namely, that the discussion must be open for both parties to criticize and evaluate on the basis of publicly accessible information.

A few remarks on omniscience as it pertains to the Mādhyamika. Once one puts into question the Mādhyamika's use of scriptural inferences to give knowledge of unfathomable karmic consequences, his appeal to the omniscience of the Buddha is also going to be in considerable trouble. In both cases one is placing much ethical debate outside the realm of criticism. However, there are also other reasons as to why a Mādhyamika should feel particularly uncomfortable in invoking a literal notion of omniscience to clinch an ethical debate. The problem arises that if the Buddha supposedly has knowledge of all things in all their details, including the unfathomable effects of karma, this looks to be tantamount to him understanding how things are in themselves, by their own intrinsic nature (*svabhāvena*). And that would be precluded by a Mādhyamika's thoroughgoing rejection of *svabhāva*—realist Buddhist schools might have some way to accept it, but it seems that the Mādhyamika would be in an especially delicate position. Literal omniscience seems in effect to be a "God's-eye point of view of the world," a view *sub specie aeternitatis*, and that is one way to formulate what an antirealism, East or West, holds to be impossible.[21]

Of course, the subject of omniscience and the many different views that

Buddhists have had about it historically are matters upon which I cannot reasonably embark here. In later Indian Buddhism and in its Tibetan successors we find, in one way or another, several versions as to what full-fledged omniscience is, and some versions would be closer to a crypto-realism than others. (There has also been, over time, an evolution from a limited conception of omniscience where an omniscient being supposedly knows one or a few essential things about everything, to a much stronger type of knowledge of knowing everything there is to know.)[22] For our purposes we'll contrast two quite remarkably different versions of that full-fledged omniscience. If we take, for example, a conception such as that of the fourteenth-century Tibetan writer Longchen Rabjampa (Klong chen rab 'byams pa), who distinguishes between "dualistic mind" (*sems*) and "primordial gnosis" (*ye shes*) or "mind itself" (*sems nyid*), omniscience is taken as primordial gnosis / mind itself rather than "dualistic mind"—dualistic mind is in fact something to be eliminated.[23] Omniscience for Longchenpa, like primordial gnosis, is a special type of understanding free from all objects (*yul*). In such a case, there seems to be no question of an omniscient being knowing each and every thing in all its details—that would *per impossibile* be a sort of dualistic mind (*sems*). Gnosis/omniscience is a type of transcendent understanding in which the very idea of a thing/object is absent. One knows everything in that there is nothing that remains unknown. This is not just a later Tibetan point of view; it is a standpoint that finds significant confirmation in Indian sūtra literature.[24] On the other hand, if we take omniscience as it seems to be understood by many Indian commentators or by Tibetan Mādhyamika writers such as Tsongkhapa (Tsong kha pa), it does seem to involve essentially an amplification *ad infinitum* of cognition of objects to arrive at all of them in all their details. It is this latter, more literal, version that might seem to run thoroughly afoul of *śūnyavāda* in demanding a "God's-eye view," where a buddha would know every detail of every existent thing as it is.

It is time to conclude. Where does this critique of the Mādhyamika appeals to track records and omniscience leave us? I think we have to admit that Prāsaṅgikas attempted the impossible in professing *lokaprasiddha* all the while trying to recuperate unfathomable karma in ways that the world itself would supposedly accept. My argument so far has been that this is not likely to work and that some hard choices therefore have to be made. Now, one of the more attractive features of Buddhism is, and has been for a long time, its openness to discussion and its emphasis on reason. We see this strongly in the present Dalai Lama's commitment to dialogue based on empirical methods and rationality—what Owen Flanagan (2006) called a "welcome mat" to open, public, debate.[25] What I think needs to be offered in ethics, in largely the same constructive spirit as that of Flanagan's article on science, is a sober note: this welcome mat will attract few long-term visitors if contemporary Buddhists, Mādhyamikas included, continue to justify their ethical views on the basis of obscure facts knowable only via a scripture whose author had omniscient knowledge.

What then would *śūnyavādin* Buddhist ethics look like without such a heavy reliance on radically inaccessible facts and God's-eye omniscience? I think a partial answer is something like the following: if moral intuitions and personal attitudes become more dominant in ethical debate, rather than scripture and omniscience, ethics becomes humanized and to quite a degree secularized; the extended welcome mat will be genuinely attractive. The present Dalai Lama has indeed regularly called for a secular ethics.[26] It is unclear to me whether he himself sees this secular ethics as necessitating significant change in Buddhist ethics and how much he is willing to do without his tradition's appeals to karma and humanly inaccessible facts in ethical argumentation. In any case, the conservative tendency in Buddhist ethical thinking, which strongly emphasizes those same karmic aspects of ethics accessible only to the church, will understandably be seen by nonbelievers as a purely religious approach, one that closes the door to rational discussion. The important feature of the Madhyamaka is that it, more than any other school, insists on the primacy of what the world acknowledges rather than on humanly unfathomable facts that are as they are for all time. This, if carried through, would be a significant move toward the humanization of ethics and away from appeals to karma and omniscience.

Notes to Chapter 8

1. In what follows, for convenience rather than conviction, I adopt the modern convention of using "Madhyamaka" for the thought and "Mādhyamika" for the thinkers. See introduction, note 1.
2. For a recent vigorous defense of Buddhist ethics as utilitarianism, see C. Goodman 2009. Keown (2001) has argued for Buddhism as virtue ethics. For my reservations on both, and on all such attempts at finding an overarching Western ethical theory present in Buddhism, Buddhist texts, Buddhist moral intuitions, and so on, see chapter 9, section IV.
3. "That 'why' is important: moralizers are happy to tell you what you ought to do—moral philosophers differ in that they aim to tell you also what makes it the case that you ought to do the things they say you ought to do" (Thomson 2001, 6).

4. I would argue that mainstream Indian Buddhism is best understood as holding what is known in analytic philosophy as a *trope theory*. Charles Goodman and others have made a persuasive case that the elements of reality—the *dharmas*, for Ābhidhārmika Buddhists—are indeed tropes. They are properties that are abstract simples but are particulars rather than universals—a blueness, a heat, or a hardness specific to one place-time and not common to several. On tropes and the varieties of trope theories, see the entry by Anna-Sofia Maurin in the *Stanford Encyclopedia of Philosophy*—http://plato.stanford.edu/entries/tropes/. C. Goodman 2004 develops a trope theory of the *dharma* in the *Abhidharmakośa*. See also Ganeri 2001, 101–2. Trope theories seem applicable in the case of Dharmakīrti and Dignāga too; see Tillemans 2011b, section 1.4. Note that analytic philosophers often characterize tropes as dependent phenomenal entities and perceptible; some trope theorists take them as powers.
5. As Jan Westerhoff (2009, 209) succinctly put it: "[Analyses] dealing with the specific ethical consequences of Madhyamaka thought are virtually absent."
6. The literature is amazingly vast. See, e.g., H. Kim 2013.
7. Rational reconstruction seems to be what, for example, Keown 2005 is doing in taking up Buddhist positions on issues such as cloning and others that medieval Indian Buddhists certainly were not aware of. Another striking example: investment guidelines for ethical investing by Buddhists in the stock market. The result of the deliberations of Gombrich et al. 2007 is what you find in the Dow Jones Dharma Index.
8. The debate about the possibility or impossibility of justification and its compatibility with śūnyavāda is certainly not a new one, and the Madhyamaka answers follow Nāgārjuna's well-worn strategy of arguing that ethical reasoning functions on the level of the customary. See Nāgārjuna's replies to the objections in *Vigrahavyāvartanī* 7–8.
9. I have taken up the idea of *lokaprasiddha* and its problems of interpretation in chapter 2. There are obviously better and worse exegeses, the worst being that truth simply is equated with what the majority of people in the world believe to be true.
10. On the tension between moral theory and intuitions, see McMahan 2000.
11. Translated and studied in Lang 2003, Sanskrit fragments in Suzuki 1994.
12. To résumé the critique in the *Catuḥśataka* (CŚ) and *Catuḥśatakaṭīkā* concerning the illusions (*viparyāsa*): the ordinary person's confidence about the future is based on self-deception about his mortality (CŚ 1.6–7); worldlings' attitudes to mourning are inconsistent (*'gal ba = viruddha*) so that they mourn what on reflection does not deserve it (CŚ 1.13); pleasure and happiness are rare, contrary to widespread opinion; upon reflection we see it is actually pain that is prevalent (CŚ 2.4); people might think that work is a source of happiness, but it is better seen as largely meaningless and slavish exertion to survive (CŚ 2.18); attitudes about beauty and cleanliness are confused and would be seen to be wrong if we reflected upon them (CŚ 3.3–5); possessiveness makes no sense (CŚ 3.11); kings (and other so-called "superior individuals") are more like social parasites, dependent upon others' work—they have no reason to feel justified of their status (CŚ 4.2); a king who is violent, corrupt, or cruel deserves to be denounced, even though he claims to provide protection or to be the "father of the people" (CŚ 4.11–13), and so on and so on.
13. For example, Dharmakīrti in PV 1.218 says that we would accept what such a superior person says "if we could know that he is superior" (*śakyeta jñātuṃ so 'tiśaya yadi*),

the point being that short of us having clairvoyance, we simply can't know who has such extraordinary knowledge and who does not.

14. On the so-called "triple analysis" (*dpyad pa gsum*) and "scripturally based inferences," see chapters 1 and 2 in Tillemans 1999; see also the introduction to Tillemans 1993 and Krasser 2013. Unfortunately there seems to be a misunderstanding here in that Krasser took my position as being that scriptural inference is somehow "hypothetical." This seems to be a misreading of a sentence in Tillemans 1999, 37, where I say "This interpretation of Dharmakīrti's account of scripturally based inferences (*āgamāśritānumāna*), which we shall term for short 'inference-like-any-other,' is not just a hypothetical possibility." My point was that seeing scriptural inference as being as probative as any other kind of inference *is not* a hypothetical possibility. Many people actually held this very position on the matter (ibid.): "Indeed, with a few minor differences, the idea of scriptural inference as being just one amongst three kinds of inferences, but as full-fledged as the others, is the way Dharmakīrti has been interpreted by many, who have in one way or another taken Dharmakīrti's account of scripture to be a surprisingly rational approach to subjects which, otherwise, would be unknowable to us."
15. Translation and text in Tillemans 1990, 1: 120 and 2: 17–19.
16. See PV 1.217: "Because he is reliable on the principal matters, we can infer [reliability] on the others" (*pradhānārthāvisaṃvādād anumānaṃ paratra*). For Dharmakīrti and his commentators, the principal matter is the four noble truths. It is striking that Āryadeva and Candrakīrti speak of the significance of getting emptiness right; it seems clear that the Mādhyamika in CŚ 12.5 is using a reasoning very similar to PV 1.217 but that the principal matter is indeed emptiness.
17. To update things a bit: the math department may be brilliant on the significant theoretical aspects of topology but unable to add up their phone bill correctly.
18. See *Mūlamadhyamakakārikā* 24.18ab: *yaḥ pratītyasamutpādaḥ śūnyatāṃ tāṃ pracakṣmahe*, "Dependent arising, that we declare to be emptiness."
19. Of course, many intelligent, scientifically minded people do hold private ideas—e.g., on medicinal remedies, on ways to ensure good luck, on CIA conspiracies, etc.—ideas that they often probably know to be unacceptable in a public discussion with their peers. Such types of dual perspectives, however, are *not* of much interest to us here, as they can be dismissed as irrational. Perhaps a Buddhist could avoid a charge of simple irrationality by saying that the intra-Buddhist consensus on karma is actually a faithful acceptance of a "white lie," a tale that the sophisticated among them know to be false but propagate to less intelligent disciples for pedagogical reasons. I should think that this would yield a more radical undercutting of karma than Dharmakīrti could easily allow, as for him karma is an objective fact, even if inaccessible to ordinary beings. On Dharmakīrti's own white lies, see Patil 2007; McCrea and Patil 2006 on the interpretation of even apoha as a white lie.
20. See Tillemans 1999, 45–46.
21. The characterization of metaphysical realism as involving the God's-eye perspective is due to Hilary Putnam (see, e.g., Putnam 1981, chapter 3).
22. See McClintock 2010.
23. Cf. Klong chen pa, *Sems dang ye shes kyi 'dri lan* (*gSung thor bu*), p. 384: *mdor bsdu na khams gsum pa'i sems byung cha dang bcas pa thog ma med pa nas brgyud pa'i bag chags can sgrib pa gnyis kyi ngo bo 'dzin cing / bskyed par brten pas spang bya yin zhing dgag*

dgos par bshad pa yin no /. "In short, the three realms' dualistic minds (*sems* = *citta*), mental factors (*sems byung* = *caitta*), and their qualities are subject to imprints coming down from beginningless [time], have as nature the two obscurations, and rely on production. As such, it is explained that they are to be eliminated and should be stopped."

24. See, e.g., the *Pañcapāramitānirdeśasūtra* D. 7a–b: *tshe dang ldan pa gang po byang chub sems dpa' sems dpa' chen po bla na med pa yang dag par rdzogs pa'i byang chub mngon par rdzogs par sangs rgyas nas rnam pa thams can mkhyen pa nyid kyi ye shes kyis gzigs te / 'di skad du nang gi'am/ phyi rol gyi'am / gzugs yod pa'am / gzugs med pa yang rung ste / gang bdag gis yongs su ma btang ba'am / ma byin pa'am / mchod sbyin ma byas pa'i chos de yang dag par rjes su mi mthong ste / gang gi phyir bdag gis dngos po de yang dag par rjes su mi mthon ba de'i phyir bdag bla na med pa yang dag par rdzogs pa'i byang chub mngon par rdzogs par sangs rgyas nas / gang bdag gis mngon par rdzogs par sangs ma rgyas pa'am / yongs su ma shes pa'i chos de yang dag par rjes su mi mthong ngo // ji ltar chos de yang dag par rjes su mi mthong ba de ltar bdag bla na med pa yang dag par rdzogs pa'i byang chub mngon par rdzogs par sangs rgyas nas chos thams cad la pha rol tu phyin pa dam pa thob ste / gang bdag gis mngon par rdzogs par sangs ma rgyas pa'am / yong su ma shes pa de ci yang med do // ji ltar gang bdag gis yongs su ma btang ba'am / ma byin pa de ci yang med pa de ltar bdag gis chos gang mngon par rdzogs par sangs ma rgyas pa'am / yongs su ma shes pa'i chos de yang dag par rjes su mi mthong ngo zhes seng ge'i sgra sgrog go //*. "Venerable Pūrṇa, when bodhisattva-mahāsattvas have awakened to unsurpassed perfect enlightenment, they understand [all things] with their omniscient gnosis. Thus they let out a lion's roar, proclaiming, 'I do not see any object whether internal or external, whether material or immaterial, that I have not relinquished, given away, or offered. Because I do not see any such phenomenon, I have awakened to unsurpassed perfect enlightenment, [7b] and now I do not see any phenomena that I do not fully comprehend or that I do not understand. Just as I do not see any such phenomena, so have I awakened to unexcelled and perfect buddhahood and obtained sacred perfection in all phenomena. Now there is nothing whatsoever that I do fully comprehend or that I do not understand. Just as there is nothing whatsoever that I have not relinquished or given away, so also do I not see any phenomena that I do not fully comprehend or that I do not understand."

25. Here is how Flanagan 2006 reformulated the Dalai Lama's invitation to dialogue. "The *Welcome Mat*: 'Come sit by my side, my Western scientific and philosopher friends. Tell me what you know. I will teach you what I know. We can debate. But in the end it is our duty, on both sides, to change our previous views if we learn from the other that what we believe is unfounded or false.'"

26. See, e.g., http://www.dalailama.com/news/post/1012-talking-about-secular-ethics-and-continuing-the-guide-to-the-bodhisattvas-way-of-life (accessed on Nov 26, 2013).

9. Reason, Irrationality, and Akrasia (Weakness of the Will) in Buddhism: Reflections upon Śāntideva's Arguments with Himself

What do we mean by rationality? We often tend to reach for a characterization in formal terms. Rationality can be seen as logical consistency, for instance. We can call someone irrational who affirms both *p* and not-*p*. By extension, someone who acts flagrantly in violation of his own interests, or of his own avowed objectives, can be considered irrational. (Charles Taylor, "Rationality")[1]

What is special in incontinence is that the actor cannot understand himself: he recognizes, in his own intentional behavior, something essentially surd. (Donald Davidson, "How Is Weakness of the Will Possible?")[2]

Why do I do the things that make me sorry? (Lyle Lovett, "Who Loves You Better than I?")

I. Irrationality and Akrasia

ONE OF THE WAYS to understand positions better on the nature and scope of reason is to look at the role, if any, they accord to irrationality in human thought and action. In the case of Buddhism, it is obvious that there is a great deal in the philosophical, doctrinal, and ethical literature that testifies to highly developed norms of rationality. We regularly find scholastic authors of various Buddhist schools advocating the strict exclusion of contradiction as a canon of right reason: contradiction is said to be a *doṣa*, a fault in thought or speech, and a *nigrahasthāna*, a point of defeat in a debate. Let us speak of a kind of "standard conception of rationality"[3] that is widespread in Buddhism, especially in its later Indo-Tibetan varieties heavily influenced by the Buddhist logical literature, but is also frequently presented in Western sources as a kind of rudimentary intuitive account of what it is to be rational. (It is what I have given above in the quotation from Charles Taylor.) Buddhists sometimes formulate this standard conception in very strong terms: in a famous passage in the *Prasannapadā*, the sixth-century Indian author Candrakīrti says that when an opponent worthy to debate with (≈ rational) has been persuaded that his own position is riddled with contradictions, he *will* give it up. Someone who does not do so is said to be *unmattaka*, "out of his mind," "demented," and hence not worth arguing with.[4] On this "standard conception" then, at least a necessary condition for people to be rational is that they strive to be consistent; thus acquiescence in—or worse, willing espousal of—inconsistency will accordingly be considered to be irrational.

Now in Western thought, there is an old conundrum that is often linked to the problem of irrationality: this is the philosophical problem, originating in Plato's *Protagoras* and in Aristotle's *Nicomachean Ethics*, of *akrasia*: weakness of the will, incontinence, the fact that people often seem to act intentionally contrary to what they also think or know to be best. In its Aristotelian presentation, akrasia is depicted essentially as a clash between reason and the emotions (*pathos*) either due to impetuosity (*propeteia*) or weakness (*astheneia*). It is the latter that primarily interests us here: contrary to the impetuous person who just acts, the weak goes through a process of deliberation to make a choice and thus is in an internal conflict. Potential examples of such weakness of the will are familiar to all and abound, from giving in to anger that one knows to be senseless to going on and on in seamy relationships while having only deep pessimism about the probable outcomes. And there are interesting philosophical consequences if such weakness is acknowledged: many socioeconomic or ethical theories, including some popular Buddhist teachings on ethics (see, e.g., Ricard 2006) take it as more or less a given that people act in a way that they are convinced will further happiness and diminish pain, be it their own or that of others: if akrasia is to be taken into account seriously, pursuit of maximal utility will be at most an idealized or simplified model, one that may well be false in describing the actual complex features of people's behavior.[5]

Finally, akratic behavior is often taken as having an epistemic counterpart too: we can know that such and such a view is wrong or false but nonetheless somehow believe in it as if we thought it true (see, e.g., Hookway 2001). Wishful thinking is an easy example; various sophisticated and seductive self-deceptions are more interesting potential cases of an epistemic version of akrasia. The problem is not just treated in works of philosophy or ethics: certain great works of literature, like Gustave Flaubert's *Madame Bovary*, explore such forms of self-deception;[6] most of the famous case studies of *mauvaise foi* that Jean-Paul Sartre so penetratingly analyzed in *Being and Nothingness* are also arguably types of akrasia. In short, an akrates is convinced that *p* is best and yet acts as if he *in some sense* believes in *not-p*; he strongly thinks that *p* is true and yet also *somehow* accepts *not-p*. Akrasia is thus often seen as a type of irrationality, or dangerously close to irrationality, given the standard conception of a rational person not acquiescing in, knowingly accepting, or promoting inconsistency.

Do Buddhists recognize any important role for akrasia in their account of how average, sane people think and act? Let us from here on put the moral and epistemic together and just speak of the problem of akrasia taken in both fashions. Of course, Buddhists do recognize that people act and think in ways that they *later* realize to be wrong, or even hopelessly incoherent—indeed this is a sad fact of life that virtually everyone is forced to admit. But do they recognize that people act and think akratically, believing things and acting in certain fashions while *at the same time* in some sense aware of being inconsistent with their own better judgment and intentionally pursuing *worse* courses of action? Let's be clear from the start: weakness of the will, in this discussion, is not just a matter of the will, as if thinking and reasons played no role. A full-fledged akrates might very well act for some seemingly powerful reasons and yet also judge that, all things considered, those reasons should not carry the day for her. The point is that, nonetheless, she would still do the *worse*. That is the philosophically interesting kind of akrasia that touches on issues of rationality.[7]

Issues of self-deception and epistemic akrasia have been taken up in connection with Chinese, Japanese, and Indian thinkers by Roger Ames, Elliot Deutsch, and others; Richard Hayes has also seen the interest of the problem in Buddhism, all the while acknowledging, as I do, that there is no treatment of it as an *explicitly* formulated philosophical theme in classical Buddhist writings.[8] My starting point and the work to which I return again and again is the *Bodhicaryāvatāra* of the Mādhyamika Śāntideva (seventh–eighth century), where, I would argue, the problem underlies the discussion in several chapters, sometimes at almost every turn. The problem comes out especially urgently in Śāntideva's self-analyses; instead of a Madhyamaka quietism, his practice clearly involves penetrating and relentless *argumentation with himself*.[9] And though the present analysis can be seen as an extended meditation on Śāntideva's tortured autointerrogation, there are other Buddhist contexts in which the problem seems to figure significantly. Still, a theme such as this is not primarily pursued by giving textual data from Sanskrit or other Asian language writings; it involves considerable interpretation and exegesis. The debt to the writings of Donald Davidson and David Wiggins and to the contemporary literature on akrasia and self-deception will become obvious.

II. Pure Rationality

To say, seemingly against the evidence, that it is utterly impossible that people act intentionally against their better judgment is to accept a version of what Donald Davidson has called a "doctrine of pure rationality," whose first clear statement in the West goes back to Socrates in Plato's *Protagoras* (see Davidson 2004b, 174–75). Here is how Aristotle summarized that view in book VII.2 of the *Nicomachean Ethics*:

> Now we may ask (1) what kind of right judgement has the man who behaves incontinently. That he should behave so when he has knowledge, some say is impossible; for it would be strange—so Socrates thought—if when knowledge was in a man something else could master it and drag it about like a slave. For Socrates was entirely opposed to the view in question, holding that there is no such thing as incontinence; no one, he said, when he judges acts against what he judges best—people act so only by reason of ignorance. Now this view plainly contradicts the apparent facts, and we must inquire about what happens to such a man; if he acts by reason of ignorance, what is the manner of his ignorance? For that the man who behaves incontinently does not, before he gets into this state, *think* he ought to act so, is evident. But there are *some* who concede certain of Socrates' contentions but not others; that nothing is stronger than knowledge they admit, but not that no one acts contrary to what has seemed to him the better course, and therefore they say that the incontinent man has not knowledge when he is mastered by his pleasures, but opinion.[10]

In short, a pure rationalist holds that when we pursue worse courses, we don't actually know what is right, and if we did, we invariably would think and act correctly. If this were also the Buddhist position, then the Buddhist might well see people as being as exclusively rational as did Socrates. As we shall see in section IV, there is a Buddhist account that goes in that Socratic direction, one that has had a certain success in popular presentations. Another textually supported account, taking seriously themes of some major Buddhist authors, does not.

III. Buddhist Sources Suggestive of Akrasia

David Wiggins began a long article on akrasia with the following astute observation: the existence of weakness of the will is not contested by ordinary nontheoretical people; it is a problem for theoreticians of rationality because they cannot see how it *could* exist and, especially, because they cannot see how it could be compatible with the other theories they espouse.[11] Indeed I suspect that many nonphilosophers, if asked, would reply (echoing Lyle Lovett) that we do sometimes, or even very often, intentionally do things that we know will make us terribly sorry, in short that we pursue worse courses and are deeply puzzled as to what reason we could have for doing so. Aristotle said that this was common knowledge, and it seems that Buddhist authors, when they are documenting or criticizing human foibles, take it as a clear fact too. Although the Buddhist will no doubt differ with us on some of the details of what is or isn't painful or seamy, there is a recurrent argumentation in texts like Āryadeva's *Catuḥśataka*, Nāgārjuna's *Ratnāvalī*, and the *Bodhicaryāvatāra* of Śāntideva to the effect that Buddhist practitioners, and indeed average people if they were to reflect a bit, actually know well that most of their actions are worse courses. Āryadeva (second–third century), for example, consecrates his first four chapters to a famous series of four "illusions" (*viparyāsa*) that are supposedly present in varying degrées in the troubled minds of Buddhist practitioners. Thus Buddhists are convinced that things are impermanent but also tenaciously and wrongly hold them to be permanent, and likewise what is actually painful is held to be pleasant, unclean things are held to be clean, and selfless things are held to have selves.[12] The logic in his treatment of these illusions is always the same: people are self-deceived; they know that permanence, cleanliness, selves, and so on are illusions, and yet they somehow think the exact opposite and act for the worse.

Śāntideva adopts a first-person perspective and again and again engages in extensive arguments with himself, contrasting fundamental Buddhist truths and norms that he (in some sense) knows with the opposite thought patterns of his own divided mind. To take two typical verses:

> Why, mind, do you protect this carcass, identifying with it? If it is really separate from you, then what loss is its decay to you?
>
> O Fool! You do not identify with a wooden doll even when it is pure. So why do you guard this festering contraption made of filth?[13]

There are many other such descriptions of seemingly inexplicable odd behavior and incoherence. The Nālandā commentator Dharmapāla (530–61), for example, illustrates the "strangeness of the world" with a list of ten "hard to fathom things" (*nan ce* 難 測), some of which (such as people coveting money all the while renouncing the world) are suggestive of akrasia (translated in Tillemans 1990, 1:171–72). Other authors, especially the writers on monastic discipline (*vinaya*), describe in considerable detail the *bizarreries* of celibate individuals who subscribe to the monastic code but nonetheless pursue (often intentionally, I suppose) quite disturbing deviations from the rules. No need to elaborate further. In any case, there seems to be ample information in texts documenting people acting intentionally in a way that they must have known, or strongly believed, to be wrong. In fact, there are more complex potential cases of akrasia where belief in errors is seen as inescapable and even necessary. These "positive" cases arise not in ethical contexts but rather in Buddhist metaphysics and philosophy of language. However, a discussion of error theories of universals and customary truths, even though they may perhaps be seen as a peculiar advocacy of epistemic akrasia, would take us too far into other matters (see Tillemans 2004 and 2011b).

It is signficant that both Śāntideva and Dharmapāla express deep puzzlement about why people do the things they do against their better judgment. But what are these two writers puzzled about, and what kind of an answer might they have expected to receive, if any? One quick, and unsatisfying, response would be to say that Śāntideva wasn't actually puzzled at all—his questions were just repeated exhortations to himself to practice Buddhism. But this unfortunately amounts to eliminating the divided mind that Śāntideva reveals throughout so much of the *Bodhicaryāvatāra*: instead of a mind in conflict, we would have an essentially indolent figure who provides himself with a series of rhetorical goads. Charity demands that we take Śāntideva's "Why?" more seriously.

Let me begin with what I think is the kind of answer that Śāntideva is probably *not* seeking. He and most other people who puzzle about why they choose worse courses (be they eighth-century Indian Buddhists or twenty-first-century country-music performers) are usually *not* seeking purely causal explanations.[14] Indeed, if the repeated "why?" (*kasmāt*) and "how is it possible?" questions that we find so often in the *Bodhicaryāvatāra* were to be taken as the search for a psychological explanation identifying causal factors that gave rise to odd behavior and beliefs, a Buddhist should have no difficulty in coming up with answers. Those answers might be intricate, especially given Buddhism's detailed discussions of karma, mental factors, dependent arising, and the other elaborations of mental causality found in Abhidharma or Pramāṇa literature, typically in connection with the question of the origin of suffering. But the answers would be forthcoming and relatively unproblematic.

In the West or in the East, there is no shortage of causal explanation as to what makes people go against their better judgment: the passions constrain people to do what they don't want to do, much like an external force or the Devil; or the psychological force of better judgment is overpowered by the force of temptation; vigilance and mindfulness are too weak against the passions; or better judgment is no match for the strength of longstanding habits and ingrained tendencies to go against it, and so on and so forth. Many of these causal explanations, and particularly the appeal to the causality of longstanding tendencies (*vāsanā*), are at one point or another invoked by Buddhists to explain psychologically how it happens that we do or think things we also know to be worse choices or errors. Indeed talk of deeply ingrained tendencies is such a Buddhist cliché that if Śāntideva or another Buddhist had simply wanted a causal account of why people go against their better judgment, it would be hard to see why any puzzlement would have arisen at all. I think it is clear that a causal explanation along the lines of "Buddhist psychology" is not primarily what is being sought; it is just too readily available.

Nor would such Buddhist psychology settle the puzzlement: invoking that type of explanation largely misses the point. Generally, when people are perplexed about why they do the things they do, they are asking for *reasons* and not just mere causes, reasons that enable them to make sense of actions by seeing them as fitting into a pattern of their thought and action that is rational and consistent. Such is, I maintain, also what seems to lie behind Śāntideva's "Why?" The puzzlement comes from the following. While Śāntideva no doubt had some all-too-human reasons for protecting his body, the Buddhist considerations outweighed them. He thus found himself pursuing a course of action (protecting his body) that he sincerely believed to be worse over one that he thought to be better all things considered, although he probably also thought, as do most of us, that people who act rationally should do what they understand to be best given all reasons available to them. Śāntideva comes to the conclusion that he acts irrationally, without adequate reasons, and thus does not understand why he does what he does.

Such is the hallmark of akrasia: the actor cannot understand herself in reasoned terms. She does an action intentionally but at the same time sincerely believes there is an alternative open to her and judges that, all things considered, that alternative would be better. She is thus left with perplexity about herself.[15] This seems to correspond to Śāntideva's predicament, for the *Bodhicaryāvatāra* is above all an intense, almost obsessive, introspection of a thinker perplexed at his rejection of what he thinks best and true.

IV. Dismissals

So much for Buddhist observations and recognition of the seemingly common phenomena of akrasia. *Theorizing* about how such phenomena are possible—making a place for the akratic in one's theoretical account of human thought and action—is quite another matter, especially given the "standard conception" of rationality that Indo-Tibetan scholastic Buddhist thinkers promote. I think that many Buddhists, in reflecting theoretically, are reluctant to acknowledge that people's thoughts and actions can be as akratic as they seem to be and feel that the appearance of akrasia needs to be explained away. I can see three basic theoretical strategies that are in accord with broad lines of Buddhist scholastic texts and popular teachings, two that would dismiss all akrasia as only apparent and one that would acknowledge it and even provide the beginning of an account of how it is possible. Each involves, inter alia, an interpretation of the key Buddhist idea that ignorance (*avidyā*) underlies moral and epistemic faults. We begin with the two dismissals.

One potential Buddhist strategy to dispel appearance of akrasia can be elaborated as follows: in the Śāntideva-style examples, four illusions, and other such cases, a Buddhist is not actually in conflict with his own clear and better understanding, because the latter is for all intents and purposes nonexistent, or too fleeting, too vague, and hence cannot enter into any such conflict. In short, there is no inconsistency between the principles that a Buddhist holds and the opposing beliefs that seem to guide how he actually behaves, because there is no real understanding of the relevant Buddhist principles at all. The would-be akrates might possibly pay lip service to those ideas and even claim that he masters them, but in fact he doesn't understand them in a way that could be said to be in genuine conflict with anything. The culprit, to put it in Buddhist terms, is the mental factor of ignorance (*avidyā*) that is at the root of the errors and misdeeds that keep sentient beings bound to *saṃsāra*, the cycle of suffering and reincarnation; ignorance clouds the mind so that understanding is weakened. Applied in a thoroughgoing fashion, this dismissal leads to a doctrine of pure rationality à la Socrates: no akrasia, no inconsistency, just the all-present "darkness of ignorance" (*avidyāndhakāra*); we're left with people (Buddhists or otherwise) who are rational and consistent but who, in their dullness, don't actually grasp the points at issue—a not very charitable depiction of serious, profound thinkers, like Śāntideva and others, who have consecrated their lives to understanding Buddhist philosophy.

Of course, this image of *avidyā* as *andhakāra*, darkness, is amply attested in Buddhist canonical literature, as are numerous other similar metaphors: ignorance as a cloud, an obscuration, a veil, fog, an eye disease. Preponderance of such imagery might seem to suggest that the ignorance that leads us astray was *invariably* interpreted as an unknowing that deprived people of better judgment, making them into "children" (*bāla*) and "fools" (*mūrkhajana*). And if that were all there was to it, then the "ignorance dismissal" would indeed put a fast end to any debate about akrasia, self-deception, and irrationality. To use Aristotle's image, people invoking ethical or philosophical principles would be like drunkards reciting verses of Empedocles that they didn't understand: such people might be stupefied, but they would not be akratic, nor would they be irrational in any interesting way.

The second potential dismissal of akrasia is a variant upon the first. It could be summarized as follows: people don't act against what they think best all things considered; due to ignorance and delusions like self-grasping, they not only don't understand what is best but erroneously believe that actions based on stinginess, indulgence in desires, and so forth are not the worse courses but are the best courses for them in that they will maximize their own utility. Similarly for cases suggestive of epistemic akrasia and self-deception: people do not actually believe that permanence, the existence of selves, and so on are illusions but believe they are real facts. In short, people may again pay lip service to Buddhist moral and philosophical principles, but they believe in something else that will maximize their own utility and that is why they pursue it. The first type of dismissal was based on people simply not understanding Buddhist principles and thus not adequately understanding what the best course of action was. The second had the additional feature that people would not actually believe that the worse course was worse, because ignorance made them take the false and worse for the true and best. The consequence of the second is in any case another variant on the Socratic principle of pure rationality: people would never intentionally pursue what they genuinely knew to be worse courses and would never believe what they knew to be false.

Who subscribes to pure rationality and its resultant dismissals of semblances of akrasia? It is above all to be found in contemporary interpretations of Buddhism as an "art of happiness" or even a "science of happiness," interpretations that often advance a position that goes strikingly in the direction of pure rationality and hence would tend to dismiss phenomena like akrasia. Indeed, what seems presupposed as a philosophy of action in this burgeoning popular literature, and is admittedly articulated with varying degrees of clarity and explicitness, is something that we can formulate along the following lines: sentient beings, by nature, will act in a way that they think maximizes their happiness; their pursuit of happiness, however, is misguided and regularly leads them to unfortunate actions because they are so deeply ignorant about what happiness really is and what leads to it.[16] This approach has no room for akrasia and precludes that there are people whose minds are divided between genuine better judgments of what is valuable and intentional pursuit of courses known to be worse.

One thing that needs to be emphasized from the outset: Buddhism as a rational "art/science of happiness" is itself a thoroughly modern interpretation of Buddhism; it often attempts to find an overarching Buddhist ethical philosophy that applies a broadly speaking utilitarian approach as a master argument to decide courses of action. Why such a philosophy has been promoted and why it might seem attractive is beyond the scope of this investigation but would involve a number of considerations about how certain Buddhists have seen their religion's possible role in the world and its compatibility with modernity. In any case, the textual sources in Buddhism underdetermine this currently promoted picture of Buddhist ethics as utilitarian, just as they underdetermine other such attempts to find a major Western ethical theory underlying Buddhism.[17] Buddhist canonical literature is extremely diverse in what it prescribes and proscribes and in the reasoning for doing so: one would need a strong philosophical or ideological stance on what Buddhism is, and especially on what it should be, to disregard that heterogeneity or take it as only apparent. Indeed, such unification is unlikely to be gained via a bottom-up approach where one reads extensively in the canon to find a clear recurring theory; rather such unification is typically "discovered" or "found" via a top-down approach that imposes a view of what Buddhism *essentially is* on very often recalcitrant texts.[18] The real issue in the quest for an overarching Buddhist ethical theory thus tends to be the philosophical pros and cons of the Western theories in question. It seems unlikely that one would make the very diverse data from Buddhist texts fit utilitarianism or virtue ethics (or any other such unifying theory) unless one were already a convinced adherent to that theory oneself.

Nor is there, as far as I can see, clear evidence in classical Buddhist literature to show that Buddhists themselves hold the background principle of the mind being governed by pure rationality, so that people will, or will invariably, act in the way they think, all things considered, to be most conducive to their happiness/utility. On the contrary, as we've seen in section III, we seem to have ample evidence that influential Buddhist authors recognize that certain people in pursuing worse courses do not act in that way: they act in a way that they themselves understand very well leads to less overall happiness for themselves and *a fortiori* less happiness for others. Indeed, following the *Bodhicaryāvatāra*, that is virtually the rule for thoughtful people embarking upon Buddhist practice. In what follows, we will seek to develop interpretations of Buddhist theoretical notions, like *avidyā* and others, that make such conflict possible and do not *explain away* those important phenomena in favor of pure rationality.[19]

There are, in Mahāyāna Buddhist philosophical literature, the makings of a more complex and rich theoretical account of akrasia, one that: (a) interprets ignorance as an active defiled intelligence, rather than an unknowing; (b) allows for conflicting networks of reasoning in different sub-systems, or different "compartments," of consciousness; (c) develops a theory of personal identity and responsibility so that compartmentalized mental states are still attributable to one agent. All these themes are present in writings of major Mahāyāna Buddhist authors. In combination they give an account of human thought and behavior in which there will be a considerable role for the all too human phenomena of akrasia in its various forms. In the remainder of this chapter, I'll sketch out some observations on each such theme in Buddhism. Hopefully the outlines of a more thorough treatment will become visible.

V. Ignorance as Defiled Intelligence

If a Buddhist wishes to defend pure rationality come what may, no doubt the easiest route for him, as we saw, is to generalize the role of ignorance as a simple unknowing: there are never any real cases of akrasia; the would-be akrates always turns out to be ignorant of what is best and true. While many Buddhists did take ignorance in that way, as a nonunderstanding (*apratipatti*), it is important to note that other major Buddhist philosophers, like the sixth–seventh-century author Dharmakīrti and the author(s) of the

Yogācārabhūmi, did *not* see the ignorance that underlies *saṃsāra* as a mere absence of understanding but as a very tenacious and even reasoned misunderstanding (*vipratipatti*). They explained it as being the wrong view that reifies persons (*satkāyadṛṣṭi*) or a "defiled intelligence" (*kliṣṭā prajñā*). I translate a relevant passage from Dharmakīrti's *Pramāṇavārttika* and *Svavṛtti* (autocommentary) in full:

> What then is the source of these [moral] faults so that they are abandoned due to the repeated cultivation of its antidote?
>
> > 222. The genesis of all the [different] kinds of faults is due to the false view that reifies the person (*satkāyadarśana*). This constitutes ignorance (*avidyā*); the attachment to the [I and the mine] is based on that. From that [attachment] come hatred and [all] the rest [of the moral faults].
>
> Indeed if someone sees that there is no I and no mine, then lacking [such] a belief, he will not be attached to anything. Nor will a detached person feel hatred for anything, for no one has any [hatred] for what is harmless to himself and his possessions or prevents harm [to them]. Thus the view reifying the self, which came about due to repeated cultivation of [a view] of the same general kind, leads to the view of there being a "mine," and these two [views] to attachment to the [I and mine], and [finally] that [leads] to hatred and [all] the rest [of the moral faults]. That is why all faults arise from the false view that reifies the person. And it is precisely that [view] that we term *ignorance* (*ajñāna*).[20]

In short, the necessary condition for the perpetuation of the world of suffering, *saṃsāra*, is ignorance taken as being a defiled intelligence reifying persons; this leads to the mistaken belief/apprehension that there is a substantial self and its possessions, to the related attitudes of self-protection and aggression, and finally, when these attitudes prevail, to the resultant worse-course behavior, like stinginess, anger, and indulgence in desires. Other thinkers, of a Madhyamaka orientation, like Candrakīrti and Tsongkhapa, also speak of active, intelligent misconstruing rather than just dullness. Thus *satyābhimāna* (the attachment that things are real), grasping at the real (*bden 'dzin*), and the like are underlying necessary conditions for our choosing worse alternatives.[21]

For philosophers who see *saṃsāra* as thus rooted in an active and defiled type of intelligence rather than a simple *unknowing* of what is best, the facile Socratic "ignorance defense" for pure rationality is not readily available: there is, rather, a clash between strongly held ways of thinking. This leaves the route open for Buddhists to say that well-cultivated practitioners, like Śāntideva, could *know* they are wrong in pursuing stinginess, anger, and other passions all while believing in permanence, cleanliness, selves, and so on. They could know those things, though their defiled intelligence strongly believes the opposite and leads them to act upon what they know to be wrong.

VI. Compartmentalization and Consistency

When we speak of an akrates going against her own better judgment, we easily attribute to her a type of inconsistency. But does that mean that an akrates who knows that generosity is the best course of action but nonetheless pursues her own stingy self-interest explicitly thinks to herself that one and the same action is both good and not good? Does she endorse a conjunction of a proposition and its negation? This seems quite unlikely and would be perilously close to what Candrakīrti calls simply "being demented," "out of one's mind" (*unmattaka*), rather than being a sane worldling in a complex tension between better judgment and defiled forms of intelligence.

Now for the Buddhist, as for Donald Davidson and many other theorists about akrasia, the way back from such looming irrationality is compartmentalization of mind: instead of one and the same mind or subject oddly holding two opposing ideas or networks of ideas—a puzzling phenomenon indeed—here are supposedly many semi-autonomous cognitive subsystems each having their own beliefs, with no substantial person linking them together.[22] I think the most plausible reconstruction of the position found in *Pramāṇavārttika* and other key texts[23] would be as follows: ignorance-qua-defiled intelligence is regularly depicted in Buddhist literature as creating a network of reasoning (e.g., "This is me," "This is mine," "This is hence essential to my happiness") with a great deal of internal cohesion and leading to a coherent series of decisions to act in certain fashions (e.g., "I should defend this," "I will be aggressive to someone who threatens me in this respect"). It is this network of reasoning and actions that leads to conflict with a competing ensemble of beliefs that there is no real I and no need to defend it. The akrates, Buddhist or otherwise, could be depicted as caught between networks of ideas leading him to endorse *p* from the perspective of one such network and *not-p* from the other, but there would be no perspective from which he endorsed both *p* and *not-p*. The inconsistency that he endorses, if any, is thus of a weaker "nonadjunctive" sort, and that need not be the same as believing the conjunction *p and not-p*; he need not endorse the stronger inconsistency that something is both good and not good.[24]

VII. The Self

Of course, this is not the end of the story: there are other major philosophical hurdles that the Buddhist must cross. Let me sketch out two of them.

First, seeing the mind as a number of subsystems is, as is often stressed in the East and in the West, particularly vulnerable to the critique that thoughts, desires, intentions, and so forth would not end up being attributed to the whole person, the unified subject that we refer to by "I."[25] Buddhists were certainly aware of that problem and had their makings of a reply. The main thrust of this philosophy, whether in the Abhidharma, in Yogācāra, or in Madhyamaka, is always that talk of the unity of the knowing subject is only a customary truth (*saṃvṛtisatya*), one due to customary transactions (*vyavahāra*)—ascription of mental states to "whole persons" thus has to be explained without ascribing these states to a real "I" that owns them. This is not the place to go into an extensive treatment of Buddhist views on personal identity—others, like Mark Siderits, have taken this up in detail, looking especially at the reductionism of Derek Parfit as well as Mahāyāna views on selflessness (Siderits 2003). Suffice it to say here that *some* such account of the unreality of substantial selves would seem to be indispensable if the Buddhist compartmentalist, or the thoroughgoing Davidsonian for that matter, is to allow for phenomena like akrasia.

Second, even if one does follow the Buddhist in relegating the unifying "I" to mere customary truth, what is also crucially necessary for philosophers who accept compartmentalization is an account of some kind of panoptic perspective, so that some or many of the mental subsystems are transparent and accessible to each other.[26] Lacking some such transparency and integrating perspective, a thinker like Śāntideva would end up *too* divided to be perturbed at all by the conflicts between his mental states. Now it may be that certain Buddhist philosophers, like Dharmakīrti, can fulfill that requirement for integration with their idea that every mental state is also aware of itself, and that this "reflexive awareness" (*svasaṃvedana*) can provide the needed panoptic perspective. However, it is not sufficiently clear to me how his account would work here, for the reflexive awarenesses of mental states are also taken to be individual and thus quite separate from each other. Curiously enough, it was not actually the Buddhist followers of Dharmakīrti who explicitly used "reflexive awareness" to integrate otherwise overly separate mental components. It was their philosophical cousins and rivals, the Kashmiri Shaivites Utpaladeva and Abhinavagupta, who accepted much of the basic scheme of Dharmakīrti's partitioning of the mind but then invoked a unitary "reflexive awareness" to give the panoptic perspective that would permit separate components to communicate.[27] The idea may hold promise for rendering the divided mental subsystems of the akrates transparent too.

VIII. Final Remarks

Buddhist philosophy of mind, in addition to compartmentalization, frequently advocates a type of stratification of the mental into conscious and unconscious strata. Indeed, a number of years ago the late Gadjin Nagao published an article in the *Felicitation Volume for Jacques May* in which he tried to look at the Buddhist *ālayavijñāna* (the storehouse consciousness) as a kind of unconscious, à la depth psychology, underlying the conscious mind, or *pravṛttivijñāna* (Nagao 1992). William Waldron has taken a similar tack with a book on the *ālayavijñāna* ("fundamental consciousness," or more literally "storehouse consciousness") entitled *The Buddhist Unconscious* (Waldron 2003). Whether we see Buddhist enlightenment in Yogācāra terms as a "revolutionary perspective" (*parāvṛtti*) on the *ālayavijñāna* or along the Madhyamaka lines of an elimination of sentient beings' "inborn grasping at things being real," progress on the Buddhist path invariably involves bringing error to the ever-increasing light of day. What place does akrasia have here?

To put things in rough and ready terms, some thoughts—like the deepest, or innate (*sahaja*), grasping at a real self, and the subtle forms of grasping at permanence and other illusions (*viparyāsa*)—could indeed be unconscious in the sense that though a person thinks *p*, he might not have the second-order understanding *that* he thinks *p* (McGinn 1979), or if he did, he might not have any understanding of the extent of its hold on his conscious life. When these thoughts are unconscious, akrasia would *not* occur in connection with them, for there is no question at this time of knowing what is best but nonetheless consciously/intentionally choosing to do or think otherwise. However, as the practitioner becomes more and more familiar with his own mind and understands better its illusions, it seems that akrasia-like conflict becomes acute. Indeed, at the first stages (*bhūmi*) of a Mahāyānist's spiritual advancement, the post-meditative (*rjes thob*, *pṛṣṭhalabdha*) consciousness is said to be under the influence of tendencies to "grasp at the real" (*bden 'dzin*) and to give rise to passions; these are termed *kleśāvaraṇa* by the scholastic, or "obscurations due to the passions." Even after their elimination after the seventh *bhūmi*, the practitioner is still subject to a subtle obscuration, namely that "phenomena appear [to him] as real" (*bden snang*). Errors that he had earlier realized to be wrong during his meditative absorptions continue to appear when the practitioner interacts with the world. The tension between meditative perspectives and post-meditative reentry into the world thus remains, albeit in more attenuated forms, until full buddhahood. What is disturbing—just as I think it was for Śāntideva—is that some type of akrasia in all its puzzling urgency seems to be the price of spiritual progress along the Buddhist path.

Notes to Chapter 9

1. Taylor 1982, 97. Note that "rational" is often used, inter alia, to describe what is simply based on reasoning, be that reasoning more or less sound or unsound, good or bad; it is also used to qualify beings that are endowed with the capacity to engage in reasoning. The adjective is also, of course, as in the passage from Taylor, used in a normative and evaluative sense, to characterize thinking, speech, behavior, and so on that are in keeping with *good* reasoning. In what follows, we are using the term in that latter sense. This is close to the use of the Sanskrit terms such as *yukta/nyāyya* and their Tibetan and Chinese translations *rigs pa*, *cheng li*, etc. Cf., however, van Eemeren and Grootendorst 2004, 123–25, where the use of the term *rational* is stipulatively limited to the first sense and the term *reasonable* is reserved for the good uses of reason.
2. Davidson 1980, 42.
3. There may be, e.g., in certain early Buddhist texts, and perhaps in certain Chan texts, nonstandard conceptions that have a greater tolerance of inconsistency. That would need a separate treatment, and I'm not going to delve into such issues here; accordingly my focus will be upon the "standard conception." There is in any case no doubt that many Buddhists do profess a standard conception of reason where avoidance of contradiction is an explicitly invoked iron-clad rule: it is abundantly attested in their own philosophical theories, their canons of debate (*vāda*), and in their polemical refutations of adversaries. On possible nonstandard conceptions, see chapters 3 and 4.
4. Candrakīrti. *Prasannapadā*, 15.9–10: *atha svābhyupagamavirodhacodanayāpi paro na nivartate, tadāpi nirlajjatayā hetudṛṣṭāntābhyām api naiva nivarteta / na conmattakena sahāsmākaṃ vivāda iti*. "But if the opponent did not desist even when confronted with a contradiction in his own position, then too, as he would have no shame, he would not desist at all even when faced with a logical reason and example. Now for us, as it is said, there is no debate with someone who is out of his mind."
5. The falsity of theories that explain behavior only in terms of maximizing utility/happiness is the consequence that David Wiggins draws from akrasia. See Wiggins 1998.
6. Emma Bovary's persuading herself that she would be swept off her feet by her lover and her elaborating numerous other romantic scenarios about love and even her own

sainthood, all the while knowing they were not so, can be regarded as case studies of epistemic akrasia. Such is the analysis in Davidson 2004b.

7. Garfield 2011 seems to think that akrasia is impossible in the case of a Buddhist, because Aristotelian akrasia is, for him, purely a conflict between knowledge of the good and desire for the ill. The culprit for Aristotle is weakness, and the solution is not more knowledge but only moral strength. On the other hand, this is supposedly not so for the Buddhist, for whom ignorance is the culprit: if action is vicious, it is because understanding is dim through ignorance. Garfield's view is a version of the "pure rationality" defense that we will take up in section II. Now it is exegetically hard to sustain that Aristotle saw *no* place for rival reasoning in cases of *akrasia*. Aristotle does talk about general syllogistic reasoning being present in the case of feelings, even if it is a kind of "feeling allied with limited reasoning" in conflict with "full-fledged reason" (Kraut 2014, §7). Modern writers on *akrasia*, like Davidson (2004a and 2004b), also bring out such competing reasons. Finally, it is quite unnecessary to read the Buddhists' idea of ignorance as being dimness. Many major Buddhists, as we shall see, take it as a type of defiled intelligence, a network of potentially quite developed, but perverse, reasonings. It looks like there can be, for them, conflicts of thinking and not just cases of dim understanding or runaway passions.
8. Although my analysis differs from that of Hayes 1996, I do agree with him on the importance, in this connection, of the Buddhist's theory of personal identity and "modularization" of the self. See section VII below.
9. On Buddhist quietism and the role of argumentation, including argumentation with oneself, see Tillemans 2008b. See also the introduction to this book.
10. Ross and Brown 2009, 119–20. Cf. the translation found in Wiggins 1998: "One may be puzzled how a man with a correct view of a situation can be weak of will. For some deny that this is possible if he really knows what is the right thing to do. For if the knowledge is present, it is strange, as Socrates thought, for something else to overcome knowledge and manhandle it like a slave. Socrates was totally opposed to that view. He denied that there was any such thing as weakness of will. For knowing that it *is* best, nobody, he said, acts contrary to the best. If he does act contrary to the best, it must be through ignorance. This account of Socrates conflicts plainly with what seems to be the case and what people say."
11. Cf. Wiggins 1998, 239–40: "Almost anyone not under the influence of theory will say that, when a person is weak-willed, he intentionally chooses that which he knows or believes to be the worse course of action when he could choose the better course. . . . But there are philosophers of mind and moral philosophers who have felt a strong theoretical compulsion to rewrite the description, rather than allow the phenomenon of weakness of will to appear as an incontrovertible refutation of the theories of mind or morality that they are committed to defend." Davidson (1980, 29) is categorical: "There is no proving such actions exist; but it seems to me absolutely certain that they do."
12. See Lang 2003 and Lang 1986. For the canonical schema of four *viparyāsa*, see *Abhidharmakośabhāṣya* ad 5.8 (translation La Vallée Poussin 1923–31, 4:21).
13. *Bodhicaryāvatāra* 5.60–61. Translation in Crosby and Skilton 1996, 39.
14. I am, of course, once again thinking of the great Texan akrates, Lyle Lovett.
15. The central idea is that of Davidson, encapsulated in one of the three quotations with which we began this article. See the elaboration in Davidson 1980, 42.

16. See Ricard 2006, 26–27: "However we go about looking for it, and whether we call it joy or duty, passion or contentment, isn't happiness the goal of all goals? . . . Anyone who says otherwise doesn't really know what he wants; he is simply seeking happiness under another name." An appeal to the self-evidence of the fact that people do what they do because they rationally (but misguidedly) calculate it will maximize their happiness is clearly found in a recent article by the American monk Thanissaro Bhikkhu (2006). On page 43 we are provided with the following diagnosis of what underlies attachment to things like alcohol: "in your calculation, the immediate pleasure derived from the alcohol outweighs the long-term damage it's doing to your life. . . . We're attached to things and actions, not because of what we think they are but because of what we think they can do for our happiness."
17. Nor could one easily appeal to the average Buddhists' ethical intuitions to decide whether Buddhism leans more to utilitarianism than to, say, virtue ethics or vice versa. Buddhist intuitions might well be about as divided on the implications of these two theories as are Western intuitions. Of course, utilitarianism has numerous well-known counterintuitive results, such as the possibility that it will justify taking an innocent life for the benefit of many. It is a safe bet that many Buddhists would find these cases as problematic as do most of us and that they would cite texts in support of their opinions. (Perhaps the most persuasive and sophisticated arguments against utilitarianism are those of Bernard Williams in his debates with J. J. C. Smart [Smart and Williams 1973].) Other scholars tend to see the emphasis on happiness as a kind of Aristotelian virtue ethics, or eudaimonism, rather than utilitarianism (see Keown 2001). Here too, however, it is strained to impose such an account as an overarching theory, as it is not at all clear that Buddhists always or even generally hold that an action is good insofar as it contributes to the agent's flourishing (*eudaimonia*). It may well be that certain Buddhists would feel that the better course of action, in some situations, would *not* be the one that made the agent flourish but the one that most benefited others.
18. It needs to be emphasized that Buddhist canonical literature is indeed extremely diverse, and is not just a series of texts corroborating our current views of Buddhist ethics. The Bka' 'gyur contains texts on everything from nonviolence and compassion to just war, torture, transgressive tantra, monastic codes of discipline, supererogatory bodhisattva ethics, and not infrequently, dismissals of all views on what is right and wrong as mere conceptual fabrications. It is unlikely that one could find clear passages that would clinch the attribution of one substantive theory to all Buddhism unless one ignores the opposing passages. Interestingly, C. Goodman 2008, although generally a defense of consequentialist ethics, recognizes this diversity of Buddhist views (p. 31): "I have presented evidence that at least *some* [my italics] Indian Mahāyāna texts hold an ethical view that is quite similar to Western consequentialism. . . . It would not be safe to extend this interpretation to all Asian societies that have accepted the Mahāyāna. . . . . The esoteric Buddhism of the *tantras* certainly can be interpreted as holding a quite different ethical position from other forms of Buddhism, though this interpretation is not necessarily forced on us." Cf. Gray 2007 on the ethical implications of tantra. A strongly recurring theme in tantra is indeed the overcoming of distinctions such as good and bad. Tantrism thus has an important nontheoretical stance, as it defends (contrary to many other Buddhist schools) the idea that there

is no decision procedure, code, standard, or theory at all that can determine what a tantrika ought to do in a given situation. Finally, it's not just tantras that present very different positions from currently prevailing ideas about Buddhist ethics. Sūtras do too. See Jenkins 2010. It is more likely that an honest, unideological reading of that canonical literature in its vast diversity—and not just the usual selection of a few well-known passages—would show that Buddhists, like most of us, are faced with what Thomas Nagel (1979, chap. 9) calls a "fragmentation of value": competing values that come into conflict, and no single criterion to decide everything.

19. Cf. Wiggins' remarks cited in note 11 above. To persist in saying that Śāntideva just cannot actually know or believe such truths is tantamount to a refusal to allow challenges to a faulty background theory.
20. *Pramāṇavārttika* 1.222 and *Svavṛtti* (ed. Gnoli 1960, 111): *kaḥ punar eṣāṃ doṣānāṃ prabhavo yatpratipakṣābhyāsāt prahīyante / sarvāsāṃ doṣajātīnāṃ jātiḥ satkāyadarśanāt // sā avidyā tatra tatsnehas tasmād dveṣādisambhavaḥ // 222 // na hi nāhaṃ na mameti paśyataḥ parigraham antareṇa kvacit snehaḥ / na cānanurāgiṇaḥ kvacid dveṣaḥ / ātmātmīyānuparodhiny uparodhapratighātini ca tadabhāvāt / tasmāt samānajātīyābhyāsajam ātmadarśanam ātmīyagrahaṃ prasūte / tau ca tatsnehaṃ sa ca dveṣādīn iti satkāyadarśanajāḥ sarvadoṣāḥ / tad eva ca ajñānam ity ucyate /.*
21. For references to the two senses of ignorance in Candrakīrti's *Pañcaskandhaprakaraṇa* and to "defiled intelligence" in the *Yogācārabhūmi*, see Seyfort Ruegg 2002, 234–35n148. For *satyābhimāna*, see Candrakīrti's *Madhyamakāvatārabhāṣya* ad *Madhyamakāvatāra* 6.28, translation La Vallée Poussin 1910, 304–5.
22. These components are mental elements (*dharma*) classified into "minds" (*citta*) and "mental factors" (*caitta*)—this is the sort of thing that is explained in extraordinary detail in scholastic texts like the *Abhidharmakośa* and so many others of the Abhidharma genre. Fragmentation of the mind into such components is also explained, or presupposed, in Yogācāra and Madhyamaka Buddhism, even if the positions on the ontological status of such elements will differ from that of the Abhidharma. Compartmentalization of the mind is, in short, part of basic Buddhism.
23. See, e.g., the passage from *Pramāṇavārttikasvavṛtti* quoted in section V above.
24. Cf. Davidson 2004b, 217: "The distinction we need here is between believing contradictory propositions and believing a contradiction, between believing that *p* and believing that *not-p* on the one hand, and believing that (*p and not-p*) on the other." I have taken up Buddhist uses of nonadjunctive inconsistencies in some detail in chapters 3 and 4 of the present book. One could even weaken the inconsistency further by saying, with Wiggins, that perspectives may embody incommensurable values. Thus for most or even all decisions, an akrates might have decision criteria as to what is best, even though he would be incapable of providing one and the same evaluative criterion that applies to all decisions. The difference is in the order of the quantifiers: "For all x, there is a y such that ϕ" may be true even though "There is a y, such that for all x, ϕ" may not.
25. In India, the objection is that of the Brahmanical schools. But see also Davidson 2004a, 171.
26. The ideas of a "panoptical scanner" and "transparency" are developed by Rorty 1988.
27. See Torella 2007. Utpaladeva takes as an example the case of the two separate cognitions in Dharmakīrti's account of nonperception (*anupalabdhi*) of a jar: that is, the cognition of an empty place, like a table, and the cognition of it being devoid of jars.

Lacking a panoptic scanner, a unitary *svasaṃvedana* that grasps both, the first cognition could not lead to the second. The example is generalized by the Shaivite to show that all separate cognitions can "communicate" with each other and enter into networks because of this illuminating consciousness.

10. Yogic Perception, Meditation, and Enlightenment: The Epistemological Issues in a Key Debate between Madhyamaka and Chan

I

TOWARD THE END of the eighth century, there occurred a debate over the future direction of Buddhism in Tibet. It happened in Samyé (Bsam yas), in the Brahmaputra Valley not far from Lhasa, and pitted an Indian side, with their Tibetan sympathizers, against a Chinese side, with their Tibetan—and perhaps even some Indian—sympathizers. The debate may have gone on for about a year in one way or another—one cannot but speculate on the formidable linguistic challenges of managing and somehow translating the polemical exchanges in Sanskrit, Tibetan, and Chinese—and the actual details of the procedures are obscure. In any case, it was not long until things took a disastrous turn. Some members of the Chinese entourage in despair of losing committed suicide; one of the prominent Tibetans allied with the Indians also committed suicide by starving to death; and the debate finally concluded with the murder of the leader of the Indian side, Kamalaśīla, at the hands of hired assassins, who supposedly "crushed his kidneys." The Chinese leader, who was known simply as Monk (Tib. *hva shang*, Ch. *he shang* 和尙) or, often, Monk of the Mahāyāna (*hva shang mo ho yen*)—henceforth simply Heshang—was ignominiously expelled from Tibet, unfairly as his side claimed. Details of the debate and its historical context, as well as a French translation of the memoir of Wang Xi (王錫) in defense of Heshang and excerpts from the *Bhāvanākrama* by Kamalaśīla, are found in the classic work of the Sinologist Paul Demiéville, *Le Concile de Lhasa.*[1] Colorful details aside, the debate, which superficially might seem to be no more than political rivalry, jealousies, and their brutally violent outcomes, is also about questions that regularly arise among Buddhists, past and present. It is in part about the efficacy of various types of meditation, but more broadly, it is about the respective *worth* of analysis and meditation as approaches to knowledge and enlightenment. The debate, as we shall see shortly, is fundamentally about epistemological issues, problems of knowledge.

II

Here is the background. The Mādhyamika thinker Kamalaśīla, in his *Stages of Meditation* (*Bhāvanākrama*), speaks of two aspects of meditation: "calmness" (*śamatha*) and "insight" (*vipaśyanā, prajñā*), the conjunction of the two being the means through which Buddhist liberation/enlightenment is achieved. As the way to develop this conjunction, he advocated that one first alternate between philosophical analysis and concentrated fixation on the conclusions of that analysis. Meditation was thus, for him, a back and forth between analytical reasoning—a kind of subtle internal debate over metaphysical issues—and concentrated absorption (*samādhi*). This is in effect the alternation between the so-called analytic meditation (*dpyad sgom*) and fixed meditation (*'jog sgom*) that would become important for later Tibetan thinkers in their theoretical account of meditation as we see, for example, in the extensive endorsement it received in the "Insight" chapter of the *Lam rim chen mo* of Tsongkhapa (1357–1419).[2] The essential point of the method was—and is still conceived to be—that the practitioner continues this alternation until he can finally conjoin calmness with insight and the object of meditation (typically a topic such as moment-by-moment change, the painfulness of phenomena, emptiness or selflessness, or uncleanliness) appears clearly without the intermediary of conceptual representation.[3] The goal is thus the development, via a series of analyses and intense concentration, of *yogipratyakṣa*, a yogin's direct perception of higher and thus liberating features about reality, features that appear to him as vividly as in a sense perception.

Such a position on meditation and the resultant yogic perception (*yogipratyakṣa*) was not at all unique to Kamalaśīla. His philosophy on yogins' knowledge and almost all other matters epistemological was derived largely from Dharmakīrti, a sixth- or seventh-century thinker who had an extraordinary influence on later Indian and Tibetan Buddhism.[4] Kamalaśīla's philosophy of meditation and *yogipratyakṣa* thus concords by and large with mainstream Indo-Tibetan Buddhist *theoretical* accounts. Not only did Buddhists from Dharmakīrti to Śāntarakṣita, Kamalaśīla, and Ratnakīrti promote it, but it was what non-Buddhists, such as Vācaspatimiśra, took to be the main Buddhist theory and criticized (see Taber 2009). And in Tibet, too, it was by and large the received theory of meditation and yogic knowledge, promoted especially intensely by the Geluk (Dge lugs) and Sakya (Sa skya) schools. Indeed, prominent twentieth-century Geluk teachers would regularly stress the importance of Kamalaśīla-style meditation and would often repeat verbatim the formulae Kamalaśīla used to ridicule the followers of Heshang.

Kamalaśīla's opponent, Heshang, on the other hand, dismissed philosophical analysis as antithetical to meditation and utterly unable to lead to liberating insight; instead he advocated a nonconceptual approach. While it is not precisely settled who his doctrinal ancestors were, it is apparent that he subscribed to major Chan (Zen) ideas and advocated a certain variant, prevalent in the Dunhuang Buddhist circles that he frequented, on *kan xin* 看心 "[nonconceptually] looking at the mind." His formulations of recurring Chan ideas are often provocative, as we see in a description of his views in the Dunhuang text entitled *The Sudden Awakening to the Originally Real* (*Cig car yang dag pa'i phyi mo'i tshor ba*). In this old Tibetan translation of an eighth-century Chinese Chan text, one is counseled to observe repeatedly the nature of thought until all appearances disappear, so that one dwells "perpetually in the source of [their] nonexistence."[5]

The details of Heshang's position on "appearances disappearing" and so on are perhaps somewhat odd and may even seem philosophically unsophisticated—interestingly enough, Heshang himself admitted to Kamalaśīla that he was no match for him, lacking scholarship and skill in debate. However, the broad outline of the position is certainly discernible from Wang Xi's memoir:

> "Looking at the mind" (*kan xin* 看心) means turning one's focus inward to the "source of the mind" (*xin yuan* 心源) and abstaining from all thought and examination (*bu si bu guan* 不思不觀), whether notions arise or not and whether they are pure, impure, empty or non-empty.[6]

There is thus no use for alternation between philosophical analysis and concentrated absorption and equally no place for a Dharmakīrtian version of yogic perception gained by strenuous effort and development of concentration; when a person directly sees the innately present nature of mind, he or she is suddenly and fully enlightened.

What do we know about the pair of key terms that Heshang used to designate this abstention from thought? As Demiéville pointed out (1987, 78–79n3), the possible Sanskrit equivalents for the terms *bu si* 不思 and *bu guan* 不觀 are many depending on the periods and the translators; among others he gives *avicāra-avitarka* ("no analysis / no rational deliberation") (Demiéville 1987, 15n1). Elsewhere, in related Tibetan or Chinese contexts treating of Heshang's views, we find terms such as *mi/myi rtog pa* and *wu fen bie* 無分別 (= *avikalpa*), which can be rendered as "no(n) conceptualization," although the Chinese quite clearly adds the nuance of "no differentiation" (Demiéville 1987, 128). Finally, when Kamalaśīla depicts Heshang's position in *Bhāvanākrama* III, he almost always uses the Sanskrit terms *asmṛti* ("not bringing to mind / no remembrance") and *amanasikāra* ("not focusing upon / not thinking about") (Tucci 1971, 15–17), which seems to be his attempt to use essentially Abhidharmic notions to translate the usual Chan terms *no-thinking* (*wu nian* 無念) and *no-mind* (*wu xin* 無心) (Demiéville 1987, 80n).

Given the plethora of terms, it may thus seem that the potential was extremely high for a debate at cross purposes. Such indeed seems to have been the conviction of Paul Demiéville, who warned:

> The protagonists of the Council of Lhasa [= the Samyé debate] must have constantly ended up in impasses because they did not attribute the same sense to the words that were always coming back again and again in the debate.[7]

If this were right, then understanding the debate would be largely a matter for philological and historical analysis, where one sought above all to sort out the (perhaps deliberate) semantic confusions; one might even eventually find (as Demiéville seems to attempt to do) a significant degree of reconciliation and common ground between the parties once the terminological misunderstandings had been cleared away.

I would venture that, fortunately, things are not quite as badly confused terminologically as Paul Demiéville seems to have thought them to be. Even though the terms are varied across three languages, sympathetically understanding this debate is not essentially or only a matter of untangling a series of misunderstandings by detailed philological and historical analyses. The various terms can be seen as attempts to express a relatively constant idea about not thinking, not analyzing, not representing things conceptually. Indeed the records of this debate bring out the parties' markedly different philosophical and religious stances; those differences are real and not simply explicable as due to "a text that is rife with terminological misunderstandings."[8] Perhaps the most basic formulation that is used to represent Heshang's views is Kamalaśīla's *na kiṃcic cintayitavyam* (Tucci 1971, 14), "one shouldn't think about anything at all." The formula is obviously very blunt and simple, but it is not fundamentally wrong, confused, or unfair to Heshang. The enemy of insight is conceptualization *simpliciter*; understanding the world via the intermediary of any concepts and representations—be they true, pure, impure, false, what have you—is thus an obstacle to spiritual insight.

III

The exchange between Kamalaśīla and Heshang was heatedly polemical. Kamalaśīla argued repeatedly in the third book of the *Bhāvanākrama* that the Chinese path, whereby a practitioner does away with all conceptual thought, results in nothing more than voluntary stupefaction; being in a state of "no thinking" (*amanasikāra*) as Heshang understands it[9]—without any dependence upon analysis or reasoning—is thus nothing noble or enlightening, as the practitioner simply does not know anything at all, *period*.

Kamalaśīla, however, went much further, and here is where things did arguably become unfair. For him, practicing Heshang's nonconceptualization would mean that all moral observances and other basic Buddhist practices would go by the wayside and that, in sum, the Buddhist path would be utterly destroyed. Let me translate a substantial representative passage from Kamalaśīla's *Bhāvanākrama* III to convey the issues and the tone of the debate.

> What [Heshang] thought, however, was the following: When sentient beings experience karmic results like rebirths in heavens, [hells,] and so forth due to the virtuous and unvirtuous karma that they produce through their conceptual thinking, they transmigrate in *saṃsāra*. But on the other hand, whosoever thinks about nothing at all and does no action (*karma*) at all will be thoroughly liberated from *saṃsāra*. Thus one should not think about anything at all (*na kiṃcic cintayitavyam*). Nor should one practice virtues such as giving and the like. Giving and other such practices were only taught for foolish people (*mūrkhajanam adhikṛtya*).
>
> [We reply:] That is tantamount to rejecting the whole of the Great Vehicle (*mahāyāna*). Now all the [Buddhist] vehicles are rooted in the Great Vehicle, so that if one rejects it, then one would end up rejecting absolutely all vehicles. Indeed, by saying that one should not think about anything, one would reject any insight (*prajñā*) that can be characterized as being an "examination of reality" (*bhūtapratyavekṣālakṣaṇā*). Because the root of all correct

> understanding is examination of reality, then by rejecting the latter one would reject [all], even transcendental, insight. And because one rejects that, one would reject omniscience (*sarvākārajñatā*). And by saying that one should not practice giving and the like either, then it is utterly obvious that one would reject methods (*upāya*) [of Buddhist morality] like giving and so forth. Now this is precisely how one can summarize the Great Vehicle: insight and methods. . . . So, therefore, one who does not respect scholars, has not learned the ways of the Tathāgata's teaching, and is himself lost and makes others lost too is refuted by both scripture and reasoning, and thus his discourse, contaminated as it is with poison, should be cast far away by anyone intelligent who desires [the best] for himself, just as if it were poisoned food.[10]

Woe to the heretic! Heshang is, in short, depicted not just as a misguided promulgator of some ineffectual methods of meditation; he is an enemy of the faith putting forth theories that are supposedly toxic to anyone who consumes them.

Kamalaśīla was no doubt irritated by what he perceived as Heshang's anti-intellectualism and disrespect for scholars, and hence the somewhat petulant remark that Heshang was "one who does not respect scholars, has not learned the ways of the Tathāgata's teaching, and is himself lost and makes others lost too." Probably a good deal of Kamalaśīla's motivation was plain conservatism. He sought to defend the Buddhist institutions of learning as found in the later Indian monastic universities, while Heshang, with his professed rejection of all conceptual thinking, at least indirectly threatened those institutions and their hierarchy. It is hardly surprising to find such politicized exchanges. The Indian party was surely *not* trying to be charitable toward Heshang or a Heshang-like position, and the Samyé debate was never destined to be consensual. The mistake would be to think that because it was strongly politicized, it was only politics and never philosophy.

IV

Let us leave aside the vested political interests of conservative religious institutions and their defenders. What could we say if we took the charitable high road? In Kamalaśīla's favor, we could certainly grant that observing moral precepts and making ethical decisions would involve thinking and intentions, the latter being (according to basic Buddhism) responsible for karma, with good intentions leading to good karmic results and good rebirths. But did Heshang mean only that a practitioner should not think conceptually when engaged in meditation, or did he actually advocate no conceptual thought *across the board*, even in more ordinary contexts where decisions, intentions, and analyses *do* undoubtedly matter? If the latter were what he meant, then Heshang would not just be a bad Buddhist, as Kamalaśīla alleges, but it is hard to see how he could function at all in most of the complex affairs of daily life and human society. Reading Wang Xi's memoir, however, gives the distinct impression that it is the former that Heshang advocated, and certainly the principle of charity would be against an *across the board* and total abstention from thinking. The provocative phrase "Giving and other such practices were only taught for foolish people," if it were interpreted more charitably than it is by Kamalaśīla, might not mean that Heshang actually advocated that the wise behave in a thoroughly antinomian fashion and reject all Buddhist morality but only that the wise would not take moral practices and the conceptual discriminations that they involve as the sum of Buddhism, as the way to enlightenment. Only fools would make *that* mistake. In short, moral concepts and actions might even be important in life, but moralizing fools go wrong in holding that they are also enlightening.

We will not pursue the passionate but seemingly confused polemic about the ethical implications of Heshang's philosophy. Instead we'll take the main issue in Samyé as whether not-thinking *in meditation* can lead to enlightenment or whether such meditation invariably results in voluntarily induced stupefaction. Kamalaśīla, of course, says that it does invariably result in stupefaction, and he repeatedly characterizes this meditative state of mind as being like the absence of thinking that occurs when someone simply faints (*saṃmūrchita*), is bereft of memory/awareness (*muṣitasmṛti*), or is utterly stupid (*atyantamūḍha*) (Tucci 1971, 16). Such a *reductio ad absurdum* of the Chinese position figures repeatedly in the *Bhāvanākrama* and in the subsequent chronicles of the Samyé debate, and it is regularly cited approvingly by later Tibetan writers such as Tsongkhapa who saw themselves as building on the victorious eighth-century dialectics of Kamalaśīla. It is, undoubtedly, at the heart of the debate.

Now, one might easily (and in the end wrongly, I think) say that this *reductio* too was no more than rhetorical intimidation, because Kamalaśīla simply begged the question as to whether there is a significant difference between the not-thinking of an unconscious individual—for example, someone who has fainted or is comatose—and the not-thinking of someone who is perfectly conscious and lucid. An intelligent follower of Heshang could of course insist that there is in fact such a difference and that Kamalaśīla was deliberately being uncharitable by disregarding it.[11] Indeed, Heshang himself seems to have allowed that the nonconceptual state he was advocating was not one of complete absence of concepts—a type of perfectly blank mind or *tabula rasa*—but one in which notions, "whether they arise or not" (see note 6), are not thought about—are not *pursued by conceptual thought*. We find roughly comparable methods of not pursuing thoughts in several schools, including Tibetan Mahāmudrā and Great Perfection (*rdzogs chen*) philosophies, which also develop the idea of "directly becoming acquainted with the nature of the mind" (*sems kyi ngo sprod*) without the intermediary of conceptual thoughts, and in the "insight meditation" (*vipassanā = vipaśyanā*) of certain modern Western practitioners as well.[12] There is no doubt a big difference between simply having a dull thoughtless *tabula rasa* and lucidly abstaining from pursuing the thoughts that arise.

Was *that* kind of distorted argumentation all there was to the debate? I do not think so. There *were* serious issues—and not just repeated question-begging—about whether not-thinking leads to meditative self-stultification. As I think it will become clear, these issues won't simply go away if we take Heshang's "not-thinking" as meaning "lucidly not pursuing thoughts." Kamalaśīla's arguments can very well be seen as undermining that position too. So let's take up two serious issues in the debate.

V

First, the Samyé debate turned in part on rival metaphysical accounts of the buddhahood, or the buddha nature, that is supposedly present in all sentient beings so that they *can* become enlightened.[13] Heshang's view was that people are all buddhas, and have been so all along, fully and *ab initio*. The innately present enlightened mind is thus to be directly disclosed or manifested; enlightenment is not something newly gained by a series of conceptual steps leading to better and more vivid understandings of metaphysical principles such as emptiness, suffering, impermanence, and so on. In reply to the objection "How does one obtain omniscience [i.e., enlightenment] if one has no notions, reflection, or analysis?" Heshang supposedly said: "If thoughts don't arise and one abstains from all notions, the true nature that exists in us and omniscience manifest by themselves."[14] The connection Heshang wishes to make between nonconceptualization and realizing innate enlightenment is thus the following: concepts distort or even preclude our understanding of that nature; it is only by avoiding them that the true innate enlightened nature—the buddha nature—can manifest.

To this, Yeshé Wangpo (Ye shes dbang po), a prominent Tibetan monk in Kamalaśīla's entourage, supposedly argued as follows, according to the sixteenth-century chronicle *Mkhas pa'i dga' ston*:

> If you [Heshang] accede suddenly [to enlightenment], then why are you still doing anything? If you are a buddha from the beginning (*dang po nas sangs rgyas*), what then is wrong?[15]

And elsewhere on the same page in this Tibetan history, Yeshé Wangpo is said to have insisted upon the absurdity of "being enlightened without having done anything at all."[16] A similar charge also figures in the *Bhāvanākrama* itself: the Suddenist's passive, nonconceptual state could not possibly constitute enlightenment, "because it would follow absurdly that everyone everywhere would be liberated."[17] The arguments against Heshang's view on buddha nature and sudden enlightenment are, in effect, a kind of appeal to gradualist common sense.

Such rival metaphysical accounts on how one is innately, or "from the beginning" (*dang po nas*), do impact significantly on the main question of whether nonconceptualization leads to spiritual progress or ever greater stupefaction. Kamalaśīla (like many mainstream Indian paṇḍits of his time) probably had a relatively "thin" description of buddha nature as a mere potential for enlightenment, so that the practitioner is not actually enlightened but can become so by following a certain step-by-step path. Heshang, on the other hand, had a very "thick" description of that nature as an enlightened state that is actual and fully present "from the beginning." For Kamalaśīla, then, simply abiding in a nonconceptual state is an obstacle to progress. One does not "see" anything soteriologically relevant, just more of the same dullness and confusion, and thus one would remain as ignorant as one is or regress even further.

With a thick description of buddha nature, on the other hand, there is something very important to be disclosed. It is not clear how Heshang himself answered the specific objection of Kamalaśīla's entourage that, if sentient beings had innate (full) buddhahood, any effort and practice would be redundant. But in one way or another the problem comes up repeatedly in traditions, such as the Great Perfection (*rdzogs chen*), that advocate such innate enlightenment and a disclosive path by which it is actualized without artifice or effort. These thinkers—often polemically tarred in later literature as close to Heshang—then had to develop their respective versions of what constituted ignorance and the path to overcome it, all the while recognizing that enlightenment was innately present all along as a type of innate awareness (*rig pa*). Disclosive artificeless paths are no doubt more elusive than their gradualist counterparts. It is not possible to take them up here in any detail.[18] Suffice it to say that Tibetan thinkers devoted deep thought to this matter and seem to have been aware of the gross absurdities to be avoided. It is hard to see that all such accounts are *a priori* precluded by "common-sense" charges of redundancy like those leveled by Kamalaśīla and his entourage.

VI

The other serious difference between the parties is on the *epistemological value* of not thinking about things and not pursuing notions analytically. Kamalaśīla repeatedly speaks of the necessity for the meditator to engage in rigorous philosophical analysis, "examination of the real/reality" (*bhūtapratyavekṣā*),[19] without which he or she falls into the trap of stupefaction (Tucci 1971, 16–17). Why would Heshang, or anyone like him, fall into that trap if he consciously abstained from rigorous analytic thinking and simply remained meditatively lucid?

In fact, what is in the background is once again a key theme in Dharmakīrtian epistemology, namely the proper way in which knowledge can be reached by "nonapprehension" (*anupalabdhi*). Kamalaśīla, as a Mādhyamika, held that no things have intrinsic natures (*svabhāva*)—natures that they would have purely "in themselves" independently of other things. This "absence of intrinsic nature" (*niḥsvabhāvatā*), which constitutes ultimate and hence liberating truth, is to be understand by means of a Dharmakīrtian nonapprehension (see Keira 2004). The meditator thus uses Madhyamaka-like reasonings—typically four or sometimes five major "reasons" (see Tillemans 1984, 361 and 371n16)—to convince himself that such natures are in fact impossible and thus that they cannot be found or apprehended (*upalabdhi*) anywhere when one engages in "examination of reality" (*bhūtapratyavekṣā*).

Now there is for Kamalaśīla (as for most people) a crucial difference between *concluding* rationally that something does not exist and simply not thinking about its existence. This is the difference between a rationally founded "nonapprehension" or "nonperception" (*anupalabdhi*, *anupalambha*, *adarśana*) of something and a "mere [rationally unfounded] absence" (*abhāvamātra*) of thinking or apprehension. In the former case, one examines the notion X and shows it to be incoherent and hence that X cannot exist, or one searches physically for X under conditions where it would normally be observable if it were there. When one does not apprehend it for appropriate reasons (e.g., that it is impossible, or that it is not observed where it should be observed), one concludes rightly that it does not exist. In the latter case, however, one does not conclude anything at all: one just does not think about the matter. The former then leads to knowledge (i.e., true understanding reached by a reliable procedure), whereas the latter does not, and indeed, so Kamalaśīla would argue, is conducive to dullness: the more it is "practiced" the less one would know. It is this latter type of meditation—mere absence of awareness and thinking (*smṛtimanasikārābhāvamātra*; Tucci 1971, 15)—that Heshang supposedly advocated and that was, for Kamalaśīla, a method conducive to indifference and dullness and nothing more.[20]

The issue is thus the epistemic worth of meditative states. Kamalaśīla's central point could be reformulated as follows: the debate is not about whether Heshang-style meditation would likely make one *become* semi-comatose or have other such damaging psychological effects. Instead, the debate is about the *value* of the Heshang-style meditative state of mind. The charge would be that, even if it were psychologically possible to be nonconceptually lucid and not pursue notions further, this would yield no knowledge. "Stultification" would then refer to the lack of knowledge that occurs when people, for one bad reason or another, fail to think things through rigorously and seek to understand by another means—a meditation that bypasses or avoids analysis. We had earlier spoken (in section IV) of the potential reply to Kamalaśīla that he might be conflating the not-thinking of an unconscious individual and the not-thinking of people who remain lucidly conscious but who abstain from, or at least do not pursue, conceptual thinking. I would hazard that for Kamalaśīla the difference is not great. His point is that, lucidly conscious or not, without a commitment to understanding based on thoroughgoing and rigorous reasoning, one will simply have no knowledge.

VII

The debate thus formulated has larger philosophical implications. What generally is the epistemic worth or epistemic contribution of a meditative state of mind when it is based upon good philosophical thinking about real states of affairs? And what is its worth if it is not? There are, broadly speaking, two recurring traditional Buddhist, as well as modern, orientations on the relationship between meditative and philosophical approaches. Roughly, the two are: (1) a "continuity thesis"—meditative understanding leads to knowledge of objects but is continuous with and dependent upon philosophical thinking—and (2) an "independence thesis"—meditative states of mind are independent of philosophy. This latter thesis has it variants: it is sometimes held that meditation is "aphilosophical," only a practical matter that does not need to be assessed philosophically; or it can be thought that meditation is radically different from, or opposed to, philosophical evaluation. In the final part of this chapter, we will consider the prospects for both these theses and their variants.

First, to take up the continuity thesis, this view is clearly what Dharmakīrti, Kamalaśīla, and other later mainstream Indian Buddhist thinkers held. So if we take the Indian discussions as instructive—as I think we should, given that these later Indian Buddhists developed the details of their position in almost unparalleled depth and subtlety—what then are the philosophical prospects for this view on meditation? The prospects would appear to be quite mixed. Of course, as we have seen, there is little doubt that meditative understanding as depicted in Kamalaśīla-style Indian accounts is indeed somehow interwoven with philosophy, but the key question is whether that version of meditative understanding could make any contribution to knowledge *distinct from* or *over and above* the contributions of philosophical thinking. If we look at the textual accounts on this, I do not think it would.

Let us, then, look briefly at the mainstream Indian Buddhist discussions of the "direct perception of the yogin" (*yogipratyakṣa*) that is supposedly the goal of meditation. Kamalaśīla's philosophical mentor, Dharmakīrti, had recognized that the direct perception of the yogin is engendered by the power of the yogin's concentration and is not caused or directly linked to an object in the world. Instead of arising *because* of the object (as in the case of sense perception), it arises because of previously developed mental powers. It seems then that the would-be "direct perception" is not very direct at all, as it is caused by factors quite different from the properties of the object—primarily by the subject's extraordinary powers of visualization.

Indians were rightly worried that, as there would be no direct causal connection with real objects (contrary to the case of sense perception, where there is such a connection), the possibility of error would loom large. What makes the would-be yogic perception more than a subjective state unanchored in reality, a *mere autosuggestion*, and hence quite possibly wrong? This doubt was also formulated by non-Buddhist thinkers such as Vācaspatimiśra and is to be taken seriously.[21]

Indeed Kamalaśīla and Dharmakīrti themselves recognized that seeming "direct perceptions" engendered by previous thought processes could well turn out to be merely self-induced hallucinations, as is the case when a man, overpowered by his intense desires, has vivid obsessive fantasies.[22] The test for Dharmakīrti, Devendrabuddhi, Dharmottara, and others as to whether a putative yogic perception was a mere hallucination or not was to see whether it could be vindicated by philosophical analysis.[23] It was to be examined by reason (*yukti*) and determined to be in accordance with other reliable sources of knowledge (*pramāṇa*). In short, yogic perception, to be genuine, had to apprehend matters that had already been confirmed rationally or would subsequently pass the tests of philosophical thinking (see Eltschinger 2009, 195ff.) This may sound like a promising approach to distinguish the genuine from the spurious, but it is surprising how little autonomy it accords meditation. It is clear that all the epistemic weight is once again on philosophical thinking and that yogic perception adds no new discoveries of truths.

One could, of course, just bite the bullet and agree that the yogic perception promoted by Kamalaśīla and Dharmakīrti *is* nothing more than a vivid presentation of conclusions reached by prior correct rational analysis. It could arguably still be important and transformative, at least psychologically. Indeed, yogic perception of a real object might well be comparable to a fictional or cinematographic re-creation of a real historical event; such re-creations, when done well, certainly do affect individuals' emotional lives and ways of understanding events. Nonetheless, just as a modern dramatization by itself adds nothing new to the historian's knowledge of the details of the event, it seems clear that yogic perception would not provide any new *information* from what had been given by philosophy. Kamalaśīla's yogic perception, in effect, appears to be neither a genuine direct perception nor a source of new knowledge but rather a type of amplification or integration of the contents of philosophical thought. Philosophy would be doing the significant epistemic work of discovering truths. This version of the continuity thesis, in effect, would relegate meditation to the status of a powerful accessory.

Second, what are the prospects for the independence thesis? There is, at the outset, a confused variant of this position that has wide currency in modern circles that promote Buddhist meditation. It is more or less the following: Buddhist meditative states are better not assessed philosophically; meditation is "aphilosophical" in that it is practical in orientation and seeks primarily improvement of the mind rather than knowledge of truths. In brief, what counts is the therapy, the cultivation of beneficial states; meditation *need not* aim for knowledge of real objects. Thus, for example, some modern applications of Buddhist "mindfulness meditation" largely pass over Buddhist philosophical positions on metaphysical issues in favor of techniques to develop calmness, increased concentration, improvement of memory, happiness, stress management, harm reduction, better decision-making, and other benefits.[24]

Whatever the efficacy of these Buddhist-based techniques might be—and

I'm not putting their therapeutic efficacy into question—interpreting Buddhist meditation in terms of psychological or neurological effects largely to the exclusion of two thousand years of rich philosophical, religious, and ethical thought is uncomfortably close to trivialization. It is very doubtful that an emphasis on psychological techniques could be taken as reflecting the essentials of Buddhist meditation. Buddhists generally hold that accomplishing the religious goal of enlightenment involves knowledge of how things are and not just psychological techniques for developing desirable states of mind and traits of character.

There is, however, a more sophisticated variant of the idea of Buddhist meditation, and Buddhism in general, as a form of therapy. People familiar with philosophies such as those of the American thinkers William James, John Dewey, and Richard Rorty sometimes argue that Buddhism is *not* indifferent to getting things right and knowing reality but that it is essentially a form of philosophical pragmatism.[25] The criterion for any state of mind being (or leading to) knowledge of real things, then, is just that it will result in maximally useful/beneficial effects or the long-term accomplishment of such human goals as liberation from the realm of suffering. In short, Buddhists are not purely practical therapists disregarding issues of knowledge; they pursue soteriological goals as *pragmatists* in their philosophies of truth and knowledge.

It has sometimes been argued that Dharmakīrti's philosophy, with its emphasis on *arthakriyā*—effective action, sometimes interpreted as "the accomplishment of human goals"—did indeed focus on a pragmatic theory of truth, and that this is even one of its more attractive features (see Powers 1994 and Cabezón 2000). I have on occasion argued against this interpretation of Dharmakīrtian thought, seeing his philosophy as involving instead a rather specific type of correspondence theory (Tillemans 1999, 6–12). Be that as it may, we need not try to settle that debate over truth theories: even if we agreed that Dharmakīrti and Kamalaśīla were somehow amenable to philosophical pragmatism, it is doubtful that they, as pragmatists, could agree that not thinking about things, or any other meditative technique, results in maximal utility *unless they had some plausible account of how it could accomplish that end.* Alas, mere unexplained data on success rates shows precious little about genuine efficacy.[26] At some point we need to fill in the gaps and account for why such and such a technique is likely to succeed when practiced in such and such circumstances, etc., and another is not. One way to see Kamalaśīla's argument is that, for him, no such account will ever be forthcoming in the case of a purely nonconceptual meditation. Right or wrong about that, at the very least he was right to demand that an advocate of non-conceptual meditation seriously address the question of how the explanatory gap would be bridged.

Finally, are there more promising defenses of the independence thesis in traditional Indo-Tibetan Buddhism that do address that gap? Already from the time of the *Madhyamakārthasaṃgraha* (attributed rightly or wrongly to the sixth-century author Bhāviveka), some Indian Buddhists promoted the idea that a propositional philosophical understanding of the ultimate differs radically from an understanding of the ultimate as it is. The former, termed *paryāya* (expedient, approximative), is a kind of philosophers' version of the ultimate; the latter, *aparyāya* (not expedient, not approximative), is genuine and beyond propositional thought. And indeed many are the Indo-Tibetan thinkers who would emphasize in one way or another the transcendence and inconceivability of genuine Buddhist knowledge of the ultimate. In the present context, however, a mere appeal to inconceivability is very short on explanation. We would need much more to address Kamalaśīla's explanatory demands.

One of the more audacious defenses of the independence thesis is that of the Tibetan polymath Longchenpa (Klong chen Rab 'byams pa, 1308–64), who made a wide-ranging distinction between "dualistic mind" / "dichotomizing thought" (*sems*) and "primordial gnosis" (*ye shes*). Propositional, philosophical knowledge is in the domain of the former, and nonobjective, nondual, ultimate understanding in the latter. Enlightenment is taken to be the disclosure of this primordial gnosis itself, while dualistic mind is in fact something samsaric to be overcome, something that obscures gnosis;[27] gnosis is a special type of understanding free from all objects (*yul*). The aim of a meditative approach would thus be knowledge of deep features of reality but not knowledge that could be said to be *of* any objects, states of affairs, or true propositions.[28]

The question will rightly arise, too, as to why one should value this "intransitive" type of meditation[29] as leading to genuine knowledge, for clearly, once philosophy has been dismissed as "dualistic thought" and is regarded as something to be eliminated, the usual epistemological ways of evaluating reliability are not available. The reasoning Longchenpa develops for the value and trustworthiness of such meditative states and gnosis does not, indeed, follow usual Buddhist epistemological strategies. Instead they appear to be essentially transcendental arguments, seeking to show that, if we accept that enlightenment is possible, then a primordial gnosis must be presupposed as underlying all samsaric thought. There is a sense in which Longchenpa stands Kamalaśīla's arguments on their head. Whereas Kamalaśīla had argued that nonconceptualization leads to stultification and that we therefore need to rely on concepts, Longchenpa begins with the premise that conceptualization and all other forms of "dualistic thinking" must be abandoned if we are to become enlightened; this he takes to be the basic recurring message of Buddhist canonical literature. However, he does not accept that enlightenment could consist in a *mere* abandonment of concepts and dualistic thinking, as this *would* lead to a stupor (*mun pa*), just as Kamalaśīla had argued. There must therefore be a more fundamental underlying understanding, a ground (*gzhi*) or innate awareness (*rig pa*) that is always present and whose disclosure is enlightenment.[30] The arguments, although they can and will be challenged at several places, would seem to turn on intriguing intuitions: that if one were not somehow actually enlightened all along, one never could become so, and that the state of *saṃsāra* and its ignorance would seem to be a form of intelligent self-deception rather than just darkness or absence of understanding.[31] It may well be that this approach—or one broadly along these lines—would hold the most promise for the independence theorist.

Notes to Chapter 10

1. Demiéville 1987 [1952]. Some of the other important publications in the considerable literature on the subject are Gomez 1983, Tucci 1986, Tucci 1971, Seyfort Ruegg 1989 and 1992, and P. Williams 1992.
2. See Tsong-kha-pa 2002, 351ff. See Tillemans 1998 on the debate in Tibet.
3. For a modern advocacy of this method of meditation, see the present Dalai Lama's "Key to the Middle Way" in Dalai Lama and Hopkins 1975.
4. On yogic perception in Dharmakīrti, see, e.g., Eltschinger 2009 and 2010, Franco 2011, Funayama 2011, Taber 2009, Woo 2003, and Dunne 2006. In Kamalaśīla's defense of yogic perception in his work the *Madhyamakāloka*, we see him regularly quoting the major definitions and ideas of Dharmakīrti; see Keira 2004, 5, 101ff.
5. *Brtag tu myed pa'i gnas*. See Tanaka and Robertson 1992.
6. See the translation of Wang Xi's memoir in Demiéville 1987, 78–80: *Question ancienne*—Qu'entendez-vous par « regarder l'esprit » [i.e., *kan xin*]? *Réponse*—Retourner la vision vers la source de l'esprit, c'est « regarder l'esprit »; c'est s'abstenir absolument de toute réflexion et de tout examen, que les notions se mettent en mouvement ou non, qu'elles soient pures ou impures, qu'elles soient vides ou ne le soient pas, etc.; c'est ne pas réfléchir sur la non-réflexion. C'est pourquoi il est dit dans le *Vimalakīrti-sūtra:* « Le non-examen, c'est la *bodhi* ».
7. Our translation of Demiéville 1987, 22: "Les protagonistes du concile de Lhasa durent constamment tomber dans les impasses parce qu'ils n'attribuaient pas le même sens aux mots qui revenaient sans cesse dans le débat."
8. "Un texte qui fourmille de malentendus terminologiques"; Demiéville 1987, 22.
9. Kamalaśīla does in fact accept a *certain* kind of *amanasikāra*—that is, not thinking about such and such things when one has understood through analysis that they

don't/can't exist. See note 11 or 14 below. But *that* of course is *not* what Heshang meant by the term. Hence the critique.

10. Sanskrit text in Tucci 1971, 13–15: *yas tu manyate / cittavikalpasamutthāpitaśubhāśubhakarmavaśena sattvāḥ svargādikarmaphalam anubhavantaḥ saṃsāre saṃsaranti / ye punar na kiṃcic cintayanti nāpi kiṃcit karma kurvanti te parimucyante saṃsārāt / tasmān na kiṃcic cintayitavyam / nāpi dānādikuśalacaryā kartavyā / kevalaṃ mūrkhajanam adhikṛtya dānādikuśalacaryā nirdiṣṭeti / tena sakalamahāyānaṃ pratikṣiptaṃ bhavet / mahāyānamūlatvāc ca sarvayānānāṃ tatpratikṣepeṇa sarvam eva yānaṃ pratikṣiptaṃ syāt / tathā hi na kiṃcic cintayitavyam iti bruvatā bhūtapratyavekṣālakṣaṇā prajñā pratikṣiptā bhavet / bhūtapratyavekṣāmūlatvāt samyagjñānasya / tatpratikṣepāl lokottarāpi prajñā pratikṣiptā bhavet / tatpratikṣepāt sarvākārajñatā pratikṣiptā bhavet / nāpi dānādicaryā kartavyeti vadatā copāyo dānādiḥ sphuṭataram eva pratikṣiptaḥ / etāvad eva ca saṃkṣiptaṃ mahāyānaṃ yaduta prajñopāyaś ca / . . . tasmād asyānupāsitavidvajjanasyānavadhāritatathāgatapravacananīteḥ svayaṃ vinaṣṭasya parān api nāśayato yuktyāgamadūṣitatvād viṣasaṃsṛṣṭavacanaṃ saviṣabhojanam ivātmakāmena dhīmatā dūrata eva parihartavyam /.*

11. There is evidence that Chan meditators were indeed confronted with the objection that their "no thought" would make them similar to wood and stones; they reply that their type of no thought has to be distinguished from the no thought of brute matter. The objection and reply figures in a Chan text attributed to Bodhidharma. See Demiéville 1987, 99n2.

12. Some might wonder if it makes any sense at all to discuss Tibetan and Chinese positions together with a Theravāda-inspired practice like *vipassanā*. Oddly enough, it probably does. The *vipassanā* and "mindfulness meditation" practiced in the West is significantly dissimilar from what is described in Abhidharma literature; it is largely a product of twentieth-century Buddhist modernist writings—e.g., works like the *Heart of Buddhist Meditation* by Nyanaponika Mahathera (Siegmund Feniger) and those of popular writers like Joseph Goldstein—that tend to downplay the cognitive and discriminative aspects of the traditional accounts. See Dreyfus 2011c. In particular, the current construal of this meditation as *purely* nonjudgmental, present-centered, bare awareness is actually quite poorly attested in the classical Abhidharma's four *smṛtyupasthāna*/*satipaṭṭhāna* contemplations. Indeed, as Dunne 2011b interestingly argues, the Western position on *smṛtyupasthāna* (mindfulness) as bare, nondual, and nonjudgmental awareness may even be, philosophically speaking at least, closer to a high-level Tibetan Mahāmudrā position than to things traditionally Abhidharmic or Theravādin. In traditional accounts of *smṛtyupasthāna* we find a considerable place for the remembrance (*smṛti*) of the usual Buddhist dogmatic themes such as impermanence, the aggregates, the four noble truths, the sense spheres, ethical principles, and so on. For example, the contemplation of the uncleanliness of the body is an obvious case where analysis and evaluation occupy a very important place in *smṛtyupasthāna*, even if the initial stages of *smṛtyupasthāna* contemplation of the physical are framed in terms of bare awareness of breath, activities, and so on. It is equally difficult to imagine that one could arrive at an understanding of the elaborate Abhidharmic scholastic schemas of aggregates, sense spheres, links of dependent origination, hindrances, factors leading to awakening, virtues, nonvirtues, and so on by bare awareness alone and *without a sustained analytical focus on those doctrinal and scholastic themes.* Cf., however, Anālayo 2003 on *vipassanā*, *satipaṭṭhāna*, and bare awareness in Theravāda.

13. By and large, metaphysics is *not* a secondary speculation that subsequent scholastic thinkers impose upon an otherwise essentially practical activity or upon an exclusively experiential state of mind. That it *is* secondary or derivative in this way is a long-standing view that has been argued by many major figures in Buddhist studies, e.g., inter alia, Constantin Regamey, Lambert Schmithausen, and Edward Conze. For critiques of this view of the derivative nature of Buddhist philosophy and the primacy of experience, see Sharf 1995 and Franco 2009. In much the same spirit as Franco (who discusses the positions of Regamey, Schmithausen, et al. in detail), I would suggest that accounts of what one should meditate upon, how one should do it, and what one will experience do vary notably with ontologies adopted about what is real, ultimate, and hence conducive to liberating experience. The Samyé debate on meditation seems to be no exception. It is, in fact, an interesting historical or cultural question as to why Westerners thought, and continue to think, that meditation somehow has to be very distinct from metaphysical speculation.
14. See Demiéville 1987, 94–95: "*Question ancienne*—Si l'on est sans notion, sans réflexion, sans examen, comment obtiendra-t-on l'omniscience? *Réponse*—Si les fausses pensées ne se produisent pas et qu'on s'abstienne de toute fausse notion, la vraie nature qui existe au fond de nous-mêmes et l'omniscience se révèlent d'elles-mêmes." Note, however, that Demiéville's translation "fausses pensées" for *wang xin* 妄心 or "fausse notion" for *wang xiang* 妄想, while literally faithful to the Chinese, might lead one to think that Heshang is advocating that one just avoid false thoughts and instead seek true ones. The point is rather that *all* thoughts or notions are, in the important sense for Heshang, fundamentally false.
15. Dpa' bo gtsug lag phreng ba, *Mkhas pa'i dga' ston*, 389; see Tillemans 1998, 406.
16. *Ci yang ma byas par 'tshang rgya ba*; Tillemans 1998, 406.
17. *Sarvatra sarveṣāṃ muktiprasaṅgāt*; Tucci 1971, 16.
18. I owe the term "disclosive path" to my former student David Higgins. Higgins 2013 is a study on Klong chen pa's key difference between conceptualizing *dualistic mind* (*sems*) and *primordial gnosis* (*ye shes*). On the paths in Jigmé Lingpa's ('Jigs med gling pa, 1730–98) works on the Longchen Nyingtig (*Klong chen snying thig*) of the Great Perfection, see van Schaik 2004. See also Read 2009 on disclosive Buddhist paths and Wittgenstein's famous ladders (or rather appearances of ladders) that are to be set aside.
19. This key term is best read as a genitive *tatpuruṣa* (i.e., a dependent determinative compound) with *bhūta* meaning "the real," "reality." We see clearly that this is Kamalaśīla's understanding of the compound when he states in *Bhāvanākrama* III, 5.17–19 (Tucci 1971): *bhūtapratyavekṣaṇā ca vipaśyanocyate / bhūtaṃ punaḥ pudgaladharmanairātmyam /*. "Now what we term 'insight' is [nothing but] the examination of the real/reality. And as for the real, it consists in the selflessness of persons and the selflessness of phenomena." The term *bhūtapratyavekṣā* has often been taken as an adjectival *karmadhāraya* compound, "correct examination," "exact analysis," etc., but whatever be the merits of that translation in other contexts, it does not seem to reflect Kamalaśīla's own understanding. I thank Martin Adam and Vincent Eltschinger for independently pointing this out to me. See Adam 2008.
20. Cf. *Bhāvanākrama* I (Tucci 1986, 211–13): *tathā coktaṃ sūtre katamaṃ paramārthadarśanam / sarvadharmāṇām adarśanam iti / atredṛśam evādarśanam abhipretam / na tu nimīlitākṣajātyandhānām iva pratyayavaikalyād amanasikārato*

vā yad adarśanam / . . . yat punar uktam avikalpapraveśadhāraṇyām amanasikārato rūpādinimittaṃ varjayatīti / tatrāpi prajñayā nirūpayato yo 'nupalambhaḥ sa tatrāmanasikāro 'bhipreto na manasikārābhāvamātram /. "As it was said in the [Prajñāpāramitā] sūtra, 'What is the perception of the ultimate? It is the nonperception of any dharmas.' Here what is meant is just this kind of [analytical] nonperception, but not a nonperception that is due to causal circumstances being incomplete or due to lack of thought, as when, for example, people close their eyes or are blind from birth. . . . Moreover it was said in the *Avikalpapraveśadhāraṇī*, 'one eliminates characteristics of form and so forth by not thinking [of them].' Here too, not thinking about them means the nonperception when one analyzes by means of insight and not the mere absence of thinking."

21. Cf. Deleanu 2010, 61, who rightly underlines how autosuggestion is a serious problem *whenever* knowledge claims are made for meditation: "To put it bluntly, how can we be certain that at least part of the cognitive content gained through, or associated with, advanced meditative states is not the result of autosuggestion rather than of genuine knowledge?"

22. The comparison between yogic perception and such hallucinations had already figured in Dharmakīrti's *Pramāṇavārttika* (3.282), and regularly recurs in later writers, including Kamalaśīla, to serve as a supposedly comprehensible worldly analogy of how yogic perception proceeds. See Eltschinger 2009, 193–94, Franco 2011, 82–86, and Keira 2004, 112–15.

23. See *Pramāṇavārttika* 3.286: *tatra pramāṇaṃ saṃvādi yat prāṅnirṇītavastuvat / tad bhāvanājaṃ pratyakṣam iṣṭaṃ śeṣā upaplavāḥ //*. "Among these [yogic understandings] we accept as a source of knowledge the meditation-induced direct perception that is reliable, like the entities that we had ascertained earlier. The rest are deluded." Cf. Franco 2011, 84–85, which adopts the reading *pramāṇasaṃvādi* instead of *pramāṇaṃ saṃvādi*. On this reading the translation would have to be changed to: "Among these [yogic understandings] we accept as meditation-induced direct perception [an understanding] that is in keeping (*saṃvādin*) with sources of knowledge."

24. Such predominantly therapeutic use of aspects of Buddhist mindfulness meditation are what we find promoted by Elizabeth Stanley, at www.mind-fitness-training.org (accessed Nov. 30, 2013), or by Jon Kabat-Zinn in his Mindfulness-Based Stress Reduction program at the University of Massachusetts. See also the web page of the Mind and Life Institute (www.mindandlife.org, accessed Nov. 30, 2013), as well as Lutz, Dunne, and Davidson 2007 for a sophisticated presentation of the neuroscience on meditation and its therapeutic implications. The essential difference between these approaches and the Buddhists is one of the importance and emphasis to be placed on knowledge of reality—i.e., broadly speaking, metaphysical concerns. True, not all Buddhist meditation is oriented to such knowledge. There were, of course, numerous Buddhist visualizations, concentration exercises, ways to pacify the mind by focusing on the breath, and other such techniques. Probably the most notorious example in the scholastic literature is the so-called meditation on the loathsome (*aśubhābhāvanā*), in which the practitioner visualizes corpses "turning blue and rotting" or skeletons; another is visualizing the whole world as earth or water. Buddhist writers concerned with epistemological issues, as well as authors of other schools, recognized fully well that the corpses and water "seen" or visualized were

unreal; the point of doing such practices was thus certainly not knowledge of the real objects on which one meditated but the psychological effects—nonattachment—that result. Nevertheless, I think that it does not need much textual exegesis—of either Hīnayāna or Mahāyāna texts—to show that, from a Buddhist point of view, the importance of such a psychological or purely therapeutic approach is quite limited if it is indifferent to questions of knowledge and reality.

25. As William James notoriously summarized his version of pragmatism: "an idea is 'true' so long as to believe it is profitable to our lives" (see R. Goodman 1995, 63).

26. The situation is not unlike people citing suggestive data on homeopathic cure rates without having an inkling as to how homeopathy could conceivably work given its use of minuscule doses of pharmacological agents. When faced with an anomaly of this sort, the homeopathist cannot just say eternally, "Well, we see that it works and that's that."

27. Cf. Klong chen pa, *Sems dang ye shes kyi dris lan*, 384: *mdor bsdu na khams gsum pa'i sems sems byung cha dang bcas pa thog ma med pa nas brgyud pa'i bag chags can sgrib pa gnyis kyi ngo bo 'dzin cing / bskyed par brten pas spang bya yin zhing dgag dgos par bshad pa yin no /*. "In short, the three realms' dualistic minds (*sems* = *citta*), mental factors (*sems byung* = *caitta*), and their qualities are subject to imprints coming down from beginningless [time], have as nature the two obscurations, and rely on production. As such, it is explained that they are to be eliminated and should be stopped."

28. In this respect, Longchenpa and other Great Perfection thinkers could be favorably compared with thinkers such as Heidegger, for whom discursive understanding and manipulation of things and propositions—the ontic—is parasitical upon a more fundamental understanding of Being.

29. I owe this classification of meditations into transitive and intransitive to David Higgins.

30. Klong chen pa, *Theg mchog rin po che'i mdzod*, 1041: *'dir mi shes pa kha cig / sems med na bems po'am mun pa ltar 'gyur ro zhes pa'ang thos pa chung ba yin te / sems med kyang ye shes yod pas rig pa 'gag pa ma yin pa'i phyir ro / de'ang ma rig pa 'khrul pa'i sems 'gags pas / ye shes gsal ba'i nyi ma 'char te / mtshan mo sangs pas nyin mo shar ba bzhin no /*. "Some ignorant people argue as follows: 'If there is no dualistic mind (*sems*), it is similar to being inanimate (*bems po*) or in a stupor (*mun pa*).' But these people have studied little. Even in the absence of dualistic mind, since primordial gnosis (*ye shes*) is present, it is not so that awareness (*rig pa*) ceases. Moreover, through the cessation of ignorance—one's deluded dualistic mind—the sun of radiantly clear primordial gnosis dawns just as with the fading of night comes the dawning of day."

31. On ignorance, self-deception, and epistemic versions of *akrasia* in Buddhism, see chapter 9 in this book (i.e., Tillemans 2008a).

Madhyamaka in Contemporary Debates

11. On Minds, Dharmakīrti, and Madhyamaka[1]

I. The Problem

Do Buddhists have a view of mind they can plausibly defend in current philosophical debates often dominated by forms of materialism? In recent years the Fourteenth Dalai Lama and a number of scientists have been meeting regularly in Dharamsala, India, to discuss and compare Buddhist and modern psychological, or cognitive science, approaches to the nature of mind. And no doubt the most difficult problem they have taken up—one that potentially significantly divides Buddhists from many major contemporary analytic philosophers and cognitive scientists—is the question of physicalism, the view that all that there is, is physical in nature or can be thoroughly explained in terms of the physical sciences.[2] The rather extreme version of physicalism that I will take up here is that of the Canadian philosophers Paul and Patricia Churchland. They do not try to show that mind and brain are somehow identical entities but argue instead that mind and the mental are just pseudo-entities accepted in "folk theories," pseudo-entities that can and (at least in the Churchlands' estimation of things) probably will end up being eliminated by better science. This stark version of the position that all is only material has a certain type of rigor appealing to the tough-minded who advocate facing facts without old notions that obfuscate. It is in one way or another taken seriously by many who would invoke science as the best or only source of knowledge. It merits attention in an East-West discussion, even if there are arguably other more sophisticated physicalisms on the market. Last but not least, it is the version of physicalism that figured in a round of the Dharamsala discussions. As Patricia Churchland participated in those discussions, what I have to say can be seen as a continuation of a contemporary comparative philosophy dialogue that has already begun and where positions have already been staked out.[3] It's time to reexamine how the Buddhists could best proceed in that debate. They may well have been betting on the wrong arguments and have more promising ways to defend mind in their philosophy.

II. Dharmakīrti

Let us first briefly go back to the Indian canonical sources to be clear on the main historical antecedents for a contemporary East-West debate on physicalism. For the Buddhist side, the physicalist school against which they (and other Indians) argued vociferously was the Cārvāka, a school that no doubt was perceived as threatening, although we have no clear image of its actual situation in India, or its institutions and the number of its adherents. Indeed we have almost nothing remaining of the Cārvāka's own writings, apart from a few fragments from its founder, Bṛhaspati (second century BC?), and a much later text, the *Tattvopaplāvasiṃha* of Jayarāśi (eighth century).[4] Nonetheless we do have in-depth refutations of their positions by their Buddhist and non-Buddhist opponents, and it is these polemical treatments that enable us to form something of an image of the broad outlines of the Cārvāka physicalist position. They held that only the material, specifically the four material elements, existed and that the mental was a type of insubstantial phenomenon, a kind of epiphenomenon, that reduced to (or perhaps was to be eliminated in favor of) the material in the same way as facts about the intoxicating potential of beer were nothing other than facts about the physical composition of beer: an account of beer's make-up in terms of its material elements adequately explains its intoxicating powers. The underlying motivation: to deny reincarnation and hence the law of karma (retribution), for Cārvākas maintained that because physicalism is so, life and consciousness must end with the destruction of one's body.

Now historically, the usual Buddhist way to refute physicalism was that of the seventh-century philosopher Dharmakīrti and his followers. Indeed, the defense of mind fell almost exclusively to the so-called *pramāṇavāda* school of Buddhist logic and epistemology, a school that advocated a type of Buddhist metaphysical realism, albeit one with a subtler ontology than most.[5] Pramāṇavādins, as well as the other schools, which largely borrowed the antiphysicalist ideas of these logicians/epistemologists, put forth a series of arguments of uneven quality essentially based on the second chapter of Dharmakīrti's major work, the *Pramāṇavārttika*. The central point was that the four elements (earth, air, fire, and water) and their combinations and configurations could not be the primary cause of the mental, in that there are mental properties—ways of thinking, character traits, and so on—that regularly vary even though the material elements remain the same.[6] For example, Pramāṇavādins sometimes argued that newly dead corpses have all the same matter as living bodies but obviously don't think and so on (see *Pramāṇavārttika* 2.51). Identical twins can have the same matter making up their bodies, because they come from the same parental sperm and blood, but they have different character traits.

We can reconstruct and abridge Dharmakīrti and his followers' basic argumentation in three steps, all controversial:

1. Minds and physical things, such as brains, are distinct kinds of real stuff/substances (*dravya*) because of having clearly different properties.
2. Like must cause like; cause and effect are between fundamentally similar kinds of things.[7]

Thus:

3. Because mind and the physical are distinct kinds of stuff, and only like can cause like, the brain and other physical things cannot be the cause of the mental; they can at most be secondary influences, auxiliary causes (*pratyaya*). A previous mind is the substantial substratum (*upādāna*) of the present mind, much like previously existing clay is the substantial substratum for the presently existing pot.

This three-step argument is not *just* supposed to convince the adversary *that* there are in fact minds: it is above all to be a proof of reincarnation. Indeed *Pramāṇavārttika* arguments become the basis for a genre of Buddhist scholastic literature known as *paralokasiddhi*, "proof of other lives," or more literally "proof of other worlds," seeking to establish that for each sentient being there is a continuum of mental states that spans past lives and will (with some rare exceptions) also extend to future lives. To put things in the formal terms adopted by the later *pramāṇavāda* scholastic: because mind and brain are distinct kinds of stuff and only like causes like, the first moment of a newborn person's mind would have to be caused by a mind, and that mind would have to be in her immediately preceding previous life.[8] The fact that it is reincarnation that is argued for, and not just the distinct existence of mind, thus brings supplementary difficulties.

In spite of the enormous respect that I, like many other orientalists and philosophers, have for Dharmakīrti, I think someone has to say honestly and clearly that steps 2 and 3 in the above reasoning—and indeed all his supporting arguments for the principle that it is mental states that primarily cause other mental states—are very difficult to defend nowadays. For example, the series of involved arguments concerning the complete physical sameness of a live and dead brain do not make much sense in the twenty-first century, when we have sophisticated detection of neural activity. The account of what happens to the brain and body at death has thus evolved, so that it would surely be unacceptable now to say that brains before and after death are physically exactly the same.

Moreover, the "like causes like" principle in step 2 may well not prove what the Buddhist wants it to prove. If it is somehow used to show that only mind is sufficiently like mind to be its main cause, an adversary might reverse the argument and say that if *that* is what follows, so much the worse for "like causes like" and its seemingly intuitive appeal. Worse yet for the Buddhist, many physicalists would *accept* the "like causes like" principle and argue that *it* is precisely the reason why mind must either be identical to, or must be eliminated in favor of, the brain. The Dharmakīrtian argument could thus be turned on its head as follows: since the brain does very clearly influence our so-called "mental states," those states must actually be physical in nature, like the brain—anything else would mean that we would have to accept a strange causality between very different sorts of stuff, so different that causality would become unintelligible. This is, pertinently, pretty much the exact argument that a physicalist like Daniel Dennett makes, calling it the "standard objection to dualism."[9]

Many of Dharmakīrti's arguments in the philosophy of mind may have made good sense, and indeed elicited rationally founded conviction, in a time when neurology and genetics were nonexistent and the physical theory of the time was rudimentary. But they are unconvincing now. It should not be surprising that his metaphysics, logic, and philosophy of language fare much better than his antiphysicalist arguments; logic and metaphysics depend very little on the science of the day. Dharmakīrti's antiphysicalist arguments, however, *do* depend on the science of his day, and that is a major reason why many of them look dated and implausible.

Naturally, not everyone would agree with that assessment. Let me, before going on, briefly take up two alternative accounts of what Dharmakīrti's philosophy of mind, as represented in steps 2 and 3, is all about.

First, Alan Wallace also seems to acknowledge that Dharmakīrti's arguments on mind, mental causation, and rebirth will not convince many. But this is, for him, because the nature of the mind is supposedly a fact only directly accessible to advanced contemplatives while to others it is a "hidden" phenomenon (*parokṣa*). Those without considerable proficiency in "contemplative science" therefore cannot validly deliberate about what mind is.[10] I suspect that Wallace is staking out his own position about contemplative knowledge and who can validly debate what. But in any event, Dharmakīrti *didn't* place those preconditions on a debate about the existence of mind as distinct from matter. Indeed, there is, as far as I can see in reading his works, no suggestion that he regarded everyone but advanced meditators as somehow incompetent to deliberate about the basic facts concerning mind.[11] He and his school do indeed hold that mind is *parokṣa* (literally "outside [the range of] the senses"), but that is only to say that it is something that needs to be understood by inferences (*anumāna*), not that it is unknowable by ordinary thinkers. Moreover his general positions on meditative understanding and yogic perception (*yogipratyakṣa*) do not place philosophical debate on important subjects like mind, the four noble truths, and others outside the competence of nonmeditators, or even non-Buddhists.[12] His arguments for mind, dualism, and reincarnation stand or fall on their own, without the entry ticket of proficiency in "contemplative science."

Second, John Taber has reexamined many of those anti-Cārvāka arguments in Dharmakīrti, and while he too concludes that they would not provide *convincing* arguments to establish dualism or rebirth nowadays, he suggests that such is not actually how they need to be taken. They are arguments showing that mind primarily causing mind and the resultant corollaries that follow from this are not *impossible* states of affairs.[13] In short, instead of a proof that mind is the primary cause of mind, and so forth, we supposedly have the much weaker demonstration that it is not impossible that it is.

Taber's argument is tied in with an elaborate exegesis of the second chapter of the *Pramāṇavārttika*, one that largely follows Eli Franco, and I obviously cannot go into that here. One would, however, hardly need forty verses of elaborate arguments to show that mind and reincarnation are "logically possible"—existent in a possible world. Most of us, even the Churchlands, I would imagine, might well agree to that right off the bat, even if we were convinced physicalists about the actual world. There are certainly weirder things in possible worlds than minds and reincarnation. The upshot is that this reading in terms of possibility appears uncharitable, as it would leave Dharmakīrti arguing for what seems to be obvious. By far the most straightforward and natural interpretation of what Dharmakīrti intended is that he saw himself as providing the best account of mind and reincarnation, indeed the true account, and not merely one, among others, that might be true.[14] Is what we can glean from Taber's discussion, then, just that he thinks Dharmakīrti's arguments should be at the table in the modern debate as a *philosophically plausible* alternative to physicalism? That would indeed be debatable, and it is in fact what I think Buddhists should be discussing, although I would maintain that Dharmakīrti will fare less well than many seem to think he will. In any case, this is obviously a different matter than the question of possibility.

Let's go back to the starting point of the three-point Dharmakīrtian reasoning. Even if mind primarily causing mind—and thus steps 2 and 3—

is problematic, it has to be said that we do find in the first step a general Buddhist strategy that is recognizable in many defenses of mind-body dualism: mind just doesn't appear to be the kind of thing that is anything like brain processes; they seem to have very different properties. Indeed, minds, for Buddhists like Dharmakīrti and many others, are inherently luminous. For example, *Pramāṇavārttika* 2.208 famously states *prabhāsvaram idaṃ cittaṃ prakṛtyā* ("Luminous is this mind by its nature"); brains and other material things are not "luminous." Minds are unobstructed in their ability to evolve and develop ever greater virtues such as compassion and wisdom; material things and the processes they undergo are invariably limited—one can learn more and more without limit, but one cannot heat water infinitely, for at a particular point in time it just boils away.

For Dharmakīrti and his followers, the two types of entities manifestly appear to be—and it is thought that they thus are—very different kinds of things. The later Tibetan tradition, for example, in its primers on Dharmakīrti's philosophy of mind, their so-called *blo rig(s)* literature, would characterize mind as "clear and knowing" (*gsal zhing rig pa*), it being understood that "clear" highlights the manifestly "immaterial" (*gzugs can ma yin pa*) character of mind and that "knowing" is in opposition to the manifestly insentient character of inanimate matter (*bem po* = *jaḍa*). And an appeal to phenomenal, or manifest, dissimilarity of the mental and the physical properties has also been a fundamental theme in many Western philosophers' defense of dualism: there would seem to be a whole lot of properties we could ascribe to mind that we couldn't easily ascribe to brains and vice versa. To put it roughly, minds have experiential contents, subjective aspects, qualia, private aspects, and so forth, whereas brains do not.

The question then arises: if we strip away the rather hopeless project of proving reincarnation and providing proofs for mind causing mind—in short, steps 2 and 3—is the remaining scaled-down Dharmakīrtian argument for mind in step 1 philosophically plausible in the current debate? The short answer: it is perhaps plausible when pitted against *some* forms of physicalism, but it will fare much less well against the radical versions we are considering. Indeed, an appeal to the fact that mind and matter have different properties may plausibly work against those Western physicalists who hold that the two are contingently *identical* entities, but it works much less well against the Churchlands' approach, what is termed "eliminativism." The Churchlands, Steven Stich, and before them Richard Rorty, with his "disappearance theory of mind," do not maintain that there are minds and that they also are identical with something material, but rather that mind is most likely a pseudo-phenomenon and hence eliminable, much like a whole slough of other pseudo-phenomena that have been eliminated by not figuring in better replacement theories of what there actually is in reality. If there is a scientifically adequate physicalist account of all that had previously seemed to require explanation in terms of mental entities, then—so argue the Churchlands—those mental entities will fall by the wayside, just as demons, occult forces, humors, astrological forces, and other postulates of superstition and outdated medicine fell by the wayside with the advent of a better-informed modern medical science. The going common-sense views about the existence and nature of mind would turn out to be an outdated and false *folk theory*.

Now, the Churchlands' eliminativist position specifically targets *propositional attitudes*—believing *that* such and such a proposition is the case, knowing *that* . . . , hoping *that* . . . , wishing *that* . . . , thinking *that* . . . , intending *that* . . . , fearing *that* . . . , and so on and so forth. According to our common-sense ideas and parlance, we do of course hold that we believe, think, fear, and so on *that* various things are thus and so, and we maintain we should believe *that* such and such is so if something else is the case. Such beliefs, thoughts, and so on are individuated by their propositional content and involve intentionality (they are directed *to* something) and normative concepts (e.g., what follows from what; what we *should* think). Many philosophers recognize that those features and others are extremely difficult to explain in a usual physicalist description of what there is. The Churchland-style eliminativist physicalists too hold that those features very likely won't be vindicated by a seamless reduction to brain states. But they go further: it's actually not even worth trying to do so. So much the worse for propositional attitudes and so much the worse for the folk theory. As Paul Churchland puts it, "[F]olk psychology is a radically inadequate account of our internal activities. . . . On his [i.e., the eliminative materialist's] view it will simply be displaced by a better theory of those activities" (Churchland 1981, 72).

Strong stuff. I think the Buddhist may be able reply to such radical eliminativism in a number of ways, but I also think that those ways, if they are to have a chance of being taken seriously, will *not* be the approach that Dharmakīrti and his followers put forward in step 1. The problem with the general Dharmakīrtian strategy is this: it doesn't matter to an eliminativist that mind and brain don't appear to be the same sorts of things, or that they have very different types of phenomenal features, or that minds would involve propositional attitudes and brains wouldn't. After all, eliminativists will retort that it doesn't matter all that much to them that demons, phlogiston, and other pseudo-entities might seem to have such and such properties, while the entities figuring in scientific theories explaining how diseases, combustion, and so forth come about don't have those properties. The real point for the eliminativist is that citing the distinct properties of demons, what they look like and so forth, is just useless deliberation about pseudo-entities; all that is worth talking about and all that is real is what figures in the physicalist account—that is all there actually is. Where Dharmakīrti was convinced that the two entities looked too different to be the same, the modern-day eliminative physicalist accepts one type of real entity and waves away all dualist intuitions about the manifest distinctness of the mental from the physical as irrelevant.

The primary issue at stake in this contemporary debate over eliminativism, then, is *not* whether mind does or does not have such and such distinct properties, but whether we could just drop the folk theory pretty much all together. How far can ordinary worldly beliefs and linguistic practices be reformed and replaced, for obviously eliminating talk of the propositional attitudes—beliefs, thoughts, feelings, intentions, and so on—is an enormous rupture? The Churchlands' view is indeed an extreme one. They, in effect, propose a wholesale error theory about our intellectual life and advocate that those errors would not figure at all when we finally have a first-class scientific upgrade.

III. Madhyamaka

It is a fact of Buddhist history that the burden of defending mind against forms of physicalism has, over time, been delegated almost exclusively to the epistemologists, the *pramāṇavāda* school, so that we find few arguments on these issues other than those (more or less) in keeping with the second chapter of Dharmakīrti's *Pramāṇavārttika*. And in the contemporary East-West dialogues on these subjects, whether in Mind-Life discussions[15] or in the Buddhist teachings that Westerners follow in Dharma centers, Dharmakīrti's thought is overwhelmingly present. But couldn't there be a more promising Buddhist approach to the mind-body problem? There is another great Buddhist philosophy that needs to be examined here, one that has a radically different stance on metaphysics from the *pramāṇavāda* school in that it does not recognize any entities whatsoever as fully or ultimately real—in effect it shuns ontology altogether. This is the Madhyamaka, the "philosophy of the middle," which stems from Nāgārjuna (second–third century), Bhāviveka (sixth century), Candrakīrti (sixth century) and other luminaries in India and Tibet, a philosophy that holds that everything, be it mental or physical, is empty of intrinsic nature (*svabhāva*).[16]

Could there be a defense of mind following Madhyamaka philosophy instead of Buddhist epistemology? Indeed, I think that there *is* a Madhyamaka case to be made in the antiphysicalist debate, one that has a significantly better chance of handling radical eliminativism than the *Pramāṇavārttika* perspective. Whether it would tell against other contemporary physicalisms is a more ambitious matter. I'm convinced that a broadly Madhyamaka-style quietistic rejection of ontology is important there, too, but I cannot go into that here (see chapter 12). In any case, radical eliminativism is one of the most uncompromisingly stark varieties of physicalism circulating these days, so it is first potentially important to see if the Buddhists have something to say to it besides rather dated Dharmakīrtian arguments. After that, one would have to take up the question of whether other prominent physicalisms somehow collapse into a type of eliminativism and how uncompromising they would be.

A Madhyamaka case for mind will largely turn on their position on the two truths, customary (*saṃvṛti*) and ultimate (*paramārtha*).[17] The particularity of their stance on the customary is that it is *global*: nothing is ultimately established; there are only customary things, things that are the way they are because of human contributions, like designations (*prajñapti*), conceptions (*kalpanā*), linguistic labeling and conventions (*saṃketa*), and customary transactions (*vyavahāra*). This is sometimes characterized as a type of global antirealism,[18] although I think it can also be convincingly regarded as a sort of *quietism* holding that the whole question of the reality or unreality of a world outside human transactions is misguided and one on which we should not take positions or hold theses (*pakṣa*).

No doubt the hardest question in interpreting Madhyamaka is how to take their idea that all things are what they are because of thought, language, and their place in human transactions. The force of that "because" will vary considerably according to different Buddhist writers, as we can see by contrasting two major Tibetan Madhyamaka approaches. One of the more extreme Tibetan schools, the Jonang (Jo nang), will in effect offer a kind of global error-theory, a strong antirealism: we *mistakenly* think and say that there are such and such things, but they are only "existent from the point of view of mistaken minds" (*blo 'khrul ba'i ngor yod pa*); customary truths "exist" because of our errors. This is starkly formulated, but it is not far from what many Indo-Tibetan Mādhyamikas held; it is what I have called "typical Prāsaṅgika."[19]

Others, such as the Gelukpa (Dge lugs pa), will say that there are right answers and sources of knowledge (*tshad ma* = *pramāṇa*) about how customary things are. Their point seems to be that customary things simply have no way they are (*sdod lugs*) *intrinsically* (*rang bzhin gyis* = *svabhāvena*) that could offer a deeper justification for why we talk and think of them in the ways we do; if we persist in demanding something real and fundamental that *makes* us at least sometimes right, we risk unintelligibility—the idea of a metaphysical undergirding for our ordinary practices turns out to be incoherent.[20] Such a quietistic interpretation is nicely put by saying that *there is no other way of establishing things ('jog byed gzhan med pa) besides, or beyond, our various customary transactions (tha snyad = vyavahāra).*[21] Antirealism and quietism are two different interpretations of the Madhyamaka, and I strongly prefer the latter, but it may be that for the present discussion we can more or less work with either.

So can customary truth, for a Mādhyamika, be reformed and replaced, and if so how much of it? As we saw, a Churchland-style physicalist would indeed advocate very radically changing our folk theories in favor of a first-class upgrade. Do the Mādhyamika have arguments, turning on features of customary truth, to show that this is neither desirable nor possible? I think that they do, especially the Mādhyamikas of Candrakīrti's school, and that this leads to a potentially more promising Buddhist defense of mind from radical eliminativism.

True, historically some Mādhyamikas, influenced by Buddhist logic and of a so-called Svātantrika persuasion,[22] did seem to maintain that *wholesale* reforms in what is recognized as customary truth *were* desirable—for example, Śāntarakṣita (eighth century) and others argued that idealism and nominalism represented needed upgrades of lower-level views on customary truth. Candrakīrti and Prāsaṅgika-Madhyamaka, on the other hand, were adamantly opposed to all such global reforms proposed by philosophers. In accepting only "what the world recognizes" (*lokaprasiddha*), Candrakīrti may perhaps accept *piecemeal changes* in accordance with the standards and procedures of the world, but it is quite clear that he has no use for across-the-board reforms such as idealism, nominalism, the logicians' ontology, their account of sources of knowledge (*pramāṇa*), and other such matters. Philosophical attempts to do better than the world in the name of metaphysics and epistemology are dismissed by him as a type of "intoxication" (*smyos pa*).[23] We can confidently suppose that he, or someone carrying on his views, would have a similar reaction if confronted with a modern-day physicalist who proposed a wholesale upgrade of ontology in the name of science.

IV. The Arguments

One can find two types of Prāsaṅgika-Madhyamaka arguments against wholesale reforms of customary truth, the first showing the enterprise to be pointless, the second that elimination of basic features of the customary is incoherent. The first is the type of argumentation that we find in

Madhyamakāvatāra 6.48, where Candrakīrti seeks to show that a wholesale reform (notably the Yogācāra rejection of the external world) is *pointless* because nothing more real is gained in this way. This seems to be a generalizable "by default" argument against wholesale reform: there is nothing ultimately real to be gained by such reforms of customary truths (given that everything is empty and thus of equal status), so why not just leave them (largely) as they are? The argument, however, is not likely to be persuasive to anyone other than a convinced "propounder of emptiness" (*śūnyavādin*). While it might work for someone who held a global view that nothing whatsoever can be intelligibly taken as fully real, it would not for a person, Buddhist or otherwise, who held that there *are* some real things and that it is our duty as philosophers to come up with an ontology that reflects that fact.

We will concentrate on the second type of argument, the incoherence of across-the-board-reform. I think that the most plausible reconstruction of a general Madhyamaka case against wholesale upgrades is one that invokes "indispensability arguments," or in other terms, "transcendental arguments," which show that such and such a proposed reform would lead to self-contradiction because if it were true, it would undercut the conditions indispensable to its truth or, at least, to our sincerely asserting it to be true. That strategy seems to figure quite regularly in Madhyamaka thought and indeed in other areas of Indian philosophy. Dan Arnold has maintained that this type of argument is what is at stake in Nāgārjuna's defence in *Mūlamadhyamakakārikā* (MMK) 24 of emptiness (and hence dependent arising) as being indispensable to any discussion whatsoever about things in the world, including whether there are four noble truths or not. Nāgārjuna's point in MMK 24.20 is that if things were *not* empty of intrinsic existence and thus were *not* dependent upon causes and conditions, there could not be anything that ever arose: a precondition therefore for any discussion about things and their status is that they be dependently arisen—that is, empty of intrinsic existence.[24]

We can also see a type of transcendental argument behind the rejection of wholesale reforms of entrenched features of common-sense/customary truth, but it is one that goes in the opposite direction of MMK 24.20. Instead of arguing that emptiness is a precondition for any discussion, it holds that leaving the customary largely intact is also a precondition for understanding emptiness. Such seems to be a key part of the argument against wholesale reform that is to be found in MMK 24.10 and Candrakīrti's *Prasannapadā* thereupon:

> But, unless one accepts what is customary in the world—what is expressed, expressions, consciousness, and objects of consciousness—one cannot teach ultimate truth [i.e., emptiness]. . . . To show this [Nāgārjuna] thus states:
>
> > The ultimate is not taught unless one bases oneself upon the customary."[25]

The *Prasannapadā* gloss of this passage contains two separable ideas. The first is obvious: arriving at a nonconceptual and nondiscursive realization of an ultimate truth beyond language is not practically, or pedagogically, possible without an initial explanation based upon language and concepts of things. But there is also a generalizable principle implicit in MMK 24.10 that can be formulated as follows: so long as we *are* in fact thinking discursively about a subject or teaching it—whatever it might be and whatever we might think about it—we must accept and rely largely upon the basic linguistic conventions and conceptual distinctions of the world. They are presupposed in the very fact of there being such thought or discussion. Whether on emptiness or another subject, the argument cannot then result in the outright *elimination* of great swaths of customary truth, on pain of undercutting the preconditions for that argument to occur at all. If that is right, then there could not be a wholesale upgrade where all of customary truth, or its essential structures, was simply *replaced* by something better.

This is, I would maintain, a transcendental argument: we cannot rationally advocate wholesale elimination of the most basic features of our ordinary conceptual scheme without a type of self-contradiction, more specifically a type of pragmatic contradiction. In the case of attempts to abandon talk of universal properties, negative states, persons, and so forth, it is indeed difficult to see how one can discuss such matters without at least recognizing that there are *in some way or another* properties that pertain to several particulars, states that do or do not obtain, and people who talk, deliberate, and so forth. Equally, we cannot even discuss the merits of eliminative physicalism without recognizing that there are thoughts about the subject and good reasons for us to think in favor or against. Nor can we accept, or assert with conviction, that something is the right position if we don't allow that we can, in a meaningful sense, come to *believe* it to be right. The incoherence, a kind of practical self-defeat, is that if such eliminativist positions were true, they would themselves all be unbelievable and unassertable.

Ever since Lynne Rudder Baker's 1987 book *Saving Belief*, this argument for the indispensability of the mental—belief is an exemplary case—has often been called the argument against "cognitive suicide."[26] A decade after *Saving Belief*, Baker explains the basic idea as follows:

> To deny the commonsense conception of the mental is to abandon all our familiar resources for making sense of any claim, including the denial of the commonsense conception. (Baker 1998, 12)

> The claim denying the commonsense conception, if true, undermines extant ideas of language and understanding; so without a new account of how language can be meaningful in the absence of belief and intention, we have no way to interpret the claim denying the commonsense conception. (Baker 1998, 15)

Is such a radically new physicalist account of our intellectual life *without* propositional attitudes forthcoming? It does not exist now, nor does it even appear to be on the horizon. Eliminative physicalists like Paul and Patricia Churchland—who are of course inclined to the extreme idea that we have never *actually* had propositional beliefs, thoughts, and so on in the first place and need to finally come to grips with that—give tentative scenarios of a weird future world in which such confusions are thoroughly eliminated from our going theory in favor of a new propositionless form of "understanding."[27]

There have been enough critiques of *those* Brave New World scenarios, and it is all too easy to pile scorn on failed attempts. A more interesting debate centers on the question: What would the failures show, if anything, about the truth of the eliminativist position? It is sometimes said that eliminativists could simply acknowledge that they cannot *as yet* explain how we make assertions in the beliefless world but that, in any case, people don't generally need to give a theoretically satisfying account of what assertions are in order to simply make them.[28] Baker replies that in the beliefless world of the eliminativist, there can be no account of how assertions could be true or false, sincere and insincere, and so on, nor even of the difference between assertions and mere emissions of sound. (In our ordinary concept of an assertion, for example, the idea that such and such is a sincere assertion of *p* presupposes that the utterance of *p* is somehow conditioned by the belief that *p* is true.) Hence her point that, *as far as we have any reason to think*, the eliminativists have no *recognizable* concept of a sincere, meaningful, or true assertion.[29] The burden of proof would fall on them to provide more than mere promissory notes.

Still, it has to be said that these debates will continue, and it should be no surprise that cognitive-suicide arguments do not just simply carry the day unproblematically. Physicalism certainly doesn't just lie down and die; it rolls with the punch. So obviously much more can be said and would need to be said to flesh out this approach. In the last section of this chapter, we'll sketch out a sample of potential Buddhist moves in some of the further debates that fairly naturally arise.

V. Some Remaining Issues

First, the radical eliminativist might perhaps retort that she could change any individual element of our folk psychology and thus arrive finally at a wholesale upgrade but that suicide only comes in if we were to try to change them all at once. She could in effect appeal to Otto Neurath's famous analogy of mariners at sea who can only repair their boat plank by plank because they need to use the boat while they fix it. Improvements to conceptual schemes would be like that boat repair. The Nāgārjunian would have to reply that *that* is not the point. Rather, the point would be that several such individual elements—beliefs, thoughts, minds, and likely universals, persons, negative states of affairs, and others—cannot, or will not, be replaced at all.

Second, let us grant, as I think we should, that it should be very difficult for the Churchlands, or anyone else, to picture convincingly a human life without thoughts, beliefs, and all the other propositional attitudes. And let us suppose, as I think is the case, that this extreme conceptual difficulty of doing without them supports the view (as far as one can reasonably see) that they are here to stay. But would the Madhyamaka position be that radical elimination of our folk psychology is incoherent (or "pragmatically self-contradictory") and thus *cannot* happen (à la Lynne Rudder Baker) or simply that it de facto *will not* happen because the most fundamental folk psychological ideas are not in any case theoretical sorts of views? Indeed, Charles Chastain (1998) has argued that the folk psychology with its various ways of speaking, thinking, and so on, is not a theory at all and is thus not going to be challenged or replaced as a bad theory by better science. Is the MMK's defense of the customary then a bona fide transcendental argument, or is it just a reasonable prediction that fundamental customary truths will largely remain unchanged whatever our theoretical deliberations? Exegetically, the former seems more likely, as there does seem to be, at the crucial points in MMK 24.20 and 24.10, a strong appeal to necessity and indispensability. These passages are not just arguing for a de facto immunity of the customary.

Third, one can imagine an intra-Buddhist objection: doesn't the Mādhyamika herself in some sense eliminate the customary when she arrives at the path of seeing (*darśanamārga*) and directly perceives only the lack of intrinsic natures, the emptiness of all things? The point is tricky. There is no doubt that Mādhyamikas maintain that customary things do not appear to the *āryas* ("noble ones") in their meditative absorption on the ultimate truth, emptiness. Nonetheless, it is quite another thing to say that Mādhyamikas eliminate customary truth or refute (*bādhā*, *gnod pa*) its existence. As I have argued elsewhere, later Mādhyamikas, like Candrakīrti, Kamalaśīla (eighth century), and others, including the fourteenth-century luminary Tsongkhapa (Tsong kha pa), have quite clearly maintained that the perspective of emptiness does *not* actually refute customary truth but only false projections, or superimpositions (*sgro 'dogs* = *samāropa*), upon it; the customary is unassailed by any ultimate perspective, be it an analysis or the resulting direct perception.[30] In fact, we can go further: it looks like this is nothing less than the mainstream position of Indian Madhyamaka from the sixth century on, be it Svātantrika or Prāsaṅgika. As, for example, Jñānagarbha (eighth century) and Śāntarakṣita argue in the *Satyadvayavibhaṅgavṛtti* and *Satyadvayavibhaṅgapañjikā*, if someone philosophically analyzes customary truth, then it is not customary truth but something else (*don gzhan*) that they are deliberating about, and thus they would end up completely refuted (*gnod pa 'ba' zhig tu zad do*) for having strayed from the main subject of debate![31] In short the Mādhyamika targets a superimposed nature of customary truths, namely that they are established intrinsically and independently, whereas the customary truth *per se* is never attacked.

Finally, would these transcendental arguments, if successful, prove any truths about what there really is and isn't in the world, or does that matter all that much to a Buddhist? They might show that there are pragmatic self-contradictions in denying the customary, but would they establish any genuine truths? I would say—perhaps surprisingly but not cavalierly—that the issue is indeed not pressing for a Mādhyamika.

Transcendental arguments are used in many areas of philosophy, and the recurring problem is invariably to evaluate what, if anything, they *prove* or if they could ever answer a skeptic. Ever since the pioneering articles of Barry Stroud on the logic of such arguments, analytic philosophers have recognized that while transcendental arguments may well show the indispensable need for us to *believe* in such and such things—persons, properties, minds, propositional attitudes—a skeptic may still retort that none of them are thereby *proven* to really exist.[32] As Stroud emphasizes, there seems to be an unbridgeable gap between us having to think that *p* is the case, on the one hand, and *p* actually being the case, on the other.[33]

Now, it has become routine in the growing philosophical literature on transcendental arguments to distinguish between strong versions that would seek to answer a skeptic head-on and prove some fact in the world that he doubted, and weaker or more moderate versions that are belief-oriented rather than fact- or truth-oriented and thus would seek to show no more than indispensability to our conceptual scheme.[34] Reading MMK 24.10 as a transcendental argument would make it come squarely down on the side of moderation, one that may show that we, by our own standards, are reasonable to hold such beliefs, even if it does not refute a persistent skeptic who holds that our standards may all be wrong and that things as they actually are could be very different from all our beliefs about them.

Is this moderate stance good enough to establish mind? Probably not for a metaphysical realist, who accepts that there is a completely belief-independent way in which *things are as they are anyway*. Suffice it to point out here that while Stroud's gap may thus well be unbridgeable for such a realist, it is difficult to see that it could tell against a Mādhyamika, who espouses the idea that how things are cannot be separated from our practices of how we conceive of them, talk of them, and act upon them. In short, when realists hold that real facts are as they are anyway, completely independent of all our beliefs, conceptions, and so on, then the move from how our beliefs invariably are to how the facts must be becomes very problematic. This would indeed be Stroud's gap. But, for better or for worse (depending upon one's attraction to metaphysical realism), it would seem that a gap like *that* can hardly exist or even be intelligible to an antirealist or quietist, East or West. The Mādhyamika approach to the realist's persistent skepticism about transcendental arguments might thus be a wise refusal to pursue the debate. And this, I should think, would not be cavalier at all but would be a significant, reasoned, Buddhist stance: mind should essentially be left "fine as it is unanalyzed" (*avicāraramaṇīya*), with no deeper justificatory account needed nor possible. This is not still yet another theory of mind; it is a Buddhist quietism about the philosophy of mind.

Notes to Chapter 11

1. The present paper, in different forms, was presented at the Centre for Buddhist Studies of the University of Kathmandu and the Department of Philosophy of the University of Kyoto. It was subsequently the keynote address of the sixteenth congress of the International Association of Buddhist Studies, Taiwan, 2011. Thanks for helpful remarks along the way to Jay Garfield and Koji Tanaka.
2. Cf. Taber 2003, 481: "[Physicalism is] the view that all phenomena including consciousness either *are* physical in nature or at least can be explained physically, in terms of the laws and principles of the physical sciences."

3. See Houshmand et al. 1999.
4. The text is studied and translated in Franco 1994.
5. On Dharmakīrti's life, works, and philosophy, see Tillemans 2011b.
6. For a translation and study of the relevant section in *Pramāṇavārttika*, 2.34–72, plus Prajñākaragupta's commentary, see Franco 1997.
7. Cf. Taber 2003, 490: "It would appear to be a basic principle of causation that like causes like: trees give rise to other trees, horses give birth to horses, milk yields yoghurt, and clay is made into pots. . . . If the body did cause cognitions, if something could give rise to something else completely different in nature, then, says Dharmakīrti, there would be 'unwanted consequences' (*atiprasaṅgāt*, P[ramāṇa]V[ārttika] II.35–36a). He doesn't tell us what these unwanted consequences are, but he may have had in mind the same possibility the Sāṃkhya believed would result from the truth of the *asatkāryavāda*, that 'anything could come from anything.'" I think that is exactly right. "Anything coming from anything" is a frequent worry in discussions of causation, Madhyamaka included.
8. See Tillemans 1993.
9. See Dennett 1991, 33ff. ("Why Dualism Is Forlorn").
10. See Wallace and Hodel 2007, 86–87: "But the origins, nature, and role of consciousness in nature presently remain hidden from the investigations of scientists and philosophers. And without comprehending the nature of the mind and consciousness, one cannot make valid inferences on the basis of Dharmakīrti's philosophy. . . . Dharmakīrti's reasoning here requires not the unquestioning assumption of his assertions about the nature of consciousness, but valid knowledge that his hypotheses are true. However, unless one is an advanced contemplative who has experientially put those hypotheses to the test, such knowledge may remain inaccessible."
11. If he had, his own anti-Cārvāka arguments would have become superfluous debates with an unqualified adversary. Note that Dharmakīrti did place entry requirements on *certain* debates about ethical matters—e.g., acceptance of Buddhist scripture is necessary to deliberate about the details of the law of karma—but he didn't do that in his defense of mind.
12. On Dharmakīrti's and Kamalaśīla's theories of meditation and yogic perception, see chapter 10 in the present book.
13. Taber 2003, 495–98. See, e.g., pages 495–96: "In the end, I do not really think that Dharmakīrti offers us anything we can use to decide the debate about consciousness. . . . Dharmakīrti has only shown that the materialist has *not* established that it is *impossible* that consciousness could exist independently of the body. . . . However, we shall see presently that this is really all he needs for the purposes of the main argument of the *Pramāṇasiddhi* [i.e., the argument in the second chapter of the *Pramāṇavārttika*]." Page 497: "[A]ll Dharmakīrti has to prove in regard to transmigration in order to establish his main thesis that the Buddha is 'one who has become a means of knowledge' is that it is possible."
14. I don't know of any other major arguments in *pramāṇavāda* philosophy that were clearly designed to show *only* that something *could* be the case in some possible world, that it is simply *logically possible* in the sense of modal logic. In *Pramāṇavārttika* 1's discussions about establishing entailment (*vyāpti*) by not seeing counterexamples, Dharmakīrti repeatedly objects that though we might not see them, "there could be / are (*sambhava, srid pa*) such counterexamples." However, here it is clear that

he did not mean logically possible but nonactual states, like sky flowers and turtle hairs. Rather he was just talking about things that people hadn't yet discovered, such as when one thinks that all the rice in a pot must be cooked because one hasn't yet happened to see any that isn't. Indeed, the idea of something being logically possible but nonetheless known to be nonactual is not taken seriously in Dharmakīrti's theory of triply characterized reasons (*trairūpya*). The point of his arguments against Īśvarasena's idea of establishing entailment by merely not seeing (*adarśanamātra*) counterexamples is essentially epistemological, namely that we are not *sure* that there aren't such things after all, for *adarśanamātra* methods of investigation are epistemically flawed—they are incomplete and undefinitive. Reading modal logic and possible worlds into Dharmakīrti is thus a hard sell. See Tillemans 2011b.

15. See, e.g., www.mindandlife.org (accessed Nov. 30, 2013). See also Flanagan 2011, chapter 3, on his arguments with the Dalai Lama about physicalism.
16. For the history, texts, and philosophy of this school, see, e.g., Seyfort Ruegg 1981; see also Seyfort Ruegg 2010.
17. To get some idea of what this is about, one can consult Newland and Tillemans, 2011.
18. See, e.g., Siderits 1988, Westerhoff 2011.
19. See the introduction and chapter 2 in this book. Note that there are no doubt better global antirealisms on the market than a global error-theory like that of the Jo nang pa. A potentially seductive interpretation of Madhyamaka and its denial of customary things being what they are "intrinsically" might be to see it in terms of Michael Dummett's global antirealism. One might then attempt a rational reconstruction of Buddhist realisms and antirealisms by saying that the former accepts evidence-transcendent ascriptions of truth and the latter does not. This might well yield a palatable global antirealism that consists in saying that there never are evidentially unconstrained truth-conditions. See Hale 1999, 283ff. It appears that Madhyamaka antirealism is largely taken in this way in Siderits 2003.
20. This is not far from the interpretation developed in Perrett 2002. It bears resemblance to a type of minimalism advocated by Mark Johnston that holds that metaphysical pictures of what there is do not (or, what is stronger, cannot) provide the justificatory undergirdings of our ordinary practices.
21. See the summary by Go rams pa Bsod nams seng ge of Tsong kha pa's views in the former's *Lta ba'i shan 'byed*, 14: *dbu ma rang rgyud pa rnams kyis tha snyad du rang gi mtshan nyid kyis grub pa'i chos khas len gyi / 'dir de khas mi len pas gang zag dang chos tha snyad du 'jog pa'i tshul ni / 'di ni lha sbyin no 'di ni lha sbyin gyi rna ba'o zhes sogs tha snyad btags pa'i tshe na / tha snyad de'i dbang gis lha sbyin dang lha sbyin gyi rna ba la sogs pa yod par 'jog gi de las gzhan pa'i 'jog byed med pa ni tha snyad du yod pa'i don no //.* "The Svātantrika-Mādhyamikas accept that on the level of the customary, things [i.e., dharmas] are established by their own intrinsic characteristics. However, here [in the Prāsaṅgika system] this is not accepted. Thus the way they establish people and things customarily is that when we apply linguistic conventions such as 'This is Devadatta,' 'This is Devadatta's ear,' we establish customarily via linguistic conventions that Devadatta, Devadatta's ear, and so forth exist. But there is no other way than that to establish them; this is what is meant by customary existence."
22. On Svātantrika-Mādhyamikas and Prāsaṅgika-Mādhyamikas, respectively, "The Ones Who Proceed by Autonomous Reasonings" and "The Ones Who Proceed by Logical Consequences [of other's views]," see Dreyfus and McClintock 2003. Note

that the terms Svātantrika and Prāsaṅgika are modern Sanskritizations of Tibetan terms for a distinction between Indian Madhyamaka subschools. The distinction is not labeled as such, nor probably even explicitly made, in Indian texts, but it is nonetheless arguably of very great importance in understanding Indian Madhyamaka. See chapter 2, p 60n7.

23. See pages 177 and 179 (sections 8 and 17) in volume 1 of Tillemans 1990.
24. See Arnold 2008.
25. Sanskrit in La Vallée Poussin's edition, p. 494. French translation in May 1959, 229.
26. See also Garfield 1988.
27. Indeed the prospects for the beliefless world are more than a little weird; for example, we may simply be without language (Churchland 1981, 88: "[S]poken language of any kind might well disappear completely, a victim of the 'why crawl when you can fly?' principle"), have bookless "neural" libraries ("Libraries become filled not with books but with exemplary bouts of neural activity."), and last but not least, we may "understand" other people only in the nonpropositional, purely causal way in which one brain hemisphere "understands" or "conceives of" the other.
28. See Chastain 1998.
29. Cf. Baker, "Reply to Chastain," in Grimm and Merill 1998, 27: "Thus, as far as we know and as far as we have any reason to think, eliminative materialism is assertible only if it is false."
30. See Tillemans 2004.
31. See Jñānagarbha's *Satyadvayavibhaṅgavṛtti*. D. 10a–b: *ci ste kun rdzob ni ji ltar snang ba yin te / de la ni ji skad bshad pa'i dpyad pa'i gnas med pa nyid do // 'di ltar / rnam par dpyod pa byed na don gzhan du song bas gnod par 'gyur // kho bo cag ni 'di la dpyod par mi byed kyi / dpyod par byed pa la ni 'gog par byed do // gal te dpyad par byas te ma rung na ma rung du zad do // ji ltar snang ba'i ngo bo kun rdzob pa la brten nas de dpyod pa byed pa ni don gzhan du 'gro ba'i phyir gnod pa 'ba' zhig tu zad do //*. "But the customary is just as it appears. There is absolutely no place for analyzing it in the [philosophical] way just explained. The point is as follows. If [you] do analyze, then [the object] is something else, and so [you] would be refuted. We [Mādhyamikas] do not analyze this [customary truth]. But if [you] analyse it, [you] are refuted. After [you] have engaged in analysis, then if something is impossible, it is nothing other than impossible. An analysis of that [object], after one has relied on the customary nature just as it appears, concerns something else, and that is why [such an analysis] is completely refuted." Śāntarakṣita, in his *Satyadvayavibhaṅgapañjikā*, accepts this view of Jñānagarbha and elaborates upon it. See D. 38b–39a: *'di ltar ji skad bshad pa'i rnam par dpyod par byed pa yin na ni // gnod pa de tshar gcad pa'i gnas su 'gyur ro // ci'i phyir zhe na / don gzhan du song bas te / skabs yin pa'i don bor na rtsod pa gzhan la brten pa'i phyir zhes bya ba'i tha tshig go // 'di rnam par 'grel bar byed de / dbu ma pa kho bo cag ni kun rdzob 'di la dpyod pa sngar ma bstan gyi / khyed kyis byed na 'gog par byed do / gal te dpyad pa byas te / de dag gi de ma rung na ma rung du zad do // kho cag la ci gnod /*. "If one were to engage in analysis of the sort just explained, then that refutation would be a point of defeat (*tshar gcad pa'i gnas = nigrahasthāna*). Why? Because it would concern something else. In other words, this is because when one abandons the object that is actually being discussed, one is then reliant upon a different debate. This is commented as follows: We (*kho cag*) Mādhyamikas have not as yet formulated any analysis of this customary [reality], but if you (*khyed*) did so, then you would be

refuted. After [you] have engaged in analysis, then if something about these [objects] is impossible, it is nothing other than impossible. What refutation would this be for us [Mādhyamikas]?"

32. See Stroud 1968 and 1994.
33. Stroud 1994, 234, put the matter as follows: "Even if we can allow that we can come to see how our thinking in certain ways necessarily requires that we also think in certain other ways . . . how can truths about the world which appear to say or imply nothing about human thought or experience be shown to be genuinely necessary conditions of such psychological facts as that we think and experience things in certain ways, from which the proofs begin?"
34. See Stern 1999, 51.

12. Serious, Lightweight, or Neither: Should Madhyamaka Go to Canberra?

HERE ARE two basic questions that arise when philosophers seek to understand what Buddhist thinkers say about ontology: (1) Are Buddhists naturalistic in their views on what there is—that is, their ontologies—or could they be? (2) If some of them, for example, the Mādhyamikas, *don't* seem to value formulating ontologies as a legitimate intellectual, or spiritual, pursuit, do they have a philosophical case for that rejection?

Often people think that Buddhism is, or should be, compatible with a form of naturalism, and that it would be a plus for Buddhism's comprehensibility if such a rapprochement could be fleshed out. Christian Coseru (2012) and Georges Dreyfus (2011a), for example, argue for a Buddhist version of "epistemological naturalism." This is the stance that asserts that empirical sciences, with their investigations of causality, can and should settle important questions about cognition, and that such questions should not remain reserved to the largely justification-oriented approach of traditional philosophy. I am sympathetic to applying such a naturalistic approach to the Buddhist *pramāṇavāda* and have argued (Tillemans 2011a) that Dharmakīrti even went some significant steps in that direction in his theory of *apoha*. Others focus on "metaphysical naturalism," the view that natural entities, or roughly the ones that science endorses, are all that there really is. They may seek parallels with aspects of physical science (for instance, there is a certain interest in quantum physics), or they may reformulate the essentials of Buddhism so that it is compatible with a naturalistic ontology, especially in the philosophy of mind. The advocates of Buddhism and naturalized mind can go two ways: either argue that usual ideas of naturalism and the ontology of science need to be broadened to include consciousness, probably largely as described in Buddhist texts, or that Buddhism needs to do without consciousness—except perhaps to say that it is a convenient fiction inferred from an object's global availability to memory, action-guidance systems, speech systems, and so on—and reinterpret itself in physicalist terms.[1]

Instead of jumping quickly and enthusiastically into such debates on metaphysical naturalism,[2] Buddhism and science, and so on, it would be better to backtrack a bit to see a larger picture. While the first question concerns specific issues in ontology, the second question takes up ontology as a whole. It is the second question about the value of ontology and metaphysics as a whole that is the most pressing to those who, like me, are sympathetic to the Madhyamaka school. If these Buddhists do have a good case here, as I think they may well have, it would be an Eastern contribution to the contemporary discussion in what is sometimes termed "metametaphysics" or "metaontology": reflection upon the foundations, methodology, and value of metaphysics/ontology in general. And if one questions the legitimacy of ontology, one questions naturalistic ontologies to boot.

Let's be clear: many naturalistic philosophers and many Buddhists alike *do* engage extensively in ontology and have no problems with it. They could be said to do "serious metaphysics." I think the term originates with the Canberran philosopher Frank Jackson, but variants like "ontological seriousness" appear too (e.g., Heil 2003, vii–viii). In any case, there is probably no better place to start than Jackson 1998, 4–5, to have an idea of how modern analytic metaphysics proceeds, whether in Australia or elsewhere:

> Metaphysics is about what there is and what it is like. But it is not concerned with any old shopping list of what there is and what it is like. Metaphysicians seek a comprehensive account of some subject matter—the mind, the semantic, or, most ambitiously everything—in terms of a limited number of more or less basic notions. . . . In sum, serious metaphysics is discriminatory at the same time as claiming to be complete, or complete with respect to some subject matter, and the combination of these two features of serious metaphysics means that there are inevitably a host of putative features of our world which we must either eliminate or locate [in a more basic theory].

Roughly, serious metaphysicians, East and West, are those that think they should seek ontologies pared down to just those entities that *deserve* to underlie our beliefs and ways of speaking about the world. What "deserve" means will take a lot of unpacking and argument, but it would be something like this: these entities are the ones that supposedly make genuine, discernible (typically causal) differences, and are thus indispensable in the most adequate and simple account of what there really is. There is another closely related idea that usually figures as an indispensable part of a serious approach, notably an abhorrence to allowing "weird" entities into our ontology of what is fully real. This is the obligation on metaphysicians to find so-called "weirdness-avoidance strategies"—the neologism is that of Paul Horwich (2006), who goes into more detail than I can here. Let's us just say for now that deserving entities, besides their other positive features, have an acceptable level of oddness. If one holds that the set of the deserving is coextensive with the set of the natural, one will be a typical naturalistic metaphysician.[3]

Undeserving things are those that can either be reduced, or seen to be errors and then eliminated, or seen to be supervenient, or in some way or another explained away because of a more basic theoretical account that satisfies the demands just mentioned. And just which entities are considered *undeserving* by contemporary Western philosophers oriented toward naturalism and serious metaphysics will vary, but the list will typically include purely normative facts (ethical properties, norms of rationality, and so on, especially if taken to be nonnatural properties), universals, instantiation relations, negative facts, mental properties, and maybe even numbers or sets. Thus some philosophers will be nominalists, others will be physicalists, others will explain away numbers as fictions, and yet others will be ethical noncognitivists, maintaining that there are no ethical properties, only attitudes pro and contra certain types of actions. Buddhist metaphysical realists (*dngos po smra ba*) share suspicion of undeservingness about some, but not all, of the same items mentioned above. Universals, negative facts, relations, even macroscopic objects like tables and chairs certainly are very suspect. But mental properties are not suspect at all. In fact the realist Dharmakīrti (sixth or seventh century) was an unabashed dualist, probably more extreme in many respects than are Cartesians, in that the bottom line of his dualism was mind being so separate from body that nothing bodily could significantly influence it at all.[4] While he and his followers were clearly serious metaphysicians, their would-be naturalism, if any, becomes a more murky issue when it is recognized that they would have no truck with physicalism; accepting their philosophies as naturalistic might thus very well necessitate significant rethinking of what we understand by the natural world.

Let us, by way of illustration, bring out what typical Buddhist metaphysical seriousness looks like with a couple of quotes from Indian texts. Dharmakīrti says the following about universals, which he sees as failing the requirements for inclusion in a proper ontology:

> It [i.e., the universal] does not come there [from somewhere else], it was not there already, nor is it produced subsequently, nor does

> it have any parts. [And even when in other places] it does not leave the previous locus. Oh my! It's just one disaster after another.[5]

Paṇḍit Aśoka, in turn, ridicules universals as follows:

> One can clearly see five fingers in one's own hand. One who commits himself to a sixth general entity fingerhood, side by side with the five fingers, might as well postulate horns on top of his head.[6]

In short, universals are depicted as weird, spooky, pseudo-entities that should not be accepted by a responsible thinker concerned with ontology. They don't come from anywhere, they are partless, aren't produced, are in several places at one time, aren't seen, wouldn't seem to have any discernible function, and so on and so on. This seems to be the intuitive starting point underlying the involved one-and-many argumentation that is used to show in detail why universals are actually impossible. The constructive explanation then comes from the *apoha* ("exclusion") theory of meaning, wherein those real universals are replaced by particulars and by fictional, double-negative stand-ins, the idea being that we can then have a trimmed-down ontology that adequately explains sameness, kinds, concepts, and so on without the extra baggage of the occult. *Apoha* is thus billed as the discriminating and complete account as well as the best weirdness-avoidance strategy available.

Of course, many nonphilosophical people, East and West, would say innocently and without much soul-searching that there are common properties, absences, good and bad, and so on. However, the reply would be short and swift: *that* type of widespread acceptance—so would say the advocates of ontological seriousness East or West—is not the point for philosophers: it's just how the world thinks; it's customary (or surface-level) truth (*saṃvṛtisatya*), folk theories, error, how things "seem to be to obscured minds" (*blo kun rdzob pa'i ngor yod pa*), and so on. Let's group these charges of being folk-theoretic, surface-level, and so forth together and speak of being "lightweight." Acquiescing in *this* lightweightness as being the best we can do—or worse, legitimizing it philosophically—is what gets the goat of the serious. At some point, so their argument goes, the deeper questions of the ontological status of these entities and the strange ways in which they would supposedly have to exist *should* become problematic in ways in which they admittedly do not for most ordinary people, nor even for many scientists. Obviously, many analytic philosophers today do subscribe to this imperative, and most of the main Buddhist thinkers in India (especially in later Indian Buddhism) certainly did too.

Now, when Buddhist thinkers *don't* subscribe to this imperative to seek ontological depth, are they offering anything more than the Eastern version of lightweightness? One can certainly maintain—and many modern writers have so maintained—that the Mādhyamika Buddhists—the followers of Nāgārjuna, Āryadeva, Candrakīrti, Tsongkhapa (Tsong kha pa), and many other luminaries—with their philosophy of emptiness (*śūnyavāda*) and disavowal of all theses, point the way to *some type* of strongly quietistic or irenic stance, the famous *āryatūṣṇīṃbhāva*, "the silence of the noble ones." Many modern writers would see this as desirable and important; some (e.g., Burton 1999) would be less enthusiastic. In any case, exactly *what* type of quietism is involved here is not obvious and needs to be investigated. Some, arguably, are indeed quite lightweight and some, fortunately, are not.

The passages in the Madhyamaka Buddhist texts that are generally cited in these discussions of thesislessness are well known. Two will suffice: namely, Nāgārjuna's famous pronouncement in *Vigrahavyāvartanī* that "I don't have any thesis and thus I don't have that fault [of which you metaphysical realists accuse me]"[7] and the oft-cited verse 50 in his *Yuktiṣaṣṭikā*: "Superior individuals have no theses (*pakṣa*, *phyogs*) and no philosophical debates; how could there be any opposing theses for those who have no theses [themselves]?"[8] These ideas are not a purely Madhyamaka invention. Far from it. Indeed they are found in the Pāli canon, where there is ample practical advice to not cling to views and to shun controversies with people who do.[9] Nonetheless, the Madhyamaka seems to interpret such a quietistic stance with a significantly different emphasis: quietism is not only the practical or prudential advice that one should stay out of useless or destructive debates but also a philosophical stance. There is a strong Madhyamaka argumentation that a philosophy of emptiness entails that one *cannot* have theses and views. That is why the Madhyamaka is of specific relevance to us here.

For our purposes, what is also especially important is the related idea of certain so-called Prāsaṅgika Mādhyamikas like Candrakīrti that a Mādhyamika thinker should not seek an account of the world that is deeper or better than what the world itself proposes. The famous passage from scripture that he cites in support is:

> The world (*loka*) argues with me. I don't argue with the world. What is agreed upon (*saṃmata*) in the world to exist, I too agree that it exists. What is agreed upon in the world to be nonexistent, I too agree that it does not exist.[10]

Candrakīrti, in *Prasannapadā* chapter 1, says clearly that he has no difficulty following the world's acceptance of universals (*sāmānyalakṣaṇa*) and particulars (*svalakṣaṇa*) alike;[11] in *Madhyamakāvatāra* 6, the external world is unproblematic for him, causality is the unanalyzed primitive notion accepted by the common man; if we believe Tsongkhapa's exegesis in the *Eight Difficult Points of the Mūlamadhyamakakārikā* (*Rtsa shes dka' gnad/gnas brgyad kyi zin bris*), Candrakīrti even accepts absences (*abhāva*) and negative facts. In other words, for Candrakīrti, a Mādhyamika should supposedly content himself with *lokaprasiddha*, "what the world acknowledges," as seeking anything else is misguided and, in a strange way, stultifying. For example, the Buddhist logicians' recurrent attempts to try to do *better* than the world are said by him (in *Catuḥśatakaṭīkā* 13) to be a type of intoxication (*smyos pa*) that actually made them no longer even know what the world does and hence become "completely unversed in ordinary matters" (*'jig rten pa'i don dag la gtan ma byang ba*).[12]

Now, both traditionally in India, and especially in Tibet, as well as in some modern writings, a frequent way to read those Madhyamaka passages about emptiness, thesislessness, and *lokaprasiddha* has been in terms of a type of antirealism, showing that nothing is real, or in other words, that all is illusory appearance created by mind as it does not stand up to philosophical analysis. Under analysis everything supposedly turns out to be nothing but "false and deceptive" (*mṛṣāmoṣadharmaka*)—the term figures often in Candrakīrti. More bluntly, things don't exist, they just appear to, and people erroneously think and talk as if they did. There are no right answers (because there are no *pramāṇas*, "sources of knowledge") about anything; at most there is just what people ignorantly think to be right, or in the phrase of the Tibetan Jo nang pa Mādhyamikas, "how things seem to be to mistaken minds" (*blo 'khrul ba'i ngor yod pa*). If one stopped at the idea that we don't possess or can't ever *know* any right answers, we would have a usual form of skepticism.[13] But we seem to go further in saying that there *can be* no right answers on anything, and that there are only answers that are found in, or extrapolated from, the "going story" on things. This suggests, in effect, an all-inclusive error theory or a global fictionalism.[14]

From here we might rather easily go to a certain type of quietism about metaphysics. If it were to be accepted that everything just *seemed* to be thus and so, but wasn't actually—and that is of course a very big *if*—one could then say that any deeper inquiry about metaphysics was pointless. After all, why would one bother to pursue any philosophy-inspired improvements to what people believe in and talk about superficially, given that in any case all is fictional or error and any would-be replacement version will be too? Suppose that, to take a very simplified analogy, ordinary people believed firmly in the reality of square circles, or to borrow from Bertrand Russell, in a barber who shaved all and only those people in his village who didn't shave themselves. Surely, it would be pointless to construct a nominalism about square-circlehood or pursue the question whether the impossible barber is enduring or momentary, external, identical with, or different from his mind and body, and so on.

But the price to be paid for *that type* of Madhyamaka combination of quietism and global fictionalism/error is potentially very high.[15] There is the usual obvious conundrum, East and West, that if people were wrong about everything, they would self-refute if they ever claimed that view to be true. But more generally, it's hard to see how they could account for the complex and evolving rational discriminations between truths and falsities that we do make, if all were just literally false and deceptive. Of course, at some point the global fictionalist or error theorist may well say that the world's *thinking* some propositions to be true and others false is based on the brute fact of some errors turning out to be *useful* to us as white lies and others remaining relatively *useless*. But while we might perhaps (like an ethical irrealist) be able to take as "true" *certain sorts* of shared white lies, like beliefs in there really being good or bad actions because such erroneous beliefs make people more respectful, gentle, and so on, it would be hard to see why many beliefs and statements—in ethics, physics, geography, or what have you—would be so useful on a wide and complex scale if one stripped them all of any truth.[16] And as I have argued (see chapter 2), things get much worse if the Mādhyamika fictionalist just refuses to take up the issue and instead adopts a *literal* interpretation of the scriptural passage where the Buddha supposedly accepts the world's mindset on everything whatsoever "as is." We then end up with an uncritical blanket endorsement of pretty much all widespread popular beliefs, from folk geography and folk economics, folk theories of medicine, to widely popular ideas about religion and so on. If that's the upshot of a Prāsaṅgika Madhyamaka, this philosophy would be more like apathy and abdication on *all* questions whatsoever and thus would be a lightweight, *bon marché*, quietism indeed.

There is, fortunately, a more sophisticated Prāsaṅgika Madhyamaka approach, one that is much closer to what I have termed "atypical Prāsaṅgika";[17] it would leave the antirealist's all-inclusive error theory largely behind and recognize that there *are* right and wrong answers but without the baggage of ontology.[18] It would thus be neither serious metaphysics nor abdication.

What does this look like? Let us grant that there are somehow right and wrong answers to be discovered and that they aren't simply to be unpacked as what the world thinks to be right. In that case, we need a different exegesis of what is meant by *lokaprasiddha*. Accepting what the world acknowledges (*lokaprasiddha*) would *not* mean that one just acquiesces in the ideas of what there is (be they harebrained or not) that might be widespread or even common sense at any given time in a given culture. Instead, limiting oneself to *lokaprasiddha* would be the recognition that one could not do anything better than description of the world's views when it comes to certain sorts of entities—that is, the ones that typically fire up philosophical discussions on ontology. We would thus need to delineate two domains of inquiry, one in which knowledge and beliefs could and should often change and another where "bettering" is misguided and where we should just leave the world as is.

Some distinctions from the philosopher Kit Fine can help to try to unpack what those two domains might be. The distinction he makes in his 2009 article "The Question of Ontology" is between quantificational and ontological questions, and it is not far from (though not completely identical with) Carnap's famous distinction between internal and external questions (Carnap 1950).[19] Thus, "Is there an *x* such that . . . ?": for example, "Are there trees in Switzerland, in Antarctica?" "Are there properties in common that define the races?" "Is there a prime number greater than seventeen that satisfies such and such an equation?" "Is there a Higgs boson?" More generally, is there an *x* such that *x* is an *F*? All these are simple quantificational questions: if one asserts that an item *a* is an *F*, it is a simple inference of no philosophical consequence to assert "There is an *x* such that *x* is an *F*." Such questions are to be contrasted with the ontological question, "Does the *x* that is *F* exist?" To put it another way, that second question is more like "Is that *x* one of the underlying real entities?" rather than just "Is there such an *x*?"[20]

Many quantificational questions are of course important, subtle, and even technically abstruse—not dumbed-down or uninteresting at all—such as when, for example, one is asking a scientific question about whether there are such and such types of subatomic particles. Many are vital: Are there weapons of mass destruction in Iraq? Is there enough food in the world to feed the growing population? It is however striking that when one asks a quantificational question about the typical matters treated by metaphysics—e.g., Are there any numbers? Are there any common properties? Are there absences? Are there thoughts, minds? Are there good or bad actions?—the answer will be a trivial "Yes, of course." Note too that this "Yes" will be forthcoming irrespective of one's deeper ontological analysis, if one has such a thing. Thus if a mathematician proves a theorem about there being numbers of such and such a sort, he trivially shows that there are numbers, no matter whether he holds a metaphysical position about math or doesn't even care about how numbers exist in any would-be deeper sense. The same applies to universals, absences, and so forth: whatever deeper view, if any, one might hold about ontology, one would not deny the trivial and innocent statements that there are things or properties in common among people, that there are tables and chairs, good and bad actions, or that there is an absence of fresh water on the moon. And significantly, this is not a matter of people commonly and somehow wrongly thinking that there are such things either; even if they are trivial, there are at least right answers about them, just as there are about nontrivial matters.

This is one way we would also get a sense for why a sophisticated Buddhist quietist could accept common characteristics and other such entities more or less as they figure in our ordinary linguistic usage. Accepting them wouldn't be any more problematic than responding "yes" to other quantificational types of questions, for to say "there are common characteristics, numbers, thoughts, and so on" is just a claim that follows immediately from a lot of very ordinary and true statements, like "Prudence is a common characteristic of the Swiss," "Seventeeen is a prime number," and "She has very interesting thoughts about life." The triviality of the "there are" statements may even be a strong indicator to the Buddhist that the questions, if pursued any deeper, will become purely metaphysical and thus go astray. And if one is nonetheless motivated by ontological seriousness to seek a deeper account, or if one wishes to ask whether the world as a whole (or perhaps the "world's conceptual scheme") is right in making these claims, then *that* is what this sophisticated quietist might call "intoxication."

Of course, most metaphysicians worth their salt, East and West, are not going to take this quietism about ontology lying down. They will probably initially whinge that a trivialization of metaphysical disputes is itself a type of superficiality and hence tantamount to lightweightness. Well, first of all, the quietists' philosophical point—and she is not apathetic to philosophy—is that nothing deeper *can* be meaningfully investigated in these cases and that this is an important, or even liberating, stance. Secondly, if her quietism is then deliberately "surface-level," or ontologically shallow, it is so in a very different way from the "all is false" variety that simply accepts in toto *all* that the world acknowledges. The more sophisticated quietism—a variety of deflationism—would lighten the burdens of philosophers by exorcising complicated debates on pseudo-issues. But that's all. It certainly wouldn't advocate blanket uncritical acquiescence in every going view. To put it another way, we conserve objectivity, rightness, discovery, and belief-revision, but about purely deflationary truths.[21]

So just why is one supposedly misguided or intoxicated in adopting the ontological perspective to evaluate and better the world instead of remaining quietistic whenever metaphysics appears on the scene? There are different answers to this in modern metaontology. Common is to suggest that "exists" is not univocal (Putnam 2004, 84–85), or (following Carnap 1950) to claim that the clear literal-versus-figurative contrast needed to say seriously what there is will not be forthcoming (Yablo 1998).[22] There is, of course, the well-developed Wittgensteinian critique of specific misunderstandings of the use of language, or "grammatical" confusions, that lead to an illusion of deliberating about real, substantive, issues. Another modern approach (e.g., Hirsch 2009 and 2011, Price 2009)—also influenced by Carnap 1950—is to say that many metaphysical disputes are purely verbal disputes about the choice of language to use.

Now, as far as I can see, none of these metaontological approaches is explicitly developed by Madhyamaka Buddhism, whatever be their merits. Still, I am quite sure that much of this could be incorporated into Buddhist quietist ends on major issues. And this would be a welcome update to the Madhyamaka program to enable it to go beyond its own argumentation about specific second-century doctrines. But that is another study—in a note I'll indicate two applications and leave it at that.[23]

A promising metaontological approach that I think *would* directly resonate with some attested Madhyamaka philosophy is to argue that the perspective needed to pursue ontology is unavailable, even though it seems constantly tempting (and hence intoxicating) in our reflections. The diagnosis of where ontology goes wrong would then go like this. There is a move that ontologists typically make at some point, although most likely it is not adequately acknowledged: they of course grant that the world *says* that there are common properties and so on and that it has its reasons for saying that such and such is a case of one; but they then proceed to ask whether the world *should* continue to speak in this fashion of common properties and so on *at all*. This latter question is not a demand for possible piecemeal changes within the world's beliefs, language, and epistemic practices. It is potentially a global upgrade, one that will be suspect to a quietist because it would seem to require a perspective that could evaluate whether the conceptual scheme we use is right as a whole, whether it matches up with how the world really is, independently of how we think and talk about it. This is the "sideways on" perspective that Wittgensteinian quietists like John McDowell or Cora Diamond diagnose as lying behind ontology.[24] We would need to place ourselves impossibly outside our scheme to evaluate it as a whole in this deeper way. In short, quietists would answer that if the ontologically serious could adopt a perspective that would compare the world's conceptual scheme with an underlying reality and examine whether it matches up or not, then they could make their enterprise work. Otherwise not.[25]

I had said that this critique of the sideways-on view could resonate with the Madhyamaka too. Madhyamaka, or more precisely, what I consider to be the most promising Madhyamaka, accepts that there are right and wrong answers about customary truth; it rejects specifically our "grasping at the real" (*satyābhimāna, bden 'dzin*), or in other words, the projection we make on customary things of them having an intrinsic nature (*svabhāva*) that is necessary for beliefs and statements about them to be true and nonarbitrary. How is the rejection of that "grasping at the real" related to the critique of sideways-on views? Well, an interesting way in which "grasping at the real or true" can be, and indeed has been, described is that it is a deep-seated demand for something like real, intrinsically existing, entities that *make* beliefs and statements true (what philosophers would now term real "truth-makers").[26] "Grasping at the real or true" thus involves a confused imperative that what we think and say, when true, must be grounded in, or be true *because of*, the way certain things are in themselves, independently of everything else, including the ways in which they figure in our customs and transactions. Buddhists, of various realist schools and stripes, especially those influenced by Dharmakīrtian *pramāṇavāda*, formulate this imperative as the need that at least some beliefs and statements—those that are the fundamental truths—must "operate in virtue of real entities" (*vastubalapravṛtta*) and are thus true because of how these entities are. On the other hand, for the Mādhyamika, no one can meaningfully account for how truth-bearers, like beliefs and statements, are made true by such entities, *vastubalapravṛtta*, that is, made true by virtue of entities that are what they are purely in themselves.[27] Such "operation in virtue of real entities" would, in effect, necessitate that there be a sideways-on view, and for a Mādhyamika that view is not available, even if our grasping at it be almost subliminal.

It might be objected that the Wittgensteinian is a quietist and the Mādhyamika more of an antirealist, or even idealist. True, Madhyamaka rejection of underlying reality is often read as a type of antirealism or idealism—namely, that all is mind-created, is an erroneous invention, or is internal to the mind. But that is not inevitable. The consequence of the rejection of underlying reality can be taken as not just a rejection of metaphysical realism but also of antirealism or idealism, for just as we cannot meaningfully talk about there being a match-up with underlying reality and real truthmakers, so we cannot adopt the view that all is error vis-à-vis an underlying reality either. It does not follow that what we talk about, in some deeper sense, is only invented by us, is a figment of the mind, or doesn't exist objectively—or in any external manner at all. Quietism and thesislessness is about staying lucidly unengaged in controversies concerning *all such matters*.

There is, however, a strategy that a metaphysician might adopt to continue the philosophical betterment of the world and yet avoid being saddled with the pernicious "grasping at truth/reality" or sideways-on perspectives. She could say that, in her way of tackling the issues of traditional metaphysics, she is just taking the world's basic beliefs and epistemic norms and applying them more rigorously and consistently than the world does in order to come up with better results. She would thus plead that metaphysics is essentially a gradual extension of what we do in any case and that a metaphysician doesn't need to concern herself with an underlying independent reality, as people may have done traditionally. Instead, one could be quietist about *that* and just rely on a thoroughgoing and comprehensive extension of worldly conventions to deal with ontological issues. This is, I think, what Mark Siderits, in his article "Thinking on Empty," meant in saying that "philosophical rationality is here [in Abhidharma and Mahāyāna Buddhism] to be thought as growing out of the worldly canon of rationality, through a process of refinement" (Siderits 1989, 233). It is, pertinently, what the Svātantrika Mādhyamika is trying to do in pursuing a Dharmakīrtian program on the level of worldly truth.

Why did some Mādhyamika Buddhist quietists reject it? Tibetans, like Tsongkhapa, argued that while Svātantrikas granted that they could not come up with ontologies capturing the underlying independently real or the "really established" (*bden grub*), they nonetheless thought there was an important difference between surface-level and deeper accounts on traditional philosophical issues, and that the latter accounts could capture how things are "intrinsically" (*svabhāvena, rang bzhin gyis*) or how they are "from their own side" (*rang ngos nas*) from a simply worldly standpoint. Tsongkhapa, however, was intransigent in his rejection of this idea that things can be "customarily established by their own intrinsic natures" (*tha snyad du rang bzhin gyis grub pa*): "intrinsically as it is" does not admit of degrees; it is an all-or-nothing affair, and there is no intelligible halfway house where things are intrinsically as they are from just a worldly standpoint but not so in the full-fledged way.[28] I think that Tsongkhapa was on the right track and even practiced a kind of weirdness-avoidance strategy. It is indeed rather weird for things to be in a halfway space where there are intrinsic natures but nothing is fully real.

This may be on the right track, but it is certainly not the end of the story. Let us go back to naturalism, but in a different garb from the metaphysical and epistemological versions. Some philosophers—especially those of a Quinean persuasion, who see philosophy as continuous with science—do maintain that they can pursue a naturalism-inspired program about how to do metaphysics. And they may well insist that questions about underlying reality don't enter into it. Elliott Sober has called it "methodological naturalism *subscript p*": "Philosophical theories should be evaluated by the same criteria that are used to evaluate scientific theories" (Sober 2009, 118). So applying those criteria—explanatory and predictive power, and especially ontological simplicity or parsimony—might seem to afford us the possibility to accept or reject various positions on issues like universals, ethical properties, and so on purely on methodological grounds. The analogy to science is as when one eliminates needless postulates like phlogiston in a theory of combustion and gains in simplicity or parsimony by reducing classical thermodynamics to statistical molecular mechanics. This would also be one way we could perhaps make sense of what a Svātantrika is doing in insisting on a difference between superficial and deep-level accounts in philosophy (and elsewhere), all the while staying quietistic about anything more underlying and independent. In short, we could just calculate the matter cleanly and disinterestedly. If the calculations turned out right, so the methodological naturalist *subscript-p* would say, we would end up with nominalism, ethical noncognitivism, and a bunch of other philosophical positions just because these theories, like other good scientific theories, explain better the phenomena and are the more sparing ways to go.

What could the quietist reply? I think the quietist would have to reply that it is doubtful that this disinterested extension of scientific criteria and reductionism to philosophy works nearly as well as it is touted to.[29] Here are a few considerations.

First, as Michael Huemer (2009) argues, four major arguments for the virtue of ontological simplicity in empirical theorizing do not extend easily to show that it is a virtue of philosophical theories.[30] Second, and more directly related to our discussion, it looks suspiciously likely that some intuitions about the nature of the underlying real come into methodological naturalism *subscript-p* via the back door. Thus, for example, the nominalist, who adopts the principle "translate what you can and then deny the truth of the rest," would try to economize on numbers by translating all mathematics into his nominalistically acceptable idiom, and when he failed—as he surely would in the case of talk of infinitely many prime numbers—he would have to reject that part as false or fictional (Sober 2009, 144–45). The ethical noncognitivist would try to economize on ethical properties by doing without them to explain why, for example, people act the way they do. (For example, people's depravity never causes them to do any of the inglorious things they do, it is the psychological events in their childhood, the societal situation, or whatever.) And he would try to find a way out of our routine and accepted use of normative propositions to explain other normative propositions (Sober 2009, 142). Indeed, he might well discount whole types of language use as just widespread popular error (e.g., Mackie 1986), because he is a priori convinced that the weird alternative, real nonnatural properties, needs to be avoided. The physicalist would try to eliminate or economize on mental entities and propositional attitudes, even if he would have significant, perhaps insurmountable, difficulties to answer "hard questions" about subjectivity and consciousness (Chalmers 1995). And so on it goes. It looks like the choice of nominalism, ethical noncognitivism, or physicalism is probably not made just because of purely disinterested science-like calculations but also, significantly, because the alternatives—namely, universals, sets, numbers, ethical or mental entities, and so on—seem to be unpalatably weird. That is why so many people bend over backward to make these choices work.

Weird in what way? Entities that are odd on scientific grounds—the Bermuda Triangle and the like—are typically felt to be so because of the improbability of the hypotheses that they exist given other things we believe, or the low likelihood of would-be observational evidence given the rest of science. Or they are just not of the sort with which we are routinely familiar, and are thus exotic. It is hard to see that universals, ethical properties, mental entities, and so on are odd or spooky in any of those ways. It is not at all clear that what is at stake in such cases is improbability and low likelihood, or even mere unfamiliarity—in most cases, we would even say that we have an intimate acquaintance with them. So to see them as odd requires a *special* type of perspective, one where we are spooked by things that normally seem quite banal and innocuous.[31]

To get a feeling for how special that perspective and its imperatives are, consider how difficult it is to do without mental entities, propositional attitudes, and the like and how motivated one has to be to try to do so. Here again Madhyamaka material is relevant. Elsewhere, in an article on a possible Madhyamaka defense of mind,[32] I had argued that Nāgārjuna in *Mūlamadhyamakakārikā* 24.10 used indispensability arguments—that is, transcendental arguments—to preclude wholesale revisions to very basic features of our language and thought. I had also argued that these arguments are significantly like the anti-"cognitive suicide" arguments that we find in some modern works of analytic philosophy (e.g., Baker 1987). Here's how I summarized that East-West argument:

> [W]e cannot rationally advocate wholesale elimination of the most basic features of our ordinary conceptual scheme without a type of self-contradiction, more specifically a type of pragmatic

> contradiction. In the case of attempts to abandon talk of universal properties, negative states, persons, and so forth, it is indeed difficult to see how one can discuss such matters without at least recognizing that there are *in some way or another* properties that pertain to several particulars, states that do or do not obtain, and people who talk, deliberate, and so forth. Equally, we cannot even discuss the merits of eliminative physicalism without recognizing that there are thoughts about the subject and good reasons for us to think in favor or against. Nor can we accept, or assert with conviction, that something is the right position if we don't allow that we can, in a meaningful sense, come to *believe* it to be right.

Now, a metaphysical realist could, and probably would, object that such a transcendental argument would not tell us how things are as they really are—that is, independently of our thought and language about them. It could only at best imply the weak conclusion that we inevitably need to believe that there are universals, minds, and the like and have a folk theory in which they would figure. *That* in itself, so it would be objected, does not imply that the folk theory is true and captures how things in reality are.

This is where the objection reveals the special and sideways-on perspective from which it arises. It would presuppose that we could meaningfully ask whether the basic necessary features of our language and thought map underlying facts, even if actually doing without them would incur repeated self-contradiction. The objector's perspective, in effect, entertains soberly the prospect that we might well have to talk the talk of our folk theory and accept the basic things in it even though that theory is in fact such a disastrous mismatch of the real that none of those basic things it "postulates" actually exists. This is the sideways-on view where one stands somewhere outside both scheme and reality and evaluates their (mis)match.

If one does make sense of such a stance, one will say that transcendental arguments, arguments against cognitive suicide, charges of self-contradiction, and the like are unsatisfyingly weak and don't show anything about the reality that is beyond how we think and talk. And one will probably have intuitions about which kinds of entities can plausibly be constituents of that reality and which kinds are just too strange to be taken seriously. There will thus be an imperative to pursue metaphysics to try to capture what is ultimately real and not just the things that figure in our talk and folk theories.[33] By contrast, thinkers who don't subscribe to any of *that*—those who lucidly avoid sideways-on views and the metaphysics they inspire—will tend to see nothing deeply strange in the basic needed features of our folk theory and thus have little reason to revise them.[34] Of course, such a quasi-Wittgensteinian "leaving everything as is" might well be waved away as bloodlessly lightweight by many Eastern and Western philosophers alike;[35] it is certainly out of step with those who demand seriousness, be they analytic metaphysicians looking to Canberra for direction, or past and present Buddhist scholars who look to Dharmakīrti. To the Mādhyamika Buddhist, on the other hand, it would be neither, but a subtle step toward peace. It is a good part of what cultivating *niṣprapañca*—"no proliferation" of concepts and positions[36]—is all about.

Notes to Chapter 12

1. The first way is that of Wallace and Hodel 2007 and the second is that of Siderits 2010. Cf. also Flanagan 2011, 3: "Imagine Buddhism without a karmic system that guarantees justice ultimately will be served, without nirvana, without bodhisattvas flying on lotus leaves, without Buddha worlds, without nonphysical states of mind, without deities, without heaven and hell realms, without oracles, without lamas who are reincarnated lamas. What would be left? My answer is that what would remain would be an interesting and defensible philosophical theory with a metaphysics, a theory about what there is and how it is, an epistemology, a theory about how we come to know and what we can know, and an ethics, a theory about virtue and vice and how best to live. This philosophical theory is worthy of attention by analytic philosophers and scientific naturalists because it is deep. Buddhism naturalized, if there is or can be such a thing, is compatible with the neo-Darwinian theory of evolution and with a commitment to scientific materialism."

   Part of the attraction toward naturalizing Buddhism is thus to be able to dispense with outmoded religious superstition and dogma. This is not my focus here, although I'm certainly sympathetic to revising Buddhism. Note that doubts about ontologies, naturalistic or otherwise, should not be construed as reinstating superstitions by a kind of back door. One could, for example, reject heavens and hells, flying bodhisattvas, or even a humanly unfathomable retributive causation (i.e., karma) stretching over countless lives because one sees no good reason to believe in them and only bad reasons for them (see, e.g., chapter 8 on karma). Good and bad reasons would be judged by our deep-seated epistemic standards. A rational person would not need a larger ontological view about what really exists to reject heavens, hells, flying bodhisattvas, and so on.
2. Let's say that at its best a discussion of "Buddhist naturalism" is a disinterested philosophical enquiry investigating how parts of a duly adapted or charitably interpreted Buddhism could fit in with science. It is, however, important to be clear at the outset that there is another recurring discussion, one that is part of Buddhist proselytizing and is even rather heavily politicized, where science is invoked to defend Buddhism essentially or as a whole, or to vindicate a traditional Buddhist culture in its confrontation with hostile modern opponents. *This* is not my focus of interest.
3. Of course the naturalistic philosophers that we are interested in here—be they hypothetical or real—*are* metaphysicians, believe that ontology is an important pursuit,

and may well have no sympathy at all for the alternatives. That's not the way it has always been—think of the logical positivists and their polemics *against* metaphysics and their rejection of all traditional ontological debates—but it is increasingly the way it is now, the turning point for many being when W. V. Quine's "On What There Is" revived the scientific respectability of the discipline. Cf., e.g., Putnam 2004, 78–79: "It [i.e., ontology] became respectable in 1948, when Quine published a famous paper titled 'On What There Is.' It was Quine who single handedly made Ontology a respectable subject."

4. See chapter 11, section II. Descartes, by contrast, notoriously saw the pineal gland as "the seat of the soul" and elaborated an obscure neurophysiological explanation of how the gland influenced sensation, memory, imagination, and the causation of bodily movement. See Lokhorst 2014.
5. *Pramāṇavārttika* 1.152: *na yāti na ca tatrāsīd asti paścān na cāṃśavat / jahāti pūrvaṃ nādhāram aho vyasanasaṃtatiḥ //.*
6. *Sāmānyaduṣana*, pp. 101–2 (ed. H. Śāstrī), translated in Chakrabarti and Siderits' introduction to Siderits, Tillemans, and Chakrabarti 2011.
7. *Vigrahavyāvartanī* 29–30 cited in Candrakīrti's *Prasannapadā* (La Vallée Poussin edition) p. 16, lines 7–10: *yadi kācana pratijñā syān me tata eva* me baved doṣaḥ / nāsti ca mama pratijñā tasmān naivāsti me doṣaḥ //.* *Johnston and Kunst's edition (see Bhattacharya 1986) reads *eṣa* ("this"), and I've followed them here.
8. *Che ba'i bdag nyid can de dag // rnams la phyogs med rtsod pa med // gang rnams la ni phyogs med pa // de la gzhan phyogs ga la yod //.* Tibetan text in Lindtner 1990, 114.
9. See, e.g., *Suttanipāta* IV (*Aṭṭhakavagga*) Norman 2001, 787 (*Duṭṭhaṭṭhaka-sutta*, verse 8): "A person who clings [to a view] indeed clings to a dispute with regard to doctrines. By what [means] and how could one dispute with one who does not cling [to a view]? For he has taken up or laid down nothing. He has shaken off all views in this very world." Norman 2001, 882 (*Pasūra-sutta*, verse 9): "If people take up a view and dispute, and say, only this is true, tell them, there is no opponent for you here when a dispute has arisen."
10. *Prasannapadā* ad MMK 18.8 and *Madhyamakāvatārabhāṣya* 6.81. On the Sanskrit and Pāli versions of this passage from *āgama*, see chapter 2, op. 58–59n1.
11. See *Prasannapadā* 1.75.2–4 (ed. La Vallée Poussin): *tasmāl loke yadi lakṣyam yadi vā svalakṣaṇaṃ sāmānyalakṣaṇaṃ vā sarvam eva sākṣād upalabhyamānatvād aparokṣam / ataḥ pratyakṣaṃ vyavasthāpyate tadviśayena jñānena saha /.* "Therefore, in the world, when any and all subjects of characterization (*lakṣya*) whatsoever, be they particulars (*svalakṣaṇa*) or universals (*sāmānyalakṣaṇa*), are visible (*aparokṣa*) because they are perceived, they are therefore established as *pratyakṣa* ('perceptible'/'perceptions'), as are the cognitions that have them as objects." See also Arnold 2005, 460–61. The point of the long discussion in *Prasannapadā* 1 is the refutation of Dignāga's position that only particulars are real as they are supposedly the only objects of perception (*pratyakṣa*), while universals are unreal, being products purely of thought. Candrakīrti does not buy this at all. Much of his discussion turns on Sanskrit grammatical considerations, although these are marshaled in support of a radical anti-foundationalist philosophical stance. Essentially, he interprets the word *pratyakṣa* to mean both "perceptible" and "perception" (which is perfectly legitimate in Sanskrit) and says that universals and particulars alike are perceptible, and the cognitions that grasp them are perceptions. This, in effect, means that universals and particulars are

on the same footing (contrary to Dignāga): both are customarily real and both are ultimately unreal. The passage has its parallel in Candrakīrti's *Catuḥśatakaṭīkā* 13, translated in Tillemans 1990, 1:175–79, and discussed on page 41ff. See Arnold 2005 for a commented translation of the whole discussion in *Prasannapadā*, and Dreyfus 1992, 42n58, for a summary of the point about Candrakīrti's recognizing universals.

12. Translated in Tillemans 1990, 1:177 and 179 (sections 8 and 17).
13. The prospects for reading Madhyamaka as *some* form of skepticism have been investigated in Dreyfus 2011b.
14. This is, in effect, what I term "typical Prāsaṅgika." It is a usual Indian and Tibetan reading of Candrakīrti. See introduction and chapter 2.
15. See chapter 2, page 56.
16. Cf. Stanley 2001, 46: "The problem facing a brute error theory of a discourse that is epistemically central . . . lies in explaining how a discourse laced through with falsity can nevertheless be useful."
17. See chapter 2, page 57.
18. First of all, one tempting way to flesh out this rejection of ontology would be to follow some modern writers in introducing REALLY as a term of art to be understood in the sense of metaphysical realism—in its typical form (what we find also in India), such realism is the position that there are things that are as they are anyway, intrinsically, irrespective of all thought and language, beliefs, and human activities. At some point this REALLY might even be distinguished from a much more innocent and ordinary use of "real" and "really." This is harder than it looks. Indeed it is a key position of many Tibetan Mādhyamikas (i.e., the followers of Tsongkhapa) that the innocent is very hard to separate clearly from the metaphysical and that metaphysical realism even appears to most of us as common sense. For our purposes we will thus stay with the sense of "realism" as metaphysical realism, the view (be it common sense or not) that there is, and we can meaningfully discuss, an underlying set of entities that are what they are intrinsically, and thus independently of any human contribution whatsoever. See Price 2009 and Horwich 2006, who make extensive use of this REALLY; see as well Priest, Siderits, and Tillemans 2011—we used the term in the context of the Buddhists' two-truth theory. Diamond 1996 chapter 1 ("Realism and the Realistic Spirit") is one of the most profound analyses of the difference between (metaphysical) Realism and realism in the ordinary sense.
19. It does need to be stressed, however, that Kit Fine himself is not pursuing a quietist antiontology line. He makes the distinction in order to better pursue ontology and analytic metaphysics without the encumbering Quinean views about quantification.
20. Of course for this distinction to work one needs to take up W. V. Quine's program for ontology in "On What There Is." We would thus need to argue against Quineans who hold that there is just one clear unambiguous sense of "there is"—for them the ontological is the same as the quantificational—and that any deviations from that clear use, such as distinctions between "there are *x*'s" and "there (really) exists an *x*," are just cases of sloppy thinking, loose uses of language, or worse, detestable double-talk. Arguing against Quine is largely what Fine's paper is about, and I won't reproduce those arguments here.
21. This Madhyamaka use of a deflationary, or minimalist, truth theory is developed in Priest, Siderits, and Tillemans 2011.
22. It might perhaps be argued that the Buddhist too, with his idea that all is *upādāya*

prajñapti ("dependent designation") is also rejecting the possibility of literalness. Jacques May, for example, translated this term as "désignation métaphorique" and took the Mādhyamika's point to be that literal description of the world was impossible. See May 1979. I won't pursue that here as I'm not sure how to spin it out clearly on the Buddhist side that *upādāya prajñapti* is indeed a global rejection of literalness. This is, however, a lead that is worth pursuing.

23. First, an interesting application of Carnap's and Hirsch's metaontology would be possible in the debates about momentariness (*kṣaṇikatva*) that we find in Dharmakīrti and his successors. A savvy modern Mādhyamika quietist could say that the classical Buddhist-Naiyāyika debate on momentariness versus permanence is recognizable as a debate between perdurantism (which holds that things are made of a succession of temporal parts) versus endurantism (which denies this), and that it could be trivialized by showing that respective sentences of a perdurantist language and an endurantist language are "truth-conditionally equivalent," in that they are true in the same possible worlds. The upshot would be that the debate is not about any deep nature of things, as it might appear to be, but just about the choice of languages, that is, perdurantist-speak versus endurantist-speak. Second, a Wittgensteinian diagnosis of grammatical confusion could well be applied to debates about reflexive awareness (*svasaṃvedana*). *Philosophical Investigations* (Wittgenstein 1953, 222): "It is correct to say 'I know what you are thinking,' and wrong to say 'I know what I am thinking.' (A whole cloud of philosophy condensed into a drop of grammar.)" Here Wittgenstein attacks the seductive idea that first-person reports of one's own conscious states must have descriptive contents because one's reports of others' states do, and the grammar of the two sentences (wrongly) seems to be the same. This might well be more a promising way to dispense with *svasaṃvedana* than the Madhyamaka's own position (in Śāntideva's *Bodhicaryāvatāra* 9.23) that reflexive awareness of what one thinks is just a higher-order understanding that one infers by abduction from other psychic data.
24. See McDowell 1981 and chapter 1 of Diamond 1996.
25. Other quietists, in a similar vein, might even invoke the basic arguments in Donald Davidson's article "On the Very Idea of a Conceptual Scheme" to provide additional semantic arguments to show that such talk of a distinct conceptual scheme—that is, one distinct from reality—is fundamentally unintelligible. See Davidson 1984.
26. The term was first coined by the Australian philosopher C. B. Martin and is now extensively used by the philosophers David Armstrong, Peter Simons, and others. See Priest, Siderits, and Tillemans 2011, where Madhyamaka is construed as rejecting real truthmakers and proceeding with a deflationary theory of truth. Cf. Heil 2003, vii–viii: "You are ontologically serious if you are guided by the thought that the ontological implications of philosophical claims are paramount. The attitude most naturally expresses itself in an allegiance to a truth-maker principle: when an assertion about the world is true, something about the world makes it true."
27. It might well be said that this "most-promising Madhyamaka" looks like it is broadly that of Tsongkhapa. I unhesitatingly plead guilty. The formulation of Madhyamaka as a rejection of *vastubalapravṛtta* is, however, not actually Tsongkhapa's position. This was how a rather interesting twelfth-century Tibetan Mādhyamika, Mabja Jangchup Tsondrü (Rma bya Byang chub brtson 'grus, ?–1185)—who did have a certain important influence on Tsongkhapa and the Gelukpa (Dge lugs pa)—

depicted what Madhyamaka philosophy was all about. He maintained that we go astray when we think that true thoughts and statements, the "sources of knowledge" (*tshad ma = pramāṇa*), must be *dngos po'i stobs kyis zhugs pa = vastubalapravṛtta*. The term is indeed very widespread in Buddhist realist accounts (e.g., Dharmakīrti's philosophy) of how beliefs and statements are true in a nonarbitrary fashion—because they "contact" real entities and are *made true* by them. Mabja's discussion on the impossibility of inference and perception "in virtue of real entities" (= *vastubala*) is translated in Dharmachakra Translation Committee 2011, 132–35.

28. See Tillemans 2003.
29. Note however that Siderits 2011 is surely right to stress that if a Mādhyamika, in the name of *lokaprasiddha*, says he has no place for *any* (even scientific) reductionism, that would be overkill. Such a philosophy with no place for *any* reduction or elimination of entities is not going to be of much interest. We need to be able to make legitimate reductions, like explaining pharmacology in terms of chemistry.
30. Here are two examples of Huemer's analyses: (1) Invoking a track record of the success of parsimony in arriving at truth may work in science but hardly in philosophy. (2) Simplicity and likelihood are typically connected in empirical theories because the simple ones are usually better supported by the observed data than the complex ones. The simpler theory makes more specific predictions of the observed phenomena than the complex—it is consistent with fewer observations than the complex. It seems doubtful that we can make sense of this in the case of realism-nominalism or dualism-physicalism debates as the rival theories will all be equally consistent with the observable data and thus equally likely. If, however, there are some things that, say, the realist can accommodate and the nominalist can't, then nominalism risks being refuted by the data.
31. One is reminded of Wittgenstein's discussion of the special type of "queerness" philosophers feel about "superlative facts"—those, for example, that supposedly would have to exist to ground necessity or rule-following. The point is developed further in chapter 1, section V. Relevant too is Mackie's "argument from queerness" against real ethical properties: this special feeling of queerness arises when one holds the view that reality can only be what is given by science and that ethics would thus have to turn into a sort of parascience. See McDowell 1998, 186ff., against applying this "bald naturalism" to ethics and thus making real ethical properties queer.
32. "On Minds, Dharmakīrti, and Madhyamaka," the keynote address to the sixteenth congress of the International Association of Buddhist Studies, Taiwan 2011. See chapter 11. The excerpt below appears on page 212 above.
33. Cf. van Inwagen 2009, 1ff.: "When I was introduced to metaphysics as an undergraduate, I was given the following definition: metaphysics is the study of ultimate reality. This still seems to me to be the best definition of metaphysics that I have seen."
34. Cf. Āryadeva, *Catuḥśataka* verse 324: *na kiṃcid āścaryaṃ viduṣāṃ vidyate bhuvi* ("Nothing on earth is strange for the wise"). Indeed, commentators on this verse of *Catuḥśataka* 13 do have a provocative dismissal of the would-be strangeness of a world in which nothing is intrinsically what it is. See Tillemans 1990, 196.
35. Wright 1994, 76: "Haven't we merely surrendered the underpinnings for such debate, committing ourselves to the kind of bloodless *quietism* for which some writers find inspiration in the later Wittgenstein?" Cf. Horwich 2006.
36. Jacques May (1959, 175n562) has the last word: "*Prapañca*, littéralement 'expansion,'

tib. *spros pa*, me paraît désigner non pas tant la fonction de pensée discursive, correspondant, sous divers aspects, à *vikalpa*, *vitarka*, *vicāra*, que l'opération de cette fonction ('expansion,' différentiation du réel global en objets et en concepts distincts . . .), et le résultat de cette opération, c'est-à-dire le monde constitué en objets et concepts distincts."

Notes on the Articles

Chapter 1: originally published as "Trying to Be Fair to Mādhyamika Buddhism," The University of Calgary, Numata Yehan Lecture in Buddhism, Winter 2001, available on http://www.ucalgary.ca/numatachair/previous_events. It was translated into Czech in *Nágárdžuna Filosofie střední cesty*, ed. Jiří Holba, Filosofické interpretace, Svazek 3 (Prague: Oikoymenh, 2012). A shortened version appeared, with the same title, in *Expanding and Merging Horizons: Contributions to South Asian and Cross-Cultural Studies in Commemoration of Wilhelm Halbfass*, ed. Karin Preisendanz (Vienna: Österreichische Akademie der Wissenschaften, Philosophisch-Historische Klasse Denkschriften, 351, Band. 2007), 507–24. The present publication is significantly different from both earlier versions.

Chapter 2: originally published as "How Far Can We Reform Conventional Truth? Dismal Relativism, Fictionalism, Easy-Easy Truth, and the Alternatives," chapter 9 in the Cowherds, *Moonshadows: Conventional Truth in Buddhist Philosophy* (Oxford: Oxford University Press, 2011), 151–65.

Chapter 3: originally published as "How Do Mādhyamikas Think? Remarks on Jay Garfield, Graham Priest and Paraconsistency," in *Pointing at the Moon: Buddhism, Logic, Analytic Philosophy*, ed. Jay Garfield, Mario D'Amato, and Tom Tillemans (New York: Oxford University Press, 2009), 83–100. It was translated into German in *Denkt Asien anders? Reflexionen zu Buddhismus und Konfuzianismus in Indien, Tibet, China und Japan*, ed. Birgit Kellner and Susanne Weigelin-Schwiedrzik (Göttingen: Vienna University Press, Verlag V&R unipress GmbH, 2009).

Chapter 4: originally published as "'How Do Mādhyamikas Think?' Revisited" in *Philosophy East and West* 63.3 (2013): 417–25.

Chapter 5 ("Prasaṅga and Proof by Contradiction in Bhāviveka, Candrakīrti, and Dharmakīrti"): newly published.

Chapter 6: originally published as "Dignāga, Bhāviveka and Dharmakīrti on Apoha," in *Religion and Logic in Buddhist Philosophical Analysis: Proceedings of the Fourth International Dharmakīrti Conference. Vienna, August 23–27, 2005*, ed. Helmut Krasser, Horst Lasic, Eli Franco, and

Birgit Kellner (Vienna: Verlag der Österreichischen Akademie der Wissenschaften, 2011), 449–58.

Chapter 7 ("What Happened to the Third and Fourth Lemmas in Tibetan Madhyamaka?"): newly published.

Chapter 8: originally published as: "Madhyamaka Buddhist Ethics," in *Journal of the International Association of Buddhist Studies* 33.1–2 (2010 [2011]): 353–72.

Chapter 9: originally published as "Reason, Irrationality and Akrasia (Weakness of the Will) in Buddhism: Reflections upon Śāntideva's Arguments with Himself," in *Argumentation*, ed. Tom Tillemans and Georges Dreyfus (Netherlands: Springer Verlag, 2008), 22.1: 149–63.

Chapter 10: originally published as "Yogic Perception, Meditation and Enlightenment: The Epistemological Issues in a Key Debate," in *A Companion to Buddhist Philosophy*, ed. Steven Emmanuel, Blackwell Companions to Philosophy Series (Oxford: Wiley-Blackwell, 2013), 290–306.

Chapter 11: originally published as "On Minds, Dharmakīrti, and Madhyamaka," in *The Moon Points Back*, ed. Koji Tanaka, Yasuo Deguchi, Jay L. Garfield, and Graham Priest (New York: Oxford University Press, 2015), 45–66.

Chapter 12 ("Serious, Lightweight, or Neither: Should Madhyamaka Go to Canberra?"): newly published.

My thanks to the publishing houses and journals for permission to reprint previously published articles.

Abbreviations

CŚ	*Catuḥśataka* of Āryadeva
CŚṬ	*Catuḥśatakaṭīkā* of Candrakīrti
D.	Sde dge Tibetan Tripiṭaka. See bibliography entry for Tibetan Tripiṭaka
KBR	*Kanazawadaigaku bungakubu ronshū, Kōdōkagakkahen—Studies and Essays, Behavioural Sciences and Philosophy, Faculty of Letters, Kanazawa University*
MHK	*Madhyamakahṛdayakārikā* of Bhāviveka
MMK	*Mūlamadhyamakakārikā* of Nāgārjuna
P.	Peking Tibetan Tripiṭaka. See bibliography entry for Tibetan Tripiṭaka
PV	*Pramāṇavārttika* of Dharmakīrti
PVSV	*Pramāṇavārttikasvavṛtti* of Dharmakīrti
PVSVṬ	*Pramāṇavārttikasvavṛttiṭīkā* of Karṇakagomin
PVV	*Pramāṇavārttikavṛtti* of Manorathanandin
TJ	*Tarkajvālā* of Bhāviveka

Bibliography

Adam, Martin T. 2008. "Some Notes on Kamalaśīla's Understanding of Insight Considered as the Discernment of Reality (*bhūta-pratyavekṣā*)." *Buddhist Studies Review* 25.2: 194–209.

Alexander, J. McKenzie. 2009. "Evolutionary Game Theory." *Stanford Encyclopedia of Philosophy* (Fall 2009 edition), edited by Edward N. Zalta. http://plato.stanford.edu/archives/fall2009/entries/game-evolutionary/.

Anālayo, Bhikkhu. 2003. *Satipaṭṭhāna: The Direct Path to Realization.* Cambridge: Windhorse Publications.

Aristotle. *The Nicomachean Ethics.* See Ross and Brown 2009.

Arnold, Dan A. 2005. "Materials for a Mādhyamika Critique of Foundationalism: An Annotated Translation of *Prasannapadā* 55.11 to 75.13." *Journal of the International Association of Buddhist Studies* 28.2: 411–67.

———. 2008. "Transcendental Arguments and Practical Reason in Indian Philosophy." *Argumentation* 22 (Springer Verlag): 135–47.

Āryadeva. *Catuḥśataka.* P. 5246, D. 3846. See Candrakīrti, *Catuḥśatakaṭīkā.*

Aṣṭasāhasrikāprajñāpāramitāsūtra. P. 734, D. 12. Sanskrit edited by P. L. Vaidya. Buddhist Sanskrit Texts 4. Darbhanga: Mithila Institute of Post-Graduate Studies and Research in Sanskrit Learning, 1960. English translation at www.84000.co.

Avalokitavrata. *Prajñāpradīpaṭīkā.* P. 5259, D. 3859.

Baker, Lynne Rudder. 1987. *Saving Belief: A Critique of Physicalism.* Princeton, NJ: Princeton University Press.

———. 1998. "Cognitive Suicide." In Grimm and Merill 1998, 1–18.

Bareau, André. 1955. *Les sectes bouddhiques du Petit Véhicule.* Publications de l'École française d'Extrême-Orient 38. Saigon: École française d'Extrême-Orient.

Barwise, Jon, and John Etchemendy. 1992. *The Language of First-Order Logic.* Stanford, CA: Center for the Study of Language and Information.

Bhattacharya, K. 1986. *The Dialectical Method of Nāgārjuna.* Translated from the original Sanskrit with introduction and notes by Kamaleswar Bhattacharya; text critically edited by E. H. Johnston and Arnold Kunst. Delhi: Motilal Banarsidass. First published 1978.

Bhāviveka. *Madhyamakahṛdayakārikā.* P. 5255, D. 3855. Citations refer to Sanskrit text in Hoornaert 2001b.

Bhāviveka. *Madhyamakārthasaṃgraha.* P. 5258, D. 3857. Translated in Lindtner 1981, 200–201n14.

Bhāviveka. *Prajñāpradīpa.* P. 5253, D. 3853.

Bhāviveka. *Madhyamakahṛdayavṛtti Tarkajvālā.* P. 5256, D. 3856. Citations refer to Tibetan text in Hoornaert 2001b.

Bodhi, Bhikkhu. 2000. *The Connected Discourses of the Buddha: A New Translation of the Saṃyutta Nikāya.* 2 vols. Boston: Wisdom Publications. See also the bibliographical entry below for *Saṃyutta Nikāya.*

Bouveresse, Jacques. 1998. *Le philosophe et le réel: Entretiens avec Jean-Jacques Rosat.* Paris: Hachette.

———. 2006. "Entretien avec Jacques Bouveresse: Défendre la vérité désarmée." *Nouveaux regards* 34: 71–74.

Bronkhorst, Johannes. 1999. *Langage et réalité: Sur un épisode de la pensée indienne.* Bibliothèque de l'École des Hautes Études, Section des Sciences Religieuses 105. Turnhout: Brepols.

Burgess, John, and Gideon Rosen. 1997. *A Subject with No Object.* Oxford: Clarendon.

Burton, David F. 1999. *Emptiness Appraised: A Critical Study of Nāgārjuna's Philosophy.* Richmond, Surrey, UK: Curzon.

Cabezón, José I. 1992. *A Dose of Emptiness: An Annotated Translation of the sTong thun chen mo of mKhas grub dGe legs dpal bzang.* Albany: State University of New York Press.

———. 2000. "Truth in Buddhist Theology." In *Buddhist Theology: Critical Reflections by Contemporary Buddhist Scholars.* Edited by Roger Jackson and John Makransky, 136–54. London: Curzon.

Cabezón, José I., and Geshé Lobsang Dargyay. 2007. *Freedom from Extremes: Gorampa's 'Distinguishing the Views' and the Polemics of Emptiness.* Studies in Indian and Tibetan Buddhism. Boston: Wisdom Publications.

Candrakīrti. P. 5266, D. 3865. *Catuḥśatakaṭīkā.* Sanskrit fragments edited by Haraprasād Śāstrī, in "Catuḥśatika of Ārya Deva." *Memoirs of the Asiatic Society of Bengal,* vol. III, 8, Calcutta, 1914. Sanskrit fragments and Tibetan in Suzuki 1994; chapters 1–4 translated in Lang 2003; chapters 12–13 translated in Tillemans 1990.

———. P. 5262, 5263, D. 3861, 3862. *Madhyamakāvatāra* and *Madhyamakāvatārabhāṣya,* edited by Louis de La Vallée Poussin, *Madhyamakāvatāra par Candrakīrti,* traduction tibétaine. St. Petersburg: Bibliotheca Buddhica 9. Reprinted Osnabrück, 1970. French translation in La Vallée Poussin 1907, 1910, 1911.

———. *Prasannapadā: Madhyamakavṛtti.* P. 5260, D. 3860. Edited by L. de La Vallée Poussin in *Mūlamadhyamakakārikās (Mādhyamikasūtras) de Nāgārjuna, avec le commentaire de Candrakīrti.* St. Petersburg: Bibliotheca Buddhica IV, 1903–13. Reprinted Osnabrück: Biblio Verlag, 1970.

Carnap, Rudolph. 1950. "Empiricism, Semantics, and Ontology." *Revue Internationale de Philosophie* 4: 20–40. Reprinted in *Meaning and Necessity* (2nd ed.). Chicago: University of Chicago Press, 1956.

Carpenter, Amber D. 2015. "Persons Keeping Their Karma Together." In Tanaka, Deguchi, et al. 2015, 1–44.

Cavell, Stanley. 1988. *In Quest of the Ordinary: Lines of Skepticism and Romanticism.* Chicago: University of Chicago Press.

Chalmers, David. 1995. "Facing up to the Problem of Consciousness." *Journal of Consciousness Studies* 2.3: 200–219.

Chalmers, David, David Manley, and Ryan Wasserman, eds. 2009. *Metametaphysics: New Essays on the Foundations of Ontology*. Oxford: Oxford University Press.

Chan, Wing-tsit. 1973. *A Source Book in Chinese Philosophy*, 4th ed. Princeton, NJ: Princeton University Press. Contains translation of Jizang's *Erdi zhang* and extracts of his *Sanlun xuanyi*.

Chastain, Charles. 1998. "Comments on Baker." In Grimm and Merill 1998, 18–26.

Churchland, Paul M. 1981. "Eliminative Materialism and Propositional Attitudes." *Journal of Philosophy* 78.2: 67–90.

Conze, Edward. 1957. *Vajracchedikā Prajñāpāramitā: Edited and Translated with Introduction and Glossary*. Serie Orientale Roma 13. Rome: Istituto Italiano per il Medio ed Estremo Oriente.

Copi, Irving M. 1982. *Introduction to Logic*, 6th ed. London: MacMillan.

Coseru, Christian. 2012. *Perceiving Reality: Consciousness, Intentionality, and Cognition in Buddhist Philosophy*. New York: Oxford University Press.

Cowherds, The (= G. Dreyfus, B. Finnigan, J. Garfield, G. Newland, G. Priest, M. Siderits, K. Tanaka, S. Thakchoe, T. Tillemans, J. Westerhoff). 2011. *Moonshadows: Conventional Truth in Buddhist Philosophy*. New York: Oxford University Press.

Crosby, Kate, and Andrew Skilton. 1996. *Śāntideva: The Bodhicaryāvatāra*. Oxford: Oxford University Press.

Dalai Lama Bstan-'dzin-rgya-mtsho, and Jeffrey Hopkins. 1975. *The Buddhism of Tibet*. London: Allen and Unwin.

Davidson, Donald. 1980. "How Is Weakness of the Will Possible?" In *Essays on Actions and Events*, 21–42. Oxford: Oxford University Press.

———. 1984. "On the Very Idea of a Conceptual Scheme." In *Inquiries into Truth and Interpretation*, 183–98. Oxford: Clarendon Press.

———. 2004a. "Paradoxes of Irrationality." In *Problems of Rationality*, 169–87. Oxford: Oxford University Press.

———. 2004b. "Who Is Fooled?" In *Problems of Rationality*, 213–30. Oxford: Oxford University Press.

Deguchi, Yasuo, Jay L. Garfield, and Graham Priest. 2008. "The Way of the Dialetheist: Contradictions in Buddhism." *Philosophy East and West* 58.3: 395–402.

———. 2013. "How *We* Think Mādhyamikas Think: A Response to Tom Tillemans." *Philosophy East and West* 63.3: 426–35.

de Jong, Jan Willem. 1950. "Le problème de l'absolu dans l'école mādhyamika." *Revue philosophique* 140: 322–27.

———. 1972. "The Problem of the Absolute in the Madhyamaka School." *Journal of Indian Philosophy* 2: 1–6.

Deleanu, Florin. 2010. "Agnostic Meditations on Buddhist Meditation." In *Zygon: Journal of Religion and Science* 45: 605–26. See www.zygonjournal.org (accessed November 30, 2013).

Demiéville, Paul. 1987. *Le Concile de Lhasa: une controverse sur le quiétisme entre bouddhistes de l'Inde et de la Chine au VIIIe siècle de l'ère chrétienne*. Paris: Collège de France, Institut des Hautes Études Chinoises. First published 1952.

Dennett, Daniel C. 1991. *Consciousness Explained*. New York: Little, Brown, and Co.

Devendrabuddhi. *Pramāṇavārttikapañjikā*. P. 5717, D. 4217.

Dharmachakra Translation Committee. 2011. *Ornament of Reason: The Great Commentary to Nāgārjuna's Root of the Middle Way by Mabja Jangchub Tsöndrü*. Ithaca, NY: Snow Lion Publications.

Dharmakīrti. *Pramāṇavārttika.* P. 5709, D. 4210. Sanskrit and Tibetan editions by Y. Miyasaka in *Acta Indologica* 2 (1972): 1–206.

———. *Pramāṇavārttikasvavṛtti.* P. 5717.1, D. 4216. Sanskrit edition in Gnoli 1960.

———. *Pramāṇaviniścaya.* P. 5710, D. 4211. References to the Sanskrit are to the edition of the third chapter in Hugon and Tomabechi 2012.

Diamond, Cora. 1996. *The Realistic Spirit: Wittgenstein, Philosophy, and the Mind.* Cambridge, MA: MIT Press.

Dignāga. *Pramāṇasamuccaya.* P. 5700. D. 4203.

———. *Pramāṇasamuccayavṛtti.* P. 5701, 5702, D. 4204.

Dpa' bo gtsug lag phreng ba. [*Mkhas pa'i dga' ston* =] *Dam pa'i chos kyi 'khor lo bsgyur ba rnams kyi byung ba gsal bar byed pa mkhas pa'i dga' ston.* Edited by Rdo rje rgyal po. Beijing: Minzu chubanshe, 1986.

Dreyfus, Georges. 1992. "Universals in Indo-Tibetan Buddhism." In *Tibetan Studies: Proceedings of the 5th Seminar of the International Association for Tibetan Studies, Narita 1989*, vol. 1: 29–46. Narita: Naritasan Shinshoji.

———. 2011a. "Apoha as a Naturalized Account of Concept Formation." In Siderits, Tillemans, and Chakrabarti 2011, 207–27.

———. 2011b. "Can a Mādhyamika Be a Skeptic? The Case of Patsab Nyimadrak." In Cowherds 2011, chapter 6.

———. 2011c. "Is Mindfulness Present-Centered and Non-Judgmental? A Discussion of the Cognitive Dimensions of Mindfulness." *Contemporary Buddhism* 12.1: 41–54.

Dreyfus, Georges, and Sara McClintock, eds. 2003. *The Svātantrika-Prāsaṅgika Distinction: What Difference Does a Difference Make?* Studies in Indian and Tibetan Buddhism. Boston: Wisdom Publications.

Dunn, J. M. 1990. "Relevant Predication 2: Intrinsic Properties and Internal Relations." *Philosophical Studies* 60, 177–206.

Dunne, John D. 2006. "Realizing the Unreal: Dharmakīrti's Theory of Yogic Perception." *Journal of Indian Philosophy* 34: 497–519.

———. 2011a. "Key Features of Dharmakīrti's Apoha Theory." In Siderits, Tillemans, and Chakrabarti 2011, 84–108.

———. 2011b. "Toward an Understanding of Non-Dual Mindfulness." *Contemporary Buddhism* 12.1: 71–88.

Eckel, M. D. 1992. *Jñānagarbha on the Two Truths: An Eighth-Century Handbook of Madhyamaka Philosophy.* Delhi: Motilal Banarsidass.

Eltschinger, Vincent. 2009. "On the Career and Cognition of Yogins." In *Yogic Perception, Meditation and Altered States of Consciousness*, edited by Eli Franco, 169–213. Vienna: Verlag der Österreichischen Akademie der Wissenschaften.

———. 2010. "Dharmakīrti." *Revue internationale de philosophie* 64.3: 397–440.

Eklund, Matti. 2005. "Fiction, Indifference and Ontology." *Philosophy and Phenomenological Research* 71.3 (November): 557–79.

Fine, Kit. 2009. "The Question of Ontology." In Chalmers, Manley, and Wasserman 2009, 155–77.

Finnigan, Bronwyn, and Koji Tanaka. 2011. "Ethics for Mādhyamikas." In Cowherds 2011, chapter 14.

Flanagan, Owen. 2006. *Science for Monks: Buddhism and Science.* Written version of the keynote lecture to the symposium "Mind and Reality" at Columbia University. See www.usc.edu/schools/college/crcc/private/flanagan_lectures/Science_for_Monks.pdf (accessed July 28, 2015).

———. 2011. *The Bodhisattva's Brain: Buddhism Naturalized.* Cambridge, MA: MIT Press.

Franco, Eli. 1994. *Perception, Knowledge and Disbelief: A Study of Jayarāśi's Scepticism*, 2nd ed. Delhi: Motilal Banarsidass.

———. 1997. *Dharmakīrti on Compassion and Rebirth.* Wiener Studien zur Tibetologie und Buddhismuskunde 38. Vienna: Arbeitskreis für Tibetische und Buddhistische Studien Universität Wien.

———. 2009. "Meditation and Metaphysics: On Their Mutual Relationship in South Asian Buddhism." In *Yogic Perception, Meditation and Altered States of Consciousness*, edited by Eli Franco, 93–132. Vienna: Verlag der Österreichischen Akademie der Wissenschaften.

———. 2011. "Perception of Yogis: Some Epistemological and Metaphysical Considerations." In Krasser et al. 2011, 81–88.

Frankfurt, Harry G. 2005. *On Bullshit.* Princeton, NJ: Princeton University Press.

Frauwallner, Erich. 1932. "Beiträge zur Apohalehre: I. Dharmakīrti. Übersetzung." *Wiener Zeitschrift für die Kunde des Morgenlandes* 39: 247–85. Reprinted in *E. Frauwallner, Kleine Schriften*, edited by G. Oberhammer and E. Steinkellner, 367–405. Wiesbaden: Franz Steiner Verlag, 1982.

French, Peter A., and Howard K. Wettstein, eds. 2001. *Midwestern Studies in Philosophy, Volume XXV: Figurative Language.* Oxford: Blackwell.

Funayama, Tōru. 2011. "Kamalaśīla's View on Yogic Perception and the Bodhisattva Path." In Krasser et al. 2011, 99–112.

Ganeri, Jonardon. 2001. *Philosophy in Classical India.* New York: Routledge.

Garfield, Jay L. 1988. *Belief in Psychology: A Study in the Ontology of Mind.* Cambridge, MA: MIT Press.

———. 1995. *The Fundamental Wisdom of the Middle Way.* New York: Oxford Press.

———. 2002. *Empty Words: Buddhist Philosophy and Cross-Cultural Interpretation.* Oxford: Oxford University Press.

———. 2006. "Reductionism and Fictionalism: Comments on Siderits's *Personal Identity and Buddhist Philosophy.*" *American Philosophical Association Newsletter* (Newsletter on Asian and Asian-American Philosophers and Philosophy) 6.1 (Fall): 1–7.

———. 2011. "What Is It Like to Be a Bodhisattva? Moral Phenomenology in Śāntideva's *Bodhicaryāvatāra.*" *Journal of the International Association of Buddhist Studies* 33: 327–51.

Glashoff, Klaus. 2004. "Using Formulas for the Interpretation of Ancient Indian Logic." In *Hōrin: Vergleichende Studien zur japanischen Kultur* 11, edited by Gregor Paul, 9–21. Düsseldorf: Iudicium Verlag.

Gnoli, Raniero. 1960. *The Pramāṇavārttikam of Dharmakīrti: The First Chapter with the Autocommentary.* Serie Orientale Roma 23. Rome: Istituto Italiano per il Medio ed Estremo Oriente. [Sanskrit edition of the text.]

Gombrich, Richard, et al. 2007. *Dow Jones Indexes and Dharma Investments to Launch New Faith-Based Indexes.* See www.djindexes.com/mdsidx/html/pressrelease/press_hist2008.html#20080115 (accessed November 30, 2013).

Gomez, Luis O. 1983. "Indian Materials on the Doctrine of Sudden Enlightenment." In *Early Ch'an in China and Tibet*, edited by Whalen Lai and Lewis Lancaster, 393–434. Berkeley Buddhist Studies Series. Berkeley: Asian Humanities Press.

Goodman, Charles. 2004. "The Treasury of Metaphysics and the Physical World." *Philosophical Quarterly* 54: 389–401.

———. 2008. "Consequentialism, Agent-Neutrality, and Mahāyāna Ethics." *Philosophy East and West* 58.1: 17–35.

———. 2009. *Consequences of Compassion: An Interpretation and Defense of Buddhist Ethics*. Oxford: Oxford University Press.

Goodman, Nelson. 1978. *Ways of Worldmaking*. Indianapolis: Hackett.

———. 1983. *Fact, Fiction, and Forecast*, 4th ed. Cambridge, MA: Harvard University Press.

Goodman, Russell B. 1995. *Pragmatism: A Contemporary Reader*. New York and London: Routledge.

Go rams pa Bsod nams seng ge. *Dbu ma spyi don nges don rab gsal*. In *Sa skya pa'i bka' 'bum: The Complete Works of the Great Masters of the Sa skya Sect of Tibetan Buddhism*, edited by Bsod nams rgya mtsho, vol. 12. Tokyo: The Toyo Bunko, 1969.

———. *Lta ba'i shan 'byed = Lta ba'i shan 'byed theg mchog gnad kyi zla zer*. Sakya Students' Union edition, Sarnath, India, 1988. (Text also appears in *Sa skya pa'i bka' 'bum*, vol. 13.) Tibetan text edited and translated in Cabezón and Dargyay 2007.

Gray, David B. 2007. "Compassionate Violence? On the Ethical Implications of Tantric Buddhist Ritual." *Journal of Buddhist Ethics* 14. http://www.buddhistethics.org. See http://blogs.dickinson.edu/buddhistethics/files/2010/05/gray-article.pdf (accessed November 28, 2013).

Grice, H. P. 1991. *Studies in the Way of Words*. Cambridge, MA: Harvard University Press.

Griffiths, Paul. 2000. Review of D. Burton, *Emptiness Appraised*. *Journal of Buddhist Ethics* 7: 22–25.

Grimm, Robert H., and Daniel D. Merill, eds. 1998. *Contents of Thought: Arizona Colloquium in Cognition*. Tucson: University of Arizona Press.

Hale, Bob. 1999. "Realism and Its Oppositions." In *A Companion to the Philosophy of Language*, edited by Bob Hale and Crispin Wright, 271–308. Oxford: Blackwell.

Hayes, Richard P. 1988. *Dignāga on the Interpretation of Signs*. Studies of Classical India 9. Dordrecht: D. Reidel.

———. 1994. "Nāgārjuna's Appeal." *Journal of Indian Philosophy* 22: 299–378.

———. 1996. "Ritual, Self-Deception, and Make-Believe: A Classical Buddhist Perspective." In *Self and Deception: A Cross-Cultural Philosophical Enquiry*, edited by Roger T. Ames and Wimal Dissanayake, 349–64. Albany: State University of New York Press.

Heil, John. 2003. *From an Ontological Point of View*. Oxford: Clarendon.

Higgins, David. 2013. *The Philosophical Foundations of Classical rDzogs chen in Tibet: Investigating the Distinction between Dualistic Mind (sems) and Primordial Knowing (ye shes)*. Wiener Studien zur Tibetologie und Buddhismuskunde 78. Vienna: Arbeitskreis für Tibetische und Buddhistische Studien Universität Wien.

Hirsch, Eli. 2009. "Ontology and Alternative Languages." In Chalmers, Manley, and Wasserman 2009, 231–59.

———. 2011. *Quantifier Variance and Realism: Essays in Metaontology*. New York: Oxford University Press.

Hookway, C. 2001. "Epistemic Akrasia and Epistemic Virtue." In *Virtue Epistemology, Essays on Epistemic Virtue and Responsibility*, edited by A. Fairweather and L. Zagzebski, 178–99. Oxford: Oxford University Press.

Hoornaert, Paul 1999. "An Annotated Translation of *Madhyamkahṛdayakārikā/Tarkajvālā* V.1–7." *KBR* 19: 127–59.

———. 2000. "An Annotated Translation of *Madhyamkahṛdayakārikā/Tarkajvālā* V.8–26." *KBR* 20: 75–111.

———. 2001a. "An Annotated Translation of *Madhyamakahṛdayakārikā/Tarkajvālā* V.27–54." *KBR* 21: 149–90.

———. 2001b. "An Annotated Translation of *Madhyamakahṛdayakārikā/Tarkajvālā* V.55–68—Bhāvaviveka's Critique of *parikalpitasvabhāva* and of Dignāga's *anyāpoha* Theory." *Hokuriku shūkyō bunka—Religion and Culture* 13: 13–47.

———. 2002. "An Annotated Translation of *Madhyamakahṛdayakārikā/Tarkajvālā* V.69–84." *KBR* 22: 113–37.

———. 2003. "An Annotated Translation of *Madhyamakahṛdayakārikā/Tarkajvālā* V.85–114." *KBR* 23: 139–70.

Horwich, Paul. 2006. "A World without Isms: Life after Realism, Fictionalism, Non-Cognitivism, Relativism, Reductionism, Revisionism, and So On." In *Truth and Realism*, edited by P. Greenough and M. Lynch, 188–202. Oxford: Clarendon.

Houshmand, Zara, et al. 1999. *Consciousness at the Crossroads: Conversations with the Dalai Lama on Brainscience and Buddhism*, edited by Zara Houshmand, Robert B. Livingston, and B. Alan Wallace; with contributions by Patricia Smith Churchland et al.; translations by Thubten Jinpa and B. Alan Wallace; with an afterword by B. Alan Wallace. Ithaca, NY: Snow Lion.

Huemer, Michael. 2009. "When Is Parsimony a Virtue?" *The Philosophical Quarterly* 59.235: 216–36.

Hugon, Pascale, and Tōru Tomabechi, eds. 2012. *Dharmakīrti's Pramāṇaviniścaya: Chapter 3 (parārthānumāna)*. Sanskrit Texts from the Tibetan Autonomous Region 8. Vienna: Verlag der Österreichischen Akademie der Wissenschaften.

Jackson, Frank. 1998. *From Metaphysics to Ethics*. Oxford: Oxford University Press.

Jenkins, Stephen. 2010. "Making Merit through Warfare and Torture according to the *Ārya-bodhisattva-gocara-upāyaviṣaya-vikurvaṇa-nirdeśa-sūtra*." In *Buddhist Warfare*, edited by Michael Jerryson and Mark Juergensmeyer, 59–76. Oxford: Oxford University Press.

Jñānagarbha. *Satyadvayavibhaṅgavṛtti*. D. 3882. Translated in Eckel 1992.

Jñānālokālaṃkāra (= *Āryasarvabuddhaviṣayāvatārajñānālokālaṃkāranāmamahāyānasūtra*). P. 768, D. 100. Sanskrit, Tibetan, and Chinese edited in Study Group 2005. English translation at www.84000.co.

Joyce, Richard. 2001. *The Myth of Morality*. Cambridge: Cambridge University Press.

———. 2005. "Moral Fictionalism." In Kalderon 2005b, 287–313.

Kalderon, Mark Eli. 2005a. *Moral Fictionalism*. New York: Oxford University Press.

———, ed. 2005b. *Fictionalism in Metaphysics*. Oxford: Clarendon Press.

Kamalaśīla. *Āryaprajñāpāramitāvajracchedikāṭīkā*. P. 5216, D. 3817. Edited by Central Institute of Higher Tibetan Studies, Sarnath, 1994.

———. *Bhāvanākrama*. P. 5310–12, D. 3915–17. Sanskrit and Tibetan texts of works 1 and 2 in Tucci 1986; texts of work 3 in Tucci 1971. French translation of work 3 by É. Lamotte in Demiéville 1987. English summary of 1 and 2 in Tucci 1986.

———. *Madhyamakāloka*. P. 5287, 3887. Partially translated in Keira 2004.

———. *Sarvadharmaniḥsvabhāvasiddhi*. P. 5289, D. 3889.

Kant, Immanuel. 1998. *Critique of Pure Reason*. Edited and translated by Paul Guyer and Alan W. Wood. The Cambridge Edition of the Works of Immanuel Kant, paperback edition. Cambridge: Cambridge University Press.

Karunadasa, Y. 1996. *The Dhamma Theory: Philosophical Cornerstone of the Abhidhamma.* The Wheel Publication 412/413. Kandy: Buddhist Publication Society.

Karṇakagomin. *Pramāṇavārttikasvavṛttiṭīkā.* Sanskrit edited by Rāhula Sāṅkṛtyāyana. In *Karṇakagomin's Commentary on the Pramāṇavārttika of Dharmakīrti.* Ilāhābād, 1943. Reprint Kyōto: Rinsen Book Co., 1982. [No Tibetan.]

Kassor, Constance. 2013. "Is Gorampa's 'Freedom from Conceptual Proliferations' Dialetheist?" *Philosophy East and West* 63.3: 399–410.

KBR = *Kanazawadaigaku bungakubu ronshū, Kōdōkagakkahen—Studies and Essays, Behavioural Sciences and Philosophy, Faculty of Letters, Kanazawa University.*

Keira, Ryusei. 2004. *Mādhyamika and Epistemology: A Study of Kamalaśīla's Method for Proving the Voidness of all Dharmas.* Introduction, annotated translations, and Tibetan texts of selected sections of the second chapter of the *Madhyamakāloka.* Wiener Studien zur Tibetologie und Buddhismuskunde 59. Vienna: Arbeitskreis für Tibetische und Buddhistische Studien Universität Wien.

Keown, Damien. 2001. *The Nature of Buddhist Ethics.* New York: Palgrave, St. Martin's Press.

———. 2005. *Buddhist Ethics: A Very Short Introduction.* Oxford: Oxford University Press.

Kim, Hyung-Hi. 2013. *La carrière du Bodhisattva dans l'Avatamsaka-sutra: Matériaux pour l'étude de l'Avatamsaka-sutra et ses commentaires chinois.* Publications Universitaires Européennes 107. Bern: Peter Lang.

Kim, Jaegwon. 1983. "Psychophysical Supervenience." *Philosophical Studies* 41: 51–70.

Klong chen pa. *Sems dang ye shes kyi dris lan* of Klong chen rab 'byams pa. In *Kun mkhyen klong chen pa dri med 'od zer gyi gsung thor bu.* Reproduced from xylographic prints from A 'dzom 'brug pa chos sgar blocks, 2 vols. Gangtok: Pema Thinley, 199?.

———. *Theg pa'i mchog rin po che'i mdzod* of Klong chen rab 'byams pa. Oddiyana Institute edition published by Tarthang Rinpoche based on blockprints from Khreng tu'u, 199? (Available from Tibetan Buddhist Resource Center, www.tbrc.org).

Kneale, William and Martha. 1962. *The Development of Logic.* Oxford: Clarendon Press.

Köppl, Heidi I. 2008. *Establishing Appearances as Divine: Rongzom Chözang on Reasoning, Madhyamaka, and Purity.* Ithaca, NY: Snow Lion.

Krasser, Helmut. 2012. "Bhāviveka, Dharmakīrti and Kumārila." In *Devadattīyam: Johannes Bronkhorst Felicitation Volume,* edited by François Voegeli, Vincent Eltschinger, Danielle Feller, Maria Piera Candotti, Bogdan Diaconescu, & Malhar Kulkarni, 535–94. Bern: Peter Lang.

———. 2013. "Logic in Religious Context: Dharmakīrti in Defence of āgama." In *Can the Veda Speak? Dharmakīrti against Mīmāṃsā Exegetics and Vedic Authority, An annotated translation of PVSV 164,24–176,16,* edited by Vincent Eltschinger, Helmut Krasser, and John Taber, 83–118. Vienna: Verlag der Österreichischen Akademie der Wissenschaften.

Krasser, Helmut, Horst Lasic, Eli Franco, and Birgit Kellner, eds. 2011. *Religion and Logic in Buddhist Philosophical Analysis.* Proceedings of the Fourth International Dharmakīrti Conference, Vienna, August 23–27, 2005. Vienna: Verlag der Österreichischen Akademie der Wissenschaften.

Kraut, Richard. 2014. "Aristotle's Ethics." *The Stanford Encyclopedia of Philosophy* (Summer 2014 edition), edited by Edward N. Zalta. http://plato.stanford.edu/archives/sum2014/entries/aristotle-ethics/.

Kripke, Saul. 1982. *Wittgenstein on Rules and Private Language.* Cambridge, MA: Harvard University Press.

Kumārila. *Ślokavārttika.* In *Ślokavārttika of Śrī Kumārila Bhaṭṭa with the Commentary Nyāyaratnākara of Śrī Pārthasārathi Miśra,* edited by D. Shāstrī. Prāchyabhārati Series 10. Varanasi: Tara Publications, 1978.

La Vallée Poussin, Louis de. 1907, 1910, 1911. "*Madhyamakāvatāra,* Introduction au Traité du Milieu de l'Ācārya Candrakīrti, avec le commentaire de l'auteur, traduit d'après la version tibétaine." *Le Muséon* (Louvain) VIII 1907: 249–317; XI 1910: 271–358; XII 1911: 235–328.

———. 1923–31. *L'Abhidharmakośa de Vasubandhu: traduction et annotations,* 6 vols. Paris: Geuthner. Louvain: J.-B. Istas. New edition prepared by É. Lamotte, Mélanges chinois et bouddhiques 16. Brussels: Institut Belge des Hautes Etudes Chinoises, 1971. The French of the 1971 edition was translated into English by Leo M. Pruden, *Abhidharmakośabhāṣyam of Vasubandhu,* 4 vols. Berkeley, CA: Asian Humanities Press, 1990.

Lalitavistara. P. 763, D. 95. Sanskrit text edited by P. L. Vaidya. Darbhanga: Mithila Institute of Post-Graduate Studies and Research in Sanskrit Learning, 1958. Translated as *The Play in Full* at www.84000.co.

Lang, Karen C. 1986. *Āryadeva's Catuḥśataka.* Indiske Studier 7. Copenhagen: Akademisk Forlag.

———. 2003. *Four Illusions: Candrakīrti's Advice to Travelers on the Bodhisattva Path.* Oxford: Oxford University Press.

Lindtner, Christian. 1981. "Atiśa's Introduction to the Two Truths, and Its Sources." *Journal of Indian Philosophy* 9: 161–214.

———. 1990. *Nagarjuniana: Studies in the Writings and Philosophy of Nāgārjuna.* Delhi: Motilal Banarsidass. First published 1982 by Akademisk Forlag as volume 4 of Indiske Studier series.

Liu, Ming-Wood. 1993. "A Chinese Madhyamaka Theory of Truth: The Case of Chi-Tsang." *Philosophy East and West* 43.4: 649–73.

Lokhorst, Gert-Jan. 2014. "Descartes and the Pineal Gland." *The Stanford Encyclopedia of Philosophy* (Spring 2014 edition), edited by Edward N. Zalta. http://plato.stanford.edu/archives/spr2014/entries/pineal-gland/.

Lutz, Antoine, John D. Dunne, and Richard J. Davidson. 2007. "Meditation and the Neuroscience of Conciousness." In *Cambridge Handbook of Consciousness,* edited by P. D. Zelazo, M. Moscovitch, and E. Thompson, 497–549. Cambridge: Cambridge University Press.

MacKenzie, Matthew. 2009. "Ontological Deflationism in Madhyamaka." *Contemporary Buddhism* 9.2: 197–207.

Mackie, John L. 1986. *Ethics: Inventing Right and Wrong.* New York: Penguin.

Magee, William. 1999. *The Nature of Things: Emptiness and Essence in the Geluk World.* Ithaca, NY: Snow Lion.

Manorathanandin. *Pramāṇavārttikavṛtti.* Sanskrit edited by Rāhula Sāṅkṛtyāyana, in appendix to the *Journal of the Bihar and Orissa Research Society* 24–26 (1938–40): part III. [No Tibetan.]

May, Jacques. 1959. *Candrakīrti: Prasannapadā Madhyamakavṛtti. Douze chapitres traduits du sanscrit et du tibétain, accompagnés d'une introduction, de notes et d'une édition critique de la version tibétaine.* Paris: Adrien-Maisonneuve.

———. 1979. "Chūgan." In *Hōbōgirin* 5: 470–93. Paris-Tokyo: École française d'Extrême-Orient.

McClintock, Sara L. 2010. *Omniscience and the Rhetoric of Reason: Śāntarakṣita and Kamalaśīla on Rationality, Argumentation, and Religious Authority*. Studies in Indian and Tibetan Buddhism. Boston: Wisdom Publications.

McCrea, Lawrence, and Parimal Patil. 2006. "Traditionalism and Innovation." *Journal of Indian Philosophy* 34: 303–66.

McDowell, John. 1981. "Non-Cognitivism and Rule-Following." In *Wittgenstein: To Follow a Rule*, edited by Steven Holtzman and Christopher Leich, 141–62. London: Routledge and Kegan Paul.

———. 1998. *Mind, Value, and Reality*. Cambridge, MA: Harvard University Press.

McGinn, Colin. 1979. "Action and Its Explanation." In *Philosophical Problems in Psychology*, edited by N. Bolton, 20–42. London: Methuen.

———. 2008. *Mindfucking: A Critique of Mental Manipulation*. Stocksfied, UK: Acumen.

McMahan, J. 2000. "Moral Intuition." In *The Blackwell Guide to Ethical Theory*, edited by H. LaFollette, 92–110. Oxford: Blackwell.

Mimaki, Katsumi. 1976. *La réfutation bouddhique de la permanence des choses (sthirasiddhidūṣaṇa) et la preuve de la momentanéité des choses (kṣaṇabhaṅgasiddhi)*. Publications de l'Institut de Civilisation Indienne, fascicule 41. Paris: Institut de Civilisation Indienne.

———. 1982. *Blo gsal grub mtha'*. Kyoto: Zinbun Kagaku Kenkyusyo (Institute for Research in Humanities, Kyoto University).

Mkhas grub Dge legs dpal bzang po. *Stong thun chen mo = Zab mo stong pa nyid kyi de kho na nyid rab tu gsal bar byed pa'i bstan bcos skal bzang mig 'byed*. In *sTong thun chen mo and Other Texts on Madhyamaka Philosophy*, vol. 1, edited by Lha-mkhar Yoṅs-dzin Bstan-pa-rgyal-mtshan. New Delhi, 1972. Translated in Cabezón 1992.

Mookherjee, S. 1980. *The Buddhist Philosophy of Universal Flux*. Delhi: Motilal Banarsidass. First published 1935 by the University of Calcutta.

Nagao, Gadjin M. 1992. "The Yogācāra Cognition Theory and Depth Psychology." In *Études bouddhiques offertes à Jacques May*, edited by K. Mimaki, J. Bronkhorst, and T. Tillemans. *Asiatische Studien / Études Asiatiques* 46: 307–22.

Nagel, Thomas. 1979. *Mortal Questions*. Cambridge: Cambridge University Press.

Nāgārjuna. *Mūlamadhyamakakārikā*. P. 5224, D. 3824. Sanskrit text in Candrakīrti, *Prasannapadā*; translation in Siderits and Katsura 2013; translation from the Tibetan in Garfield 1995.

———. *Vigrahavyāvartanī*. P. 5228, D. 3828. Sanskrit text critically edited by E. H. Johnston and Arnold Kunst and translated by K. Bhattacharya. See Bhattacharya 1986.

———. *Yuktiṣaṣṭikā*. P. 5225, D. 3825. Edited and translated in Lindtner 1990.

Newland, Guy. 1992. *The Two Truths in the Mādhyamika Philosophy of the Ge-luk-ba Order of Tibetan Buddhism*. Ithaca, NY: Snow Lion.

Newland, Guy, and Tom Tillemans. 2011. "An Introduction to Conventional Truth." In Cowherds 2011, chapter 1.

Norman, Kenneth R., trans. 2001. *The Group of Discourses: Sutta-Nipāta*, 2nd ed. Oxford: Pali Text Society.

Oetke, Claus 1991. "Remarks on the Interpretation of Nāgārjuna's Philosophy." *Journal of Indian Philosophy* 19: 315–23.

———. 1996. "Ancient Indian Logic as a Theory of Non-Monotonic Reasoning." *Journal of Indian Philosophy* 24: 447–539.

Paṇḍit Aśoka. *Sāmānyadūṣaṇa.* In *Six Buddhist Nyāya Tracts in Sanskrit,* edited by Haraprasād Śāstrī. Bibliotheca Indica 185. Calcutta: The Asiatic Society, 1910. [No Tibetan.]

Pañcapāramitānirdeśasūtra. P. 848, D. 181. English translation in preparation for www.84000.co.

Patil, Parimal. 2007. "Dharmakīrti's White-Lie." In *Pramāṇakīrtiḥ: Papers Dedicated to Ernst Steinkellner on the Occasion of his 70th Birthday,* part 2, edited by B. Kellner, H. Krasser, M. T. Much, and H. Tauscher. Wiener Studien zur Tibetologie und Buddhismuskunde 70.2, 597–619. Vienna: Arbeitskreis für Tibetische und Buddhistische Studien Universität Wien.

Paul, Gregor, ed. 2004. *Hōrin: Vergleichende Studien zur japanischen Kultur,* vol. 11. Düsseldorf: Iudicium Verlag.

Perelman, Chaïm, and Luci Olbrechts-Tyteca. 1958. *Traité de l'argumentation: La nouvelle rhétorique.* Paris: Presses Universitaires de France.

Perrett, Roy W. 2002. "Personal Identity, Minimalism, and Madhyamaka." *Philosophy East and West* 52.3: 373–85.

Pind, Ole Holten. 2009. *Dignāga's Philosophy of Language: Dignāga on anyāpoha. Pramāṇasamuccaya V, Texts, Translation, and Annotation.* Dissertation, University of Vienna. Philologisch-Kulturwissenschaftliche Fakultät. Betreuerin: Steinkellner, Ernst. Available at http://othes.univie.ac.at/8283/ (accessed August 15, 2015).

Powers, John. 1994. "Empiricism and Pragmatism in the Thought of Dharmakīrti and William James." *American Journal of Theology and Philosophy* 15.1: 59–85.

Price, Huw. 2009. "Metaphysics after Carnap: The Ghost Who Walks?" In Chalmers, Manley, and Wasserman 2009, 320–46.

Priest, Graham. 1999. "Negation as Cancellation, and Connexive Logic." *Topoi* 18.2: 141–48.

———. 2002. *Beyond the Limits of Thought.* Oxford: Oxford University Press.

Priest, Graham, Mark Siderits, and Tom Tillemans. 2011. "The (Two) Truths about Truth." In Cowherds 2011, chapter 8.

Putnam, Hilary. 1981. *Reason, Truth and History.* Cambridge: Cambridge University Press.

———. 2004. *Ethics without Ontology.* Cambridge, MA: Harvard University Press.

Read, Rupert. 2009. "Wittgenstein and Zen Buddhism: One Practice, No Dogma." In *Pointing at the Moon: Buddhism, Logic, Analytic Philosophy,* edtied by Jay L. Garfield, Tom J. F. Tillemans, and Mario D'Amato, 13–23. New York: Oxford University Press.

Rescher, Nicholas. 2001. *Paradoxes: Their Roots, Range and Resolution.* Chicago and La Salle: Open Court.

Rescher, Nicholas, and Robert Brandom. 1980. *The Logic of Inconsistency.* Oxford: Basil Blackwell.

Ricard, Matthieu. 2006. *Happiness: A Guide to Developing Life's Most Important Skill.* New York: Little Brown.

Robinson, Richard H. 1972. "Did Nāgārjuna Really Refute All Philosophical Views?" *Philosophy East and West* 22: 325–31.

Rorty, Amélie Oksenberg. 1988. "The Deceptive Self: Liars, Layers, and Lairs." In

Perspectives on Self-Deception, edited by Brian P. McLaughlin and A. O. Rorty, 11–28. Berkeley: University of California Press.

Ross, David, and Lesley Brown. 2009. *Aristotle: The Nicomachean Ethics.* Translated by David Ross, revised with an introduction and notes by Lesley Brown. Oxford World's Classics Paperback. Oxford: Oxford University Press. First published 1980.

Saitō, Akira. 2004. "Bhāviveka's Theory of Meaning." *Indogaku Bukkyōgaku kenkyū—Journal of Indian and Buddhist Studies* 52.2: 24–31.

Saṃyutta Nikāya. Edited by M. Léon Feer in *The Saṃyutta-nikāya of the Sutta-piṭaka.* London: Published for Pali Text Society by Henry Frowde, Oxford University Press, 1890. For an English translation, see Bodhi 2000.

Śāntarakṣita. *Satyadvayavibhaṅgapañjikā.* P. 5283, D. 3883.

Śāntideva. *Bodhicaryāvatāra.* P. 5272, D. 3871. Sanskrit edition in Vaidya 1960. English translation in Crosby and Skilton 1996.

Samādhirājasūtra. P. 795, D. 127. Edited by P. L. Vaidya. Buddhist Sanskrit Texts 2. Darbhanga: Mithila Institute of Post-Graduate Studies and Research in Sanskrit Learning, 1961. English translation in preparation for www.84000.co.

Se ra Rje bstun Chos kyi rgyal mtshan. *Skabs dang po'i spyi don = Bstan bcos mngon par rtogs pa'i rgyan 'grel pa dang bcas pa 'i rnam bshad rnam pa gnyis kyi dka' ba'i gnad gsal bar byed pa legs bshad skal bzang klu dbang gyi rol mtsho zhes bya ba las skabs dang po'i spyi don.* Blockprint, textbook (*yig cha*) of Se ra byes Monastery, Byllakuppe, Mysore district, Karnataka, India, 1970s. Translation of an extract on the "neither one nor many argument" in Tillemans 1984.

Seyfort Ruegg, David. 1977. "The Uses of the Four Positions of the *Catuṣkoṭi* and the Problem of the Description of Reality in Mahāyāna Buddhism." *Journal of Indian Philosophy* 5: 1–71. Reprinted in Seyfort Ruegg 2010, 37–112.

———. 1981. *The Literature of the Madhyamaka School of Philosophy in India.* Wiesbaden: Otto Harrassowitz.

———. 1983. "On the Thesis and Assertion in the Madhyamaka / dBu ma." In *Contributions on Tibetan and Buddhist Religion and Philosophy*, edited by E. Steinkellner and H. Tauscher, 205–40. Wiener Studien zur Tibetologie und Buddhismuskunde 11. Vienna: Arbeitskreis für Tibetische und Buddhistische Studien Universität Wien.

———. 1989. *Buddha-Nature, Mind and the Problem of Gradualism in a Comparative Perspective: On the Transmission and Reception of Buddhism in India and Tibet.* London: School of Oriental and African Studies.

———. 1992. "On the Tibetan Historiography and Doxography of the 'Great Debate of bSam yas.'" Reprinted in Seyfort Ruegg 2010, 253–66.

———. 2000. *Three Studies in the History of Indian and Tibetan Madhyamaka Philosophy*, part 1. Wiener Studien zur Tibetologie und Buddhismuskunde 50. Vienna: Arbeitskreis für Tibetische und Buddhistische Studien Universität Wien.

———. 2002. *Studies in Indian and Tibetan Madhyamaka Thought, part 2. Two Prolegomena to Madhyamaka Philosophy: Candrakīrti's Prasannapadā Madhyamakavṛttiḥ on Madhyamakakārikā I.1 and Tsoṅ kha pa Blo bzaṅ grags pa / rGyal tshab Dar ma Rin chen's dKa' gnad/gnas brgyad kyi zin bris.* Wiener Studien zur Tibetologie und Buddhismuskunde 54. Vienna: Arbeitskreis für Tibetische und Buddhistische Studien Universität Wien.

———. 2010. *The Buddhist Philosophy of the Middle: Essays on Indian and Tibetan Madhyamaka.* Studies in Indian and Tibetan Buddhism. Boston: Wisdom Publications.

Sgom sde Lha ram pa Thub bstan bsam grub. 2013. *Sgom sde tshig mdzod chen mo.* Taipei: The Corporate Body of the Buddha Educational Foundation.

Sharf, Robert. 1995. "Buddhist Modernism and the Rhetoric of Meditative Experience." *Numen* 42.3: 228–83.

Siderits, Mark. 1988. "Nāgārjuna as Anti-Realist." *Journal of Indian Philosophy* 16.4: 311–25.

———. 1989. "Thinking on Empty: Madhyamaka Anti-Realism and Canons of Rationality." In *Rationality in Question: On Eastern and Western Views of Rationality*, edited by Shlomo Biderman and Ben-Ami Scharfstein, 231–49. Leiden: Brill.

———. 2003. *Personal Identity and Buddhist Philosophy: Empty Persons.* Ashgate World Philosophies Series. Aldershot, Hampshire, UK: Ashgate.

———. 2007. *Buddhism as Philosophy: An Introduction.* Ashgate World Philosophies Series. Aldershot, Hampshire, UK: Ashgate.

———. 2010. "Buddhas as Zombies: A Buddhist Reduction of Subjectivity." In *Self, No Self? Perspectives from Analytical, Phenomenological, and Indian Traditions*, edited by Mark Siderits, Evan Thompson, and Dan Zahavi, 308–31. New York: Oxford University Press.

———. 2011. "Is Everything Connected to Everything Else? What the Gopīs Know." In Cowherds 2011, chapter 10.

Siderits, Mark, Tom Tillemans, and Arindam Chakrabarti, eds. 2011. *Apoha: Buddhist Nominalism and Human Cognition.* New York: Columbia University Press.

Siderits, Mark, and Shōryū Katsura. 2013. *Nāgārjuna's Middle Way: Mūlamadhyamakakārikā.* Classics of Indian Buddhism. Boston: Wisdom Publications.

Silk, Jonathan, ed. 2000. *Wisdom, Compassion, and the Search for Understanding: The Buddhist Studies Legacy of Gadjin M. Nagao.* Honolulu: University of Hawai'i Press.

Smart, J. J. C., and Bernard Williams. 1973. *Utilitarianism: For and Against.* Cambridge: Cambridge University Press.

Sober, Elliott. 2009. "Parsimony Arguments in Science and Philosophy: A Test Case for Naturalism." *Proceedings and Addresses of the American Philosophical Association* 83.2: 117–55.

Śraddhābalādhānāvatāramudrāsūtra. P. 867, D. 201. English translation: www.84000.co.

Stanley, Jason. 2001. "Hermeneutic Fictionalism." In French and Wettstein 2001, 36–71.

Steinkellner, Ernst. 1971. "Wirklichkeit und Begriff bei Dharmakīrti." *Wiener Zeitschrift für die Kunde Südasiens* 15: 179–211.

———. 1984. "Svabhāvapratibandha Again." In *Studies of Mysticism in Honor of the 1150th Anniversary of Kōbō-Daishi's Nirvāṇam. Acta Indologica* 6: 457–76.

Stern, Robert. 1999. "On Kant's Response to Hume." In *Transcendental Arguments: Problems and Prospects*, edited Robert Stern, 47–66. Oxford: Clarendon.

Stroud, Barry. 1968. "Transcendental Arguments." *Journal of Philosophy* 65: 241–56.

———. 1994. "Kantian Argument, Conceptual Capacities, and Invulnerability." In *Kant and Contemporary Epistemology*, edited by Paolo Parrini, 231–51. Dordrecht: Kluwer.

Study Group. 2005. *Jñānālokālaṃkāra: Transliterated Sanskrit Text Collated with Tibetan and Chinese Translations.* Edited by the Study Group on Buddhist Sanskrit Literature, The Institute for Comprehensive Studies of Buddhism. Tokyo: Taishō University.

Sutta-Nipāta. See Norman 2001.

Suzuki, Kōshin, ed. 1994. *Sanskrit Fragments and Tibetan Translation of Candrakīrti's Bodhisattvayogācāracatuḥśatakaṭīkā.* Tokyo: Sankibo.

Taber, John. 2003. "Dharmakīrti Against Physicalism." *Journal of Indian Philosophy* 31: 479–502.

———. 2009. "Yoga and our Epistemic Predicament." In *Yogic Perception, Meditation and Altered States of Consciousness*. Edited by Eli Franco, 71–92. Vienna: Verlag der Österreichischen Akademie der Wissenschaften.

Tanaka, Koji. 2003. "Three Schools of Paraconsistency." *Australasian Journal of Logic* 1: 28–42.

Tanaka, Koji, Yasuo Deguchi, Jay L. Garfield, and Graham Priest, eds. 2015. *The Moon Points Back*. New York: Oxford University Press.

Tanaka, K. T., and R. E. Robertson. 1992. "A Ch'an Text from Tun-huang: Implications for Ch'an Influence on Tibetan Buddhism." In *Tibetan Buddhism: Reason and Revelation*, edited by Steven D. Goodman and Ronald. M. Davidson, 57–78. Albany: State University of New York Press.

Tanji, Teruyoshi. 2000. "On *samāropa*: Probing the Relationship of the Buddha's Silence and His Teaching." In Silk 2000, 347–68.

Taylor, Charles. 1982. "Rationality." In *Rationality and Relativism*, edited by M. Hollis and S. Lukes, 87–105. Cambridge, MA: MIT Press.

Thanissaro Bhikkhu. 2006. "The Integrity of Emptiness." *Buddhadharma: The Practitioner's Quarterly*, Winter: 42–47.

Thakchoe, Sonam. 2007. *The Two Truths Debate: Tsongkhapa and Gorampa on the Middle Way*. Boston: Wisdom Publications.

Thomson, Judith J. 2001. *Goodness and Advice*. Princeton, NJ: Princeton University Press.

Tibetan Tripiṭaka, Dergé (Sde dge) edition. Reproduced in A. W. Barber, ed., *The Tibetan Tripiṭaka: Taipei Edition*. Taipei: SMC Publishing, 1981. Sde dge par phud edition available at www.tbrc.org.

Tibetan Tripiṭaka, Peking edition. Tokyo-Kyoto: Tibetan Tripiṭaka Research Institute, 1955–61. See www.tbrc.org.

Tillemans, Tom J. F. 1984. "Two Tibetan Texts on the 'Neither One nor Many' Argument for *Śūnyatā*." *Journal of Indian Philosophy* 12: 357–88.

———. 1990. *Materials for the Study of Āryadeva, Dharmapāla and Candrakīrti: The Catuḥśataka of Āryadeva, Chapters XII and XIII, with the Commentaries of Dharmapāla and Candrakīrti: Introduction, Translation, Sanskrit, Tibetan and Chinese Texts, Notes*, 2 vols. Wiener Studien zur Tibetologie und Buddhismuskunde 24,1–2. Vienna: Arbeitskreis für Tibetische und Buddhistische Studien. Reprinted, in one volume, Delhi: Motilal Banarsidass, 2008.

———. 1992a. "Tsong kha pa *et al.* on the Bhāvaviveka-Candrakīrti Debate." In *Tibetan Studies*, Proceedings of the 5th Seminar of the International Association for Tibetan Studies, NARITA 1989. Monograph Series, Occasional Papers 2, 315–26. Narita: Naritasan Shinshoji.

———. 1992b. "Note liminaire." In *Études bouddhiques offertes à Jacques May*, ed. Johannes Bronkhorst, Katsumi Mimaki, and Tom Tillemans. *Asiatische Studien / Études Asiatiques* 46.1: 9–12.

———. 1993. *Persons of Authority: The sTon pa tshad ma'i skyes bur sgrub pa'i gtam of A lag sha Ngag dbang bstan dar. A Tibetan text on the central religious questions of Buddhist epistemology*. Tibetan and Indo-Tibetan Studies 5. Stuttgart: Franz Steiner Verlag.

———. 1998. "Issues in Tibetan Philosophy." In *Routledge Encyclopedia of Philosophy*, edited by Edward Craig, vol. 9: 402–9. London: Routledge.

———. 1999. *Scripture, Logic, Language: Essays on Dharmakīrti and His Tibetan Successors.* Studies in Indian and Tibetan Buddhism. Boston: Wisdom Publications.

———. 2000. *Dharmakīrti's Pramāṇavārttika: An Annotated Translation of the Fourth Chapter (parārthānumāna)*, vol. 1 (k. 1–148). Vienna: Verlag der Österreichischen Akademie der Wissenschaften.

———. 2001a. "Trying to Be Fair to Mādhyamika Buddhism." The Numata Yehan Lecture in Buddhism, Winter 2001: 1–29. Calgary: Religious Studies Department, University of Calgary. Shorter version in *Expanding and Merging Horizons: Contributions to South Asian and Cross-Cultural Studies in Commemoration of Wilhelm Halbfass*, edited by Karin Preisendanz, 507–24. Philosophisch-Historische Klasse Denkschriften 351. Vienna: Österreichische Akademie der Wissenschaften, 2007.

———. 2001b. Review of Silk 2000. *The Eastern Buddhist* 33.1: 181–85.

———. 2003. "Metaphysics for Mādhyamikas." In Dreyfus and McClintock 2003, 93–123.

———. 2004. "What Are Mādhyamikas Refuting? Śāntarakṣita, Kamalaśīla *et alii* on Superimpositions (*samāropa*)." In *Three Mountains and Seven Rivers: Prof. Musashi Tachikawa's Felicitation Volume*, edited by S. Hino and T. Wada, 225–23. Delhi: Motilal Banarsidass.

———. 2008a. "Reason, Irrationality and Akrasia (Weakness of the Will) in Buddhism: Reflections upon Śāntideva's Arguments with Himself." In *Argumentation*, vol. 22.1, edited by T. Tillemans and G. Dreyfus, 149–63. The Netherlands: Springer Verlag.

———. 2008b. "Introduction: Buddhist Argumentation." In *Argumentation*, vol. 22.1, edited by T. Tillemans and G. Dreyfus, 1–14. The Netherlands: Springer Verlag.

———. 2009. "How Do Mādhyamikas Think? Notes on Jay Garfield, Graham Priest and Paraconsistency." In *Pointing at the Moon: Buddhism, Logic, Analytic Philosophy*, edited by J. Garfield, T. Tillemans, and M. D'Amato, 83–100. New York: Oxford University Press.

———. 2011a. "How to Talk about Ineffable Things: Dignāga and Dharmakīrti on Apoha." In Siderits, Tillemans, Chakrabarti 2011, 50–63.

———. 2011b. "Dharmakīrti." *Stanford Encyclopedia of Philosophy* http://plato.stanford.edu/entries/dharmakiirti/.

———. 2013. "Yogic Perception, Meditation and Enlightenment: The Epistemological Issues in a Key Debate." In *A Companion to Buddhist Philosophy*, edited by Steven M. Emmanuel, 290–306. Blackwell Companions to Philosophy. Oxford: John Wiley.

Torella, Raffaele. 2007. "Studies on Utpaladeva's Īśvarapratyabhijñāvivṛti, part I: Anupalabdhi and Apoha in a Śaiva Garb." In *Expanding and Merging Horizons: Contributions to South Asian and Cross-Cultural Studies in Commemoration of Wilhelm Halbfass*, edited by K. Preisendanz, 473–90. Philosophisch-Historische Klasse Denkschriften 351. Vienna: Österreichische Akademie der Wissenschaften.

Trisaṃvaranirdeśaparivarta (chapter 1 of the *Ratnakūṭasūtra*). P. 760.1, D. 45.

Tsong-ka-pa. 2002. *The Great Treatise on the Stages of the Path to Enlightenment*, vol. 3. Translated by the Lamrim Chenmo Translation Committee, edited by Guy Newland. Ithaca, NY: Snow Lion.

Tsong kha pa (Blo bzang grags pa). *Collected Works (gsung 'bum).* dGe ldan gsung rab mi nyams rgyun phel Series 79–105. Delhi: Ngag dbang dge legs bde mo, 1975–79.

———. *Byang chub lam rim chen mo.* In *Collected Works*, vol. *pa*. Translated in Tsong-kha-pa 2002.

———. *Rtsa ba'i shes rab kyi dka' gnas chen po brgyad kyi bshad pa. Collected Works*, vol. *ba*. Sarnath: Pleasure of Elegant Sayings Press, 1970.

———. *Rtsa she ṭīk chen = Dbu ma rtsa ba'i tshig le'ur byas pa shes rab ces bya ba'i rnam bshad rigs pa'i rgya mtsho. Collected Works*, vol. *ba*. Sarnath: Pleasure of Elegant Sayings Press, 1973.

Tucci, Giuseppe. 1971. *Minor Buddhist Texts*, part 3. Serie Orientale Roma. Roma: Istituto Italiano per il Medio ed Estremo Oriente.

———. 1986. *Minor Buddhist Texts*, part 2. Containing the first *Bhāvanākrama* of Kamalaśīla. Sanskrit and Tibetan texts with introduction and English summary. Delhi: Motilal Banarsidass. First published 1956 by Istituto Italiano per il Medio ed Estremo Oriente.

Uddyotakara. *Nyāyavārttika*. In *Nyāyadarśanam*, edited by Taranatha Nyayatarkatirtha. Calcutta: Amarendramohan Tarkatirtha, 1936.

Vajracchedikāprajñāpāramitā. P. 739, D. 16. See Conze 1957.

Vaidya, P. L. (Parasuram Lakshman). 1960. *Śāntideva: Bodhicaryāvatāra, with the commentary Pañjikā of Prajñākaramati*. Buddhist Sanskrit Texts 12. Darbhanga: Mithila Institute of Post-Graduate Studies and Research in Sanskrit Learning.

Vasubandhu. *Abhidharmakośa* and *Abhidharmakośabhāṣya*. D. 4089, 4090. Sanskrit edited by P. Pradhān, *Abhidharma-Koshabhāṣya of Vasubandhu*. Patna: K. P. Jayaswal Research Institute, 1967. French translation in La Vallée Poussin 1923–31.

van Eemeren, Frans H., and Rob Grootendorst. 2004. *A Systematic Theory of Argumentation*. Cambridge: Cambridge University Press.

van Inwagen, Peter. 2009. *Metaphysics*, 3rd ed. Boulder, CO: Westview Press.

van Schaik, Sam. 2004. *Approaching the Great Perfection. Simultaneous and Gradual Methods of Dzogchen Practice in the Longchen Nyingtig*. Studies in Indian and Tibetan Buddhism. Boston: Wisdom Publications.

Waldron, William S. 2003. *The Buddhist Unconscious: The Ālayavijñāna in the Context of Indian Buddhist Thought*. New York: Curzon.

Wallace, B. Alan, and Brian Hodel. 2007. *Contemplative Science: Where Buddhism and Neuroscience Converge*. New York: Columbia University Press.

Wang Xi 王錫. *Dun wu da cheng zheng li jue* 頓悟大乘正理決 [= "Wang Xi's memoir"]. See Demiéville 1987.

Watanabe, Toshikazu. 2013. "Dignāga on *Āvīta* and *Prasaṅga*." *Journal of Indian and Buddhist Studies* 61.3 (March): 171–77.

Westerhoff, Jan. 2009. *Nāgārjuna's Madhyamaka: A Philosophical Introduction*. Oxford: Oxford University Press.

———. 2011. "The Merely Conventional Existence of the World." In Cowherds 2011, chapter 12.

Wiggins, David. 1998. "Weakness of Will, Commensurability and the Objects of Deliberation and Desire." In *Needs, Values, Truth*, 3rd ed., 239–68. Oxford: Oxford University Press.

Williams, Michael. 1988. "Scepticism without Theory." *Review of Metaphysics* 41.3: 547–88.

Williams, Paul. 1992. "Non-Conceptuality, Critical Reasoning and Religious Experience: Some Tibetan Buddhist Discussions." In *Philosophy, Religion, and the Spiritual Life*, edited by M. McGhee, 189–210. Cambridge: Cambridge University Press.

———. 1995. "Identifying the Object of Negation: On *Bodhicaryāvatāra* 9:140 (Tib. 139)." *Asiatische Studien / Études Asiatiques* 49.4: 969–86.

Wittgenstein, Ludwig. 1953. *Philosophical Investigations.* Oxford: Basil Blackwell.

———. 1978. *Remarks on the Foundations of Mathematics.* Oxford: Basil Blackwell.

Woo, Jeson. 2003. "Dharmakīrti and His Commentators on Yogipratyakṣa." *Journal of Indian Philosophy* 31: 439–48.

Woods, John. 2006. "Pragma-Dialectics: A Retrospective." In *Considering Pragma-Dialectics*, edited by Peter Houtlosser and Agnès van Rees, 301–11. Mahwah, NJ and London: Lawrence Erlbaum.

Wright, Crispin. 1994. *Truth and Objectivity.* Cambridge, MA: Harvard University Press.

Yablo, Stephen. 1998. "Does Ontology Rest on a Mistake?" *Proceedings of the Aristotelian Society, Supplementary Volume* 72: 229–61.

———. 1999. "Intrinsicness." *Philosophical Topics* 26: 479–505.

———. 2000. "Apriority and Existence." In *New Essays on the A Priori*, edited by Paul Boghossian and Christopher Peacocke, 197–228. Oxford: Oxford University Press.

———. 2001. "Go Figure: A Path through Fictionalism." In French and Wettstein 2001, 72–102.

Yongs 'dzin Phur bu lcog (Byams pa thul khrims rgya mtsho). *Yongs 'dzin bsdus grwa = Tshad ma'i gzhung don 'byed pa'i bsdus grwa'i rnam bzhag rigs lam 'phrul gyi lde'u mig* (3 vols: *chung*, *'bring*, *che ba*). Included in T. Kelsang and S. Onoda, *Textbooks of Sera Monastery for the Primary Course of Studies.* Biblia Tibetica 1. Kyoto: Nagata Bunshodo, 1985.

Yon tan bzang po. *Rgyu 'bras theg pa mchog gi gnas lugs zab mo'i don rnam par nges pa rje jo nang pa chen po'i ring lugs 'jigs med gdong lnga'i nga ro.* Beijing: Mi rigs dpe skrun khang, 1990.

Index

A few remarks on the index. First, some terms in the book have multiple translations of more or less equal accuracy—we do not give all those variants in the index. Second, page references in italics indicate a more detailed discussion of a term; notes are generally only mentioned in the index when the information they give is relatively substantial, not purely bibliographical. David Higgins deserves heartfelt thanks for his work in preparing the index.

About the Author

TOM J. F. TILLEMANS is professor emeritus of Buddhist studies in the Faculty of Letters at the University of Lausanne in Switzerland. Born in 1950 in the Netherlands, he initially studied in Canada, and then in India, Switzerland, and Japan. Buddhist logic and epistemology, Madhyamaka philosophy, and comparative philosophy have been his longterm research interests. He now serves as editor in chief for the 84000 project, tasked with translating the scriptures of the Tibetan Buddhist canon. Tom Tillemans divides his time between Switzerland and Gabriola Island, on the west coast of Canada.

Studies in Indian and Tibetan Buddhism
Titles Previously Published

Among Tibetan Texts
History and Literature of the Himalayan Plateau
E. Gene Smith

Approaching the Great Perfection
Simultaneous and Gradual Methods of Dzogchen Practice in the Longchen Nyingtig
Sam van Schaik

Authorized Lives
Biography and the Early Formation of Geluk Identity
Elijah S. Ary

Buddhism Between Tibet and China
Edited by Matthew T. Kapstein

The Buddhist Philosophy of the Middle
Essays on Indian and Tibetan Madhyamaka
David Seyfort Ruegg

Buddhist Teaching in India
Johannes Bronkhorst

A Direct Path to the Buddha Within
Gö Lotsāwa's Mahāmudrā Interpretation of the Ratnagotravibhāga
Klaus-Dieter Mathes

Foundations of Dharmakīrti's Philosophy
John D. Dunne

Freedom from Extremes
Gorampa's "Distinguishing the Views" and the Polemics of Emptiness
José Ignacio Cabezón and Geshe Lobsang Dargyay

Himalayan Passages
Tibetan and Newar Studies in Honor of Hubert Decleer
Benjamin Bogin and Andrew Quintman

Luminous Lives
The Story of the Early Masters of the Lam 'bras Tradition in Tibet
Cyrus Stearns

Mipham's Beacon of Certainty
Illuminating the View of Dzogchen, the Great Perfection
John Whitney Pettit

Omniscience and the Rhetoric of Reason
Śāntarakṣita and Kamalaśīla on Rationality, Argumentation, and Religious Authority
Sara L. McClintock

Reason's Traces
Identity and Interpretation in Indian and Tibetan Buddhist Thought
Matthew T. Kapstein

Resurrecting Candrakīrti
Disputes in the Tibetan Creation of Prāsaṅgika
Kevin A. Vose

Scripture, Logic, Language
Essays on Dharmakīrti and His Tibetan Successors
Tom J. F. Tillemans

The Svātantrika-Prāsaṅgika Distinction
What Difference Does a Difference Make?
Edited by Georges Dreyfus and Sara McClintock

Vajrayoginī
Her Visualizations, Rituals, and Forms
Elizabeth English

About Wisdom Publications

Wisdom Publications is the leading publisher of classic and contemporary Buddhist books and practical works on mindfulness. To learn more about us or to explore our other books, please visit our website at wisdompubs.org or contact us at the address below.

Wisdom Publications
199 Elm Street
Somerville, MA 02144 USA

We are a 501(c)(3) organization, and donations in support of our mission are tax deductible.

Wisdom Publications is affiliated with the Foundation for the Preservation of the Mahayana Tradition (FPMT)